MURDER HOUSES OF
LONDON

MURDER HOUSES OF
LONDON

JAN BONDESON

AMBERLEY

First published 2014
This edition published 2015

Amberley Publishing
The Hill, Stroud
Gloucestershire, GL5 4EP

www.amberley-books.com

British Library Cataloguing in Publication Data.
A catalogue record for this book is available from the British Library.

ISBN 978-1-4456-4706-7 (paperback)
ISBN 978-1-4456-1491-5 (ebook)

Typesetting and Origination by Amberley Publishing.
Printed in Great Britain.

Contents

Contents

Introduction

I shall hope to write a book one day on the subject of 'Murder Houses of London'.
Guy Logan, *Verdict and Sentence*

Thus wrote the old crime author Guy Logan, whose knowledge of London's criminal history was second to none.[1] Regrettably, old age and a lawsuit instigated by a vindictive baroness put paid to Guy Logan's plans to publish a monograph on the Murder Houses of London, but I have decided to follow in his footsteps and produce a comprehensive account of London's topography of capital crime: houses inside which celebrated murders have been committed.[2] Since there is no shortage of London murder houses, this volume will deal with Westminster, Kensington, Chelsea and Fulham, the Bloomsbury and St Pancras areas, Marylebone and Paddington, Islington, and the Tower Hamlets. A second volume will deal with the remainder of the metropolis, mainly south of the river.

In modern Britain, it sometimes happens that houses within whose walls particularly heinous and repulsive murders were committed are demolished. Thus went No. 16 Wardle Brook Avenue, Hattersley, home to Ian Brady and Myra Hindley's murderous campaign, and the Soham school caretaker's cottage where the double child murderer Ian Huntley had once been at work. But from Victorian and Edwardian times, there are very few recorded instances of murder houses being demolished. Instead, various other strategies were made use of to disguise the identity of the house, and to protect the respectability of the neighbourhood. In 1849, the lodger John Gleeson Wilson murdered Mrs Henrichson, her two children and servant girl in a bloodbath at No. 20 Leveson Street, Liverpool. The name of the street was promptly changed to Upper

Greville Street, and the murder house became a hotel. Guy Logan used to stay there when he was in Liverpool, to have a look at the bloodstain on the grate, and study the landlord's scrapbook about the murders.[3]

There are also some Victorian instances of celebrated murders causing the names of London streets to be changed. The two unsolved murders of old Mrs Samuels and Annie Yates at No. 4 and No. 12 Burton Crescent meant that the name of this gloomy Bloomsbury backwater was changed to Cartwright Gardens, and the unsolved murder of Matilda Hacker at No. 4 Euston Square prompted the change of name of the southern part of this square to Endsleigh Gardens. A particularly gruesome trunk murder at No. 45 Ladysmith Road, Kensal Rise, resulted in its name being changed not to Trunkville Road, as suggested by some jokers, but to Wrentham Avenue. There are a few verified instances of houses being renumbered after a celebrated murder was committed, but not very many: people wanted their mail delivered accurately, and no other person would of course want the sinister number of the murder house. To encounter another strategy to disguise the identity of a murder house, you should try to make your way to 'Acid Bath' Haigh's old workshop at No. 79 Gloucester Road, or perhaps read a few more chapters in this book to receive proper directions on where to find it.

There do not appear to be any London murder houses that are relics of crimes perpetrated prior to 1800.[4] The rapid slum clearances in Victorian times led to the demolition of many a notorious rookery in Westminster, St Giles, and the City. Thus Tanfield Court, near the Temple church off Fleet Street, where the Irish servant girl Sarah Malcolm murdered her mistress Mrs Lydia Duncomb in 1732, is no more. As late as 1973, Ivan Butler was able to visit Fleur-de-Lys Court, off Fetter Lane, where Elizabeth Brownrigg had tortured and murdered her female apprentices back in 1767, but road widening and development destroyed what remained of this notorious alleyway in 1974.[5] Another celebrated murder house, the old shop at No. 29 Radcliffe Highway, where the Marr family was murdered in 1811, stood as late as 1928, but has since been destroyed.[6] But the late Georgian and Victorian builders knew their trade: they were able to produce quality houses that would stand for centuries to come. The historic garden squares of Chelsea and Belgravia testify to their ability and architectural prowess, as do the elegant town houses of Kensington and Marylebone. Even houses intended for the poor were built to last, as evidenced by many of the humble terraces of Hammersmith and Fulham surviving to this day, in good order.

The historic murder houses of London have faced a trinity of enemies: decay, the Luftwaffe and the developer. Clearances of low-quality slum tenements have deprived London of a fair few murder houses. Mr Hitler's concerted effort to rearrange London's architecture meant that his Luftwaffe destroyed many a murder house, not only in the East End, but all over the metropolis. The developer has accounted for even more of them. The two aforementioned murder houses in Burton Crescent are no more, since the entire eastern terrace was demolished to allow the expansion of the University of London. The house at No. 13 Park Lane, where Madame Riel was murdered by her servant Marguerite Dixblanc in 1872, stood for many decades. At one stage, it became part of Old Park Lane when the houses were renumbered, but it was later a victim to the hotel-building craze in those parts. The elegant Bloomsbury town house at No. 11 Montague Place, site of the unsolved murder of Elizabeth Jeffs in 1828, was demolished when the British Museum was extended in 1904.

But even when you have ascertained that a murder house is still standing, it is not always entirely straightforward to find it. Many London streets have been renamed, and house numbers have changed. Moreover, in Victorian times, a 'Terrace' was a row of terraced houses in a certain road, similar in build and structure. Sometimes, the Terrace (sometimes called Villas, Place or Row) was named after the builder, sometimes after the road itself, and at other times from patriotic motives. The profusion of 'George Terraces', 'Queen's Terraces' and 'King's Terraces' in every street confounded the Victorian postmen, since provincial letter writers often did not include the name of the road on which the Terrace stood. Furthermore, the naming of roads also had serious deficiencies at the time, since there was a 'George Street', a 'King Street' and a 'Victoria Street' in every district and suburb. In the 1880s and 1890s, when the London street nomenclature and house numbering had become insufferably confused, there was a determined move to abolish all these 'Terraces', 'Places' and 'Rows', to rename the streets in a more imaginative manner, and to renumber the houses going from the centre to the periphery. This makes it a challenge to find some of the older murder houses, although the Ordnance Survey maps and Post Office directories are useful allies to the enterprising murder house detective.

For a crime to qualify as 'murder', it must have been treated as such during some stage of its investigation and/or prosecution. For a house to qualify as a 'murder house', the murder must have been committed within its walls, not out in the street or in the garden. Moreover, the building in question must survive relatively intact: thus this book makes no mention of Dr Crippen's murder house at No. 39 Hilldrop Crescent, nor of No. 10 Rillington Place, where John Christie piled up the bodies, since both these houses have been completely demolished. Nor is there a vestige left of Miller's Court, or of any other building associated with Jack the Ripper, although the old house at No. 29 Hanbury Street, where Jack murdered Annie Chapman in the rear yard, stood until 1970. Public buildings, like the Tower of London – home to various royal murder intrigues in olden times – and the House of Commons – where Prime Minister Spencer Perceval was murdered in 1812, are not included. I have tended to prefer older, historical murder cases to more recent outrages. Unsolved murder mysteries have been preferred to simple slayings. The murderous activities of the present-day yobs and knife-wielding young thugs have been avoided altogether. There are numerous instances of women dying after botched abortions, or deluded mothers killing their babies or young children, but although these tragic incidents were classified as murders at the time, they do not belong in this book.

Armed with this book and a good London map, you will be able to do some murder house detection work of your own. Why not go for a stroll round Soho to investigate the curiously little-known Soho Stranglings of the 1930s, and the sanguinary exploits of another possible serial killer called by some the Soho Ripper, active in the 1940s? A tour of some elegant murder houses of St James's, Belgravia and Knightsbridge is of course a must, including Lord Lucan's house in Lower Belgrave Street. A walk through the murder houses in Kensington and Chelsea's elegant garden squares should end at the former Cross Keys public house in Lawrence Street, where the landlady Mrs Buxton was mysteriously murdered in 1920. Nor do Marylebone and Paddington have any shortage of murder houses commemorating brutal unsolved murders, some of them celebrated crimes, others virtually unknown. A tour of old Bloomsbury will allow the reader to find out exactly why, in Victorian times, the sinister streets and squares of these parts went under the name 'the Murder Neighbourhood'. Vile and unspeakable crimes, many of them unsolved to this day, were committed in the flyblown lodging houses and decaying old terraces of this part of London. Islington has its own 'murder neighbourhood': over the years, a surprising number of murders have been committed in a relatively small area to the east of Islington Green. After visiting the house in what is today No. 2 Ivor Street, Camden Town, where Mrs Pearcey murdered her rival Phoebe Hogg in 1890 and dispatched her young daughter as well for good measure, follow her route through the cobbled streets to dispose of the dismembered remains of her victims, which she had put in a large perambulator. It leads through a spooky old tunnel underneath the railway line from Camden Road station. It seems almost a certainty that, on dark, foggy October evenings, the place is haunted by the sound of the creaking wheels of a heavily laden Victorian perambulator.

Above: The murder house at No. 4 Burton Crescent, where Mrs Samuels was murdered in December 1878. The main suspect, the muscular servant Mary Donovan, was tried for the murder but acquitted, although the police detectives were convinced that she was guilty. From the *Illustrated Police News*, 28 December 1878.

Below: The murder house at No. 12 Burton Crescent, where the prostitute Mary Ann Yates was murdered in March 1884. No clue as to the identity of the culprit ever emerged. From the *Illustrated Police News*, 22 March 1884.

Above left: The murder house at No. 4 Euston Square, said to have been haunted by the ghost of Miss Hacker for many decades.

Above right: The house in No. 13 Park Lane where Madame Riel was murdered by Marguerite Dixblanc in 1872. From the *Illustrated Police News*, 20 April 1872.

Opposite page: Six of London's houses of mystery, from Lincoln Springfield's article about 'London's Undiscovered Murders' in *Harmsworth's Magazine* for December 1898. In order of appearance: No. 12 Great Coram Street, where Harriet Buswell was murdered in 1872; No. 4 Burton Crescent, where Mrs Samuels was murdered in 1878; No. 4 Euston Square, where Miss Hacker was murdered in 1879; No. 139 Harley Street, where the body of an unknown female murder victim was found in 1880; No. 136 Lever Street, where the baker Urban Napoleon Stanger was suspected to have been roasted in his own oven in 1882 and No. 92 Bartholomew Road, where another Mrs Samuels was done to death in 1887. The Harley Street murder house is the only one standing today.

The Crippen murder house at No. 39 Hilldrop Crescent, from F. Young (ed.), *The Trial of H.H. Crippen* (London, 1933).

1

Westminster

The mysteries of modern London are like the sands of the seashore. The mighty city itself is a mystery. The lives of thousands of its inhabitants are mysteries. In the glare and clamour of the noonday, as in the darkness and silence of the night, the mysteries arise, sometimes to startle the world, sometimes to attract so little attention that the story of them never reaches the public ear.

George R. Sims, *Mysteries of Modern London*

In this book, I have defined 'Westminster' roughly as the constituency of the Cities of London and Westminster, thus excluding Marylebone, Paddington and the north-western chunk of the enormous borough that is today the City of Westminster. It is a very diverse area, ranging from some of the most affluent areas in the world, like Belgravia and St James's, to the few remaining seedy parts of Soho and Covent Garden. This is reflected in the nature of the murders taking place. Among the wealthy 'West Enders', disagreements and violence among the servants account for a not inconsiderable part of the murders. In two grand houses, butlers were murdered in 1925 and 1970, but both killers were caught after first-class police work.

It is remarkable that the City of London itself does not appear to have a single historic murder house standing. This is not only because of the law-abiding nature of the inhabitants of those parts, but also because the many office buildings are not inhabited at night, and the area has been developed, with comparably few older houses remaining. The old warehouse at No. 2 Cannon Street West, where Mrs Sarah Millson was murdered in 1866, stood for decades as a relic of the City's most mysterious unsolved murder, but it was demolished after wartime damage.[1] When I did some murder house detection work in the late 1990s, it was still possible to see where it had once stood, just by Budge Row, but in recent years, the entire area has been extensively developed.

In contrast, Soho has no shortage of murder houses. A population that included a generous proportion of prostitutes, pimps and gangsters made sure that violence abounded: the majority of the victims connected with the Soho murder houses were actually prostitutes. There are two clusters of unsolved murders of prostitutes in Soho: one in 1936 and another in 1947–8, and there has been speculation that two previously unknown serial killers had been at work.[2] Read about the murders, visit the remaining murder houses, and make your own mind up about these matters.

Some of Westminster's most famous historic murder houses are no more. No. 14 Norfolk (now Dunraven) Street, just off Park Lane, where Lord William Russell was murdered by his valet Courvoisier in 1840, no longer exists, although some remaining Georgian town houses in this street give an indication of what it must have looked like. Nor does No. 9 Portland (now Noel) Street, where a man named William Bousfield murdered his wife and three children in 1857, remain today. No. 13 Park Lane, where Lord Lucan's mistress Madame Riel was murdered by her servant Marguerite Dixblanc in 1871, stood for many decades after the event, and was admired by the author and amateur criminologist George R. Sims, who could report that it had been restored and enlarged: 'A lady comes out with a lap-dog, from the premises where not long ago a woman lay strangled, and from which a murderess fled.'[3] But since that time, No. 13 Park Lane has become yet another casualty of the frenetic hotel-building along this famous London avenue.

The Cadogan Place Murder, 1839

One of the criminal sensations of 1839 was the 'Cadogan Place Murder'.[4] The magistrate Henry Edgell lived in the large Georgian terraced house at No. 21 Cadogan Place with his family and a full staff of servants. On Friday, 17 May 1839, Mr Edgell and his family went for an excursion to Kent in their carriage, to visit some friends. They left four servants to remain in the house: the cook, the upper housemaid, the eighteen-year-old footman William John Marchant, and the young under housemaid Elizabeth Paynton. The two former individuals took advantage of the absence of their master, and also went out for some fun, leaving Marchant and the girl Paynton alone in the house.

On their return to No. 21 Cadogan Place, the cook and the housemaid were unable to obtain admittance to the house, since the front door was securely locked. Fortunately, the coachman and the upper footman soon returned from Kent. The coachman scaled the garden wall and broke open the door of the back kitchen. He let in the other servants, and they proceeded to examine the house to find out why nobody had been answering the doorbell. When they reached the drawing room, they saw Elizabeth Paynton lying on the floor, her throat dreadfully cut. A bloodstained razor lay by her side, and this was clearly the weapon with which she had been killed. When it was ascertained that Marchant had absconded from No. 21 Cadogan Place, suspicion at once attached to him.

Two days later, Marchant gave himself up to a police inspector in Hounslow and confessed to the murder. He was in a dreadful state of anxiety, claiming that he could hear the ghost of the murdered girl pursuing him. A newspaper reporter described Marchant as a 'slight puny youth' who cried incessantly and seemed to be 'in a state of dreadful agitation'. Jemmy Catnach, London's leading producer of catchpenny poems, soon published a handbill entitled 'The Life and Death of John William Marchant':[5]

> I lived as servant in Cadogan Place,
> And never thought this would be my case,
> To end my days on the fatal tree:
> Good people, pray drop a tear for me.
> Elizabeth Paynton, the servant maid,
> Of me was never in the least afraid:
> She never thought, with a deadly knife,
> John Marchant would take her life.

When on trial at the Old Bailey for the murder of Elizabeth Paynton, Marchant pleaded guilty. The motive was supposed to be unrequited love, since the other servants said that, although Marchant had been very partial to the attractive Elizabeth Paynton, she had been disposed to laugh at him. There were obvious signs of a struggle in the drawing room, suggesting that Elizabeth Paynton had fought for her life. Some hair held clutched in her right hand matched that of Marchant.

Above: Cadogan Place, a postcard stamped and posted in 1904.

Below: The execution of William Marchant, from a worn old handbill.

Now every hour, as you shall hear,
Appeared before me this maiden fair;
She would not leave me by night or day –
Then to justice I gave myself straightaway.

Marchant himself hinted that, after he had made advances on Elizabeth, she had angrily repulsed him, threatening to make sure that he lost his job. In a fury, he had murdered her, before locking up the house and absconding. William John Marchant was hanged at Newgate Prison on 8 July 1839. There was a surprising amount of newspaper publicity about the murder, including at least two 'execution broadsides'. The murder house at No. 21 Cadogan Place still stands, on the east side of this famous square.

The Pimlico Murder, 1876

In 1876, No. 99 Stanley (now Alderney) Street, Pimlico, was home to the wealthy fifty-eight-year-old builder John Collins. He was known for his financial astuteness, his considerable property portfolio, and his reluctance to spend sixpence if he could avoid it. Although his terraced Pimlico town house was quite large, the only live-in servant was an elderly cook, and there were several lodgers. Mrs Collins had to perform quite a few of the household chores herself. Since Mr Collins did not trust banks, he kept his entire fortune locked away at the house.

On 14 December 1876, Mr and Mrs Collins were visited by a young man named Frederick Treadaway, to whom they had been introduced

Portraits in connection with the Pimlico murder, from the *Illustrated Police News*, 30 December 1876.

Above: Frederick Treadaway and other features of the Stanley Street murder, from the *Penny Illustrated Paper*, 30 December 1876.

Left: The murder house at No. 99 Stanley Street, from the *Illustrated Police News*, 30 December 1876.

by some relations. The following morning, Treadaway unexpectedly returned to No. 99 Stanley Street without an invitation. Mr Collins was out at the time, but his wife showed Treadaway downstairs to the dining room. Since he complained of feeling tired, as he had been 'walking about all night', she suggested he should take a nap, and kindly put some pillows on the back of one of the chairs. When John Collins returned home for luncheon, he was surprised to see Treadaway sleeping on one of his dining room chairs. He woke the young man up and Mrs Collins could hear them having a conversation. As luncheon approached, Mr Collins said, 'What do you say to broth?' and Treadaway replied, 'I'll have some.'

Mrs Collins went into the back kitchen to help the cook serve at table. All of a sudden, she heard the report of a firearm. Running back to the dining room, she was confronted by the wild-eyed Frederick Treadaway, who was brandishing a shiny revolver. He took a shot at her but missed. Seeing that her husband sat slumped in his chair with blood pouring from his head, she bravely seized Treadaway by the collar to prevent his escape. He then thrust his thumb into her mouth and tore her cheek, before knocking her down and making his escape from No. 99 Stanley Street. In spite of the punishment she had taken, Mrs Collins pursued him out into the street, shouting, 'Stop thief!' A young man pursued the gunman as far as Eccleston Square, but lost him in the crowd.

When the local constable came to No. 99 Stanley Street, he found John Collins dying from a revolver shot to the head. Mrs Collins was alive and conscious, and she provided the name and description of the fugitive murderer. Inspector Bishop, who took charge of the case at the College Road police station, made sure that Treadaway's description was widely circulated to police forces throughout London and the Home Counties. It was presumed that the gunman had planned to murder both Mr and Mrs Collins, and possibly the old cook as well, in order to be able to search the house with impunity, and steal the money that the capitalist builder had hoarded on the premises. Frederick Treadaway's parents, who were both respectable people, faced some searching questioning as to where their son might be hiding.

In the hunt for the Stanley Street murderer, railway stations and omnibus terminals were kept under police surveillance, as were the homes of known friends of the Treadaway family. It turned out that Frederick had been staying with a lady friend, Mrs Milton, at her house in Castle Street for two days before the murder. He returned there after the murder, cut off his whiskers, and replaced his deerstalker with a tall hat. The police kept watch at the Isleworth cottage owned by a close friend of Frederick Treadaway's, and, indeed, a whiskerless cove in a tall hat was observed to come up to this very cottage. As Treadaway was leaving, he was arrested by some sturdy constables.

It turned out that, after he had murdered John Collins, Frederick Treadaway had been tramping aimlessly around London for twenty-four hours. He was entirely penniless, and the motive of his visiting the Isleworth friend had been to borrow £1. Young Treadaway had once been working as a hosier's assistant, but his lack of industry and punctuality had earnt him the sack. He was fond of drinking and partying, a talented singer and pianist, and very popular among his fun-loving friends. He was just twenty-two years old and looked even younger; the journalists marvelled that this unmanly looking, neatly dressed youngster stood accused of a callous murder. The police were much praised for having apprehended the fugitive within twenty-four hours. The murder house at No. 99 Stanley Street, where the body of Mr Collins had been laid out in one room and his widow was recovering from her injuries in another, was daily visited by a thousand curious people.

On trial at the Old Bailey for the wilful murder of John Collins, things were not looking good for Frederick Treadaway. There was no doubt that he had shot Mr Collins with a pistol purchased beforehand. The only tactic open for the defence to try was the 'insanity card'. Treadaway's father testified that several of his relatives were quite insane, including the prisoner's sister. Young Treadaway had once fallen down, foaming at the mouth, and he often suffered from headaches. His mother had once heard him speak of committing suicide. Both the defence and the prosecution called medical witnesses, but their opinions diverged wildly. The defence argued that Treadaway suffered from 'epileptic vertigo'. He had purchased the pistol to commit suicide. Inside the Collins house, he had one of his epileptic fits, and murdered the Pimlico miser in an unconscious state. During the first day of the trial, one of the witnesses had made a derogative remark to young Treadaway, who immediately began shaking uncontrollably.

The prosecution pooh-poohed all these concerns: there was no convincing family history of insanity, no doctor had diagnosed Treadaway with epilepsy before the murder, and they suspected that there was a good deal of hysteria mixed up with the theatrical fainting fit inside the courtroom. In his summing-up, Mr Justice Lush was scrupulously fair: he said that if the jury believed that the prisoner had not been aware of committing a crime, they should acquit him on grounds of insanity. But after deliberating for half an hour, the jury returned a verdict of guilty. Mr Justice Lush accordingly sentenced Frederick Treadaway to death.[6]

There was a good deal of debate in the medical journals about the Treadaway case. Some doctors argued that the Stanley Street murderer had really suffered from epilepsy, and that a great miscarriage of justice had been committed. Others claimed that, at most, he suffered from 'vertigo' or 'hysteria'.[7] Treadaway was to be executed at Newgate on 26 February 1877. All preparations had been made to carry out the death sentence, and the executioner Marwood was in readiness. But two days before the planned execution, the Governor of Newgate received a message from the Home Secretary, saying that, after a careful medical inquiry, Treadaway had been respited from the capital sentence. The prisoner 'was very much affected, and appeared deeply sensible of the mercy that had been extended to him'. The last we hear of Frederick Treadaway is in the 1881 census, which lists him as a prisoner in HM convict prison, Chatham, and in the 1891 census, he was still listed as a convict at Portsea. There has been Internet speculation that he was the George Frederick James Treadaway who married in 1894, was listed in the 1911 census, and died in 1939.

The medical debate concerning Treadaway has continued into the present time. Dr J. P. Eigen has argued that Treadaway was justly respited, since he suffered from epilepsy and committed the murder in a state of automatism, snapping out of his dazed state after having assaulted Mrs Collins.[8] But Eigen's account contains some obvious errors: Collins was no friend of Treadaway, just an acquaintance, and Treadaway was not arrested at the crime scene, but disguised himself and fled London. He may well have suffered from some variant of epilepsy, but this is irrelevant, since there is evidence of premeditation (the purchase of the pistol beforehand), motive (Treadaway was as poor as a church mouse, and Collins known to be a wealthy miser), and planning of the crime (disguise and flight). Frederick Treadaway was a lucky man to escape the hangman's noose.

In 1878 or 1879, Stanley Street was renamed Alderney Street, quite possibly because of the murder. According to the relevant Post Office directories, the houses were not renumbered. The murder house at No. 99 Alderney Street still stands, and looks virtually unchanged since the time of the murder.

Murder in Greek Street, 1883

In 1883, the first-floor flat at No. 55 Greek Street was inhabited by the thirty-nine-year-old harness maker William Crees. For some time, he had been behaving very strangely. Twice, he had been in hospital with headaches and confusion, but the doctors could do little for him. Still, William Crees was healthy enough to get married in November 1883 to twenty-three-year-old Eliza Ann Horsman, daughter of a Worthing confectioner. When Mr John Horsman brought his daughter to London for the wedding, Crees had appeared quite lucid. William Crees had given Mr Horsman and his daughter an optimistic account of his flourishing business and elegant living accommodation, but it turned out that he was quite a poor man, living in a shabby Soho flat. Nor was his wife particularly impressed with his mental balance: without even being drunk, he might go dancing in the street, whooping aloud, and being a nuisance.

In the early morning of 30 November, William Crees came up to police constable Henry Dyer, who was on patrol in the Soho streets, grasping him by the sleeve and saying, 'The doctor told me to do this!' He seemed quite incapable of explaining what he was referring to, as he danced around the startled policeman, laughing aloud. When asked where he lived, Crees gave the correct reply, and the policeman frogmarched him there, hoping that some person on the premises might take this madman off his hands. But in the cramped, dirty flat, Eliza Ann Crees was lying on her back on the floor, quite dead and covered in blood. A knife and a poker were lying nearby. Constable Dyer now knew exactly what event Crees had been alluding to when he hailed him in the street.[9]

At the coroner's inquest, the respectable confectioner John Horsman, who had come to London to identify his daughter's body, faced several unpleasant surprises. Firstly, Crees's history of mental problems, and his several hospital stays, were exposed. Secondly, it turned out that his marriage had been bigamous, since Crees already had a wife and four children alive. The murderer himself had nothing intelligible to contribute to the proceedings: he seemed quite mad, and when asked to explain what had happened, he just said, 'It is on the mantleshelf!' Several people testified as to Crees's various peculiarities, including the landlady at No. 55 Greek Street. Another lodger at the premises had heard an angry quarrel in the Crees apartment just before William went out in the small hours of 30 November.

The coroner's inquest returned a verdict of wilful murder against William Crees. He was to be tried at the Old Bailey, but since both his mental and bodily health were failing, he ended his days in a hospital. A little research shows that William Sellick Crees had been born in Blandford, Dorset, in 1844. In 1871, he was a gunner on board the *Royal Alfred*, in Grassy Bay, Bermuda. He married Lucy Werry in 1872 and settled down in Torrington, North Devon. They had the children Sidney, William, Thomas and Lucy. William then deserted his wife and family, and married Harriett Potter in Kingston in 1880, under the name William Sellick-Crees. This stratagem was not enough to fool the authorities, however, and he was convicted of bigamy. His marriage to Eliza Ann Horseman was thus his second bigamous one; there is nothing to suggest that Lucy Crees had expired in the meantime. The 1881 census finds him a convict at HM prison, Lewes. In 1891, he was a Broadmoor inmate, however, and he died there in 1932 aged eighty-five.

Another question is, of course, what was wrong with William Crees? There is no evidence that he was an alcoholic, and at the inquest a doctor confidently ruled out delirium tremens. Instead, the same doctor stated, 'In the condition of the pupils of his eyes I believe there has been a great deal of brain irritation going on.'[10] This obtuse statement might refer to what is today known as Argyll Robertson pupils: bilateral small pupils that constrict when the patient focuses on a near object, but do not constrict when exposed to bright light. They are a highly specific sign of neurosyphilis, a common disease at the time and one that might explain his rapid mental decay.

The Great Windmill Street Murder, 1887

In 1887, the terraced house at No. 29 Great Windmill Street, Haymarket, was a small lodging house. On the ground floor was a shop, and upstairs every room was crammed full of various needy individuals. One of them was the thirty-two-year-old German Franz Schultz, who worked as an interpreter when he felt like it, which was not particularly often. Separated from the *Eisbier* and *Schnapps* of his fatherland, the thirsty German made do with London bitter and gin instead, often returning home to No. 29 Great Windmill Street in a very intoxicated condition. Schultz lived with a sluttish young woman named Amelia Pottle, who liked to call herself 'Mrs Schultz' although the German cad stubbornly refused to marry her. Amelia was a part-time prostitute, who entertained various 'gentleman friends' in her bedroom when Schultz was out interpreting, or more often drinking. The other lodgers often heard angry quarrels from the Schultz rooms on the first floor, with the drunken German shouting at his wife in his guttural voice, and the sound of heavy blows when he disciplined her using his fists.

On Sunday 29 May 1887, Franz Schultz returned home in his usual drunken state. Amelia, who had also been refreshing herself, together with her most recent 'customer', was in a cantankerous state of mind, and the two soon started quarrelling. Mrs Theresa Marshall, who lodged on the second floor, heard the sound of blows and furniture breaking. She resolutely went downstairs to investigate. When Schultz opened the door, he looked worse for wear from drink. In his guttural voice, he complained that Amelia was a dirty beast, and that her 'gentleman friend' had only paid her ten shillings. Mrs Marshall told the German pimp that ten shillings was better than nothing, and asked him whether he had broken a chair that was lying on the floor. Before Schultz could answer, Amelia came into the room, saying, 'You shall not break any more of my furniture, it belongs to me, and I paid for it!' The German angrily seized hold of her, threw her on the bed, and made to strike her with the back of the chair, but Theresa Marshall snatched it away from him and threw it under the table.

Having persuaded Schultz to calm down, and to leave poor Amelia alone, Mrs Marshall returned to her own room. Schultz and his 'wife' went to sleep, and peace returned to No. 29 Great Windmill Street. But in the middle of the night, at around 1.30, the German again went on a rampage, moving furniture about and shouting angrily in his own language. At first, the other lodgers did nothing, being so very used to Schultz beating up his 'wife'. But after Amelia had screamed 'Murder! Police!' and run downstairs pursued by Schultz, the cutler Peter Bulstrode, who slept in a small bedroom behind the ground-floor shop, looked out of the window. He saw poor Amelia lying in the back yard enveloped in flames, and Schultz kneeling down by her side. The German took her up in his arms and carried her down into the basement, where he tried to put out the flames with water. He clearly heard Amelia say, 'I am dying! Take me to the hospital, I will say I did it myself!'

A pastry cook named George Darter, who was just passing by No. 29, heard the cry 'Murder! Police!' and ran to investigate. He made sure Amelia was sent to Middlesex Hospital in a cab. When he asked Schultz what had happened, the shifty-looking German muttered, 'She threw the lamp at me!' but Darter asked why, if that was the case, she was so much more badly burnt than himself.

Probably worried that Theresa Marshall might give damning evidence against him, Schultz tried to convince her that Amelia's burns were just an accident, but she did not believe him. The slimy German then asked if he could come to her room to sit down, but she was not having any of that. Franz Schultz was probably contemplating leaving London, but first he wanted to make sure that Amelia did not actually recover. When he came to Middlesex Hospital, he was told that she had just died from her terrible burns. There was a police presence at the hospital, and Inspector Edmund Burke took Schultz into custody. On trial at the Old Bailey for murdering Amelia Pottle, the German cut a sorry figure: a string of witnesses testified that he was a drunkard, a cad and a pimp, and that he had habitually mistreated poor Amelia. Peter Bulstrode, George Darter and Theresa Marshall all provided damning evidence about his activities on the morning of the murder.[11]

What saved Franz Schultz from the gallows was that, just like the heroine in a sentimental novel, the terribly burnt Amelia kept her final promise to the German scoundrel she had cohabited with: she told the casualty house surgeon that she had thrown the lamp at Schultz and burnt herself by accident, and the young doctor gave evidence in court to that effect. As a result, the German pimp walked free; the life of young Amelia Pottle was clearly not very highly valued. When interviewed by a journalist, Schultz said that he wanted to emigrate to the United States. Four years later, at the time of the 1891 census, he was still in London, however, as a patient in Middlesex Hospital.

Richard Prince in court, from the *Illustrated Police News*, 25 December 1897.

The murder of William Terriss, from the *Illustrated Police News*, 25 December 1897.

Justice for Prince! From the *Illustrated Police News*, 22 January 1898.

The Murder of William Terriss, 1897

William Charles James Lewin was born in London in 1847, and educated at Bruce Castle School, Tottenham. He then studied at Jesus College, Oxford, but left without taking a degree. After trying the merchant service, silver mining in America, sheep farming in the Falkland Islands, and tea planting in Bengal, he returned to England and took to the stage, adopting the stage name William Terriss. His handsome looks, sonorous voice and gallant bearing made him very popular. He was noted for his portrayals of heroes, which earned him the nickname 'Breezy Bill'. He was popular offstage as well, being noted for his generosity, especially towards fellow actors. One night, he arrived at the theatre dripping wet, as his contemporary Ellen Terry recalled. He shrugged off the usual jokes (Is it raining, Terriss?), and it was only later that everyone learned that the valiant actor had just dived into the Thames to rescue a child in danger of drowning.

By the early 1880s, William Terriss had established himself as one of Britain's most popular actors. He acted in a wide range of plays, from Shakespeare's *Othello* and *Romeo and Juliet* to overblown Victorian melodramas like *The Bells of Haslemere*, *The Harbour Lights* and *Black-Eyed Susan*. The part of Black-Eyed Susan herself was played by the young actress Jessie Millward. She and Terriss established themselves as romantic leads together. Although Terriss already had a wife and family, he and Jessie became lovers, and toured Britain and America together for some years. A friend of Henry Irving, George Bernard Shaw and W. S. Gilbert, William Terriss remained one of London's most famous actors well into late Victorian times. Even at the age of fifty, he was still a handsome, athletic man with a full head of hair. Tall and barrel-chested, he was able to 'ham it out' with the best of the Victorian leading men.

If William Terriss was one of the most successful actors in London, the same could not be said for the talentless Scottish oaf Richard Archer Prince. Although Prince had a high opinion of himself and his acting ability, all he got was simple bit parts. As was his custom, the benevolent Terriss helped the struggling younger actor to find work in various productions that he had a hand in. Prince's sister, a celebrated London courtesan, also helped him with money from time to time. Over the years, the frustrated Prince drank to excess and became mentally unstable. During the run of the play *The Harbour Lights*, in which Prince had a minor role, Terriss took offence at some insulting remark that

Prince had made about him, and made sure he was dismissed from the theatre. He kept sending small sums of money to Prince via the Actors' Benevolent Fund, however, and continued to try to find him acting work. By the end of 1897, Prince was destitute and desperate for work, but as a result of his drunken incompetence he had become unemployable. After an angry quarrel, even his sister wanted nothing to do with him. On 13 December, Prince was forcibly ejected from the foyer of the Vaudeville Theatre, and he and Terriss were later seen to argue in the latter's dressing room in the Adelphi Theatre. On 16 December, Prince asked for money at the office of the Actors' Benevolent Fund, but was told that his request could not be considered that day. He then met his sister, who had just picked up a 'gentleman friend' in the Empire Promenade, and appealed to her for money, but this heartless woman said that she would rather see him dead in the gutter than give him a farthing. The paranoid Scot, who blamed his benefactor Terriss for all his disappointments, crossed the street and waited for Terriss in Maiden Lane, behind the Adelphi Theatre.

On 16 December 1897, William Terriss went to the Adelphi Theatre to prepare for the evening's performance of the play *Secret Service*. But as he entered the theatre via the former royal entrance in Maiden Lane, Prince sneaked up to him and stabbed him in the back. As Terriss turned to face him, Prince stabbed him in the side, and then again in the back. William Terriss cried out, 'My God, I am stabbed!' and fell down in a pool of blood, as his cowardly murderer tried to abscond. The other actors took care of the stricken Terriss, who was still alive when Jessie Millward came down to see him. His last words are reported to have been, 'I will come back.' The murder of William Terriss became a sensation in the London press. When Prince was caught, he told the police, 'I did it for revenge. He had kept me out of employment for ten years, and I had either to die in the street or kill him.' On trial at the Old Bailey for the murder of William Terriss, Prince was found guilty but insane and sent to Broadmoor, where he staged his own plays for the other inmates, invariably playing the leading role himself.[12] He was a friend of the even more notorious veteran inmate Ronald True, and distinguished himself further by conducting the prison orchestra until his death in 1937.

True to his word, William Terriss has indeed come back. His ghost has been seen at the Adelphi Theatre and in Maiden Lane, as well as making frequent appearances at the Covent Garden underground station. Terriss was murdered ten years before this station opened, but it is said that he used to buy goods from a bakery that stood where the station is now. In 1955, the ticket collector Jack Hayden saw the ghost of Terriss wearing an opera cloak and gloves, and holding a cane. Another time, the ghost entered the former cafeteria through a closed door. He stood, silent and unmoving, before leaving through the same closed door; the employees were terrified.

Several Adelphi employees witnessed Terriss's last appearance at the theatre, in 1950. The ghost appeared from a green mist, frightening them very much. The last sighting of the ghost in Covent Garden station occurred in 1972, but staff members still hear footsteps and whispering. A 2005 Channel 5 documentary on ghosts on the London Underground reported that a ghost had been seen many times at Covent Garden station, and identified it from an old photograph of William Terriss.[13]

Murder at Bridgewater House, 1901

Bridgewater House, near St James's, was redesigned by Sir Charles Barry in 1840 in the then fashionable Italian palazzo style for the Earl of Ellesmere, the son and heir of the Duke of Bridgewater. A very large, impressive town house, it is built from Bath stone, with three stories and a basement. In this very basement, a large staff of servants were hard at work back in 1900: one of them was the forty-year-old footman Walter Leigh, another the nineteen-year-old kitchen maid Nellie Kitchener. Leigh was known as a taciturn, reticent man, and had been footman at Bridgewater House for seventeen years. A steady, competent servant, he had made a habit of always doing what he was told, and showing respect to his betters.

In September 1900, when the servants were at the earl's country residence near Doncaster, Walter Leigh made overtures to young Nellie, but she firmly told him to cease. She later told a friend that, although she wanted to be friendly to a fellow servant, she had no feelings for Walter, who was more than twice her age and not particularly attractive. The gloomy Walter Leigh went on with his duties without mentioning the rebuff he had received. Since Nellie mostly worked in the kitchen, they met only at meals.

On the morning of Sunday 24 March 1901, the servants of Bridgewater House had their breakfast as usual. They were all sitting comfortably at table, chatting about the South African war. After breakfast, Nellie went into the pantry. She was followed in there by Walter Leigh. The other servants were startled as three revolver shots rang out, one after the other. When they went into the pantry, they saw Nellie lying on the floor, shot through the head and quite dead. Walter Leigh was lying nearby, shot through the head as well, although he was still breathing. He was removed to St George's Hospital, where he expired a few hours later from his two self-inflicted wounds.

At the inquest into the deaths of Nellie Kitchener and Walter Leigh, the butler and under-butler at Bridgewater House testified that Nellie

DISCOVERY OF THE BODIES.

Walter Leigh shoots himself after murdering Nellie Kitchener, from *Illustrated Police News*, 30 March 1901.

Kitchener had been a very good servant, popular and well liked by the staff. They knew nothing about any intimacy between her and Leigh. Walter Leigh had also been a good servant, but very reserved and with few friends. A housemaid who shared a bedroom with Nellie was the only person who had heard of the shy Walter Leigh's attempt to speak to Nellie Kitchener when they were in Doncaster. The inquest returned a verdict of murder and suicide, the state of mind of the murderer left as an open question.

Walter Leigh's room had contained a sealed envelope, with a will dated 4 March 1901 leaving all his possessions to his nephew, except £60 in Bank of England notes and £5 in gold inside the envelope, which were left to his brother. The fact that this letter was dated nearly three weeks before the murder and suicide seemed to indicate that the footman had been planning to murder Nellie for some time. The motive is likely to have been unrequited love and jealousy.[14]

Bridgewater House was damaged in the Second World War, and later adapted into offices. In 1981, the Greek shipping tycoon John Latsis bought this fine building for £19 million and restored it to its former glory. Royalty and heads of state attended the lavish parties he gave there. Latsis was a firm friend of the Conservative Party, whose coffers benefited from some generous donations from him. Latsis died in 2003, but Bridgewater House, London's grandest and most exclusive murder house, at No. 14 Cleveland Row, is still owned by his family.

The Murdered Moneylender of Maddox Street, 1921

The thirty-eight-year-old Mr Stanley Theeman lived in Elgin Court, Maida Vale, but had his office as a moneylender on the first floor of No. 7 Maddox Street, off New Bond Street. On 22 December 1921, business was brisk at his little office, since, just like today, many people wanted loans to be able to afford some small luxuries for Christmas. But one of the customers waiting, a taciturn, foreign-looking young man, had other, more sinister plans. Once he was alone with Mr Theeman, he produced a small automatic pistol and handed the startled moneylender a pencilled note containing the following words: 'Silence, or you are a dead man! This is my last hope. If you do not give me a chance, you and I will die together. Remember, delay is fatal! I need £300.'

Mr Theeman's response to this extraordinary situation is not known, but it is unlikely to have been to produce a wad of £300 in cash for his

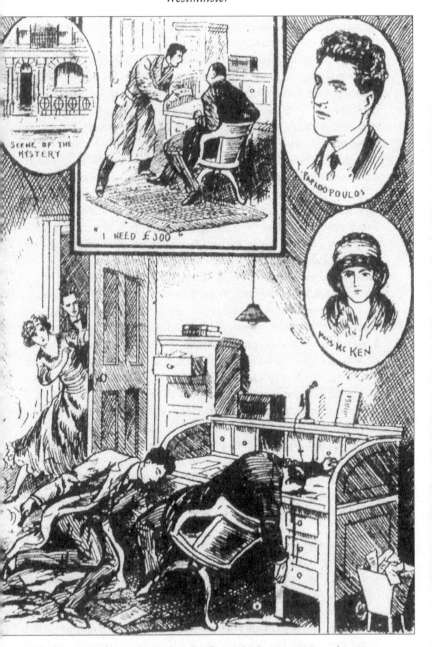

Murder of a West-End moneylender, from the *Illustrated Police News*, 29 December 1921.

sinister visitor, since his secretary Miss Ivy McKen was startled to hear three pistol shots in rapid succession, and the sound of a heavy fall.

When Miss McKen opened the door to Theeman's office, the foreign-looking young man was lying motionless on the floor with a large gunshot wound to the head. Next to him was the still-smoking pistol. Mr Theeman was also down on the floor, exclaiming, 'He has killed me, Miss McKen, he has killed me! He has hurt my leg!' Indeed, the moneylender was bleeding from two gunshot wounds, to the chest and the leg. Both men were rapidly removed to hospital, but the murderer died the same evening, and Mr Theeman the following day.

At the coroner's inquest on Stanley Theeman, his murderer was identified as the twenty-eight-year-old Theodore Papadopoulos, a Greek citizen who had been living in London for a few years. He had once been a private soldier in the Greek army but, after both his parents had been killed by the Turks, he had deserted and become a thief. He then joined the British army as an interpreter. To avoid being caught by the Greek military police, who did not take kindly to deserters, he took refuge in London in 1918. Here, the lazy, work-shy young Greek made a perilous living as a small-time crook and swindler. He posed as a photographer and persuaded various 'mugs' to invest in his business. He was also good at telling sob stories about his sufferings during the war to various kindly old bodies who took an interest in the relief of distressed foreigners, and then he spent their money quickly.

Papadopoulos had often spoken of destroying himself when his mood had been low, but he had shown no indication of committing any rash act prior to his desperate attempt to rob Stanley Theeman. He had never met Theeman before, and appears to have chosen his victim more or less at random. The inquest, which relentlessly exposed all the Greek's previous misdeeds, returned a verdict of murder against Theodore Papadopoulos, who had then committed *felo de se*.[15]

Murder and Madness in Lowndes Square, 1922

In 1922, the large and elegant town house at No. 30 Lowndes Square, Knightsbridge, belonged to Colonel Charles W. Trotter. He employed a full staff of servants, headed by the butler James Pellant, to look after it. In 1920, the fifteen-year-old Ernest Albert Walker had been employed as footman at No. 30, straight after leaving school. Mr Pellant thought him a very good young lad, being the son of a Kent police constable, and both reliable and industrious. At Christmas 1921, Ernest Albert Walker was informed that his mother had just died of influenza. Understandably, this made the young footman very depressed, and he took out Colonel Trotter's gun-case to shoot himself. The other servants impeded him, however, and he was harshly spoken to by Mr Pellant for this attempt at self-destruction; no person seems to have suggested that he perhaps needed to see a doctor, or a psychiatrist.

After his mother's death, Ernest Albert Walker became a changed man, or rather boy. Although he kept doing his job to the full satisfaction of Mr Pellant, he had strange, perverted fantasies of committing murder. In April 1922, he carefully drew up a list on black-edged writing paper:

1. Rung up Sloane-street.
2. Waited at front door.
3. Invited him in.
4. Bring him downstairs.
5. Ask him to sit down.
6. Hit him on the head.
7. Put him in the safe.
8. Keep him tied up.
9. Torture.
10. Prepare for the end.
11. Sit down, turn on gas.
12. Put latter out.
13. Sit down, shut window.
14. Kensington 2059.

The demented Ernest Albert Walker followed this list to perfection. On 22 April, when Colonel Trotter and the Hon. Mrs Trotter were away, he telephoned the district messenger office in Sloane Square, asking that a messenger boy should be sent to No. 30 Lowndes Square. When the fourteen-year-old Raymond Davis came knocking at the door, Ernest Albert Walker followed his murderous plan, hitting Davis on the head with an iron fire bar and then tying him up, although he had never seen the boy before. The other servants had been given the day off, and the demented footman could do what he pleased in the large, empty house. After leaving his hapless victim in a gas-filled room, Ernest Albert Walker escaped to Tonbridge. But once he was away from London, the enormity of what he had done seems to have dawned on him, and he went up to a police constable saying that he had just committed murder at No. 30 Lowndes Square.

Initially, the Tonbridge constable thought that he was the victim of a practical joke, but eventually he collared Ernest Albert Walker, took him to the local police station, and communicated with his London colleagues. When arrested on a charge of murder, the footman said, 'Yes, sir. I do not know what made me do it; I do not think I knew what I was doing at the time.' Indeed, when a party of London constables searched the premises on No. 30 Lowndes Square, they found the unconscious Raymond Davis. Amazingly, considering the amount of punishment he had received, he was still alive. The unfortunate lad even regained consciousness for a while, and told how he had been knocked down by an unknown assailant, only to briefly awake, bound and gagged, in a gas-filled room, before passing out once more. He expired the following morning, from gas poisoning and his other injuries. At the coroner's inquest on Raymond Davis, the bizarre 'murder list' was read aloud, as was a letter that Ernest Albert Walker had written to the butler:

> I rang up Sloane-street office for them to send a messenger to 30, Lowndes-square. He came to the front door. I asked him to come in and wait. I brought him to the pantry and hit him on the head with a coal hammer. So simple. I killed him – not with the gas. Then I turned the gas full on. I am sane as ever I was, only I could not live without my dear mother. I didn't half give it to that damned boy. I made him squeal. Give my love to dad, and all my friends. I remain yours truly, Ernest.

At the inquest, a verdict of wilful murder was returned against Ernest Albert Walker. There was a history of insanity in his family: his great-uncle had died in an asylum, as had his great-aunt and her two feeble-minded daughters. The young footman himself had been considered mentally deficient when attending Newington school, but the teachers in another school had not agreed with this harsh verdict. There was no doubt that the death of his mother had affected him very much, and disturbed his fragile mental equilibrium. On trial for murder at the Old Bailey, he was found guilty but insane, and committed to Broadmoor.[16] In 1937, he was released after fifteen years in the asylum, and disappeared into obscurity.[17]

As for the murder house, old Ordnance Survey maps show that it stood on the eastern extremity of the southern terrace of Lowndes Square. The houses on the eastern side ended with No. 28, and No. 29 was approached from Lowndes Street to the south of No. 30. But in the early 1930s, several of the large, old-fashioned houses on the south side of Lowndes Square were internally remodelled to become a fashionable block of flats. Thus, the present-day Lowndes Court at No. 34 Lowndes Square encompasses the old houses at No. 29–No. 34, including the murder house at the corner with Lowndes Street.

The Murder of Sir Henry Wilson, 1922

Field Marshal Sir Henry Wilson was a distinguished soldier, who had served in the Third Anglo-Burmese War and the Second Boer War. After playing an influential role in the First World War as a staff officer and army corps commander, he was made a Field Marshal in 1919. He retired as Chief of the Imperial General Staff in 1922, and unwisely decided to dabble in Irish politics. In a by-election victory, he became MP for North Down, Ulster. A firm enemy of the Irish Republic, he travelled to Belfast in June 1922 to advise the Northern Irish authorities on how to deal with the Republican bomb outrages.[18]

Returning to London, Sir Henry unveiled the Great Eastern Railway war memorial in a ceremony at Liverpool Street station on 22 June 1922. Returning home to his elegant Belgravia house at No. 36 Eaton Place wearing full dress uniform, he paid the cab driver and walked up the steps to the house. But two IRA members, Reginald Dunn and Joseph O'Sullivan, both of them ex-servicemen, were waiting for him, carrying loaded revolvers. Hit in the arm by two bullets, Sir Henry tried to draw his dress sword, but his attackers gunned him down without mercy. Hit by nine bullets in all, Sir Henry expired on the stairs of his house as the two gunmen made their escape down Ebury Street.

Joseph O'Sullivan, who had a wooden leg, soon struggled, but Dunn stayed with him. The two IRA men commandeered a cab and then a victoria, firing at their pursuers and wounding two police constables. In the end, they were pulled from their vehicle by a furious mob, and would have been lynched had not the police intervened. Found guilty of the wilful murder of Sir Henry Wilson, Dunn and O'Sullivan were sentenced to death and executed together at Wandsworth Prison.[19] They were buried in the prison grounds, as was the custom, but in 1976 their

The murder of Sir Henry Wilson, from the *Illustrated Police News*, 29 June 1922.

remains were repatriated to Ireland. Sir Henry Wilson was buried in the crypt of St Paul's Cathedral. The murder house at No. 36 Eaton Place has been subdivided into flats.

Murder at the Savoy Hotel, 1923

The Savoy was London's first proper luxury hotel. It was constructed by the successful entrepreneur Richard d'Oyly Carte in 1889, and was the first London hotel with electric lights and electric lifts. Expensive and opulent, it attracted a wealthy international clientele. One of them was Oscar Wilde, but he later was the cause of the first of several unsavoury episodes in the annals of the Savoy Hotel, when it transpired, at his trial for gross indecency, that he had been entertaining a succession of rent boys in Room 361.

In July 1923, yet another wealthy and noble couple came to stay at Suite 41 at the Savoy Hotel: the Prince and Princess Fahmy. Prince Ali was just twenty-two years old; he was a dapper-looking Egyptian playboy who led an idle life while squandering a not inconsiderable allowance. He came from a wealthy and noble family, but it can be debated whether he was really entitled to the title of prince. Princess Marguerite was ten years older; she was a pretty French divorcee who had been a Paris good-time girl when she met the young prince. They had married in Egypt, first in a civil ceremony on 26 December and then in a Muslim wedding in January 1923.

When Marguerite Fahmy had been staying at the Savoy Hotel for a few days, she summoned the Savoy's doctor, complaining she was suffering badly from haemorrhoids. She alleged that her husband had 'torn her by unnatural intercourse' and was 'always pestering her' for this kind of sex. Already thinking about possible future divorce proceedings she repeatedly asked the doctor for 'a certificate as to her physical condition to negative the suggestion of her husband that she had made up a story'. The doctor, who was not a specialist in haemorrhoids and other disagreeable diseases of the rear passage, did not feel inclined to write her one, however.

The Fahmys were often at loggerheads, and their quarrels sometimes ended in blows. He gave her a knock or two if he thought she had been too cheeky, and she sometimes repaid the compliment by scratching his face. In the evening of 9 July, the Fahmys went dining as usual, elegantly dressed. But soon there was another argument and it was not

The Cecil and Savoy hotels, from an old postcard.

Madame Fahmy.

long before Marguerite retired to Suite 41 after refusing the offer of a dance with her husband. The gloomy-looking Ali followed her a little later. A night porter passing their door after midnight saw Fahmy burst from the room in agitation, his face badly scratched. 'Look at my face!' he shouted. 'Look at what she has done!' But the porter, who did not know that he was addressing a prince, merely reminded this excitable foreigner that he ought to keep quiet, since there were respectable people sleeping nearby.

Just seconds later, three shots rang out. The porter rushed back to the room, where he saw Marguerite throw down a black handgun. Ali sat slumped against the wall, bleeding profusely from a wound on his temple, from which bone splinters and brain tissue protruded. 'Qu'est-ce que j'ai fait, mon cher?' (What have I done, my dear?), Marguerite kept saying over and over again. When the police arrived, and the bleeding Ali was taken off to hospital, Marguerite had thoughts only for herself. As she stood next to her fallen husband, she said, 'Oh, sir, I have been married six months, which has been torture for me. I have suffered terribly.' But since it was obvious that she had gunned down her husband, she was taken into custody.

Ali Fahmy died soon after, and the case was now one of murder. Marguerite was in a very difficult position indeed. There was no denying that she had shot him dead, and she was fully compos mentis. Even if she escaped the gallows, a lengthy prison sentence would be likely to come her way. She is not the only killer in this book to have been very well served by the brilliant Edward Marshall Hall. Pulling out all the stops, this eloquent gentleman soon had the jury eating out of his hand. Playing on their inherent racism and xenophobia, he depicted Ali Fahmy as an Oriental degenerate, and a homosexual as well, whose perverted sexuality had made poor Marguerite's life unbearable. Marshall Hall went on to remind them that, as an Oriental man, his wife to him was no more than a belonging and that however much he may have acquired the outward signs of urbanity and sophistication, he was forever an Oriental under the skin. He boldly claimed that the night Marguerite had shot him, this unnatural man had advanced at her, gun in hand, but she had wrestled it away from him and then pulled the trigger of the Browning .32-caliber pistol herself.

When Marguerite took the stand, she was encouraged by the Great Defender to describe her life as a Muslim bride, and the case soon turned her way. She told how she had been sitting 'in a state of undress in which her modesty would have forbidden her facing even her maid', she had noticed a strange noise and she pulled aside the hangings that screened an alcove and 'saw crouching there, where he could see every move she made, one of her husband's numerous ugly, black, half-civilized manservants, who obeyed like slaves his every word'. She screamed for help, but when her husband appeared from an adjoining room, he only laughed, saying, 'He is nobody. He does not count. But he has the right to come here or anywhere you may go and tell me what you are doing.'

Marshall Hall took the murder weapon and demonstrated the shooting for the benefit of the jury. For an instant he pointed the weapon at them, acting out the role of Prince Ali, advancing on his wife in a threatening manner. Marshall Hall crouched and snarled in what he thought was a convincing imitation of the murderous Ali Fahmy. The hushed courtroom then watched him drop the gun to the floor. The great barrister later insisted that that part was an accident, but it had a powerful effect on the jury, which returned a verdict of not guilty after only an hour's deliberation.[20] The jurors all but ignored the fact that Marguerite had shot her husband at point-blank range.

Although there were some, Egyptians in particular, who objected to Marshall Hall describing their country as the haunt of perverted, homosexual degenerates who preyed upon Western women to degrade them and destroy their values of decency, the great barrister could exult that he had saved yet another client from the gallows. The acquittal of Marguerite Fahmy had been cheered not only by the spectators inside the Old Bailey, but also by a large crowd outside. The newspaper press also ate from his hand, praising him as the saviour of a pure, innocent Frenchwoman who had escaped a fate worse than death at the hands of her perverted husband. The *Daily Mirror* cautioned against marriages between Western women and Eastern men, claiming that the Fahmy case 'should serve as a lesson to our young emotionally impressionable daughters who have yet to acquire a certain sophistication'. *Lloyd's News* wrote that 'the white woman who seeks love from men not of her race, whether they are yellow, brown or black, enters a world against which her nature must rebel when she learns the truth', and the *Sunday Pictorial* commented that the Madame Fahmy case held little surprise for those who were familiar with the manifestations of the Oriental mentality.

The defence of Marguerite Fahmy was one of Marshall Hall's most formidable bravura performances in court. The prosecution, who appear to have been spellbound by the great barrister's oratory themselves, were not even allowed to cross-examine Marguerite. A recent TV documentary has made the spicy suggestion that the reason for this might well have been that Marguerite possessed a wad of compromising letters from her former lover Edward, Prince of Wales, the contents of which might have done considerable harm to the reputation of that foolhardy young royal. A cross-examination would also have found out that Marguerite had once been a Paris prostitute, and that she was the mother of an illegitimate child. Known for her lesbian tendencies, she had sometimes catered to female clients as well. Enjoying the limelight after her ordeal at the Old Bailey, this wicked woman became a minor celebrity for a while, and even acted in a couple of films. Since Ali Fahmy had not written a will, Marguerite did not inherit any of his wealth, although she tried yet another one of her tricks, namely to pretend that she was pregnant with her late husband's child. But this stratagem did not have the desired effect, and she sunk back into obscurity, dying a Paris recluse in January 1971. The Savoy Hotel would remain murder free until 1980, when Tony Marriott murdered the prostitute Catherine Russell in Room 853.[21]

Murder of Sir George Lloyd's Butler, 1925

In 1925, the prestigious address of No. 24 Charles Street, Mayfair, belonged to the distinguished politician and colonial administrator Sir George Lloyd, who had just been appointed High Commissioner of Egypt.[22] The house was (and still is) an elegant mansion, situated in a quiet Mayfair cul-de-sac. Sir George was not staying there in June 1925, preferring to spend some time at his country estate in the warm summer months. The house was looked after by a butler, the twenty-six-year-old Frank Edward Rix, and a domestic staff of six. Rix was a trusted family servant, appreciated for his efficiency in running the household.

At 7.30 in the morning of 7 June 1925, one of the housemaids came into Rix's basement bedroom to give him his breakfast and a cup of tea. She was horrified to see that the butler had been brutally murdered by repeated heavy blows to the head and face. The police were promptly called, and a team of Scotland Yard detectives began their investigation, led by the veteran Chief Constable Frederick Westley. Their search for

Above: Charles Street, from an old postcard.

Opposite above: Bishop gives himself up for murdering the butler, and a sketch of the murder house in Charles Street, from the *Illustrated Police News*, 18 June 1925.

Opposite below: The murdered butler Rix's room is investigated by the police, from the *Illustrated Police News*, 11 June 1925.

the murder weapon was not a lengthy one: a large, bloodstained hammer was lying on the floor of the murder room. The first blow from this formidable instrument had probably been sufficient to stun the hapless butler, but the murderer had kept belabouring Rix's head with the heavy hammer, inflicting terrible injuries. It was considered extraordinary that the murderer had been able to beat Rix to death without any person waking up; after all, the basement was full of sleeping domestics, one of them in the room next door to the butler's pantry. A gold ring inscribed 'F.E.R.', a watch, some money and a pair of boots had been stolen from the butler's cupboard. 'Sir G. Lloyd's Butler Murdered in Mayfair House!' exclaimed a headline in the *Daily Mirror*, illustrated with a photograph of the prominent politician, rather than the murder victim. The *News of the World* instead reproduced a photograph of the murder house at No. 24 Charles Street, showing it looking exactly as it does today.

Questioning Sir George Lloyd's surviving domestics, the detectives soon found a vital clue. A seventeen-year-old pantry boy named Arthur Henry Bishop had been employed at No. 24 for six months before Rix had fired him for his incompetence and dishonesty. In spite of his tender years, Bishop had seemed like a nasty piece of work, and he had greatly resented being sacked. Before leaving, he had stolen £1 from Rix, and a silver cigarette case from one of the footmen. The plan had been for Rix to procure alternative employment for Bishop at some house or hotel, but this plan never came to fruition, perhaps because the butler did not want to foist such an incompetent recruit onto one of his respectable Mayfair colleagues. The line of thought that the murderer had been in league with one of Lloyd's other domestics was gradually discarded, since none of them seemed to have any particular sympathy for young Bishop. The police sent out a description of the absconded Bishop: a stocky lad 5 feet 6 inches in height, with a full face and a blotchy complexion, and usually dressed in a blue serge suit.

The very next day, an alert woman shopkeeper in Shoreham, a village between Swanley and Sevenoaks in Kent, saw a lad exactly answering this description. She telephoned the Sevenoaks police, and detectives were dispatched to look for the suspect. It turned out that the former pantry boy had had enough of his life of crime, however: two hours later, he quietly gave himself up to the village policeman. Bishop later made a full confession to the detectives. He had been drinking hard on the evening of 6 June, he said, ruminating on his misfortunes and cursing the miserable butler who had ended his career in Sir George Lloyd's household. He got the idea to rob the house at No. 24 Charles Street to take revenge, and entered the basement by forcing a window. Having armed himself with the hammer, he crept into the butler's room and ransacked his cupboard. Thinking that Rix was about to wake up, he hit the sleeping butler hard with the hammer, and then continued beating him about the head until he was dead.

Young Bishop knew a prostitute named Margaret Stewart who used to walk her beat in Jermyn Street, and it turned out that she was still 'available' even in the wee hours of 7 June, when Bishop came searching for her. Bishop took her to a nearby hotel for some late-night 'fun'. When she saw that he was wearing two watches and a ring, and commented that he seemed to have a good deal of money, he said he was a prosperous farmer from Kent. When the observant girl also noticed that the initials on the ring did not match his own, he told her that he had just purchased it.

Arthur Henry Bishop was duly tried and convicted for the murder of Frank Edward Rix. There was no recommendation to mercy from the jury, nor any comment from Mr Justice Rigby Swift before he sentenced Bishop to death. An appeal was later made on grounds of insanity. It spoke in Bishop's favour that he was very young, that he had been intoxicated at the time of his crime, and that he had no previous criminal record. On the other hand, he was a nasty piece of work, and his crime a dastardly and premeditated one. Accordingly, the appeal failed and Bishop was hanged at Pentonville Prison on 14 August 1925. He was one of only four eighteen-year-olds executed in Britain in the twentieth century.[23] The murder house still stands, and still appears to be a private residence at one of London's most exclusive addresses. The nearby No. 20 Charles Street is a small palace, with a blue plaque announcing that it was once inhabited by the Prime Minister, the Earl of Rosebery.

Sir George Lloyd became Lord Lloyd not long after the murder of his butler, and remained active as an elitist right-wing Tory politician for many years. He was a friend of traditional British values, and fond of architecture, but it does not appear that he remained very long in the murder house at No. 24 Charles Street; when employing the aesthete James Lees-Milne as his private secretary some years later, he lived in a large Georgian house at Portman Square. Lord Lloyd was clever enough to appreciate the threat of the Nazi regime in Europe, something that did not help his career during the years of appeasement. But when Winston Churchill came to power in 1940, Lord Lloyd was appointed Leader of the House of Lords and Secretary of State for the Colonies. Sadly, he died in office the year after.

Murder at the Union Club, 1926

Charles Emile Berthier was a dodgy Frenchman, active in London as a car dealer. His business was not very successful, and his gambling and card playing devoid of good fortune. In happier days, he had lent money to another, even dodgier Frenchman named Charles Baladda. This individual had been a pilot in the First World War, but was invalided out of the French air force after being badly wounded in action. Baladda later went to England, where he was suspected to be an international criminal and deported. He clandestinely returned to London, however,

A Soho street market near Frith Street.

living under various aliases and successfully evading the police. In the 1920s, Baladda moved back and forth between France and England. His main legitimate business was said to be representing certain French winegrowers. A strong, muscular man, nicknamed 'Big Arms', he was fond of drinking, gambling and partying, spending much time in various Soho clubs. Although this mystery man was known to have money, he showed no inclination at all to repay his debt to Berthier.

On the evening of 7 April 1926, the thirty-six-year-old Charles Emile Berthier went to the Union Club, situated at No. 24 Frith Street, Soho. The gloomy Frenchman went up to the card-playing table, where Baladda sat gambling with some cronies. Berthier shook hands with the men, before saying, rather threateningly, 'I am broke. My friends, I respect them, but those who owe me money will have to pay or I shall do them an injury!' Baladda stared at him and replied, 'You must not speak like that. One does not say those things, one does them!'

'What is the matter with you, "Big Arms"?'

Baladda rose to face Berthier, replying, 'And what is the matter with you?' As he was about to put his hand on Berthier's shoulder, the latter pulled a revolver from his raincoat pocket and shot his burly opponent three times. Baladda clutched his chest and collapsed.

The frenzied Berthier ran out of the room, but he was caught by an Italian named Luigi Dionigi, who pushed him into the billiards room and hit him hard on the head with a billiards cue. Berthier went down for the count, but when Dionigi went to seize hold of him he leapt up again. Screaming 'Don't kill me!', he dashed past the Italian and out of the club. A man saw Berthier running up Frith Street, his ear bleeding profusely from the blow he had received. He was screaming 'L'hôpital! L'hôpital!', and the passer-by gave him directions to the French hospital. It does not appear as if Berthier made it to the hospital, however. Instead, the shaken Frenchman recovered his *sangfroid* and returned to the motor garage. Making use of one of the more roadworthy of his vehicles, he set out for Newhaven, but was arrested on board the ferry to Dieppe.

On trial at the Old Bailey for the murder of Charles Baladda, things were not looking good for Charles Emile Berthier. Numerous eyewitnesses had seen him shooting Baladda and making his escape from the Union Club. The defence played the insanity card: Berthier had been very depressed after the failure of his business and the recent death of his wife. One of his uncles was in a lunatic asylum, and his brother had committed suicide. The jury found him guilty, but they added that he had been insane at the time he committed the murder, and not responsible for his actions. Mr Justice Salter ordered the prisoner to be detained at Broadmoor until His Majesty's pleasure be known. This was not particularly long, since Berthier was repatriated to France by April 1928. To prevent further mischief, it was stipulated that he should not be allowed to re-enter the United Kingdom.[24] The murder club at No. 24 Frith Street is today the 'Dodo' supermarket.

Two Suicide Pacts at the Regent Palace Hotel, 1932

The Regent Palace Hotel, situated just by Piccadilly, was constructed in 1914; it was the largest hotel in Europe at the time, with 1,028 beds. In 1932, it became the epicentre of London's hotel-related murders, with two domestic tragedies in rapid succession. In June 1932, Captain John Blockley of the Indian Army Service Corps booked into the Regent Palace with a young woman named Helen Diamond, whom he presented as his wife. The problem was that there was already a Mrs Blockley; the captain had married Helen bigamously at the Glasgow Sheriff Court, promising to take her with him to India. But the couple had spent their honeymoon in Margate, and when they booked into the hotel, they were in a far from happy mood. The day after, Captain Blockley shot his 'wife'

The Regent Palace Hotel, from an undated postcard.

dead and then committed suicide. Nobody heard or reacted to the shots, and the bodies were not discovered until twelve hours later.[25]

There was more carnage to come at the Regent Palace Hotel. Mabel Jones, a native of Bradford, married the textile engineer Herbert Victor Hill in 1924, but in March 1931 they separated by mutual agreement. Although Mabel was now thirty-two years old, she began 'walking out' with the twenty-one-year-old motor engineer Herbert Turner. In October 1932, the two lovers were in a gloomy state of mind. Herbert suggested that they should commit suicide together, and purchased a bottle of prussic acid. They went to London and took a room at the Regent Palace Hotel. On 30 October 1932, a hotel maid noticed that 'Mr and Mrs Turner' did not answer the telephone, or respond to a knock on the door, although she knew they were in the room. She informed the management, and when the door was opened with a master key Mabel Hill was found dead, but Herbert Turner was still alive. Having recovered from his rash attempt at self-destruction, Herbert Turner faced a murder trial. There was no doubt that he had purchased the prussic acid, nor that Mabel Hill's death was the result of poisoning with that substance. After long deliberation, the jury found him guilty, but added a strong recommendation to mercy. Mr Justice Stephens passed sentence of death on the prisoner, but added that he agreed with the recommendation to mercy. Turner's sentence was duly commuted to penal servitude for life.[26] It is surprising that, according to a newspaper account, he was out of prison as early as December 1934.[27] The Regent Palace Hotel appears to have been murder-free since the two 1932 tragedies.

The Soho Stranglings, 1935–1936

In November 1935, the forty-one-year-old Soho prostitute Josephine Martin was found strangled in her room at Nos 3–4 Archer Street (the house no longer stands). She was a veteran prostitute who had been walking the Soho streets for decades. Although of Russian descent, she called herself 'French Fifi'. No worthwhile clue to the identity of Fifi's murderer was ever found, although it was presumed that she might have been killed by a 'customer' who wanted to steal her savings.

Marie Jeanet Cotton was born in France in 1892, but she moved to London in 1920 to become a domestic servant. In 1924, she married a man named Louis Cousins, but he deserted her the year after and died in 1929.

Old Compton Street, from an old postcard.

Marie Jeanet made a decent living for herself as a servant and restaurant waitress, and there is no evidence that she ever turned to prostitution. In 1936, she was employed as the domestic servant of a barrister in Savile Row. She lived in a three-room flat at No. 47 Lexington Street, sharing it with her lover, the Italian chef Carlo Lanza, and his fifteen-year-old son Remo, who worked as a kitchen boy. A newspaper photograph of her shows a thin, handsome, dark-haired woman, with something of a refined appearance in spite of her lowly position in society.

In the evening of 16 April 1936, Marie Jeanet Cotton was found dead at No. 47 Lexington Street by the lad Remo. Just like French Fifi, she had been strangled, and a silk scarf was tied round her neck. 'Yard Hunt for Maniac!' exclaimed the *Daily Mirror*, convinced that a serial killer was on the loose in Soho. Chief Inspector F. D. Sharpe, the officer in charge of the murder investigation, found nothing to suggest that Marie Jeanet had ever been involved in the vice trade, however. Many prostitutes went to the police with various tips about Fifi and Marie Jeanet. The man Lanza was said to have sometimes kicked 'Madame Cotton' when they quarrelled, but he had a cast-iron alibi for her murder. Both Fifi and Marie Jeanet were said to have gone in fear of some mysterious enemy who had threatened to kill them, but the identity of these individuals was never discovered.

The most promising lead in the Lexington Street murder investigation was a man named James Allan Hall. In 1935 and early 1936, he had lived in the house at No. 47 after leaving his estranged wife, whom he had often treated violently. He was bisexual, and partied hard with various dodgy individuals. During one of these orgies, a mattress belonging to 'Madame Cotton' was badly damaged in some unspeakable manner. She wanted compensation, but Hall absconded to other lodgings in Craven Street. She tracked him down there, and was supposed to have met him the day before the murder, but Hall did not come. When questioned by the police, he did not have an alibi for the murder. At the inquest on Marie Jeanet Cotton, he seemed shifty and evasive, and gave a most unfavourable impression. Still, there was no direct evidence against him, and the verdict was one of murder against some person or persons unknown.[28]

Some of the police detectives investigating the Lexington Street murder were convinced, for some reason or other, that Hall was the guilty man. They kept a track on his movements and activities as late as 1939, but without succeeding in building up a case against him. Chief Inspector Sharpe instead suspected another, unnamed man, who was an acquaintance of 'Madame Cotton', but there was not enough evidence to charge him with the murder. The serial killer panic in Soho caused by the murders of French Fifi and Marie Jeanet Cotton would reach its peak when, in early May 1936, a third woman, the young prostitute Leah Hinds, was found strangled in Old Compton Street. The newspaper writers at the time were convinced that some mysterious 'Jack the Strangler' was active in Soho, completing the work of his Whitechapel namesake forty-eight years earlier. The Georgian terraced murder house at No. 47 Lexington Street, said to have been quite dilapidated back in 1936, today looks very well cared for.

The Murder of Leah Hinds, 1936

Constance May Hinds had a very unpromising start in life. She was born in 1912, the illegitimate daughter of the female career criminal Kathleen Hinds, who had many convictions for theft, receiving stolen goods and vice crime. Constance May was taken care of by her grandmother, but she soon turned out to be as vicious as her mother, leaving home in her early teens to make a living on the Soho streets as a cheap prostitute. She had a number of dubious 'boyfriends', some of whom doubled as

JEANETTE COTTON
THE VICTIM.

REMO LANZA.
WHO DISCOVERED
THE CRIME

SCENE OF
THE MURDER

THE BOYS DISCOVERY.

The murder of Madame Cotton, from the *Illustrated Police News*, 23 April 1936.

her pimps, including the black entertainer Jim Rich, who 'kept' her from 1930 until 1932. In 1931, she gave birth to a baby, which was adopted away. In June 1933, she married the Margate waiter Robert Thomas Smith, but she left him the following year.

Constance May Hinds changed her address very frequently, moving in and out of various cheap lodgings. For some reason or other, she also changed her name on a regular basis, alternating between 'Leah Hind', 'Leah Hines', 'Connie Smith' and 'Connie May Hine', among other pseudonyms. She was known as 'Dutch Leah', since she sometimes wrongly claimed Dutch ancestry, and as 'Stilts Leah' for her habit of wearing high-heeled shoes. In April 1936, she met a street conjurer named Stanley King and moved in with him at Little Pulteney Street. He found out that she was a prostitute, but continued the relationship nevertheless. Perhaps at one stage he had hoped to 'reform' the devious Leah, but not with any degree of success. Since he himself worked in the evenings, he could not keep a watch on her, and she made sure she had charge of the sole set of keys to their room, so that he would not be able to 'catch her in the act'.

In May 1936, Stanley King and Leah Hinds (as most people knew her) lodged in a second-floor room in a dilapidated house at No. 66 Old Compton Street (it still stands), right in the centre of Soho's prostitution racket. The house, consisting of three stories above a shop, was crammed full of needy lodgers; there were even two men living in the basement. Leah was a regular visitor to various sleazy nightclubs nearby. She regularly touted for customers in Cambridge Circus, and had eight convictions for soliciting.

On the evening of Friday 8 May 1936, Leah was out partying in Soho as usual. Close to midnight, she found a 'customer' and brought him back to No. 66 Old Compton Street. Three witnesses – a restaurant porter and two young girls of doubtful virtue – saw the well-known Leah return home with her 'gentleman friend'. They described him as slim, tall and clean-shaven, with long hair and a slouching gait. He wore a dark raincoat, but not a hat. The next morning, Stanley King came to pick up Leah at No. 66, but she did not open the door when he knocked. He could hear her puppy whining inside the room. Worried that something might be seriously wrong, he went to a local restaurant, where he met a labouring man named Adams. Since Stanley did not have a key to the door to the room, he persuaded Adams to break down the door.

The murder of Leah Hinds, from the *Illustrated Police News*, 14 May 1936.

Inside, they found the puppy alive and well, but Leah had been strangled to death with thin wire. She had clearly tried to fight off her departed assailant, since her face had been battered with a series of heavy blows. She had probably been murdered shortly before 1 a.m.

Chief Inspector Sharpe, who was in charge of the investigation of the murder of Marie Jeanet Cotton, also led the Leah Hinds murder task force. He thought the motive might well have been theft, since Leah had boasted, during the evening, that she had money, and her handbag had been ransacked. Leah's and Stanley's fingerprints were found inside the murder room, and also an unknown print, either from the murderer or from a previous 'client'. This print did not match any kept on file at Scotland Yard. The tabloid newspapers quickly spread their conviction that a serial strangler was at large in Soho. 'Maniac's Three Soho Women Victims! Girl's Friends Fear to Talk!' exclaimed the *Daily Mirror*, although the second part of that headline was falsified already in the article itself: there was in fact no shortage of people who had known Leah and who told the police and journalists a variety of more or less true stories about her. The special correspondent of the *Mirror* could report that 'A friend of Constantine Hinds said to me, "I was with Dutch Leah only three nights ago. Even while we were talking, she kept looking around her with an expression of fear in her eyes. She had many enemies, and it was a common saying among her friends that Leah had it coming to her."' Another dubious tabloid scoop described the exhortations of a Danish ex-jockey named George Killik, who fancied himself as a medium: he proclaimed that the murderer was a thin, impoverished man with large hands, and saw another girl in danger of her life.

Eschewing such tabloid sensationalism, the police made a determined effort to find some link between the three murdered women – French Fifi, Marie Jeanet Cotton and Leah Hinds – but without success. Chief Inspector Sharpe did not believe that Leah had been murdered by some former pimp or old enemy; rather, he believed it had been by a random stranger with homicidal tendencies, whom she had had the misfortune of picking up on the night in question. He thought that, although Fifi and Leah might have been murdered by the same random robber of prostitutes, 'Madame Cotton' had probably been killed by a person she knew.[29]

In 1937, there was yet another spate of murder mania, after the prostitute Elsie McMahon was found murdered in her room at No. 306 Euston Road (the house no longer stands). Again, the tabloids did their best to fuel a serial killer scare, although the police never linked the McMahon murder with the three Soho stranglings. As late as May 1938, the *Chicago Tribune* published a feature on London's mysterious serial killer of prostitutes. Although this article published a photograph of the house at No. 306 Euston Road, with a helpful arrow indicating Elsie McMahon's window, its grasp of London topography was not strong, with Soho extending as far north as Euston Road in its transatlantic author's imagination.[30] There were no further murders of prostitutes in the years leading up to the Second World War, however. The serial killer Gordon Cummins, known as the Blackout Ripper and discussed elsewhere in this book, started his career in 1942 (or quite possibly late 1941), but his *modus operandi* differed very considerably from that of the Soho Strangler, nor did he fit the description of the man seen with Leah Hinds. Today, very few people know about this strange series of unsolved murders in 1930s London, however.

The Murder of Red Max Kassel, 1936

In the 1920s and 1930s, Soho was home to a considerable population of gangsters. Juan Antonio Castanar, the Argentinian tango dancer, was a leading member of the prostitution racket, operating from his dancing academy in Archer Street. His major rivals were Casimir Michelotti, the notorious Lisle Street gangster; another sinister Frenchman known only as 'Le Marsellais'; and a mystery man who called himself Emil Allard, alias Max Kassel, alias 'Red Max'. In 1929, Castenar and Michelotti were both arrested and deported back to their respective countries of origin, as undesirable aliens. As for 'Le Marsellais', he came to grief in Canada a few years later, quite possibly at the hands of Red Max or one of his henchmen.

In the 1930s, Red Max took advantage of the disappearance of his three major rivals, and became Soho's king of vice. As befitting a man of mystery, he used several different names, and alternately claimed Latvian, French, German or Canadian nationality. He had come to London as early as 1913, on the run from the French police. A suave, well-dressed, foreign-looking cove, and a multiple bigamist, Max specialised in the trafficking of prostitutes. He exported English girls to brothels in Paris and the South of France, and imported French 'hostesses' to work in his Soho nightclubs and strip joints. Scotland Yard had a large dossier about him, containing some spicy revelations. In 1924 the French acrobat Martial Le Chevalier had been murdered in Air Street, Piccadilly; he had been involved in the vice trade, and there were rumours that Red Max had put out a contract on him. The police also knew that Josephine Martin, alias French Fifi, murdered in her Archer Street flat in 1935, had acted as a 'hostess' for foreign prostitutes smuggled into London by Red Max, and again there was murmuration that she might have paid the penalty for being disloyal to this Soho supervillain.

Contemporary photographs of Red Max Kassel, and of the murder house.

But before the Scotland Yard detectives were ready to take on Red Max and his organisation, a dead man was found underneath a hedge near St Albans on 24 January 1936. He had been shot six times in the abdomen. A sturdy bloke, wearing a flashy suit and with a scar across his face, he was identified as Red Max. Although the detectives were unlikely to have mourned this sudden and unexpected demise of Red Max, they investigated his murder with their usual thoroughness. There were tyre marks near where the body had been found, indicating that Max had been shot dead somewhere else, presumably in some Soho den of vice, and then 'taken for a ride' out into the countryside. It seemed very likely that some rival gangster had decided to eliminate him in order to take over his profitable brothels and nightclubs.

The police followed up every lead in the hunt for the murderer. One of the detectives had a lucky break when he saw some broken glass outside Cambridge Dairy at No. 36 Little Newport Street, Soho, emanating from a defect in the window pane of the second-floor flat. When this flat was searched, the police found extensive bloodstains, among other indications that Red Max had met his end in here. The owner of the flat was the French pimp and gangster Charles Lacroix, also known as Roger Vernon. He lived there with the prostitute Suzanne Bertrand, who had married an Englishman named Naylor. Both these individuals had gone on the run after the murder, but the French police tracked them down in Paris.

It also turned out that the police had a star witness: a young French girl named Marcelle Aubin, who served as maid to the aforementioned 'Mrs Naylor'. She had been at No. 36 Little Newport Street when the now fifty-five-year-old Red Max came calling about a small debt he owed. He does not appear to have been armed, which was an unexpected oversight on his part. After an angry quarrel, the dangerous Frenchman 'Vernon' gunned his opponent down at point-blank range. Max tried to call for help, and smashed two panes in the window, but he was bleeding badly and Vernon was able to restrain him. The cold-blooded killer telephoned a French garage proprietor named Pierre Alexandre, who drove him to St Albans where they got rid of Red Max.[31]

The French authorities were unwilling to extradite Vernon and Mrs Naylor, and they went on trial at the Seine assizes in Paris in April 1937. By this time, young Marcelle Aubin had died mysteriously, but the driver Alexandre was willing to testify against his former partner in crime. Roger Vernon, who was exposed in court as a thief, drug smuggler, white slave trafficker and Devil's Island escapee, was found guilty and sentenced to ten years of penal servitude, but Mrs Naylor was acquitted. Maître Legrand, the lawyer who had defended Vernon in court, later challenged the public prosecutor to a duel, being incensed by some ribald remarks this worthy had made about his professional integrity.[32]

The Red Max murder house at No. 36 Little Newport Street had been presumed to have been destroyed, and there was certainly no house of a similar description in what is today Newport Street. But after reading that some houses at the end of the former Little Newport Street are today part of Newport Place, I went to have another look, and cor blimey! There it was. The present-day No. 11 Newport Place looks very much like it did when Red Max met his end on the premises, except that the ground floor is now home to the 'Canton' Chinese restaurant rather than to the Cambridge Dairy.

Murder at the Coach and Horses, 1940

In December 1940, London was full of military men from the Dominions awaiting transfer abroad. The vast majority of them were looking forward to doing their bit in the great conflict, but the Canadian military policeman James Forbes McCallum had other ideas. The Coach and Horses is a traditional pub situated at No. 42 Wellington Street, Covent Garden. One day, Lance Corporal McCallum came bursting into the pub, army revolver in hand. He aimed at the startled barman, Morris Schulman, and called out, 'Paper money!' McCallum tried to swing the glass screen at the counter, but he did not understand its mechanism and injured himself in the process. All of a sudden, a shot rang out and Schulman fell dead, with a fatal bullet wound in the throat. When arrested, McCallum said that the gun had gone off by mistake. He was tried for murder, found guilty and sentenced to death. 'Canuck Soldier Faced Execution for Murder!' exclaimed the newspapers in his native land, but McCallum received a late reprieve from the Home Secretary and was imprisoned for life.[33]

The Murder of 'Little Hubby' Distleman, 1941

In wartime Soho, various gangster types kept fighting for power and influence. The Italian mob was making inroads at the expense of various gangs of Jewish and East End villains. One of these tough Italian gangsters was Antonio 'Babe' Mancini. His gang owned more than half of the gambling machines in Soho, and these machines had all been fixed so that the high prizes could not be won. Babe and his gang threatened shop and restaurant owners that their premises would be smashed up if they did not allow him to install his machines, and very few of them dared to stand up to a villain of his reputation.

A rival gang, mainly consisting of assorted Jewish and East End riff-raff, had one of their strongholds at No. 37 Wardour Street, where they kept a club and a small restaurant. One member of this gang was Harry Distleman, known as 'Little Hubby' to differ him from his brother 'Big Hubby' Distleman. Under normal circumstances, Mancini would not have gone anywhere near this rival club, but he had gambling machines set up in another club in the very same building, and he needed to empty them of money. On 20 April, the rival gangs began mouthing off in Wardour Street. Babe received reinforcements from his own mob, and managed to evict the opposition from his club without any significant bloodshed. On 1 May, the rival gangsters vandalised Mancini's club. Worried that serious damage had been done to the premises, Babe rushed over there, along with only a few of his henchmen.

Sure enough, when Mancini and his men emerged from the club after having surveyed the damage, one of the hoodlums cried out, 'There's Babe! Let's knife him!' Being severely outnumbered, Babe and his men took refuge in their own club, but after reinforcements had arrived, they decided to fight their way out. The rival gangsters fought back with bludgeons and billiards cues. A man named George Fletcher came running at Babe swinging a chair, but the agile Italian crook dived under his blow, drew his stiletto and slashed his opponent's wrist. 'Little Hubby' Distleman tried to interfere, also swinging a chair, but Mancini stabbed him hard in the left shoulder, killing him.

On trial for murder at the Old Bailey, Mancini was badly served by his legal team. Instead of following the obvious path of having their client plead guilty to manslaughter, the Italian was allowed to plead not guilty to both murdering Distleman and stabbing Fletcher. He had only injured Fletcher in self-defence, and had never touched Distleman, he claimed. Quite a few people had seen the fight, but many of them were afraid to testify against a villain of Mancini's calibre. Nevertheless, it was clear that Distleman had been stabbed to death by Mancini's stiletto, and the Italian was found guilty of murder and sentenced to death. Amazingly, both the Court of Criminal Appeal and the House of Lords turned down his appeal, and Mancini was hanged on 17 October 1941. This was a very harsh verdict, considering that it was not contested that Fletcher and Distleman had attacked Mancini, but at the time there was little sympathy for a hardened Italian gangster.[34]

Pistols at Dawn at Denbigh Street, 1943

Count Ludomir Cienski grew up in comfortable circumstances in his native Poland. The German invasion in 1939 changed all that, however. The count, who was a lieutenant in the Polish Army Reserve, fought bravely for his country, and managed to escape to London after his country's defences had collapsed, to continue his fight for a free Poland. He was employed at the Polish army headquarters, and lived with his wife Paulina in a small ground-floor flat at No. 58 Denbigh Street, Victoria.

In early 1943, Count Ludomir began to suspect that Paulina was having an affair. His duties took him away from home quite often, and he noticed that his wife appeared cold and strange when he returned. Their marriage had never been particularly happy: in particular, Count

Ludomir, an angry, short-tempered man, very much resented his much younger wife consorting with other Polish military men. It turned out that the errant countess was indeed having an affair with another officer, Lieutenant Jan Buchowski of the Polish Navy. He was younger and more prepossessing than the histrionic Count Ludomir, and was a decorated war hero who had been awarded the DSO for bravery in the field.

When Paulina demanded a divorce from her husband and announced her intention to marry Buchowski instead, Count Ludomir wrote his rival an angry and threatening letter. Buchowski wrote back accusing the cuckolded nobleman of being a cad who had stolen and read his letters to his wife. Count Ludomir decided to confront Buchowski face to face at No. 58 Denbigh Street. After they had gone into the sitting room and closed the door, there were three gunshots. The landlord heard the noise and rushed into the room. He found Buchowski slumped in an armchair. A yard or two away stood the count, holding a smoking revolver in his hand.

When the police arrived, Count Ludomir gave a calm and coherent statement. He had tried to persuade Buchowski to promise not to see his wife again, but the naval officer had refused. The histrionic nobleman then handed Buchowski his revolver and asked him to shoot him, since, if his wife was taken from him, his life no longer mattered. Buchowski immediately grabbed the revolver and fired at his rival, missing by a narrow margin! Realising that his opponent was no gentleman, and that he was in serious danger, Count Ludomir leapt at his opponent and caught the hand holding the revolver. There was a struggle, and two more shots were fired. Buchowski fell back into the chair.

The detectives examined the room and the body to see how much the nobleman's story could be relied upon. They had some doubts about it, since the landlord had said that the three shots came in quick succession, whereas Cienski's story suggested that there should have been an interval between the first one and the other two. The revolver had three empty chambers. There were two bullets in the body of the dead man and one had smashed into the wall opposite the chair in which the corpse was lying. It seemed reasonable to accept the story that Buchowski had fired in the direction of Cienski with the first bullet. The position of the gun when the other two were fired became vitally important, for it was not easy to accept that the man holding the gun had been so easily overcome that it was turned on himself. How could

Buchowski have struggled fiercely against his antagonist if the first bullet had gone straight through his heart?

Cienski was charged with murder and in due course stood trial at the Old Bailey, where Sir Patrick Hastings defended him. A fine figure of a man, wearing his uniform and decorations, he looked younger than his forty-three years. As the case proceeded, an amazing lapse on the part of the police were revealed. The existence of the dead man's fingerprints on the revolver, as well as those of Cienski, would have gone a long way to confirm the defendant's story; in contrast, the absence of the dead man's prints might well have sent Count Ludomir to the gallows. Shamefacedly, the police had to admit that, through an oversight, the weapon had not been examined for fingerprints until some foolish person had cleaned it.

In his eloquent summing-up, Mr Justice Humphreys stressed the fact that the prisoner was a foreigner of excitable temperament and old-fashioned notions of morality. Thus, a story that would have sounded preposterous coming from the lips of an Englishman might still be the truth. If the prisoner's story was unacceptable, and the jury considered that the fatal shots had been fired in a state of excitement and without the deliberate intention of killing, it was open to return a verdict of manslaughter. The jury was out for just under an hour, before returning a verdict of not guilty.[35] Count Ludomir was very lucky to leave the Old Bailey a free man, and to be able to give the *Daily Express* an interview praising the fairness of British justice.[36] He fought for his country throughout the war, divorced his wife, and instead married Veronica Evelyn Jurkiewicz in 1946; hopefully, she did not go 'chasing the lads' to give her trigger-happy husband another excuse to make use of his shooting skills. Count Ludomir and his wife remained in London after the war; since it is recorded that the adventurous nobleman finally expired in August 1988, he survived his dice with death at the Old Bailey by more than forty-five years.

The Murder of Evelyn Hatton, 1944

Evelyn Hatton was a quiet London housewife, who had been married to cinema attendant James Frederick Hatton since early 1922 and lived in Colville Terrace, Bayswater. In the 1940s, when she was in her early forties, she was still quite youthful-looking and attractive: a brunette with slightly greying hair, and always smartly dressed. Her neighbours wondered how such a fashionable lady had ended up with the humble cinema usher, but these two seemed to get on very well together. Their daughter, a beautiful young actress on the West End stage, had married an army captain.

In December 1944, a property agent looking after the upstairs flat at No. 44 Duke Street, St James's, came to repair a leaky washbasin. He saw a woman lying on the floor in the bedroom of the expensively furnished flat, but did not investigate any further. On his way out, he dropped a note to Miss Evelyn Clayton, who rented the flat, saying that she ought not to allow drunken friends to sleep up there! Three days later, a rent collector came to get the weekly rent from Miss Clayton. When nobody answered his call, he opened the front door with his own master key to find Miss Clayton's dead body on the floor; she had been strangled with a silk scarf and her feet bound together with a sheet from her bed.

There was consternation when the police discovered that the mysterious 'Evelyn Clayton', well known as a fashionable West End prostitute, was in fact identical to the forty-four-year-old Bayswater housewife Evelyn Hatton. For two decades, she had been entertaining customers in various Piccadilly flats and hotels without her husband suspecting that anything was amiss. Evelyn had been renting the elegant and well-located Duke Street flat for five weeks, paying nine guineas a week for it. Poor James Frederick Hatton was questioned at the Savile Row police station, and later taken to the mortuary to identify the body of his wife. Sir Bernard Spilsbury then conducted a post-mortem indicating that Evelyn Hatton had died from strangulation. She had been dead for at least three days before being discovered; the foolish actions of the property agent had given her murderer a three-day head start on the police. A journalist noted that, although a 'To Let' sign had been hung outside Evelyn Hatton's flat, no person seemed particularly keen to become the next tenant of the Duke Street murder flat.

Nor was it exactly easy for the Scotland Yard detectives to reconstruct the crime, or to find out more about Evelyn Hatton's strange double life. She had been active in the West End *demi-monde* for at least twenty years, and had always been a very popular, upper-class prostitute, with many affluent and discreet customers, some of them from the very highest levels of society. Evelyn had no close friends, and it was difficult to track down the men who used to come and see her in the Duke Street flat. She liked to go partying in the London clubs, but even when drunk and jolly, this strange, secretive woman confided in no one. As for the scenario of the murder, it might be that Evelyn had returned after an evening of partying to find a burglar ransacking her flat. To prevent her from screaming, this individual had strangled her using the scarf. It might also be that a 'customer', possibly an American serviceman, had accompanied her home with the intention of robbing her and ransacking the flat. But would the prudent Evelyn Hatton, who preferred customers she knew and trusted, really trot along with some dangerous young American whose intentions she did not know?[37]

The Scotland Yard detectives, led by Superintendent Parker, spent much time questioning other members of the West End *demi-monde* who had known the elusive Evelyn Hatton, but without finding any clue to the identity of her murderer. In recent decades, St James's has become home to many high-class art galleries and antique shops. In 1993, art connoisseur Jay Jopling opened his celebrated White Cube gallery in Evelyn Hatton's old flat at No. 44 Duke Street, but today the ground-floor shop at No. 44 is Paolo Brisigotti Antiques, and the flats above may well be residential property.

Murder of a Lonely Woman, 1945

In early 1945, the thirty-two-year-old Mrs Audrey Irene Stewart was leading a very lonely life. Her parents were both dead, her two sisters lived in the United States, and her divorced husband was serving with the RAF in Canada. A miserable, friendless woman, she led a vegetating existence in a first-floor bed-sitting room in a lodging house at No. 17 St George's Drive, Victoria. In the late evening of 2 January, the landlady of No. 17 left a lamp in the hall to be used by any boarder who came home late. At 10 a.m. the following morning, she was surprised to see this lamp outside Audrey Irene Stewart's room. The door stood ajar, and Mrs Stewart was found on the bed, naked and unconscious. She was removed to Westminster Hospital, where the doctors were appalled by her extensive head injuries. She lingered for twenty-one days without regaining consciousness, before finally expiring.

The police investigation of the murder of Audrey Irene Stewart made little headway. The landlady said that Mrs Stewart had at least once been visited by a soldier who had (falsely) claimed to be her husband. A few days before the murder, her bag had been stolen, but later recovered with one small key stolen. Had this been the key to the front door of the house, used by the killer to enter the premises? Audrey Irene Stewart's total savings of £12 10*s* had been stolen by her killer. Another hypothesis was that one of the other lodgers had murdered her. It was considered extraordinary that, although the killer had used excessive force battering his victim's head, no other person in the crowded apartment house had heard anything suspicious on the night of the murder. A Belgian woman who lodged in the house had heard two women talking around midnight, one of them opening the front door with a key. But there was never any serious suspect, and the murder remains unsolved.[38] The relevant police file at the National Archives is closed until 2021.

In October 1946, an American soldier under arrest in Germany hinted that he could give vital information about the unsolved murder of a woman in England. This led to the reopening of several unsolved murders of women in wartime London, including those of Evelyn Hatton and Audrey Irene Stewart, but it turned out that the soldier had nothing relevant to say.[39]

A King Stumbles on Murder, 1946

King George II of Greece had succeeded to the throne in 1922 following the abdication of his father, but he reigned for little more than a year before a republican uprising forced him to abdicate. For a while, he lived at Brown's Hotel in London and became quite an anglophile. Recalled to the throne in 1935, George II was the reigning monarch when the Italians invaded Greece in 1940. The Greek army fought back, and actually pursued Mussolini's troops into Albania, but the following year the Germans invaded. After the country had been overrun by the formidable Nazi military machine, King George was forced back into exile in England. For bravery under German fire while escaping from Greece, he was awarded the Distinguished Service Order – the only king ever to receive this honour.

Even after the Nazi empire had collapsed and the Germans and Italians had been evicted from Greek soil, it still looked like King George's exile would become a lengthy one: the republicans had returned to power, and he was once more a king without a country. He took the lease of an elegant terraced house at No. 45 Chester Square, Belgravia, where he hoped to live quietly with his long-term mistress. A housekeeper, Miss Elizabeth McLindon, was employed to get the house ready. When King George came to inspect the house on 9 June 1946, he found that the preparation of the house left much to be desired and that Miss McLindon was nowhere to be found. The king tried to force his way into the servants' quarters, but he was thwarted by a locked door, to which none of the king's men possessed a key. In an angry temper, King George left No. 45 Chester Square. The Greek courtiers reported the case of the missing housekeeper and the locked door to the police, and a few days later the door was forced by some policemen. It turned out that when the king had been knocking at Elizabeth McLindon's door, she had been lying dead at the other side, murdered by a revolver shot to the head.

It is not every day, even in London, that someone is murdered inside the house of a king. There was much media speculation about the Chester Square murder mystery: had some disgruntled Greek republican broken into the house to murder the king, but shot the housekeeper by mistake? The Scotland Yard detectives retorted that there were no signs of a forced entry: the housekeeper had clearly let her killer into the house. There was also evidence that the forty-one-year-old Elizabeth McLindon had been 'chasing the lads' in a manner quite unbecoming to a royal housekeeper. A wealth of correspondence from various 'gentleman friends' was found in her lockers. One of them was 'Arthur', identified by Miss McLindon's sister as Arthur Robert Boyce, a Brighton house-painter. During the trawl of Elizabeth McLindon's boyfriends, Boyce was interviewed by the police in his home town. He seemed very much dejected that the Chester Square housekeeper, whom he claimed he wanted to marry, had been murdered in London. A tall, thin, gloomy-looking man, he looked very unlike a murderer. However, the police discovered that Boyce was a convicted bigamist, and that he was wanted for questioning over the illicit cashing of cheques. One of these had been altered after the signature of M. Papanicolau, secretary to the King of Greece!

When Arthur Robert Boyce had been painting Brighton Pier together with a party of other workmen, he had been bragging that he had once owned a revolver, but that he had thrown in into the sea. The police thought he was referring to the disposal of the murder weapon, which, if he were telling the truth, never would be seen again. When Boyce was arrested on the cheque fraud charge, his Brighton lodgings were thoroughly searched. The police trawled his friends and acquaintances, and one of them, the Welsh army soldier John Rowland, said that when he had shared lodgings with Boyce he had lost a .32 automatic pistol, the same calibre as the cartridge case found in the servants' quarters of No. 45 Chester Square next to the body of Elizabeth McLindon. Rowland still had another cartridge case from his old pistol; the forensic technicians showed that it had been fired from the same gun that had killed the Chester Square housekeeper.

It turned out that the bigamist Boyce had been up to his old tricks again: after seducing Elizabeth McLindon, he had promised to marry her. When he proposed to her, he had shown a bank balance that had been altered to show £2,075 in credit, a fair amount more than the true balance of just £75. The cheque with which he wanted to buy the engagement ring had bounced. This latter mishap made even the dim-witted Elizabeth McLindon suspicious. She looked through the pockets of Boyce's coat and found an invitation to a wedding between Boyce and another woman. Writing to the woman in question for an explanation, she found out that shortly after the wedding, Boyce had been arrested for bigamy! She told Boyce that the wedding was off, and hung up on him when he tried to phone her at No. 45 Chester Square. On 8 June, when Boyce told her he was coming to see her, she ran out of the house, but he pursued her and persuaded her to return to the royal residence. When she insisted on double-checking with the jeweller that his cheque had not bounced again, Boyce knew that he would shortly be caught in yet another lie; he pulled the revolver and shot her dead.

On trial at the Old Bailey for the murder of Elizabeth McLindon, things did not look good for Arthur Robert Boyce. When questioned, Boyce said that he had given the revolver to Elizabeth McLindon for protection against the republican Greeks who he claimed were regularly calling at No. 45 Chester Square to threaten the king. Surely, one of these men must have taken the gun and used it against her. His defence counsel tried an alternative hypothesis: perhaps one of Elizabeth McLindon's other lovers had become furious when he heard that she was going to marry Boyce, and shot her as revenge. The jury, however, remained quite impressed by the technical evidence against Boyce: he was convicted of murder and hanged at Pentonville Prison on 1 November 1946.[40]

King George II of Greece remained at the Chester Square murder house only for a few more months. In September 1946, he was invited to return to Greece after a plebiscite had supported the monarchy. On arrival, he is said to have remarked, referring to his several periods in exile, that the most important tool for a King of Greece was a capacious suitcase. After King George died in 1947, he was succeeded by his younger brother Paul. In 1967, after the Greek government had been overturned by a group of military officers, King Constantine II and his family were exiled to London. Since that time, the Greeks have continued to misrule their country without any royal involvement; the exiled King Constantine and his family remain in London today. The murder house at No. 45 Chester Square still appears to be a private residence.

The Soho Prostitute Murders, 1947–1948

In the evening of 8 September 1947, the thirty-three-year-old prostitute Rita Green was patrolling her Soho 'beat'. At 6 feet tall and known as 'Black Rita' for her raven tresses, she was a popular and relatively successful prostitute. Although the daughter of a police constable, she had deviated from the 'straight and narrow' from an early age, preferring the Soho *demi-monde* to a life involving hard graft and honest toil. She might have been married once, possibly to a man named Driver, but he had long ceased to play any part in her life.

Later in the evening, gunfire was heard from Rita Green's first-floor flat at No. 42 Rupert Street, Soho. The manager of the ground-floor café, and some other bystanders, ran up the stairs to Rita's flat and knocked at the door, but there was no response. The police were quickly at the scene and broke the door down to discover Rita lying on the floor with gunshot wounds to her neck and abdomen. She died shortly after being taken to Charing Cross Hospital.

The police at first presumed that Rita Green had been murdered after a quarrel with her late night 'customer'. A man had been seen to leave the flat in a hurry after the shots had been heard, but no witness could provide a good description of him. In the afternoon on the day of the murder, Rita had been seen talking to a neatly dressed man in a dark blue suit, carrying an attaché case. The crime reporter Duncan Webb found a witness from the Soho underground who had seen Black Rita walking home with a 'student type' shortly before she was murdered. There was also gossip that Rita had a new boyfriend, a gangster who was known to carry a revolver. But these leads failed to provide any vital breakthrough in the murder investigation, and the murder of Black Rita is still unsolved.

There have been several hypotheses about the unsolved Soho murder of Rita Green. It is of course quite possible that she was murdered by a random 'customer', but how common was it for clients of Soho prostitutes to carry loaded revolvers around with them? There were rumours that Black Rita had been a police informant, and that some Soho gangsters had made her pay dearly for this. In 1947, the violent and unpredictable Messina brothers, and their gang of pimps and 'enforcers', were making their presence felt in the Soho underworld. They put some of the local pimps out of action and took over their girls, and were also known to rough up various freelance prostitutes who refused to share their earnings with them. Had they murdered Black Rita to frighten the other Soho streetwalkers, and make them more amenable to join the Messina pimping operation?

Another hypothesis is that Rita Green was the first known victim of a serial killer of Soho prostitutes. On 5 September 1948, the sixty-year-old prostitute Helen Freedman, known as 'Russian Dora', was stabbed to death at her third-floor flat at No. 126 Long Acre. Later the same month, her forty-one-year-old colleague Rachel Fennick, nicknamed 'Ginger Rae', was stabbed to death with a long-bladed knife in her second-floor front room at No. 46 Broadwick Street. 'Jack the Ripper Stalks Streets of London Again!' exclaimed the headline of an American newspaper commenting on the carnage in Soho. In 1946, a woman named Margaret Cook had been stabbed to death outside a nightclub near Oxford Circus; had she been the first victim of this sinister 'Soho Jack'?

The police failed to make much headway in the 'Ginger Rae' case, except that a number of other prostitutes had seen her soliciting on the evening she was murdered. A tailor's cutter named Edwin George Peggs, who had befriended 'Rae', was briefly a suspect before being written off. As late as 1962, the pervert and criminal George Hobson incriminated his friend Gordon Arthur Wood in the 'Rae' murder. Wood's movements could be traced until 1957, but not any longer. When Hobson was himself in prison for rape in the 1970s, the police put pressure on him to tell all he knew about the murder of 'Ginger Rae', but this hardened villain 'clammed up' and the police file was closed in 1975.[41]

Since some of the relevant police files are still closed, it is not possible to assess how seriously the police took the serial killer scenario. The reason for this secrecy is likely to be that the veteran prostitute Helen Freedman doubled as a blackmailer and a police informant. One of her roles was to spy on Irish nationalists active in London, so here we have yet another motive to murder her. Had Black Rita and Ginger

Rae been her accomplices in this operation? The newspaper publicity about the Soho murders in 1947–48 was mostly confined to the tabloids, and uncharacteristically subdued, probably because the police made sure there were no leaks of information. The reason for this might well have been that Russian Dora's list of blackmail victims contained some very unexpected names. It might also be that the 'Irish connection' was considered particularly sensitive, and that Special Branch was content with losing some low-level police informants in exchange for information about 'bigger fish'.

All three murder houses still stand and are in good condition; this part of Soho has improved very considerably in recent years due to the tourist trade, and the bad old days of prostitutes and gangsters seem far away. It takes only a very short walk to visit the three houses, perhaps indicating that Soho Jack, whoever he was, liked to operate within a close range of his secret hideout in some brothel or undercover club.

Murder of the 'Maltese Barber', 1948

The infighting between the French gangsters in Soho, which culminated in the murder of Red Max Kassel in 1936, meant that other organised criminals were in a position to take over. They were the Messina brothers: five dangerous Maltese gangsters who soon controlled most of the important prostitution racket. The Messinas were treated with respect by the Soho mob, and there were not many who dared to cross them. One of these men was another Maltese pimp named Amabile Ricca. He had shot a man dead back in Malta in 1932, but claimed it was an accident and got off scot-free. Known as the 'Maltese Barber', he had a fearsome temper and was always armed with a stiletto and a handgun.

In June 1948, Amabile Ricca had just emerged from prison after serving eighteen months for malicious wounding. Many people were dismayed to see this dangerous character hit the streets again, and they may well have decided to take pre-emptive action. On 18 June, when the Maltese Barber was playing billiards at a Maltese social club at No. 3 Carlisle Street, the Maltese brothers Francis and Joseph Farrugia burst in to the club. After an angry altercation, they shot Ricca to death. All the other Maltese ran away in a wild stampede, and the two Farrugias also made themselves scarce. Joseph, who had gunned Ricca down, gave Francis the pistol, which he hid in Soho Square nearby.

Since the Maltese colony in London stuck together, and since they did not like the police, it turned out to be very difficult to get hold of reliable witnesses to the murder of Amabile Ricca. But the detectives 'leant on' some influential leaders of the Maltese, and soon they got a tip about Francis Farrugia's involvement. After he had heard that his brother had been arrested, Joseph Farrugia gave himself up to the police, and confessed to shooting Ricca. The gun was found where Francis said it had been hidden. Joseph said that Ricca had given him a steely glare, and put his hand in the pocket where he kept his own firearm; these sinister actions had prompted him to make a pre-emptive strike. Many members of Soho's gangland were pleased to see the end of the dangerous and unpredictable Amabile Ricca. In the end, Joseph Farrugia received a sentence of five years in prison for manslaughter, and his brother, who had helped him get rid of the gun, got off with six months in prison.[42]

Student and Blonde Found Shot, 1956

Derek Roberts was a competent and hard-working medical student at St Thomas's Hospital. Normally, his life should have mimicked those of the jolly young doctors depicted in Richard Gordon's early novels: the long, hard student years, the carefree time as a roving young doctor, and then either the brass plate on the door as a country GP or the struggle to become a successful hospital specialist with Harley Street aspirations. But in 1955, when Derek was just twenty-one years old and still without prospects in life, he met the beautiful nineteen-year-old fashion model Valerie Murray, and fell deeply in love with her. The daughter of an army colonel, Valerie came from a wealthy and privileged background. One of London's most successful models, she was earning £1,000 a year. Obviously flattered by Derek's attentions, she encouraged his suit for a while, but as her modelling career really took off she left the penniless student behind. A shapely young blonde, Valerie Murray displayed swimsuits at a London fashion show, modelled hats in February 1956 to great acclaim, and was crowned 'Bride of the Year' just a few weeks later after showing off wedding dresses in a leading woman's magazine.

Derek Roberts remained determined to marry his faithless Valerie, however. He proposed to her more than once, but she always turned him down. Valerie Murray lived in an elegant basement flat at No. 61 Cadogan Place, a very short walk to the south of where the footman William Henry Marchant had murdered Elizabeth Paynton back in

Cadogan Place, from an undated postcard.

1839. One of London's must sought-after social butterflies, she kept attending various lavish parties. The young men she was flirting with were older, wealthier and better-looking than poor Derek. The young medical student was becoming increasingly frantic: he kept calling at the Cadogan Place flat, embarrassing Valerie and her two flatmates. On 14 March 1956, Valerie took Derek out for dinner and told him that she could never marry him, and that she did not want to see him again. He should stop pestering her, and get on with his own life instead. The morning after, Derek went out and bought a shotgun, telling the gun shop manager that he needed it to shoot rabbits.

Worried about what the jilted Derek Roberts might be up to, Valerie Murray had made plans to leave the Cadogan Place flat, where he had pestered her in the past. All her belongings were packed up and she was ready to move. On the morning of 15 March, the other two girls living in the flat, one of them Valerie's sister Pamela, left for their office jobs. Valerie stayed behind in the flat, listening to the radio. Later the same day, Derek drove to Cadogan Place, bringing the shotgun with him. Although Valerie had told a friend that she was 'almost afraid' of what the frantic student might be capable of, she let him into the flat. What happened next we do not know, but Valerie was later found dead at No. 61 Cadogan Place, with a gunshot wound to the side of the head.

It looked as if she had been trying to let somebody out of the flat, when this person had shot her. The body of Derek Roberts was also found in the flat's front room, with a self-inflicted gunshot wound.

As could be expected, the murder of Valerie Murray attracted much tabloid press publicity. '"Bride of the Year" Model Shot!' exclaimed the *Daily Express*, with a large picture of Valerie Murray overshadowing features on Prime Minister Harold Macmillan's economic policy, and Archbishop Makarios in Cyprus. In rather poor taste, the *Daily Mirror* illustrated its large feature on the murder with a photograph of Valerie Murray wearing a swimsuit, and another snapshot of her coffin being carried out of the murder flat. Various relatives of the murdered girl spoke of her virtues, and the journalist marvelled that a 'girl with the world at her feet' had 'died for love'. It was also briefly noted that Derek Roberts' widowed mother had left her home in Salisbury to help with police inquiries.

In contrast, *The Times* afforded the Cadogan Place murder only two paragraphs, one of them dealing with the coroner's inquest, held at Westminster on 23 March. Witnesses told that Derek Roberts had been very worried and depressed the weeks prior to the murder, and that he had feared that his exam results would suffer. He had once threatened to commit suicide, but Valerie Murray had not taken him seriously. The remarkable ease with which a clearly disturbed young man had been able to get his hands on a shotgun and ammunition was but lightly touched upon. The verdict reached was the obvious one: Valerie Margaret Murray had been murdered by Derek Cay Roberts, who had then taken his own life while the balance of his mind was disturbed.[43]

The Antiques Shop Murder, 1961

Cecil Court, situated just off Charing Cross Road, was originally constructed in the late seventeenth century. In the 1890s, when the houses were becoming increasingly dilapidated, Cecil Court was completely reconstructed, and the old rookeries replaced with two neat rows of late Victorian houses with shops on the ground-floor level. From an early stage, the Cecil Court shops were favoured by the sellers of books, prints and antiques, and the pedestrian arcade remains a haven for wealthy collectors today.

In 1961, the shop at No. 23 Cecil Court was Louis Meier Antiques. On 2 March, a customer came into the shop, taking an interest in a curved ornamental dress sword and some oriental daggers. An ugly, scruffily dressed youth, he did not look like he could afford a sword costing £15. He told Mr Meier that his father was an Indian, and that it was common to carry a dagger in that country.

The next day, a young apprentice signwriter came into Louis Meier Antiques wanting to purchase a billiards cue. He was surprised to see that there was no one in the shop. Behind a partly open curtain, he could see what he thought was perhaps a dummy lying on the floor, or a woman who had fainted. Being a foolish, timorous youth, he did not dare to investigate further. Shortly after, Mr Meier himself came into the shop to find his assistant Elsie May Batten lying dead on the floor, with the blade of an ivory-handled dagger buried in her chest.

Elsie May Batten was the wife of Mr Mark Batten, President of the Royal Society of Sculptors. The post-mortem showed that she had been brutally murdered by repeated hard stabs from the razor-sharp dagger. When Mr Meier was asked if anything untoward had happened in the shop recently, he immediately thought of the swarthy youngster with an interest in swords and daggers. He was able to provide a good description of this individual, as was a gun dealer in St Martin's Lane, where a person strongly suspected to be the murderer had tried to sell a sword stolen from Mr Meier's shop. Their descriptions were used to produce two 'identikit' images of the suspect. The two images were so very similar that it was considered well-nigh certain that they depicted the same man. They were distributed to all police forces, and also released to the press.

On 8 March, a police constable walking his beat in Old Compton Street saw a swarthy youth who exactly fitted the identikit image come walking along with his girlfriend. He promptly arrested both of them. The seventeen-year-old blonde girlfriend turned out to be completely innocent, but twenty-one-year-old Edwin Bush was a nasty piece of work. He was a well-known thief and burglar whose larcenous habits had remained unchanged after several spells in borstal. Bush brazenly denied any involvement in the Antique Shop Murder, although admitting that the identikit image looked a bit like him. He relied on his mother to provide an alibi, but the mother's story did not agree with his own. In an identification parade at the Bow Street police station, Mr Meier was unable to make a positive identification, but Mr Roberts from the gunsmith's shop immediately picked out Bush. The youngster then made a full confession of the murder, adding that the world would be better off without him, and here he may well have been right.

On trial at the Old Bailey for the murder of Elsie May Batten, Edwin Bush tried playing the 'racism card', claiming that the shop assistant had not liked Indians; she had made use of various insulting epithets until he stabbed her in a fit of rage. The jury remained unimpressed, however, and Bush was found guilty and sentenced to death. Edwin Bush was the last person to hang at Pentonville Prison, on 6 July 1961.[44] The murder shop at No. 23 Cecil Court is today part of Goldsboro Books, an upmarket bookshop for signed first editions. Perhaps you will be able to buy a signed copy of *Murder Houses of London* in there?

The Murder of 'Big Tony' Mella, 1963

Antonio Benedetta Mella, a native of Italy, was one of the kingpins of Soho's seedy nightclub world in the 1950s and 1960s. In 1963, he owned quite a club empire, all staffed with scantily clad 'hostesses' selected by Mella himself. A tall, muscular man, 'Big Tony' Mella was usually treated with respect by the other denizens of Soho's underworld. In 1963, he purchased the Grill Club at No. 48 Dean Street, and renamed it the Bus Stop Club. He made sure that above the club comfortable offices were constructed for himself and for the club's manager, his long-time friend and henchman Alfred Melvin. The Bus Stop Club was situated in classic Soho gangster territory, and its clientele were hardly spring chickens. No. 82 Dean Street, not far away, had been the site of a gangster murder in a porn shop in 1956 (the house no longer stands).

On the evening of 28 January 1963, Big Tony Mella suddenly came running out of the Bus Stop Club. He collapsed in the street and never rose again. The police found that he had been shot three times in the back. Inside the club, Alfred Melvin lay dead from a gunshot to the head. A small-calibre Browning automatic pistol was lying on the floor. At first, it was presumed that some rival gangsters had made a raid on the Bus Stop Club, and murdered Mella and Melvin. A waiter at the August Moon restaurant nearby had heard two loud pops and a good deal of shouting and noise; when he looked out, he had seen Big Tony lying in the gutter close to Romilly Street, and there had been a lot of blood about. The club hostesses had only heard a sound like an exploding cigar, before Mella came tearing out into the street. 'Yard hunt Soho gun gangsters!' exclaimed the headline of the *Daily Mirror*.[45]

But the breast pocket of Melvin's jacket was found to contain a letter to his wife, detailing how he had decided to shoot his boss after Big Tony had refused to repay him a £400 debt. He had been pressing the club owner for this money for some time, but although Mella had plenty of money he had treated Melvin in a bullying manner that infuriated the club manager. Melvin had procured a .22 automatic pistol, and shot down Mella from behind before committing suicide. In the end, Mrs Melvin sent a wreath to Mella's funeral, and Mrs Mella did the same for Melvin, also generously declaring that she had forgiven her husband's murderer. The showgirls and club hostesses from Big Tony's clubs split into two groups and formed the majority of the mourners when the two men were buried on 18 February. The ground floor of the murder house at No. 48 Dean Street is today a small Thai restaurant, and Big Tony's former offices appear to be flats.

The Murder of Paddy O'Keefe, 1964

Paddy O'Keefe was a thirty-seven-year-old Irish barman at the White Horse Hotel, situated at the corner of Rupert Street and Archer Street. He had previously worked in another, rougher pub near the Elephant and Castle, and boasted that he was a 'crook-tamer' who could pacify aggressive customers with ease.

In the evening of 14 June 1964, a young man leapt over the counter at the White Horse, pulled out a large revolver, and shouted, 'This is a hold-up! I want the money!' He rifled the till and seized hold of £47 in all. When the brave but foolhardy Paddy O'Keefe confronted him, the robber gunned him down and fled the premises. The police found O'Keefe dead, and the hue and cry was on for the robber turned murderer.

The police soon caught the twenty-one-year-old private soldier Lawrence Winters, a tough character who belonged to the Parachute Regiment. He had purchased a revolver from another soldier for £5 and planned a robbery, since he 'wanted some money to take home'. The gun had gone off accidentally, he claimed. A psychiatrist described Winters as an abnormal man with violent psychopathic tendencies, and he was found guilty of manslaughter on the grounds of diminished responsibility.[46] Sentenced to life imprisonment, the name of this violent, unpredictable Lawrence Winters again hit the headlines in 1973, after he took an active part in violent riots at Peterfield jail in Scotland, where he was one of the inmates. Along with three other ringleaders, he had six years added to his sentence.[47]

Another Butler Bites the Dust, 1970

Wilton Crescent is one of the most prestigious addresses in London. An elegant crescent of late Georgian houses, it surrounds well-kept mature central gardens. Whereas the houses on the northern part of the crescent are stone-clad, those in the southern part are entirely stuccoed. They have a semi-basement, four main floors, and a fifth floor with servants' bedrooms. The substantial No. 32 Wilton Crescent is the odd house out among these grand Georgian terraces, however: it is double-fronted, comprises only a basement, two main stories and some attic bedrooms, and is built in a vaguely neo-Elizabethan style.

The wealthy businessman Sidney Lewis Bernstein, who founded Granada Television in 1953, was awarded a life peerage in 1969 as Baron Bernstein. As befitting such a distinguished television magnate, Lord Bernstein resided in the grand house at No. 32 Wilton Crescent.[48] His butler, the sixty-five-year-old Dutch national Julian Sesee, lived in the basement flat. A tall, distinguished-looking man, Sesee seemed the perfect butler, a Jeeves in real life and a true 'gentleman's gentleman'.

On 18 December 1970, Lord Bernstein was going on a holiday to Barbados. The butler was seen loading the suitcases into his lordship's Rolls-Royce. In the morning of 21 December, when Lord Bernstein's cleaner arrived to do some pre-Christmas tidying-up in the large house, Sesee was not there to let her in. When his lordship's secretary arrived with a key, the two women were shocked to see that the house seemed to have been broken into: the furniture was turned upside down, and desks and cupboards had been ransacked. In the basement flat, they found Sesee's dead body lying on the floor. He had been stabbed hard in the stomach.

'Peer's Butler is Murdered!' exclaimed the first page of the *Daily Mirror*. 'Perfect Butler Mystery!' echoed the *Daily Sketch*. Detective Chief Superintendent John Hensley, one of Scotland Yard's leading murder investigators, took charge of the investigation. His detectives soon made some very curious discoveries. Firstly, there were no signs of a forced entry: Sesee must have invited his murderer into the house. Secondly, nothing valuable seemed to have been stolen. Thirdly, it was considered curious that Sesee's stomach had been wrapped in towels, as if the murderer had desperately tried to stem the flow of blood. Fourthly, it transpired that Sesee had been leading a double life: the respectable, immaculately dressed butler had been a homosexual, and he had often invited various dodgy 'gentleman friends' to join him for some 'fun' in the basement flat at No. 32 when Lord Bernstein was away. A witness had seen a foreign-looking young man near No. 32 Wilton Crescent the evening Sesee had been murdered, and the police were keen to track down this individual.

A few weeks later, the police struck lucky. The young Irish hotel waitress Jean Fitzgerald contacted the Sesee murder detectives with a most remarkable story. Her boyfriend, the twenty-seven-year-old Moroccan male nurse Mustapha Bassaine, had been bisexual, and she knew that he had had a relationship with the sixty-five-year-old butler, something she had disapproved of very much. The night of the murder, Bassaine had telephoned Jean, asking her to come and join him at No. 32 Wilton Crescent, but she had suspected that he was up to no good and refused to go. When Bassaine had returned home to their flat, she saw that there was blood on his clothes, and that he was wearing a pair of trousers that were much too large for him. The day after the murder, Bassaine had said that he wanted to go for a visit home to Morocco, and she had seen him off to the airport. He had not returned, and the police suspected he was probably not intending to do so in a hurry, since he had bought a one-way ticket.

When the coroner's inquest on Julian Sesee was concluded in October 1971, it returned a verdict of murder against Mustapha Bassaine. It was feared that he would not face a trial, since there was no extradition treaty between Britain and Morocco. For a while, it was hoped that the Moroccans would get fed up with Bassaine's activities, or that the Foreign Office would think of some cunning plan to get the suspected butler killer back to London to stand trial. Instead, the foolish and imprudent Bassaine went on a trip to Rotterdam where he was promptly arrested, since he was wanted by Interpol. The Dutch returned him to London, where he stood trial for murder at the Old Bailey in March 1973. All Sesee's dirty laundry was exposed in court, as were Bassaine's own bisexual tendencies. The Moroccan's legal team alleged that Jean Fitzgerald, the girlfriend, had been insanely jealous of Sesee, and that she had murdered the butler and then 'framed' Bassaine for the crime. But there was rock-solid evidence against the Moroccan. His fingerprints were found in Sesee's flat and on Lady Bernstein's desk, from which he had stolen £80. Bassaine had discarded his bloodstained trousers in Sesee's washing machine, and stolen a pair of the sturdy butler's own trousers to use instead. Bassaine was found guilty of murder and sentenced to imprisonment for life.[49] It was not immediately clear if he had quarrelled with Sesee and murdered him in a rage, or whether he had planned to murder the butler and ransack the house. What fate this sinister Moroccan had intended for Jean Fitzgerald, if she had really come to meet him on the night of the murder, will never be ascertained. The murder house at No. 32 Wilton Crescent, one of the most exclusive addresses in London, is still standing today.

Murder at Moreton Place, 1972

In 1972, the sixty-nine-year-old Albert Charles Cox was living alone in a small bed-sitting room at No. 7 Moreton Place, Pimlico. He had been a night porter at a hotel, but was now retired. A lifelong bachelor, he had become something of a recluse as he got older. Eschewing the current fashion, he liked to wear a trilby hat and old-fashioned spectacles. For some reason or other, Albert Charles Cox was also in the habit of carrying a large sum of money in his wallet, and there were rumours that he was a wealthy man, and that he had hoarded a good deal of money and valuables back at Moreton Place.

On 4 March 1972, the neighbours at No. 7 Moreton Place alerted the police, since they had not seen Albert Charles Cox for several days. They had knocked at his door, but there was no response. Cox was not known for going on holidays; in fact, he had always been very reluctant to leave his tiny flat. When the police had broken down the door, they found Cox lying face down in a chair, bound, gagged and dead. An intruder had clearly overpowered the old man, bound him with his own ties, and ransacked the room for money and objects of value. A post-mortem examination by Professor Keith Simpson showed that Cox had been murdered around 28 February; the cause of death was that he had been suffocated by the gag.

The murder of Albert Charles Cox received very little media attention: nobody bothered much that an obscure old man had been done to death for sordid motives in a shabby little Pimlico bed-sitting room. Only the *Westminster & Pimlico News* took any particular interest in the murder investigation. This newspaper reported that Cox's nephew had been sent for from Chalfont, Buckinghamshire, to identify the body. When the coroner Gavin Thurston concluded the inquest, a verdict of wilful murder against some person unknown was returned. Although hundreds of people had made statements in connection with the murder of Albert Charles Cox, the murder squad at the Rochester Row police station remained clueless. Not a single person appears to have been a serious suspect for the crime.

Today, No. 7 Moreton Place looks like an elegant and well-kept Georgian terraced house, its bad old days as seedy 1970s bedsits long forgotten. It has a blue plaque, since it is the birthplace of William Morris Hughes, the seventh Prime Minister of Australia. There is no memorial to Albert Charles Cox, a harmless old bloke in a trilby hat who was brutally done to death by some callous thief for the sake of a few hundred pounds.[50]

Murder at the Royal Automobile Club, 1972

Founded in 1897 with the aim of encouraging the development of motoring in Britain, the Royal Automobile Club is today one of London's exclusive private members' clubs. Its clubhouse at No. 89 Pall Mall contains extensive dining and sporting facilities, including a capacious swimming pool. In 1972, a young lady named Sarah Gibson was employed there as an assistant housekeeper. Her father was an army colonel turned racehorse trainer, and her brother a professional jockey. Sarah seems to have liked her job at the club, and enjoyed London life. But in the early morning of 3 July 1972, her naked body was found in her bedroom (Room 519) on the fifth floor of the clubhouse. She had been sexually assaulted and strangled.

The police concluded that Sarah Gibson had been tied up, sexually molested and deliberately strangled with her own nightdress. At first, it was presumed that she had known her killer, perhaps a young man she had met when taking a walk in Piccadilly. Or else, one of the club members might have stayed behind after the club closed at midnight. Sarah had been seen with a slim, good-looking man in his early thirties, and it was presumed he might have been her secret boyfriend. This individual was tracked down by the police, but he turned out to have a solid alibi. Nor was any evidence found to incriminate the respectable club members. A number of petty objects had been stolen from Sarah's room, including her bracelet and lighter, and a Churchill crown. A man's socks and shirt had been left behind by the murderer. Had a thief entered the club with intention to steal, and had Sarah woken up when he ransacked the room? It was a chilling thought that a young woman was not safe even in the heart of London's most exclusive gentlemen's clubs. No signs of a break-in were found, however, and the club was supposed to be well guarded at night.

In late July, the police received a mysterious anonymous letter about the murder at the Royal Automobile Club. A person alleging to be the murderer claimed that, since he felt no remorse or guilt for the murder, he hoped that the police would catch him before he could kill again. He added that if the police saw fit to give him a list of all drug pushers in the country, he would do the coppers a favour by killing them all, one by one, since he had seen the misery these dealers caused. The police did not take the mystery man up on this offer, however, particularly since the letter ended, 'The man you want is at the Centre Point.' Having searched the unoccupied skyscraper by that name without finding anything suspicious, the police remembered that there was also a Soho homeless shelter known as the 'Centre Point'. Here, they found the homeless thief and vagabond David Frooms. He was identified as the person who had cashed a Churchill crown at a bank, and sold Sarah's bracelet and lighter for £2.50 to a Soho jeweller. Frooms had numerous convictions for petty theft. It turned out that on the night of the murder he had been lurking around at the back of the Royal Automobile Club; here he found a ladder, which he made use of to enter the club dining room. Undisturbed by the club's security guards, he then rummaged around the clubhouse at will, stealing from the cash till and entering several empty bedrooms. It had been mere chance that led him to enter Sarah's room. He could remember tying her up and stealing from the room, he said, but not murdering her, he asserted.

Since Frooms seemed like a very nasty piece of work, the latter part of his story was not believed. His fingerprints were found in the murder room, and psychiatrists proclaimed him fit to stand trial. Nor was there any suggestion that he had been under the influence of alcohol or drugs at the time of the murder. When Frooms was on trial at the Old Bailey in December 1972, things were not looking good for him. The prosecution had a simple task, and attempts from the defence to allege manslaughter were wholly unsuccessful, since there was no evidence Frooms had intended to kill Sarah Gibson. Passing sentence of imprisonment for life,

Mr Justice Forbes told Frooms, 'Nothing but a monster could have done this. You have been found guilty of murder under the most terrible of circumstances.' What happened to the creature Frooms after the verdict is not known, but hopefully he was caged for a substantial period of time.[51] The Royal Automobile Club denies that there have ever been any ghostly manifestations in Room 519 in their stately clubhouse, which is still very much in existence at No. 89 Pall Mall.

A Murder Amusement Arcade, 1974

On 4 September 1974, all seemed well at the Golden Goose amusement arcade, situated at No. 36 Old Compton Street, Soho. One of the regulars at this rather sleazy arcade was the gangster Alfredo Zomparelli, known as 'Italian Tony'. He was in the employ of Albert Dimes, a leading gangster who was reputed to be the American mafia's man in London. Not long before, Zomparelli had got into a fight with a man named David Knight, and the tough Italian 'enforcer' had stabbed his opponent to death. Knight's brother Ronnie, the 'celebrity gangster' who was once married to Barbara Windsor, had sworn revenge against Zomparelli, and a gangster named Nicky Gerard had offered to 'neutralize' Italian Tony. Not only was Gerard keen to get his hand on the large wad of cash that Ronnie Knight had offered him, he was also seeing Zomparelli's wife, a former stripper, and was keen to take out Italian Tony as a precautionary measure, before the cuckolded husband could exact his revenge.

As Zomparelli was amusing himself at the Golden Goose, Nicky Gerard came sneaking up to him from behind. Without hesitation, he gunned down Italian Tony, before rapidly making himself scarce. There was strong suspicion against Nicky Gerard and Ronnie Knight, and they both stood trial for the murder, being acquitted due to lack of evidence. In his autobiography *Memoirs and Confessions*, Knight later admitted putting out a contract on Zomparelli to avenge the murder of his brother.

Nicky Gerard's reputation as a hard man increased after the successful hit on Zomparelli. Whereas Ronnie Knight was a relatively prudent man by 1970s London gangster standards, Gerard took many risks, one of them making an enemy of a dangerous gangster named Tommy Hole, who objected to the imprudent Gerard 'muscling in' on his East End 'manor'. In June 1982, two masked men gunned Gerard down outside his house in Canning Town. Hole was a strong suspect, but again he walked free from the Old Bailey. Tommy Hole went on to become a very wealthy and influential East End gangster. He served time for armed robbery and for attempted murder, but emerged from prison with his empire intact.

On 5 December 1999, all seemed well at the Beckton Arms, a nondescript modern pub near Barking Road. Tommy Hole and his friend Joe 'the Crow' Evans sat at the bar enjoying a quiet afternoon drink. At three o'clock, a stranger came into the pub, had a look around, and then quickly left. If Tommy and 'the Crow' had possessed the instincts of their younger days, they would have sensed danger, but both men were now approaching retirement age. All of a sudden, two men came bursting into the pub and shot Hole and Evans dead. This was clearly a gangland contract killing, and there was much speculation about the motive. Could some long-minded gangster have wanted to avenge Nicky Gerard, shot dead seventeen years earlier?[52]

The murder amusement arcade at No. 36 Old Compton Street was for a while 'Play 2 Win', a more modern and up-to-date arcade than the Golden Goose, but today it is a small restaurant. The obscure Beckton Arms murder pub also still stands.

The Lucan Mystery, 1974

So, which is London's most famous murder house? Some would say Jill Dando's house in Gowan Avenue, others George Joseph Smith's house in Waterlow Road, and yet others would point out the murder houses left behind by the perverted Dennis Nilsen and the prolific serial killer Patrick Mackay. Aficionados of murder in high life would favour Lord Lucan's house at No. 46 Lower Belgrave Street, where the nanny Sandra Rivett was murdered on 7 November 1974. Mystery still surrounds the motive for the murder, the identity of the culprit, and the whereabouts of John Bingham, 7th Earl of Lucan, who went missing after the murder, never to be seen again.[53]

The Binghams are a well-known aristocratic family, and one of them was made the 1st Earl of Lucan in 1795. The 3rd Earl became notorious for his lack of military prowess in the Crimean war, and the 4th Earl squandered much of the family fortune. Richard John Bingham, the future 7th Earl of Lucan, was born in 1934, the son of an army officer. He was educated at Eton and Sandhurst, and became a competent young officer, serving in Germany for a while before retiring from the Coldstream Guards in 1955. Unlike his parents, who both had socialist leanings, John was a staunch right-wing conservative. An incorrigible snob and racist, he deplored the attempts from various Labour oiks to erode the privileges of his own class, and their failure to keep various greasy dagoes and golliwogs in their proper place. Even some of John's upper-class contemporaries thought his archaic political opinions quite over the top.

Already at Eton John had been fond of gambling, and in the army he had 'fleeced' more than one of his fellow subalterns at the gaming table. After leaving the military, he got a job as an investment banker, with a salary of £500 a year. His parents were happy that he had settled down to a career, but unbeknown to them John continued to gamble. He maintained himself in a comfortable bachelor flat, kept an Aston Martin sports car, and raced his powerful speedboat with some degree of success, although it once sank under him when he was the leader of a race. A handsome man with masculine, aristocratic good looks, John was fastidious with regard to his choice of female company, preferring society women to the late-night floozies of the Soho nightclubs and the less reputable camp followers of the Brigade of Guards. Many of the attractive women he dated would surely have been very happy to marry such an eligible bachelor, who was the heir to an earldom, but John was reluctant to settle down. His parents were not happy when he retired from the bank after winning £26,000 at a gambling party in 1960, to become a professional gambler.

The London ladies who had designs on the dashing Lord Bingham received some very bad news late in 1963, when he married Veronica Mary Duncan, the daughter of Major Charles Moorhouse Duncan, MC. They settled down in an elegant Georgian terraced town house at No. 46 Lower Belgrave Street, and soon had two daughters and a son. After the untimely death of John's father, he inherited the earldom in 1964 and took his seat in the House of Lords. Most evenings, he took his seat at the upmarket Clermont gambling club instead, however, and all poor Veronica could look forward to was to watch him amusing himself at the gaming tables. Once, his nickname had been 'Lucky' Lucan, but his luck gradually ran out and he began squandering the family fortune. His marriage suffered as a result, and so did Veronica's mental health. Her husband took her to see various psychiatrists, and made sure that she was dosed with lithium and other drugs. Once, the earl took her to a large, forbidding-looking building, without telling her what they were doing there. It was a private asylum, and he wanted her to become an inpatient there! Veronica made sure that she made a rapid escape from these premises, however. Not without reason, she began to suspect that her husband was up to no good; was he not exaggerating her mental health problems in order to secure custody of the children if she divorced him?

In early 1973, Lady Lucan separated from her husband. She kept custody of the children, and remained in the comfortable house at No. 46 Lower Belgrave Street. Lord Lucan moved into a large flat at No. 72A Elizabeth Street nearby. He had high hopes to recover the children, to whom he was devoted. John had applied to the High Court for an order, claiming that Veronica's mental health problems rendered her unsuitable to look after them. He employed a firm of private detectives to spy on his wife, and to help him kidnap the children and bring them back to the Elizabeth Street flat in triumph. Pending the High Court hearing, he had the right to take care of them. John then made sure his private detectives followed Veronica almost around the clock; when they went off duty, he himself sat spying in his large Mercedes sedan outside No. 46, disguised in dark glasses and a hat. At times, he rang the bell at the house and did his best to provoke an argument with his estranged wife, recording her furious outbursts with a hidden tape recorder. But in spite of his sneaky tactics, the caddish earl was taught a hard lesson when the High Court proceedings began in July 1973. Veronica was a convincing witness, there was nothing to suggest that she was an incompetent mother, and her psychiatrist gave her unexpected support. Her sister, Christina Shand Kydd, who the earl had hoped would provide damning testimony, instead supported Veronica. Not without reason, the judge found John's methods sordid and ungentlemanly, and his private detectives far from convincing witnesses. In the end, Lucan's barrister had to concede the case. This was a hard blow for the arrogant, padded nobleman: his wife had outwitted him, he had lost custody of his beloved children, and all he was left with was a bill for £40,000 in legal fees.

Lord Lucan's gambling cronies found him a changed man after his humiliation in court. He looked gloomy and careworn, drank to excess, and lost heavily at the gaming table. Obsessed with his children, he sat spying in his car outside No. 46 whenever he found the time. His bank accounts were all heavily overdrawn, and he was making arrangements to sell the family silver to stave off his creditors. Once, when drinking with his friend Greville Howard, he described his impossible situation. Howard advised him to go bankrupt, but Lucan thought this would mean further humiliation for his family. Instead, he said he would not mind murdering Veronica, and disposing of her body in the Solent. When Howard told him not to be silly, since his children would suffer even more when their father was in court for murder, Lucan replied that he did not intend to get caught.

At 9.45 p.m. on Thursday 7 November 1974, Lady Lucan burst into the Plumber's Arms, the pub at No. 14 Lower Belgrave Street. She was bleeding profusely from the head, and screamed, 'Help me, help me, help me, he is in the house, he has murdered my nanny!' This must have been a very unexpected emergency for the pub landlord in this very affluent part of London, but he promptly called the police and an ambulance. When the police searched No. 46, they found a bloodstained towel in one bedroom and a large pool of blood with a man's footprints on the floor of the basement. They searched the basement and discovered broken crockery and walls splashed with blood. They found an American canvas mailbag, inside which was the body of Sandra Rivett, nanny to the Lucan children, who had been brutally murdered by repeated blows to the head from a blunt instrument. It is likely that the instrument in question was a bloodstained length of lead pipe wrapped in surgical plaster, which was found nearby.

At the hospital, Lady Lucan named her husband as the attacker. Sandra Rivett had put her head round the door and asked Lady Lucan if she would like a cup of tea, before going downstairs to the kitchen. After a quarter of an hour had passed, Lady Lucan began to wonder what had happened to the tea. When she went downstairs, calling Sandra's name, a man emerged from the cloakroom and hit her with a heavy object. She screamed, and when he told her to 'shut up', she recognised the voice of her husband. Lucan shoved three gloved fingers down her throat to silence her, but she tweaked his private parts hard and managed to get free. The bewildered earl stopped his attack, and accompanied her upstairs. When she asked him where the nanny was, he said that she was dead. Their daughter, ten-year-old Lady Frances Bingham, was surprised to see her parents come upstairs. When Lucan went into the bathroom to get a cloth to clean his wife's face, she seized her opportunity to escape to the Plumber's Arms.

At around 10 p.m. on the evening of the murder, Lucan's friend Mrs Madeleine Florman, a wealthy lady who lived nearby in Chester Square, was awakened by someone ringing her doorbell. She ignored it, blaming local youths, and twenty minutes later received a phone call from an agitated Lucan, who soon hung up. Police later found bloodstains on her doorstep. A few minutes later, Lucan called his mother and told her that he had been passing No. 46 when he saw a man attacking his wife through the basement window. 'There was something terrible in the basement,' he added. 'I couldn't bring myself to look.' Lucan had borrowed a Ford Corsair from a friend, and he made use of this vehicle to drive down to Uckfield, East Sussex, to the house of his friend Susan Maxwell-Scott. By this stage, he had 'improved' his story somewhat, telling her that, after seeing an intruder attack his wife, he had entered the house and gone to the basement, where he had slipped in a pool of blood. The assailant fled in some unspecified manner. Lady Lucan screamed that the man had killed Sandra Rivett, and accused Lucan of hiring the mystery intruder to murder herself. After realising his difficult position, Lucan had decided to abscond, since he was worried that his vengeful wife would accuse him of hiring the assassin. Lord Lucan had a stiff whisky and some Valium sedatives before leaving Mrs Maxwell-Scott's house and driving off into the night. The Ford Corsair was later found in Newhaven. In the boot was another length of lead pipe wrapped in surgical plaster. Lord Lucan was never seen again.

At the coroner's inquest on Sandra Rivett, the damning evidence against the vanished earl was compiled. It turned out that Lucan had asked his daughter Lady Frances which was the nanny's day off, and by mistake she had wrongly told him Wednesday instead of Thursday. Lucan's brother-in-law Bill Shand Kydd read out a letter he had received from Lucan, in which the fugitive nobleman repeated his story of interrupting a fight in the house. His wife would blame him for hiring the assailant, he asserted, adding that she had demonstrated her hatred of him in the past and would do anything to see him accused. Lady Lucan gave her evidence calmly and convincingly. Her account was supported by the forensic evidence. The blood found in the basement had been mainly Group B (Sandra Rivett's group), while that found on the basement stairs was mainly Group A (Lady Lucan's group), and both types had been found on the lead pipe. There was no technical evidence to support the existence of another assailant. The coroner's jury returned a verdict of 'Murder against Lord Lucan'. The nobleman has the dubious honour of being the last person ever to be declared a murderer by an inquest jury, since this procedure was outlawed by the Criminal Law Act of 1977.

So what happened to Lord Lucan? Some say that he committed suicide, possibly by boarding a ferry from Newhaven and leaping overboard, but no person saw the tall and distinctive-looking nobleman in Newhaven, nor was his body ever found. Some of his friends thought it likely that he chose death before dishonour, but others found it unlikely that this inveterate gambler would destroy himself instead of having another roll of the dice. Although it is highly likely that Lucan left Uckfield in the Ford Corsair, there is no conclusive evidence that it was he who parked it in Newhaven. There have been many alleged sightings of Lord Lucan all over the world. In December 1974, police in Australia arrested a man they believed was Lucan but who was in fact the crooked politician John Stonehouse, who had faked his suicide a month earlier. In September 2003, the book *Dead Lucky* by Duncan MacLaughlin, a former Scotland Yard detective, claimed that Lucan fled to Goa, India, where he became known as Barry Halpin. However, ludicrously, it turned out that 'Jungle Barry' had in fact been a Liverpool folk musician and schoolteacher before becoming a beach bum in Goa.[54] In 2012, there was a revival of interest in the Lucan case after a woman claimed that she had arranged for Lucan's two eldest children to visit Gabon and Kenya twice between 1979 and 1981, for their fugitive father to see how they had grown up. Lady Lucan, however, who is still alive today, told the newspapers that the children had not been anywhere near Africa at that time. When interviewed, Lucan's brother Hugh Bingham also said he believed that Lucan had fled to Africa after the killing, although he denied having had any contact with Lucan or his children, and had no solid evidence to back up his theory.[55]

Over the years, there has also been a good deal of debate concerning Lord Lucan's guilt. The extreme pro-Lucan lobby has asserted that the earl has been telling the truth all the time: there had really been a second man on the premises, and Lady Lucan had either deliberately perjured herself, or been too shocked to distinguish the assailant from her husband. Lord Lucan saw the struggle when he passed by the house and ran in to help, only to be accused of the murder by his wife. The proponents of this theory, mainly the journalist Sally Moore who wrote *Lucan: Not Guilty*, have a point in that it is strange that the murderer did not realise that he was attacking the wrong woman. Furthermore, both Lady Frances and Susan Maxwell-Scott testified that Lucan's clothes were only slightly bloodstained, something not consistent with him wearing them during the savage attack on Sandra Rivett. But on the other hand, this version ignores that Lucan clearly was planning an attack on his wife beforehand, and asked which was the nanny's day off. His story of seeing his wife being assaulted in the basement is untrue, since Lady Lucan said she never set foot down there, and here she is again supported by the forensic evidence. It is also very dubious whether any person walking or driving past the murder house would be able to see a person being attacked in the basement, since its front window is set very low.

Another theory, put forward by author Patrick Marnham in *Trail of Havoc*, is that Lord Lucan had employed a contract killer to murder his wife, but that this individual had bungled the job, killing the nanny instead. When Lucan came to the house to help get rid of the body, the killer had left and his wife was still alive. This theory neatly fits some of the evidence, but it may be objected that it is natural for a person employing a contract killer to make sure he has a solid alibi for the time of the murder, instead of turning up at the murder scene himself. Lord Lucan had a motive to want to get rid of his wife, he was at the murder house at the relevant time, and Lady Lucan's damning testimony against him is supported by technical evidence. Lucan's own confused statements on the night of the murder can be proven to contain several falsehoods. The case against Lord Lucan for murdering Sandra Rivett is a formidable one, but I do not believe that he planned and executed the murder alone.

Nor do I believe that Lord Lucan committed suicide, since this act would have been contrary to his temperament: would this inveterate gambler not have tried his luck with one final roll of the dice? Even though the plot to murder Lady Lucan went badly wrong, this does not imply that the second part of the plan, namely to smuggle Lucan (and in the original version also the children) out of the country, was equally unsuccessful. The reason that Lucan left his own passport behind in his flat might well be that he had no need for it, since he had made sure that he had a faked passport under another name. Aided by one or two other people, he might have gone to Rhodesia or South Africa, two large countries with indifferent policing, where Lucan might have had a friend or two among the wealthy landowners. His brother Hugh Bingham is said to have told a TV journalist that the fugitive peer died in 2004, and that his grave was in Africa.[56] This statement may well be close to the truth.

2

Kensington

Houses wherein have been enacted notorious crimes must always be of interest to the student of criminology. It would be interesting to know, how many buildings with such a sinister history are still standing in England, but many of them the writer has himself inspected, and can, therefore, vouch for their continued existence.

Guy Logan, from *Famous Crimes Past & Present*

In this book, I have defined Kensington as the non-Chelsea part of the Royal Borough of Kensington and Chelsea. Kensington thus covers a vast expanse of West London, from the elegant garden squares of South Kensington to the fashionable and expensive parts of Bayswater and Notting Hill. Looking at the expensive houses and flats in these parts, and the profusion of valuable cars and shops selling luxury goods, it is easy to forget that parts of Kensington have had a distinctly seedy reputation in the past.

One of London's most notorious murder houses was of course No. 10 Rillington Place, Notting Hill, where John Reginald Christie piled up the corpses between 1943 and 1953. A necrophilic serial killer, Christie murdered three prostitutes, had intercourse with their corpses, and buried their remains in the tiny garden of his ramshackle end-of-terrace house. After the war, the Welsh van driver Timothy John Evans moved into the top-floor flat at No. 10. An unbalanced young man of mediocre intellect, he admitted murdering his wife and baby daughter, and was executed for these crimes. However, in 1953, Christie was arrested for the murders of six women, one of them his own wife. He willingly admitted murdering Mrs Beryl Evans, and is likely to have dispatched the baby as well. It is amazing but true that the old house at No. 10

The Black Lion, from a postcard stamped and posted in 1920.

Rillington Place stood for another seventeen years after these gruesome murders. A West Indian landlord bought the old house and sublet the rooms to various penurious countrymen. The murder house was pulled down in early 1970, along with the remainder of Rillington Place, as a part of a slum clearance.

Another of Kensington's lost murder houses was No. 89 Addison Road, where little Vera Page was outraged and murdered in 1931; although a man named Percy Orlando Rush was strongly suspected by the police, there was not enough evidence to put him on trial. No. 52A Cromwell Road, where the painter Ernest Castlelein was murdered by an unknown assailant in 1945, no longer stands; nor does No. 28 Appleford Road, where Brian Burdett murdered his wife Moira in 1956, but otherwise the architecture of capital crime has lasted quite well in these parts. Visit the murder houses of the prostitute-killing 'toff' Ronald True; the calculating serial killer 'Acid Bath' Haigh, who had his own method of dissolving the remains of his victims; and the bestial sadist Neville Heath. Also make sure that you do not miss London's oldest murder pub, the Black Lion at No. 123 Bayswater Road.

London's Oldest Murder Pub, 1800

On 30 January 1800, a troop of soldiers from the first regiment of guards went to the Black Lion public house, Bayswater, to have a few pots of ale and porter. The thirsty soldiers emptied the pots at a rapid pace. One of them, George Scott, invited another soldier, James Hartley from the third regiment of guards, to join them. A certain Henry Kendrick objected to Hartley drinking with them, but Scott was adamant that they should show good manners, and allow the stranger to join their company.

Some pots of beer later, the soldiers were getting quite drunk. George Scott suggested that they should have 'a parting pot' before returning to the barracks, but when Kendrick wanted the truculent Hartley to contribute a penny to it the stranger replied that he would see him damned first. Kendrick did not want any quarrel, and Scott said that, since he was the reason Hartley had come into their company, he would pay the penny for him. Having enjoyed plenty to drink, he needed to 'go out and make water' before quaffing more beer, however. When George Scott walked towards the door, Hartley stabbed him hard with a short sword, and Scott collapsed on the tavern floor.

There was much uproar at the Black Lion at this unprovoked attack. As Kendrick knelt down by his fallen comrade's arms, Scott could only say, 'Oh Lord, Kendrick, I am killed, I am dead!' As Hartley tried to escape, he was struck hard in the face, first by a hawker named Davis, and then by a soldier named Rudkin. George Scott died within fifteen minutes of being stabbed, and James Hartley was arrested by the beadle and constable of Paddington parish.

On trial at the Old Bailey for the wilful murder of George Scott, on 19 February 1800, James Hartley alleged that he had been struck in the face by Kendrick, Rudkin and Scott, and that he had defended himself with the sword to avoid further ill-treatment. Colonel Peyton, commanding the third regiment, and eleven other witnesses, all gave him a good character. However, Kendrick and Rudkin stoutly denied that any person had struck Hartley before he stabbed Scott to death. Hartley's barrister tried his best to show up some contradictions, mainly that Rudkin had told a witness that Hartley and Scott had been playing dominoes for beer, and quarrelled about the reckoning, something he had denied when giving evidence in court. Was there rivalry between the guards regiments, and were Rudkin and Kendrick lying about knocking Hartley around?

What sealed James Hartley's fate was that the hawker Davis, who entirely lacked military connections, gave evidence that agreed perfectly with Kendrick and Rudkin's version of events. Hartley was found guilty of wilful murder, sentenced to death, and hanged at Newgate on 24 February 1800.[1] The Black Lion, a Bayswater country pub in 1800, is today situated right in the middle of the tourist district, and enjoys a very healthy trade due to its 'olde worlde' atmosphere.

The Child That Did Not Scream in the Night, 1867

James Mooney was a young workman of Irish descent, who lodged at No. 9 Pembroke Place. In 1867, this small alley, situated off Earl Street (today's Earl's Court Road) was a crowded and none too salubrious part of London. Mooney usually got on reasonably well with his wife Ann and their two children, but in May 1867 there was serious marital strife. On Tuesday 23 May Ann walked out on 'Jem', as he was called, and the Irishman consoled himself with a lengthy drinking binge. On Saturday night, the drunken Jem went out to look for his wife. He found her outside a nearby pub, talking to a young man with whom she was clearly on very friendly terms! She had obviously been drinking. Jem challenged the guilty pair, but Ann obstinately refused to return home, perhaps hoping that her paramour would stand up for her. However, the interloper did not have the bottle to face up to the fierce Irishman, who angrily seized hold of his wife and frogmarched her all the way home to No. 9 Pembroke Place.

Once back home, Jem threw Ann down on the bed, damning and blasting her in the meanwhile. Their daughter was away, but their little son John James, aged just six, cried, 'Mother, hide under the bed, father will kill you!' This pathetic outcry did nothing to pacify Jem. He thrashed his wife with his fists, and then tore her clothes off and threw them into the fire. Finally, Ann managed to tear free from her demented husband. Dressed in only one undergarment, she took refuge with her friend and neighbour Elizabeth O'Bryen at No. 2 Pembroke Place. Jem kept on cursing and damning her eyes, but he did not pursue her.

The following morning, Jem Mooney came to call on the O'Bryens, looking much the worse for wear. They thought he was looking for his wife, but instead he asked Mr O'Bryen to help carry his child to the hospital. The following remarkable conversation ensued:

> Mrs O'Bryen: What is the matter with him?
>
> Jem: He is ill.
>
> Mrs O'Bryen: He was well yesterday.
>
> Jem: Well, he's burnt. [To his wife, who came to join them.] Go and see the state of your child!
>
> Ann: He was well enough when I left home yesterday!
>
> Jem: Had you remained in your own home your child would not have been burnt!

Berating the sullen Jem for his callousness, Mrs O'Bryen accompanied him back to No. 9 to have a look at the child. When Jem removed the blanket from the child's bed, she could see that little John James was horribly burnt. She asked the little boy if he was in much pain, but he was incapable of answering her. When berated for neglecting his little boy, Jem seemed more than a little shifty and evasive, saying that what had happened was the fault of the child's mother for not looking after him properly! Little John James was removed to hospital, where he soon died. Jem was taken into custody by the police.

At the coroner's inquest on John James Mooney, his wife described how Jem had beaten her up. Hannah Penton, who also lodged at No. 9, had heard the row, with Ann screaming, 'Jem, don't!' and then running out of the house in a nearly naked condition. Ann Hayes, who lived at No. 8, testified that early on Sunday morning she had seen that the door to No. 9 was open. She had gone in and seen the child lying in bed. He had said, 'Poor mother ran away, and naughty father burn me.' This was hearsay evidence, and ruled out as not admissible. Jem said that the night John James had got burnt, he had seen an extinguished candle lying on the child's bed, and he lighted it with a lucifer match. Then he saw that the quilt was on fire, and put it out. Since the bed was wet, he turned it around. John James said that his feet felt hot. Then Jem went to bed himself. In the morning, the child had said, 'Father, I am dying.' Without investigating the cause for this remarkable statement, Jem had run over to No. 2 to fetch help. On the second day of the inquest, Elizabeth O'Bryen provided some damning evidence concerning Jem's callous attitude. To her, he had said nothing about putting out any fire and turning any bed around: he had just seen the candle lying on the bed, and lit it.

On trial at the Old Bailey for the wilful murder of his son, Jem looked to be in a good deal of trouble. When Mr Daly opened for the prosecution, the court was of the opinion that there was hardly a case for the jury, and Mr Daly then offered no evidence. Jem was tried and convicted of common assault on his wife, and sentenced to six months in prison.[2] He had been saved by the murderer's greatest friend, the law ruling out hearsay evidence. Might there in fact have been some underhand compromise, with the charge of murdering the child being dropped, but the charge of assault proceeded with?

It must be said that even though it was not immediately possible to reconstruct the events leading to John James Mooney's death, Mr Daly and his colleagues acted with culpable negligence when conducting the prosecution. Firstly, the medical evidence was pathetic: at the inquest, a young doctor had briefly described John James's terrible burns on the buttocks, thighs and legs, but made no comment on how to interpret these injuries. It was not queried whether there might be other injuries, or whether the child was conscious when receiving the burns. The state of the child's bed was not investigated, except for a muddled remark from a police inspector that he had seen no mark of a candle on it. This would seem to imply that the bed was in good condition, and certainly not a charred, smoking wreck. Importantly, two young, alert and sober people, one of them actually lodging in the same house, had testified that no scream had been heard from the Mooney rooms that fateful night. Elizabeth O'Bryen testified that when she had told Jem that he must have been very drunk not to have heard the little boy scream, he had just blamed the incident on his wife.

The most likely turn of events is that the furious Jem, having just trashed and stripped his wife, was infuriated by some pathetic remark from his little son, who clearly took his mother's side. In a drunken rage, he stunned John James with a blow and put him on the fire, which was blazing merrily away consuming poor Ann's wearing apparel. This was why his buttocks and thighs were so very badly burnt. Jem had then lifted the child up, thrown him onto the bed and put the blanket over him. When John James regained consciousness, he was too weak to cry out, since he was already dying from burn-induced shock. To save himself, Jem told some obvious lies, and his version of events did not at all tally with Mrs O'Bryen's recollections of what he had said on Sunday morning.

There were too many James Mooneys for it to be possible to reconstruct what this dismal wife-beater and infanticide did after emerging from prison. If Ann took him back, she is unlikely to have been kindly treated for, albeit reluctantly, having testified against him in court. Pembroke Place is today a pleasant, old-world alley of neat little houses, situated just off the busy Earl's Court Road. The murder house at No. 9 is still standing and appears to be well looked after. Is it haunted by the pathetic moaning of a terribly burnt child?

Murdered by an Army Sergeant, 1876

Charles O'Donnell became a soldier when he was only in his teens. He remained in the army until he retired at the age of fifty-three in 1872, with the rank of sergeant. Two years later, he married Mrs Elizabeth Tibbs. Civilian life did not agree with Charlie O'Donnell, however. He did no work at all, drank to excess, and shouted at his wife if she dared to disobey him. His behaviour became so unbalanced that Elizabeth had to have him confined in Colney Hatch asylum. The sergeant remained there for six long months, before emerging as angry and mean-spirited as before. In particular, he was keen to lay his hands on Elizabeth's not inconsiderable savings, and she began to suspect that this money was the prime reason he had married her in the first place. She refused to part from her savings, knowing that he would soon spend them on drink. Charlie did not like this at all, and there were some angry quarrels between the two. After he had horsewhipped her in a drunken rage, they separated and continued to live apart until early October 1876, when a reconciliation took place and Charlie moved in with his wife in a lodging house at No. 46 Rawlings Street, Kensington.

For a few weeks, Charlie seemed a changed man, but even when he was on his best behaviour Elizabeth did not trust him. Fearful that he would steal her savings, she entrusted a parcel of coins and banknotes to another lodger. On 26 October 1876, Charlie and Elizabeth quarrelled incessantly from the early morning until six in the afternoon, the angry old soldier bellowing at his wife and she screaming back at him. The quarrel suddenly subsided, and to the relief of the other lodgers at No. 46 Rawlings Street there was no further racket from the O'Donnell flat for several days. In fact, things seemed unnaturally quiet, with Charlie coming and going, often in a very drunken condition. On 29 October, Charlie turned up at No. 28 Lower George Street, where he had previously lodged with the clockmaker Charles Christian Scherer. He looked very dejected, and Scherer asked him if he had quarrelled with the missus again. The friendly clockmaker invited Charlie inside, but even after being given a glass of whisky, the old soldier still looked very gloomy. When asked where his wife was, he replied, 'I hope she is in heaven!' He then wanted to write his will, and the puzzled Scherer gave him a piece of paper. Charlie wrote, 'I trust you will see us buried as soon as you can. Pay yourself, and give my respects to your wife and child. C.D.'

Realising that his friend might well have done something terrible, Scherer sent a lodger to the police station. When Inspector William Marsh forced the door to the lodgings at No. 46 Rawlings Street, he found the dead body of Elizabeth O'Donnell, murdered by repeated blows to the head with a heavy pair of tongs. The bedclothes were saturated with blood. The policemen were aghast that the demented Charlie had slept in this ghastly bed for three nights, next to the decomposing body of his wife. Both mirrors in the room had been smashed: had the skulking murderer been fearful of seeing his own face? Not less than £48 in gold was found in a cupboard, as well as a bankbook representing another £30.

At the coroner's inquest on Elizabeth O'Donnell, a verdict of wilful murder was returned. On trial for murder at the Old Bailey, the prosecution alleged that, infuriated by his wife's refusal to hand over her savings, Charlie had deliberately murdered her. The only argument from the defence was that Charlie must surely have been insane at the time. It was divulged that he had in fact been in Colney Hatch a second time, for two weeks in early 1876, but whatever treatment he had received had clearly not done him any good. After deliberating for more than an hour, the jury returned a verdict of 'guilty'. Baron Hawkins, the notorious 'hanging judge', calmly sentenced him to death, observing that he entirely concurred in the verdict. Charlie O'Donnell was hanged at Newgate on 11 December 1876.[3] The murder house at No. 46 Rawlings Street still stands.

The Bayswater Tragedy, 1895

In early 1895, a young lady calling herself Miss Gertrude Hilyer applied to rent a room at Mrs Elizabeth Wills' lodging house at No. 53 Talbot Road, Bayswater. The snobbish landlady emphasised that this was a very superior boarding house; in fact, she *let suites* to various respectable and well-bred people, among them a titled lady and an officer and his wife. Still, Miss Hilyer looked very respectable herself: a tall, good-looking young woman who said that her father had been a naval officer. Having been approved by the landlady, she moved her few belongings into the vacant top-floor back room at No. 53. The nosy landlady found her something of a woman of mystery. She had a marked aversion to doing any work, and often hinted that she had seen better days, and toured the world as a famous actress and singer.

After a few weeks at No. 53 Talbot Road, Miss Hilyer had something confidential to tell Mrs Wills. Her real name was Mrs Gertrude Mayston, and she asked permission for her husband to move in with her. The suspicious landlady did not at all like the sound of this, and demanded to see their marriage certificate. After Mrs Mayston had produced this document, Mrs Wills grudgingly allowed the husband to move in. The landlady was shocked to see that Frank Mayston was a short, shabby-looking fellow, who spoke with a pronounced cockney accent and appeared to be quite stupid and uneducated. When she asked Frank what business he was in, she nearly had a fit when he showed her his cabman's badge. A humble cabbie living in her respectable house!

Frank Mayston murders his wife, from the *Illustrated Police Budget*, 31 August 1895.

Above left: A drawing of Gertrude Mayston, from *Lloyd's Weekly Newspaper*, 1 September 1895.

Above right: The murder room at No. 53 Talbot Road, from *Lloyd's Weekly Newspaper*, 1 September 1895.

But it turned out that Frank was actually an *unemployed* cab driver. Just like his wife, he seemed quite reluctant to do any work. Gertrude constantly nagged her husband, berating him for his cockney rhyming slang, his coarse language, and his lack of both manners and education. Still, Frank was humble and subservient to his overbearing wife. The shopkeepers used to laugh at him, as he came walking a few steps behind his tall, dignified-looking wife, carrying all her parcels for her.

Gertrude told the landlady that she had married much beneath her station in life, and that her respectable relations not only refused to recognise Frank as her husband, but actually threatened to disinherit her. Her own habits of life were not beyond reproach, however. She often came home late, in such a drunken state that Mrs Wills had to help her to bed, so that she did not make a racket on her way up, or fall downstairs. Poor henpecked Frank, who was not allowed to accompany her on these nocturnal expeditions, worried that she was 'carrying on' with other men. His concerns deepened when he found a letter addressed to her from an unknown gentleman, enclosing £10.

After Mrs Wills' other lodgers had complained about Mrs Mayston's noisy and drunken habits, the landlady was seriously considering evicting her from the premises. However, early in the morning of 20 August 1895, four pistol shots rang out from the Maystons' second-floor room. When the landlady opened the door, she saw Gertrude's dead body on the floor. She had been shot in the head, with blood still pouring from a terrible bullet hole in the right temple. Frank was lying in a pool of blood, with a smoking revolver nearby. When a doctor arrived, he was surprised to find that, although the former cabbie had three bullet wounds to his head, he was still alive and conscious. He identified himself and provided his father's name and address, before saying, 'I did it. She caused me a deal of trouble.'

Frank Mayston was taken to St Mary's Hospital, where he was daily expected to expire. After all, one bullet had travelled right through his brain, and two others remained lodged within that organ. Surprisingly, however, Frank made a good recovery, only to be charged, at the coroner's inquest, with murdering his wife and attempting to commit suicide. Mrs Wills gave interviews to the press, complaining that 'The Bayswater Tragedy' had completely ruined her once prosperous business: all her other lodgers, the officer and the titled lady included, had promptly moved out of the murder house!

At the coroner's inquest, more details emerged about Gertrude Mayston's strange life. She was the daughter of a naval officer who was now dead, and her mother had remarried. Disapproving of her daughter's marriage to such a common little man, this snobbish lady had broken off all contact with her. Gertrude had once been a young lady of superior intelligence and breeding, and a talented singer and pianist. She had gone on the stage under the name 'Gertie Hilyer', and even played with the Gaiety Company in the United States in 1894. Frank's father, a retired publican living in Barnes, testified that his son had been working on and off, as a barman or a cab driver. Frank had never told his father that he was married.

When Frank Mayston was on trial for murder and attempted suicide at the Old Bailey on 21 November 1895, further painful details emerged about his unhappy mésalliance with Gertrude. Mrs Wills testified that she had constantly been nagging him, and treating him with disdain.

Once, when he had objected to her drunken habits and questionable nocturnal habits, she had replied, in a commanding voice, that she should go where she liked and do what she liked. Another time, when she had fallen downstairs in a state of intoxication, she had said that she wished she had broken her neck.

As a result, there was considerable sympathy for the henpecked Frank, whose married life had been so very unhappy. The doctor described his injuries, adding that, although he was currently in a stable condition, inflammation of the brain resulting from his wounds might well have fatal results. Changing his story in a short statement to the jury, Frank said that he had decided to leave his faithless wife and go to America, and that he had bought the revolver for his personal protection. He had showed the loaded weapon to his wife, and she had grabbed hold of it; the next thing he remembered was waking up in St Mary's Hospital. The prosecuting council objected that the theory of Gertrude shooting Frank and then committing suicide was quite inconsistent with the sworn facts of the case. Nevertheless, the jury found Frank Mayston not guilty of murder; on the count of attempting suicide, no evidence was offered, and the prisoner walked free.[4]

At the coroner's inquest, a mystery woman had stood up and exclaimed, 'And I know who the father of the child is!' but she had been hushed down. There is another newspaper reference to a child born to Gertrude Mayston, and 'farmed out' to some nurse. A little research shows that Gertrude Annie Haines had married Frank Mayston in mid-1893. Just a few months later, she gave birth to a daughter! The child was 'farmed out' and Gertrude Mayston went to America with the Gaiety Girls, leaving her husband behind. The reason Gertrude had married Frank is likely to be to avoid the disgrace of being an unmarried mother. He, on the other hand, appears to have been genuinely in love with her, and much in awe of her good looks and refined mannerisms. Although she bullied and tormented the humble Frank, he refused to leave her, and she was stuck with him. Gertrude's tour with the Gaiety Company seems to have induced her already flighty morals to plumb novel depths: she drank to excess and consorted with other men. Poor Frank had finally had enough in August 1895, ending the unnatural half-life of the woman he loved, and doing his best to put an end to his own miserable existence as well.

So what happened to Frank Mayston in the end, I can hear the reader ask. Did he buy another revolver to increase the number of bullets inside his brain, or did he leap headlong into the Thames from the seat of his cab, clutching some locks of his faithless Gertrude's hair? No, it turns out that Frank refrained from further rash actions: the 1901 census lists him as a building society agent, and the 1911 census has him living in West Ham, where he expired in 1925, aged sixty. Thus, Frank Mayston survived his suicide attempt by thirty years. If he was autopsied in 1925, the doctors must have received a shock when they detected the bullets lodged in his brain!

Murder by an Army Doctor, 1919

Norman Cecil Rutherford was born in Bradford in 1882. He attended school in Yorkshire and studied medicine at London University. When still a medical student, he fell in love with the beautiful young Alice Maud Roberts, daughter of the wealthy Yorkshire magnate Sir James Roberts. Sir James was not amused by the idea of his daughter marrying a penniless medical student, particularly since he had already arranged for her to marry a Polish nobleman. However, the headstrong Norman abducted Alice from her Baildon home and they were married in Scotland. After Norman had qualified in 1903, Sir James paid for him to go to South Africa with his wife. After spending some time as a *locum tenens* in Port Elizabeth, he became assistant surgeon at the Middelburg Military Hospital, in the Cape Province. The spoilt Alice did not like living among the rough South Africans. She wrote many letters to her father complaining of her hardships, and after a couple of years Sir James invited the Rutherfords to return to Yorkshire. He had decided that it was not right for his son-in-law to be working as a doctor in a godforsaken part of the globe. Instead, the magnate pontificated, Norman would be employed as a manager in his business, and provided with a house on his estate. This arrangement only worked for a few months, however; after a quarrel with his overbearing father-in-law, Norman took his wife and family back to South Africa.

This time, Norman got a job as assistant district surgeon in Zastron, a small agricultural town in the Oranje Free State. He liked South African life and amused himself by hunting lions and other animals, and studying their comparative anatomy. His wife disliked living in such a dismal outback, and urged him to return to England. These differences did not prevent them from raising a large family. It was not until 1908 that Alice managed to persuade Norman to return to Britain. He resumed

Sketches from the murder of Major Seton, from the *Illustrated Police News*, 23 January 1919.

his postgraduate studies in Edinburgh, and became a Fellow of the Royal College of Surgeons of London a few years later. He decided to become a medical scientist, and published several papers on embryology and anatomy. In 1911, he was senior assistant to the Professor of Anatomy at the Royal College of Surgeons of Ireland. A member of the Royal Zoological Society, he could enter Dublin Zoo for free, and put his children into the den to play with the lion cubs. Although lacking the contacts to become a success in the nepotistic medical world, Norman did reasonably well and kept his large family in the style to which they were accustomed. In 1914, he was teaching embryology and comparative anatomy at London University, again in a junior position. Perhaps sensing that war was inevitable, he took an interest in military medicine and became a captain in the London University Medical Corps.[5]

On the outbreak of the First World War, Norman Cecil Rutherford's undoubted talents were finally made use of. A vigorous young doctor with useful knowledge and experience in military medicine, he was employed at various mobile ambulances at the front line. His courage and competence, and the high death toll among the other army doctors, meant that he was rapidly promoted. In September 1917, when Lieutenant-Colonel Rutherford was in charge of an advance dressing station, tending to the wounded under heavy shelling, he was awarded the DSO for conspicuous gallantry in the field. In early 1919, when he had been promoted to Commissioner of Medical Services at the Ministry of National Service, his future seemed brighter than ever before.

One problem was still preoccupying Norman Cecil Rutherford, however, namely his suspicions that his wife had been unfaithful to him during his many years of service on the Western Front. Although they had now been married for seventeen years, and had six children alive, Norman knew that Alice was of a somewhat flighty character, and that her mind was full of conceit and snobbery. Her sister had married into the aristocracy, and the silly Alice had been talking about divorcing her husband and following suit. When he was home on leave, the jealous Norman cross-examined the housemaids about what 'gentleman friends' had come to see his faithless wife. There were angry scenes between the Rutherfords, and Alice alleged that Norman had more than once treated her cruelly.

In January 1919, Norman used the 'third degree' on his frightened housemaids in his usual bullying manner, extracting the information that Alice had often been visited by another military surgeon, Major Miles Seton. This drove him over the edge, since Seton was actually a good friend of his, and the godfather of one of his children. He also knew that Seton came from a wealthy family: he was the cousin of Sir Malcolm Seton, and lived in his large house at No. 13 Clarendon Road, Notting Hill. In the evening of 13 January, Norman armed himself with a revolver and went to seek out Seton at his cousin's house. He was admitted by the unsuspecting servants and went in to see Major Seton in Sir Malcolm Seton's dining room. The two doctors had a brief and sinister conversation, before Norman pulled the revolver and emptied its contents into his rival. Sir Malcolm and Lady Seton heard the shots and ran downstairs. They saw the tall, uniformed Norman standing over the body of the interloper, who was groaning with pain. 'Did you do this?' asked Sir Malcolm. 'Yes!' replied Norman, with satisfaction, putting the revolver on a table before adding, 'I only wish I had another bullet for myself!'

Hoping that his cousin's life could be saved, Sir Malcolm Seton went to fetch medical assistance, leaving his wife alone with the gunman and his victim. As Lady Seton tried to comfort the dying major, she heard a clicking noise behind her. Turning around, she saw Norman holding the revolver. This must have been a somewhat sinister situation, but Lady Seton's upper-class *sangfroid* did not desert her. 'Put that down at once!' she ordered, and Norman meekly obeyed her. There has been speculation that he had tried to shoot or intimidate her, but he might just as well have been considering suicide; in either case, the revolver was empty. When Sir Malcolm returned to No. 13 Clarendon Road with a doctor and a police constable in tow, Major Seton was found to be dead, and Norman Cecil Rutherford was taken into custody.

From all classes of society, there was widespread sympathy for Colonel Rutherford. Had Major Seton not been a howling cad, and had Mrs Rutherford not behaved in a blameworthy manner, 'carrying on' with another man when her husband was away fighting for his country? When he was on trial at the Old Bailey for murdering Major Miles Seton, however, things could have been looking better for Norman Cecil Rutherford. There was no doubt that he had murdered his colleague, with premeditation. Housemaids spoke of his angry, bullying manner, and they had often heard him shouting at his wife. Other housemaids spoke of Major Seton's many visits to Mrs Rutherford when the colonel had been away. Alice Rutherford herself did not give evidence, although some unsympathetic letters of hers were read in court, demanding a divorce from her husband and denying him access to their children. These letters made it clear that she cared very little for him, and was determined to marry another man (probably Seton).[6]

Norman Cecil Rutherford was found guilty of the murder of Major Miles Seton, and sentenced to death. An appeal on grounds of insanity was successful, however, and he was incarcerated in Broadmoor for an indefinite period of time. It seems as if the authorities were very reluctant to have such a brave, capable officer end his days on the scaffold; although Norman was perfectly sane, the only way to get him a reprieve was by means of the 'insanity' argument. With unseemly energy, Mrs Rutherford kept trying to divorce him. She had initial success, but the decision was reversed by the Court of Appeal.[7] When she appealed to the House of Lords in 1922, she did so with the bitter words: 'I asked so pitifully, when I knew insanity was to be the defence, "Can nothing be said at the trial to clear me?" and I was told that all Norman's past life must be kept back, or it would so harden the jury that he would be hanged. So I saved his worthless life, but at what a price! I, the woman who is now branded for life, the wife of a murderer, the mother of disgraced children, can you do nothing for me?' Their lordships could not, although Lord Birkenhead, sitting as Lord of Appeal, found it 'unfortunate' that she would remain 'tied for life to a dangerous, violent and homicidal lunatic after having for many years suffered both in body and in spirit from his unfaithfulness and cruelty.' All Alice Rutherford could do, though, was to change her name back to Roberts by deed poll, which she did in 1927. She is said to eventually have married another man, and lived on to be nearly 100 years old.

Norman Cecil Rutherford, the sanest inmate in Broadmoor, remained there for many years. Many people rightly found it shameful that a perfectly sane man would have to dwell with dangerous lunatics, and the National Archives contain a large file full of appeals and petitions to free him.[8] There was a petition among London doctors, and another among MPs. Norman's loyal brother Squadron-Leader Percival Rutherford also appealed, but although Norman promised to join the French Foreign Legion he was not released. It is telling that Sir James Roberts, who was still alive, also corresponded with the Broadmoor authorities, with the purpose of prolonging his son-in-law's incarceration as far as possible, so that his daughter would be protected against her insane husband. It was not until 1928 that Norman was finally liberated from Broadmoor. A newspaper described him as a sturdy, jovial man, robust and bearded. He had enjoyed playing cricket for the Broadmoor team, and once scored a century against a strong Berkshire side.

After his release, Norman did not get hold of a horsewhip to beat up his faithless wife, but behaved with restraint and *decorum*. After successfully appealing to be reinstated on the Medical Record, he went to Vienna to teach anatomy. Forming a low opinion of Nazi Germany, he persuaded several Jewish colleagues to escape to London, where they were safe from the clutches of the Nazi regime. After the Second World War, he worked in Persia for a while, before settling down into retirement in a Yorkshire cottage. A quiet life was not to the globetrotting doctor's liking, however, and he once more returned to South Africa, where he died in Kloopf, Natal, in late 1951 and was buried in his old tin hat as he had requested. The murder house at No. 13 Clarendon Road still stands, as a memorial to a once famous crime in London society that has since become totally forgotten.

Officer and Daughter Shot, 1921

Roderick McKenzie, a native of Aberdeen, enlisted in the Durham Light Infantry in 1894, when he was just seventeen years old. He served in India and in Sierra Leone, rose to the rank of Sergeant-Major, married and had two children. He retired in 1912 and held a commercial appointment in London for a while. At the outbreak of the First World War, he rejoined the army and secured a temporary commission. He served in the Tank Corps and advanced to become lieutenant and quartermaster of the corps at Wareham, where he resided in the officers' quarters with his wife and children. Tragedy struck in 1918 when McKenzie's wife died. Heartbroken, the now forty-one-year-old lieutenant let his mother take care of his young son. He retired from the army in 1919 and moved into an elegant ground-floor flat at No. 19 Glazbury Road, North Kensington, with his daughter Dorothy, or 'Dolly' as he had nicknamed her.

However, it was not easy for Roderick McKenzie, who had spent most of his life in the Army, to adapt to civilian life in the 1920s. He lived on his pension and his not inconsiderable savings, but idleness did not suit him and he started drinking heavily. He set his daughter Dorothy up in her own milliner business when she was just a teenager, but she was

DOROTHY McKENZIE.

LIEUTENANT QUARTERMASTER
RODERICK McKENZIE

SCENE OF THE CRIME.

Double tragedy in a Kensington Flat, from the *Illustrated Police News*, 25 August 1921.

not capable of running it. Instead, Dorothy got involved with a West End 'fast set', attending late-night parties and consorting with some very harum-scarum young men. Roderick McKenzie, who was very fond of his daughter and who had old-fashioned ideas about how teenage girls ought to behave, did not like this one little bit. However, when the ex-lieutenant tried to lock Dorothy up in her room, she escaped and went to the party nevertheless, and when he turned up at a fashionable West End party blind drunk to take his daughter home, she pushed him over and ran away.

After a while, the flighty young Dorothy McKenzie returned to the flat at No. 19 Glazbury Road, but her habits remained very 'fast': she sometimes partied all night, and three different boyfriends came calling at the flat. When poor Roderick McKenzie lectured to her about her late mother's virtues, she did not listen; when he hid her evening dresses to prevent her from going to parties, she sneaked out nevertheless. In the end, Roderick McKenzie could take it no longer. He wrote to his brother and to another friend, hinting that since his daughter was keeping such evil company he intended to destroy himself. On 20 August 1921, the bodies of Roderick and Dorothy McKenzie were found in the Glazbury Road flat. He had shot her through the chest and then taken his own life with a shot to the head.

At the inquest on Roderick and Dorothy McKenzie, his brother George, a wholesale meat seller in Aberdeen, described him as a physical wreck, ravaged by malaria and alcoholism. A pathetic letter from the gloomy ex-lieutenant was read out in court: 'Sorry, old man. I have done my best, but lately Dolly has got beyond me. My affairs are in order, and there are still a few hundreds left. Let my mother down as lightly as you can. – Your loving brother, Rod.'

Another letter, to an old family friend, contained the bitter words:

> Dear Barnard – I have tried to keep her off the streets, apparently without avail. I have offered every inducement and every sacrifice for the sake of her mother's memory. But it is no use. To-day I have tried to lock her clothes up to prevent her going away again. Evil company has done it, I am afraid.

A neighbour in Glazbury Road testified that he had often seen Roderick McKenzie drunk, and that his daughter had been afraid of him. The verdict was the obvious one: Roderick McKenzie had murdered his daughter, and then shot himself while temporarily insane.[9]

A Scandal in the Peerage and a Celebrated Murder, 1922

Arthur French, 4th Baron de Freyne, a forthright English aristocrat, owned a large estate in County Roscommon, Ireland, which he ruled with an iron hand from the family seat at stately French Park. He was widely detested for his reactionary and anti-Irish views, and his cruel mistreatment of his many tenants. In 1902, his tyranny led to full-scale revolt: the tenants refused to pay him rent, and mass evictions followed. Lord de Freyne then took some leading members of the Irish Party to court for influencing his tenants to rise up against him.

Lord de Freyne ruled his family with an iron hand as well. In November 1902, his eldest son and heir, Lieutenant the Hon. Arthur Reginald French, wanted to marry a young lady named Annabelle Angus. Lord de Freyne did not approve of her, thinking she looked rather like a floozie. Investigating her past, he found that she was a former barmaid and the divorced wife of another officer, and that she had also given birth to a bastard child fathered by another man. Lord de Freyne forbade the wedding, and when Arthur Reginald married Annabelle without his permission, the angry nobleman cut him off without a penny.

Unable to keep himself in the style to which a British officer was accustomed, Arthur Reginald had to resign his commission in the Royal Fusiliers. Leaving his wife behind, he sailed to America in early 1905, planning to become a trooper in the North West Mounted Police. Instead of becoming a Mountie, Arthur Reginald stayed in New York for a while, going drinking in the Bowery and consorting with various dodgy transatlantic types. One day, he failed to return, and there was speculation in the newspapers that he might have been murdered or kidnapped. Lord de Freyne made no exertions to find his errant son, but the New York police managed to track him down at Fort Slocum: he had enlisted as a private in the US Army.[10] Selling his fashionable civilian attire to pay for expensive dinners, he soon became known as 'The Dook of Fort Slocum'!

In 1913, old Lord de Freyne died. Once more, his obscure son was searched for, and this time he was tracked down serving with his regiment in the Philippines, still a private soldier. He could now throw away his humble soldier's cap and don an elegant tall hat, since he had inherited his father's title and fortune.[11] He settled down at French Park, but did not invite his wife to rejoin him. In the First World War, the 5th Baron de Freyne served with distinction as an officer in the South Wales Borderers, and was killed in the Battle of Aubers Ridge in 1915.

In the meantime, Annabelle Angus, or rather Lady de Freyne, had plenty of problems of her own. Her illegitimate son Ronald True, born in Chorlton-on-Medlock, Manchester, in June 1891 as the result of a short-lived teenage romance with some bloke, presumably named True, was a thoroughly bad hat. An alcoholic and a morphine addict, he had failed in numerous professions, including a short but disastrous stint as a pilot in the Royal Air Force, during which he had crashed three aeroplanes and narrowly escaped with his life. Posing as the war hero 'Major True', he went to America, where he married a young actress. In San Francisco, he was sentenced to eighteen months in prison for issuing worthless cheques under the name Baron de Freyne.

Released from the San Francisco prison, Ronald True returned to London, where he descended into a whirl of alcohol and drug abuse. Many people thought him quite insane, particularly after he had developed the fixed idea that another man, also named Ronald True, was issuing false cheques in his name. Lengthy inpatient stays in various clinics and psychiatric hospitals, paid for by Lady de Freyne, who was genuinely fond of her worthless son, did nothing to improve his condition.

Ronald True liked to have casual sex with various prostitutes, one of whom was Gertrude Yates, who called herself Olive Young and received her customers in a basement flat at No. 13A Finsborough Road, Fulham. They first spent the night together on 18 February 1922, but Olive did not care much for her sinister 'client'. After she discovered that he had stolen £5 from her handbag, she refused to have anything further to do with him. True was persistent, however, making many telephone calls to her and appearing unannounced at 13A Finsborough Road on 5 March. For reasons unknown, Olive let him in, which was not a good decision. The next morning, when Olive's maid came to clean the flat, True was just leaving. He told her not to disturb Miss Young, since she was in deep sleep after a busy night. When the maid opened the bathroom door, she found Olive's dead body battered to death with a rolling pin. Most of her jewellery and money had been stolen by the murderer.

Due to the maid's observations, Ronald True was the main suspect, and he was arrested by the police at the Hammersmith Palace in King

Street, where he was watching a music hall show. A bluff cove with an upper-class accent, he told them all about this infernal 'other' Ronald True, who issued dud cheques and murdered young women, but they did not believe him. Tried at the Old Bailey for the wilful murder of Gertrude Yates, a.k.a. Olive Young, he was found guilty and sentenced to death.[12]

The case of Ronald True caused a massive outcry from the popular press. The reason was that another London murderer, the pantry boy Henry Jacoby who had murdered Lady White at the Spencer Hotel, had been found guilty and sentenced to death in spite of a strong recommendation to mercy from the jury. The day after Jacoby was executed, medical experts declared that True was insane, and he was reprieved from the death sentence and indefinitely committed to Broadmoor. Surely, there was one law for the well-to-do son of a peeress, who had murdered a prostitute, the journalists wrote, and another law for the working-class killer of a titled lady! Here they disregarded that Jacoby's crime had been a premeditated and dastardly one, and that True had showed signs of mental derangement for several years before

Above left: Ronald True, from G. Pollock, *Mr Justice McCardie* (London, 1934).

Above right: Olive Young from G. Pollock, *Mr Justice McCardie* (London, 1934).

Ronald True and Richard Archer Prince amusing themselves in Broadmoor, from the *Illustrated Police News*, 31 December 1925.

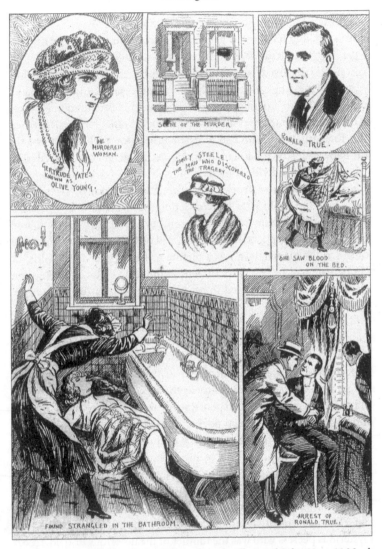

Sketches from the murder of Olive Young, from the *Illustrated Police News*, 16 March 1922.

the murder. At the time he murdered Olive Young, Lady de Freyne was actively looking for him, to have him incarcerated in a lunatic asylum to get long-term treatment for his disastrous addiction to drugs.

Ronald True lived on at Broadmoor for many years. After being weaned off the drugs and the alcohol, his mind cleared considerably, and there were those who called him the sanest man in Broadmoor. He took an interest in running the entertainments for the other inmates, together with Richard Prince who had murdered the actor William Terriss. He was allowed his own batman, a Yorkshire murderer named Frederick Owen, but this individual hanged himself in 1934, whether from the strain of looking after True's various needs is not known.[13] True's wife never saw him again after his conviction, but Lady de Freyne visited him regularly, and allowed him an income of £250 a year. His room was furnished with Chippendale furniture, and pictures by Picasso lined the walls. On the mantelpiece was a picture gallery of the Gaiety Girls, of whom True had been a close student in the early 1920s. In 1939, some friends of Ronald True tried to get him released from Broadmoor by petitioning the Home Secretary, but without success.

Ronald True's only son was killed in the Second World War, but both the murderer and Lady de Freyne lived into the 1950s. True became one of the veteran Broadmoor inmates: a keen gardener, an excellent bridge player, and a great raconteur of true or false yarns from his extraordinary career. He was busy as the Broadmoor Sports Secretary, and also ran a weekly football pool until he was sacked for swindling £85 of the proceeds into his own pocket. A heavy smoker for many years, Ronald True died from a heart attack in the Broadmoor medical ward in January 1951, mourned only by his seventy-six-year-old mother. Her name had been exposed in some American papers, including the *San Francisco Examiner*, but it had not been divulged in the British press. An article in the *Daily Mirror* said that now only one person, the Medical Superintendent of Broadmoor, would know the secret of 'Lady X', the mysterious peeress who was the mother of the notorious Ronald True.[14] As we have seen, however, that worthy paper underestimated the efforts of future generations to make obscure American newspapers available online.

The murder flat at 13A Finsborough Road has survived all the actors and actresses in the Ronald True drama: it still stands, a memorial to a long-forgotten scandal of the peerage, and to a sordid and brutal murder.

Murder at Pembridge Square, 1928

Mr Alfred Webb, a well-to-do West London accountant, lived in an elegant flat in a converted detached Victorian town house at No. 20 Pembridge Square. In the evening of 9 February 1928, he was returning home with his son Clifford and a friend named Mr Sweeney. Flat No. 3, the Webb family home, was on the first floor of the large, impressive house. In the communal hallway outside the flat, Mr Webb was aghast to see that a pane of glass had been broken in his front door: somebody was clearly burgling the flat! He called to Clifford and Mr Sweeney for assistance, and cautiously advanced to have a look inside. The door was unlocked, but inside was a very short, stout man who tried to push past him. With a hearty goodwill, Mr Webb collared the burglar. For a moment, Clifford saw his father struggling with the intruder, but then there was a shot from a revolver and Mr Webb fell to the ground with blood pouring from his head. The short, bowler-hatted gunman dashed past Clifford and Mr Sweeney out into the street. Clifford pursued him, shouting, 'Stop thief!' as he saw the gunman disappearing down the southern side of Pembroke Square. There were still quite a few people about, and for a while an entire crowd was chasing the fugitive, although the fog meant that they did not have much of a clue where he had gone.

The Pembridge Square burglar managed to escape, possibly through jumping onto a bus or hailing a cab. Mr Webb was taken to hospital, where he died the following morning. Scotland Yard was called in, and Detective Chief Inspector John Horwell took charge of the murder investigation. One of the witnesses, a man who had nearly been run into by the absconding murderer while walking along Pembridge Square, had seen him throwing something into a front garden. Horwell had the gardens along the killer's escape route carefully searched, and a .32-calibre automatic revolver was retrieved. The second round in this weapon had jammed in the breech, so the murderer had actually tried to fire a second shot at Mr Webb. The Webb flat was expertly searched, and a good deal of jewellery and other valuables had been stolen, so the killer was definitely a professional burglar. Gun crime was uncommon in London in the 1920s, however, and a loaded revolver was definitely not part of the typical burglar's kit.

Chief Inspector Horwell had his men make house-to-house inquiries to find out if any burglar had been 'sounding the drum' in the neighbourhood. This was police parlance for the miscreant knocking at

Sketches from the murder of Alfred Webb, from the *Illustrated Police News*, 16 February 1928.

Opposite above: The execution of Stewart, from the *Illustrated Police News*, 14 June 1928.

Opposite below: Pembridge Square, from a postcard stamped and posted in 1908.

SCENE of the MURDER

STEWART WALKING TO HIS DEATH

FREDERICK STEWART.

THE VICTIM

MR. ALFRED WEBB.

the front doors of houses in the hope of finding an empty house or flat that was ripe to be broken into. Indeed, an old lady could remember a very short man calling at her house. He had asked for the chauffeur, saying he was from the 'Warwick Garage'. Chief Inspector Horwell asked all his detective colleagues if they had any pint-sized burglar with some association with 'Warwick' in their 'manors'. One of them replied that he knew a certain Frederick Stewart, a bookmaker's clerk and part-time burglar. He was very short, liked wearing large bowler hats, and used to hang about near Warwick Mews, Kensington.

Frederick Stewart was also known for being very fond of betting on the dogs and the horses. His favourite dog-track at Southend-on-Sea was staked out, and sure enough, the pint-sized burglar was taken into custody in a public house nearby. When questioned by Chief Inspector Horwell, Stewart admitted the burglary and the possession of the gun, but claimed that the gun had gone off by accident when Webb had struck him. During his trial at the Old Bailey, the same defence was made use of, but the fact that a second round had jammed in the breech spoke in favour of deliberate murder by the cornered burglar, and Stewart was found guilty and sentenced to death. An appeal was made, but the Lord Chief Justice found the case as clear as could be, and there was little sympathy for an armed burglar shooting a harmless householder in cold blood. A true betting fanatic, Stewart sat poring over the racing magazines even as he languished in the death cell. When he heard that he was to be hanged on Derby Day, 6 June 1928, he asked for the execution to be postponed so that he could learn the result of the races, but to no avail: he was hanged early in the morning, seven hours before the 'Off'. As he was led to the scaffold, he gave the prison warders a final tip: 'Have a few bob on Felstead today!' The horse won, at 33 to 1, but Stewart would never know this.[15]

Murder at Pembridge Villas, 1929

James Achew was born in Cincinnati, Ohio, in 1873, of mixed American and Japanese parentage. He moved to England in 1895, and became a cabaret performer and singer. He took the name 'James Starr', married a woman named Nina Leslie, and performed with her in the club swinging act 'Starr and Leslie' until 1911. He then moved to Australia, where he took a hotel at Woolagong, near Sydney, but he soon gave it up and returned to London with very little money. Nina had had enough of him by this time, and left him without any maintenance. Instead, James Achew moved in with the singer Sybil da Costa, who was twenty-two years his junior. It is not known if they performed together. Many people, including Sybil's brother Algernon da Costa, thought that Sybil could have done much better than cohabiting with the unprepossessing, foreign-looking 'James Starr'. He was reluctant to work, fond of strong drink, and becoming quite ugly by the time he reached early middle age, his hair and teeth falling out fast. Nevertheless, Sybil supported him and their little daughter Peggy throughout the 1920s.

In 1929, Sybil became the housekeeper at a hotel at No. 110 Westbourne Terrace. One of the guests there, Miss Agnes Blackhall, lent Sybil some money, allowing her to open her own boarding house at No. 6 Pembroke Villas, Bayswater. Miss Blackhall became the first paying guest. James and Sybil themselves had Bedroom 6, on the first floor. Sybil Starr, as she called herself, was quite a success as a boarding-house keeper. She attracted a better class of lodgers to No. 6 Pembridge Villas: medical students, nurses, and a young South African author named William Plomer. Many of these guests contrasted the young, attractive and hard-working Sybil with her idle, prematurely aged husband. James did no work on the premises, drank throughout the day, and spied on the residents, in the belief they had designs on his 'wife'. Sybil made sure a doctor was consulted about his morose and depressed condition, but this obtuse medical man had no good ideas how to treat him, and did not consider him sufficiently deranged to be certified as a lunatic.

Due to James's incessant spying, several of the guests left No. 6 Pembridge Villas, since they did not know what this sinister-looking man might be capable of. Just like Basil Fawlty, he hid in the guests' wardrobes to find out what they were up to. Sybil was becoming worried that the business would suffer. She confided in her brother Algernon, but he did not have any suggestion for how to make James see sense. In November 1929, James became convinced that Sybil was having an affair with the author Plomer. Early in the morning of 14 November, he tried to make her confess, and when she denied any wrongdoing, he cut her throat with a razor. One of the lodgers found her dead body at the top of the stairs; James had pursued her there, and she had ten razor slashes on her throat and neck. James Achew was found in the kitchen with his head inside the gas oven. More squeamish with his own throat than with that of his wife, he only had a slight wound that hardly bled, and his attempt to gas himself was equally unsuccessful.

James Achew's injuries did not prevent him from attending the coroner's inquest on Sybil da Costa, otherwise Starr. Her brother Algernon was one of several witnesses to state that Achew's suspicions that Sybil was unfaithful to him were wholly unfounded. A verdict of wilful murder was returned, and at the Central Criminal Court Achew was found guilty and was sentenced to death.[16] An appeal was turned down, but at the very last minute he was respited by the Home Secretary on grounds of mental deficiency, and sent to Broadmoor, where he died in 1952, aged seventy-nine.

As for the author William Plomer, he was fortunate to be staying at a friend's house the night of the murder. Pondering his narrow escape, he wrote a novel, *The Case is Altered*, based on the grisly murder at No. 6 Pembridge Villas. Even in his novel, Plomer did not mention the reason he had not 'fancied' his landlady Sybil in the first place: namely that he was a closet homosexual.[17] If the demented James Achew had been more thorough in spying on him, much mischief would have been averted.

Murder by the 'Monocle Man', 1941

Harold Dorian Trevor was a well-known con artist, mostly active in London and along the South Coast. A tall, gentlemanly looking fellow, he liked to dress in elegant clothes and wear a monocle. His aliases included Commander Herbert, Sir Francis Ford, Captain Gurney, Captain Strong, Commodore Crichton and Sir Charles Warrent. Even as a young man, he hired a brougham and two servants, and went to the best hotel in Windsor, where he presented himself as Lord Reginald Herbert. Here, he enjoyed a sumptuous luncheon, paid for by a bad cheque. He then invited the hotel owner and his wife for a ride in the brougham; they returned to find the cash register empty. Trevor used the money to take a young actress out for dinner, but when she discovered that he had stolen her purse from her handbag Trevor was arrested and sentenced to six months in prison.

In 1925, Trevor stole £18 from a woman's apartments in Tavistock Place. It turned out that an army major was practically his double, including the elegant clothes and the monocle, and several witnesses identified the unfortunate officer as the thief. After fingerprint evidence had been secured, the major proved his innocence and Trevor was once more jailed. Trevor made it his business to prey on women with money. Many a trusting hotel proprietor and boarding-house keeper had reason to wish they had never crossed the Monocle Man's path. In 1936, Trevor was sentenced to five years in prison for a long series of swindles; the newspapers expressed relief that the Londoners would be safe from this pest until 1941.[18]

The Monocle Man emerged from prison in October 1941. He made his way to a large maisonette at No. 71A Elsham Road, whose owner, Mrs Theodora Jessie Greenhill, had advertised a room for rent. She had no idea that the suave and charming 'Doctor Trevor' who wanted to rent a room had in fact spent forty of his sixty-four years inside prison cells. Her opinion of the good 'doctor' changed quickly, however, when she saw him pocket a silver cigarette-box. As she was going to telephone the police, Trevor knocked her down with a heavy bottle, and then strangled her to death.

Probably aghast at what he had done, the Monocle Man, who had previously never used violence in his long criminal career, hastily made himself scarce. However, he had run out of luck. Unexpectedly, Mrs Greenhill's daughter returned from America just an hour after the murder. She discovered the body and alerted the police. Since a witness had seen the dapperly dressed, monocled Trevor leaving the premises, the police knew who they were dealing with, particularly since the clumsy murderer had left behind a receipt for the rent, with the name Dr H. D. Trevor on it. A fingerprint on the bottle used to murder Mrs Greenhill matched one of Trevor's, kept in the police records. The desperate murderer absconded from London, travelling north and selling Mrs Greenhill's belongings on the way. Caught hiding inside a Rhyl telephone box in early 1942, Harold Dorian Trevor was found guilty of murder at the Old Bailey and sentenced to death. He was executed at Wandsworth Prison on 11 March 1942.[19] The murder house still stands.

The Acid Bath Killer of Gloucester Road, 1945–1949

John George Haigh was born in 1909, the son of respectable religious parents. A bright lad when he applied himself, he won a scholarship to the Queen Elizabeth Grammar School in Wakefield, and became a choirboy in Wakefield Cathedral. However, he did not take his studies seriously, and showed an early tendency to thieving and dishonesty. After school he was apprenticed to a firm of motor engineers, and then

John George Haigh.

drifted between various short-term jobs in insurance and advertising, until he was sacked after being suspected of stealing from a cash box.

In 1934, Haigh married a young woman named Beatrice Hamer, but she left him after he had been sentenced to thirteen months in prison for fraud. She gave birth while he was in prison, but gave the baby girl up for adoption. Likewise, Haigh's conservative family ostracised him from that point onwards. In 1937, another, larger-scale fraud earned Haigh four more years in jail. Released in 1941, this inveterate scoundrel was soon back behind bars, this time serving twenty-one months for looting and theft from bombed-out houses. This time, though, Haigh was aspiring to better himself, not through adhering to the 'straight and narrow' but through becoming a master criminal. In prison, Haigh kept reading various law books. He became convinced, quite wrongly, that if the victim's body no longer existed the killer could never be charged with murder. He had access to a workshop where chemicals were stored, and was delighted to find that the carcase of a dead mouse, which he had put in a container of sulphuric acid, was dissolved within half an hour.

After he had been released from prison in 1944, Haigh met a friend named Donald McSwan, a wealthy owner of amusement parlours who had employed him as a chauffeur back in the 1930s. The unsuspecting McSwan introduced Haigh to his parents, who mentioned that they had invested in property. Greedy to lay his hands on their money and valuables, the clever and enterprising Haigh made plans to murder the

An old postcard showing Gloucester Road; the premises where 'Acid Bath' Haigh murdered and disposed of some of his victims is on the right side, past Gloucester Road underground station.

McSwans one by one. He rented a workshop in the basement of No. 79 Gloucester Road, Kensington, and made sure that he had a good supply of acid handy. On 6 September 1944, Haigh invited Donald McSwan to No. 79 Gloucester Road, allegedly to show him a pinball machine he had invented. Haigh bludgeoned McSwan to death, put his body in a 40-gallon drum, and poured concentrated sulphuric acid into it. Two days later he returned to find the body reduced to sludge, which he poured down a manhole.

Haigh moved into McSwan's house and began selling his belongings. When the old McSwans wondered what was happening, he told them that their son had fled to Scotland to avoid being called up for military service, and that he himself was looking after the house while his friend was away. When they became suspicious, he lured them to No. 79 Gloucester Road, where they were murdered and disposed of in the same manner as their son. The brazen Haigh used his forgery skills to obtain the title to all the houses and other property owned by the McSwans. In 1945, he moved into the Onslow Court Hotel at Nos 109–113 Queen's Gate (today the Kensington Hotel), bringing with him a cool £8,000 of ill-gotten gains.

In spite of his successful caper exterminating the McSwan family and robbing them of their assets, the unsuccessful gambler Haigh was already running short of money in 1947. He found another couple to murder and rob: Dr Archibald Henderson and his wife Rose, whom he met after purporting to show interest in a house they were selling. The experienced murderer rented a small workshop at 2 Leopold Road, Crawley, West Sussex (it no longer exists), and moved his supply of acid and drums there from Gloucester Road. On 12 February 1948, he drove Henderson to Crawley on the pretext of showing him an invention. When they arrived, Haigh shot Henderson in the head with a revolver he had earlier stolen from the doctor's house. He then lured Mrs Henderson to the workshop, claiming her husband had fallen ill, and shot her dead without any further ado. After disposing of the Hendersons' bodies in oil drums filled with acid, he forged a letter from them and sold all of their possessions for £8,000 (except their dog, which the cynophile murderer decided to keep).

In early 1949, the hard-spending John George Haigh had once more run out of cash. He could hardly even pay for his room at the Onslow Court Hotel. The personable, well-dressed Haigh, who was an experienced con artist, made friends with fellow resident Olive Durand-Deacon, the wealthy widow of a solicitor. He invited her down to the Crawley workshop in February 1949, where he shot her in the back of the head, stripped her of her valuables, and put her into the acid bath. This time, however, this normally reliable and professional killer had been both clumsy and unlucky. Two days later, another old lady at the hotel made a fuss about her friend's disappearance, and reported her missing. She suspected that Haigh was involved. Haigh had been seen in Crawley with his victim, and Mrs Durand-Deacon's fur coat and jewellery were produced by the cleaner and jeweller with whom Haigh had deposited them. Detectives soon discovered Haigh's record of theft and fraud and searched the Crawley workshop. They found Haigh's attaché case containing a dry cleaner's receipt for Mrs Durand-Deacon's coat, and also papers referring to the Hendersons and McSwans. Further investigation of the sludge at the workshop by the pathologist Keith Simpson revealed three human gallstones and part of a denture (which was later identified by Mrs Durand-Deacon's dentist). Thus modern forensic technology was instrumental in bringing to justice an extremely cunning and dangerous serial killer.

In the end, Haigh confessed to the earlier murderers, adding some spicy inventions, like that he had drunk the blood of his victims. This, it was hoped by his defence counsel, would aid the 'insanity defence', but a board of medical experts appointed by the Home Secretary declared Haigh sane. During his trial, Dr Henry Yellowlees, who claimed Haigh had a paranoid constitution, declared, 'The absolute callous, cheerful, bland and almost friendly indifference of the accused to the crimes which he freely admits having committed is unique in my experience.' It took only minutes for the jury to find Haigh guilty. Mr Justice Humphreys put on the black cap and sentenced him to death. The humourist murderer, a cool customer if there ever was one, wrote to his solicitor that 'it was an effort to refrain from audible laughter when the judge donned his black cap. He looked for all the world like a sheep with its head peering out from under a rhubarb leaf.' It is not known whether 'Acid Bath' Haigh produced any further witticisms when he was led to the gallows and hanged at Wandsworth Prison on 10 August 1949.[20]

What happened to the murder house, or rather murder basement, at No. 79 Gloucester Road, though? Some careless writers have accused the Kentucky Fried Chicken restaurant at No. 81 Gloucester Road of being Haigh's old haunt, but this is not the case. It is not *always* that the house following No. 77 is No. 79. The reason for this is that the numbering of the houses in that part of Gloucester Road is more than a little odd, with No. 75 followed by No. 77A, No. 77 and No. 81 (the latter the KFC fast-food shop). The experienced murder house detective is not taken in by such simple stratagems: the old No. 79 is of course identical to the present-day No. 77, and No. 77A is the former No. 77. The murder house's characteristic portico has survived, and so have some of the railings, but Haigh's old basement has been paved over. A spy I sent into the building could report that the basement itself is likely to have survived, although it is kept securely locked; the dark secret of 'No. 77' appears to be kept well guarded.

Murder in Pembridge Gardens, 1946

Neville Heath was born in Ilford in 1917, the son of a barber. His father made sure that he received a decent education, so that he could enter the Royal Air Force as a cadet in 1937. He made good progress as an aviator, but was sacked from the RAF for being absent without leave, and embezzling money. A handsome, plausible young man, Heath took to life as a professional con artist, obtaining credit by fraud, and passing bogus cheques. During these escapades, he called himself 'Lord Dudley' or 'Lieutenant-Colonel Armstrong'. The law caught up with him and he was sent to borstal, but he emerged in 1939 after war had broken out, to enlist as a private soldier in the Royal Army Service Corps. He soon obtained a commission, and served in the Middle East for a while, but was caught passing worthless cheques, arrested and shipped home to be court-martialled. On the way to Britain, he escaped and went to Johannesburg, where he joined the South African air force. This time, he took his military duties more seriously, and rose to the rank of captain, but was court-martialled for wearing decorations to which he was not entitled. He married, but deserted his wife and went back to London after the war.

In London, Neville Heath resumed his old life as a conman. He preyed on women, hoping to marry well or at least to deprive his various lady friends of some of their savings. In June 1946, when he was living at the Pembridge Court Hotel, situated at No. 34 Pembridge Gardens, Kensington, his current girlfriend, or perhaps rather victim, was young Yvonne Symonds. He had proposed to her and she had accepted him, also agreeing to share his hotel room on at least one occasion. At some

Pembridge Gardens, from a postcard stamped and posted in 1905. The future murder house at No. 34 is the last house in the terrace to the left.

stage in his career, Heath had acquired a taste for sexual sadism, and he knew an older woman, thirty-two-year-old Margery Gardner, who was a masochist who liked to be beaten with a whip among other perverted practices. She was a part-time actress who had left her husband and daughter to seek her fortune in the London *demi-monde*. The previous month, Heath had beaten her at another London hotel, but she had been saved by a hotel detective. After they had spent the evening of 20 June dancing at the Panama Club in Kensington, Neville Heath and Margery Gardner returned to Room 4 at the Pembridge Court Hotel. The following day, her body was found naked on the bed, her wrists and ankles bound. There were seventeen slash marks on her body, her nipples had been savagely bitten, and an instrument had been inserted into her vagina. The whip that had inflicted the slash marks on her body was nowhere to be seen. These marks showed the distinctive diamond pattern of a woven leather riding crop. Forensic pathologist Professor Keith Simpson told the police, 'Find that whip and you've found your man.'

However, 'Lieutenant-Colonel N. G. C. Heath', the gentleman who had reserved the hotel room, was nowhere to be found. He had gone to spend some time with Yvonne Symonds and her parents in Worthing. They were quite impressed with the plausible 'Lieutenant-Colonel', but he chose to leave abruptly when his name appeared in the newspapers in relation to Margery Gardner's murder. He went to Bournemouth and took a room at the Tollard Royal Hotel, under the extraordinary alias 'Group Captain Rupert Brooke'. A few days later he met Doreen Margaret Marshall, who was staying at the Norfolk Hotel. After he had gallantly offered to walk her home to the hotel, she was never seen again. As for the poetic 'Group Captain', he climbed into his own hotel room through the window. Had Heath made a speedy getaway, he might still have been saved, but he decided to brazen it out. As the last person who had spoken to Doreen Marshall, he was questioned by the police. One of the Bournemouth detectives thought the 'Group Captain' very much resembled the man Neville Heath, whose photograph had been reproduced in the newspapers as the main suspect in the murder of Margery Gardner. The next morning, the 'Group Captain' admitted that he was Heath. The whip, which he had unwisely not discarded, was found among his possessions. On 7 July, Doreen Marshall's mutilated body was found by a rhododendron thicket in Branksome Dene Chine.

On trial for the murder of Margery Gardner, Heath wanted to plead guilty. His counsel, J. D. Casswell KC, questioned this, and so the the suave murderer changed his mind, saying, 'All right, put me down as Not Guilty, old boy!' Casswell wanted to use the insanity defence, and so didn't call Heath to give evidence; this proved unsuccessful, however. It was acknowledged that Heath was a sexual pervert and a psychopath, but both doctors called to give evidence agreed that he was not insane. He was found guilty and sentenced to the death penalty.[21] On 16 October 1946 he was hanged by Albert Pierrepoint at Pentonville Prison. When Heath was offered a whisky just before his execution, he coolly replied, 'Considering the circumstances, better make it a double'. The elegant murder hotel at No. 34 Pembridge Gardens is today a private house, quite possibly undergoing a conversion into flats.

The Chalk Pit Murder of Beaufort Gardens, 1946

Thomas John Ley was born in Bath in 1880, the son of unremarkable working-class parents. In 1888, the Leys emigrated to Australia, where Thomas became clerk to a firm of solicitors. He did quite well, advancing to become partner in the firm. This enabled him to enter politics, and he became a member of the New South Wales parliament in 1917. In the early part of his career, he had been known as 'Lemonade Ley' for his alleged teetotalism, but later it became evident that he was taking bribes from the brewery industry. He served as Minister of Justice for New South Wales from 1922 until 1925, when he was elected to the federal House of Representatives. There was scandal when his opponent in this election alleged that Ley had offered him a £2,000 bribe to stand down! When this individual took Ley to court, the case collapsed from lack of evidence when he failed to turn up in court. In 1927, another of Ley's political opponents was found dead after apparently jumping from a precipice. Yet another Australian politician who had objected to some of Ley's dubious business dealings fell overboard and drowned when travelling on board ship.

After being defeated in the 1928 election, Thomas John Ley moved back to England. It may well be that once he was out of political office he was fearful that the full extent of his bribery and corruption would be exposed. Leaving his wife behind in Australia, he instead took with him his mistress Maggie Brook, whose husband had also died mysteriously, from being stung by a swarm of bees. In London, Ley tried to keep a low profile. A wealthy man after his successful Australian business deals, he invested his cash in property, and gambled on the stock market. In 1934, he won £5,000 damages against a man named Hamilton who had published some insulting letters relating to Ley's political exploits in Australia, but the year afterwards the verdict was reversed by the House of Lords.[22] In 1940, after falsely accusing another business man of bribery, Ley and his son Keith were convicted of libel and slander, with £12,000 damages.[23] During the Second World War, Ley's disastrous career plumbed novel lows when he was convicted of black-marketeering. A large, stout man of sinister aspect, he rather resembled Uncle Fester of the *Addams Family*.

In 1946, Ley lived in a large house at No. 5 Beaufort Gardens, Kensington, which he was converting into flats. Maggie Brooks had had enough of him by this stage, and she had moved into a flat at No. 3 Homefield Road, Wimbledon (it still stands). The jealous Ley was worried that she was having an affair with the barman Jack Mudie, who lived in a bed-sitting room at the same address. With time, this belief developed into an obsession, and the ruthless Australian decided that Mudie had to die.

Since Jack Mudie was an able-bodied man, the obese, unfit Ley decided to recruit some accomplices. The first of them was the joiner's foreman Lawrence John Smith, who was in charge of the building works at No. 5 Beaufort Gardens. Ley told him that Mudie had seduced Mrs Brooks, and that he was now blackmailing her. Smith willingly agreed to help teach the blackmailer a hard lesson. Next to be sworn into the plot were a chauffeur named John William Buckingham and his son with the same name. Buckingham's friend Bill Bruce, a Putney bus driver, also agreed to take part in what he perceived to be a vigilante action against a blackmailer.

The cunning Ley suggested that Mrs Bruce should contact Mudie at the pub where he was pulling pints, the Reigate Hill Hotel. She should pose as a society lady who needed an experienced barman to help at a cocktail party she was arranging at No. 5 Beaufort Gardens. Mudie, who was keen to get his hands on some extra cash, agreed to take part. When he turned up at No. 5 on 28 November 1946, the conspirators were waiting for him. Smith and the elder Buckingham seized hold of Mudie, frogmarched him down to the lower ground floor, and tied him to a chair. Buckingham was paid £200 in cash, which he was to share with his son and the Bruces. After he had left, either Ley or Smith murdered Mudie by slowly strangulating him.

On 30 November, Jack Mudie's body was found in a chalk pit near Woldingham in Surrey. A polisher's rug was wrapped round his neck, and a pickaxe was found nearby; both were later traced to the building works at No. 5 Beaufort Gardens. As soon as the story of the 'Chalk Pit Murder' was out in the newspapers, the two Buckinghams and Mrs Bruce called at Scotland Yard. They told all about the mysterious Mr Ley who had sworn them into a 'Bulldog Drummond'-style plot to punish a blackmailer. When Smith was arrested and questioned, he corroborated the story told by the Buckinghams and Mrs Bruce, but stated that when he had left Mudie alone with Ley the barman had still been alive. Unfortunately for him, two witnesses had seen his rented car at the chalk pit before the murder took place, indicating that he had been planning the crime beforehand and looking for a suitable place to dispose of the body. Ley himself denied everything, but the case against him looked very strong, particularly after the Buckinghams and Mrs Bruce had agreed to become principal witnesses for the Crown.

On trial for murder at the Old Bailey on 19 March 1947, Lawrence John Smith seemed like a rather stupid, ordinary workman. In contrast, Thomas John Ley, who had managed to lose much weight on the prison 'grub', was dapper and articulate. The evidence against them was formidable, however, and they were both found guilty and sentenced to death.[24] Later, Smith's sentence was commuted to life imprisonment, and Ley was declared insane and sent to Broadmoor. A gloomy, rotund figure, he was said to have been its richest inmate ever. He died there in July 1947.[25] The murder house at No. 5 Beaufort Gardens still stands; just like Ley had originally intended, it has been converted into flats.

Another Murder in Finsborough Road, 1948

The forty-one-year-old George Cyril Epton, an unemployed engineer's assistant, led an idle and immoral life, largely spent chasing various floozies, and drinking to excess when he could afford it. He lodged in the first-floor flat at No. 17 Finsborough Road, Kensington, and spent his day visiting the Labour Exchange, and picking up prostitutes for some 'fun' back home in his flat.

Early in the morning of 6 May 1948, a lifeless woman was found on the steps down to the basement flat at No. 17 Finsborough Road. She was declared dead at St Stephen's Hospital and the police were called in. Detective Inspector Albert Webb saw that the small balcony of the first-floor flat was directly overlooking the place where the woman's body had been found. When he called on Epton, this individual replied, 'I suppose you have come about the murder?' He denied all knowledge of the woman found on the basement steps, but Webb saw that there were bloodstains both in the bedroom and on the stone floor of the balcony. Epton said that his wife had died from tuberculosis, and that she used to spit blood, but the experienced detective was not falling for that one: he took Epton with him, and the luckless engineer was held in the cells overnight.

According to the *Daily Express*, all Finsborough Road was watching the detectives working outside No. 17 except the oldest resident, sixty-seven-year-old scientist William Leigh-Sharp, who had been living there since 1922, when Ronald True had murdered Olive Young at No. 13. Clearly no close student of the murder houses of London, this misanthropic scientist told the *Express* reporter, 'My housekeeper told me about the True murder at breakfast. I was having breakfast today when my housekeeper told be about the murder at No. 17. I did not go out to look then or now!'[26]

From material found in her handbag, the murdered woman was identified as the twenty-six-year-old Winifred Mulholland, who lived in a Brixton lodging house and worked as a part-time prostitute in central London. According to her landlady, she was in the habit of wearing a rather odd-looking fur coat made of dyed rabbit skins. Epton denied all knowledge of her. Instead, he had now suddenly remembered that on the morning of the murder, he had heard the doorbell ring, and the sound of a car racing off. Could this perhaps have been the murderers dumping the body? However, Winifred Mulholland had been wearing no shoes when found, and a pair of partly burned shoes had been found in Epton's flat. He said that they had belonged to his late wife, and that he had burned them because he had no use for them.

The autopsy on Winifred Mulholland showed that she had been beaten with repeated blows from two different blunt instruments. A bloodstained hammer and flat iron were found in Epton's flat. Dyed rabbit hairs from her fur coat were found on the bloodstained rug, on Epton's bloodstained trousers, and on the balcony. Since things were not looking good for Epton, he changed his story. He had picked Winifred

Mulholland up in Piccadilly the evening before the murder, and taken her back to No. 17 Finsborough Road. After they had had intercourse seated on a chair, he had retired to his bedroom. When he found that Winifred had stolen £9 from his hip pocket, he returned to the living room and demanded the money. When she refused to return it, he had struck her hard on the head. Although she was obviously dying, he made no attempt to go for help, but instead tipped the body out from his balcony early in the morning.

Found guilty of murder at the Old Bailey, George Cyril Epton was sentenced to death by Mr Justice Birkett. This was the first death sentence to be passed after the House of Commons had voted to abolish capital punishment, a vote that was later overturned by the House of Lords. Epton did not hang, however: in spite of the sordid callousness of his crime, his sentence was commuted to one of life imprisonment.[27] A Cyril Epton is recorded to have died in Wandsworth in 1973. The murder house at No. 17 Finsborough Road, just two doors from No. 13 where Ronald True had murdered Gertrude Yates back in 1922, still stands.

The Murder of Christine Granville, 1952
Krystyna Skarbek was born in 1908, the daughter of a Polish count. Although there was not much money in the family, she was able to lead a relatively carefree existence prior to the Second World War, becoming an expert skier and horsewoman. In 1938, she married the Polish author and diplomat Jerzy Giżycki, who took her with him to a diplomatic posting in Ethiopia.

On the outbreak of war, Krystyna Skarbek went to London with her husband, intent on fighting the German enemy that had invaded her country. She was accepted by the Secret Intelligence Service and went to Poland to organise a system of couriers to transmit intelligence out of the occupied country. In Hungary, she met a Polish officer named Andrzej Kowerski, who called himself Andrew Kennedy. She followed suit and changed her name to Christine Granville. When she and Kowerski were captured by the Gestapo, she saved them by pretending to suffer from tuberculosis, and biting her tongue to fake coughing up blood.

Christine Granville went on to distinguish herself as a Special Operations Executive intelligence agent in occupied France. Showing exceptional bravery, she once saved several agents captured by the Germans by pretending to be General Montgomery's niece and threatening fearsome reprisals unless the prisoners were released. This happened in August 1944, when the Germans were very much concerned with their safety after the occupation of France had ended, and through a bribe she managed to free all the prisoners. For this caper, she was awarded the George Medal, and later also an OBE.[28]

In spite of her gallant service, Christine Granville was ungenerously treated after the war; after refusing to accept a desk job, she was dismissed with one month's wages. To make ends meet, she became a stewardess on board an ocean-going liner, but she found this job far from congenial. On board ship, she met the forty-one-year-old bathroom steward Dennis Muldowney, a backward and slow-witted cove who fell deeply in love with her. In time, Christine Granville realised that Muldowney was far from sane; fed up with his obsessive stalking, she told him she did not want to see him again. On 15 June 1952, he was waiting for her at the foot of the narrow stairs of the Shellbourne Hotel, Lexham Gardens, where she used to stay when in London. He stabbed her hard in the chest with a long-bladed knife, and she was dead before medical help arrived.

Christine Granville was buried in St Mary's Roman Catholic Cemetery at Kensal Green in north-west London. Following his death in 1988, the ashes of her comrade-in-arms, Andrzej Kowerski, were interred at the foot of her grave. The creature Muldowney pleaded guilty to murder and was hanged at Pentonville Prison on 30 September 1952.[29] One of his few coherent utterances was, 'To kill is the final possession.' As for the Shellbourne Hotel at Nos 1–3 Lexham Gardens, it is today the Lexham Gardens Hotel.

Murder at the Aban Court Hotel, 1954

Kenneth Gilbert and Ian Arthur Grant were two young petty criminals, aged twenty-one and twenty-four respectively in 1954, and both living with their parents in Harwood Road, Fulham. Although habitually larcenous and dishonest, neither of them had ever committed any serious crime. They both worked as factory porters, but hard graft for low wages was not to their liking. Gilbert and Grant were disgruntled young men, envious of their betters and making plans to 'get rich quick'. One of these plans involved robbing a hotel by knocking down the night porter and ransacking the premises for money and valuables. Such a scheme would only work in a small- or medium-sized hotel, where the porter would be unable to summon reinforcements. The two ruffians

Aban Court Hotel, from an old postcard.

knew one that fitted the bill: the Aban Court Hotel at No. 25 Harrington Gardens, Kensington.

In the late evening of 8 March 1954, Gilbert and Grant took up their positions outside the Aban Court Hotel. At midnight, they burst into the hotel and seized hold of the night porter George Smart, known as 'Cockney George'. They made use of their coshes until Smart lay unconscious in a pool of blood. The two ruffians were dismayed to find that recent business had apparently been very low at the old hotel: less than £2 in cash was kept at the premises, and no valuables apart from a few packets of cigarettes. The following morning, George Smart was found in the hotel lobby, bound, gagged, and dead from severe head injuries.

The police detectives investigating the murder of George Smart soon closed in on Gilbert and Grant. These two were known thieves, and as such were included in the massive police trawl through the West London underworld. When their rooms were ransacked, a quantity of cigarettes was found. Although protesting their innocence, they were both arrested. Solid fingerprint and forensic evidence was soon compiled against the two young thugs, and their solicitor advised them to admit the robbery and plead guilty to manslaughter. They denied entering the hotel with the intention to murder Smart, but when he caught them thieving they had knocked him down. In an eloquent speech, their barrister Mr Crowder asked for his clients to be given the benefit of the doubt: there was a 'no man's land' between murder and manslaughter, and he urged the jury to find Gilbert and Grant not guilty of murder. Mr Justice Glyn-Jones's summing-up was very much against the accused, however. He reminded the jury that if they were satisfied that the two ruffians had entered the hotel premises with the intent to commit a felony, and that violence had been used resulting in Smart's death, it was their duty to find Gilbert and Grant guilty of murder.

Kenneth Gilbert and Ian Arthur Grant were duly found guilty of murder and sentenced to death. There was no appeal or respite, since their crime had been a dastardly one: to brutally murder a harmless hotel porter for the sake of a paltry sum of money. They were the last pair of murderers to be hung together, at Pentonville Prison on 17 June 1954, before the Homicide Act of 1958 outlawed the old tradition of multiple hangings.[30] The old Aban Court Hotel still stands, although it is today part of the larger Harrington Hall Hotel at Nos 7–25 Harrington Gardens.

Murder in Onslow Square, 1954

Michael Rennie, the celebrated film and television actor, was born in 1909. After working as a car salesman for a while, he became the manager of his uncle's rope factory. In 1935, he decided to try his luck as an actor, initially with moderate success only. In the Second World War, he served as a flying officer in the RAF. After the war, the career of the tall and handsome Michael Rennie took off big time. He starred in a number of Hollywood films, including the 1951 science fiction blockbuster *The Day the Earth Stood Still*.

In 1947, Michael Rennie married the actress Margaret McGrath as his second wife. She was a beautiful blonde who had enjoyed an adventurous career of her own as one of the vaudeville performers at the Windmill Theatre in Soho. This theatre boasted of never closing, in spite of the Blitz. More than once, the scantily clad performers at the Windmill had to take cover when some bombs exploded nearby. Another time, Margaret saved six horses from certain death, leading them out of their burning stables. She and the other 'Windmill Girls' later toured various military establishments to raise the morale of the troops. 'Never has so much been shown by so few to so many' was the way in which an officer in the Brigade of Guards memorably summarised their performance.[31]

Michael and Margaret Rennie led a happy family life, and soon had a son named David. In April 1954, Michael was acting in the Italian

Onslow Square, from an old postcard.

film *Mambo*, and Margaret wanted to take a holiday in France. Her mother, the sixty-four-year-old Mrs Violet McGrath, agreed to look after their flat at No. 59 Onslow Square, Kensington. Mrs McGrath's own flat needed redecorating, and while the work was being done she thought she would do very well living in her daughter and son-in-law's much more salubrious flat in one of London's historic garden squares.

Mrs McGrath lived at No. 59 Onslow Square for several weeks. She was fond of visiting various pubs nearby to have a drink or two, and the publicans noticed that she consorted with some very undesirable types, hinting that she was living in a flat at Onslow Square, and mentioning her son-in-law's acting success. On 10 May 1954, Margaret Rennie returned home to the flat. She found the door jammed by some object. Forcing it open, she found the dead body of her mother. Violet McGrath had been strangled to death with one of her own stockings. Nothing was missing from the flat, and it did not appear to have been searched for valuables.

Since Michael Rennie was quite a celebrity, the Onslow Square murder received its fair share of newspaper publicity. Violet McGrath's past life had been blameless, and it seemed unlikely that she had been targeted by some old enemy or avenger. A dark-haired, foreign-looking woman had been seen leaving the flat, but she was never identified by the police. Instead, the police concentrated on the shady clientele of some of the pubs nearby. They thought the naïve Mrs McGrath had confided in some impecunious, desperate criminal, who had murdered her and intended to ransack the flat, only to panic and kill her before escaping from the house.

An important clue came from Harold Frank Hammond, the painter and decorator who was renovating Mrs McGrath's own flat. He had seen her with a man named Walter Hensby at the Gloucester Arms public house, and Hensby had later asked him for her telephone number. Hammond had found it notable that, although Hensby was a drunken barfly, he had referred to Mrs McGrath as 'Vi'. He was an aircraft electrician by trade, but seems to have spent much of his time playing billiards in pubs and betting on the horses. Interestingly, he had some recent cuts on his arm, quite possibly resulting from scratches from a woman's fingernails. When questioned by the police, Hensby did not seem evasive, but freely admitted knowing Mrs McGrath. He had last visited her in the Onslow Square flat on 6 May, he said. He gave an account of his doings the following days, largely consisting of incessant drinking and gambling. The injuries to his hands had happened at work, he said. The police were interested to find that he had repaid various small debts after the murder, but Hensby said that, after winning £8 at the dog-track, he had settled a number of bar bills and gambling debts.

At the coroner's inquest on Violet McGrath, the forty-six-year-old Walter Hensby was questioned at length about his activities the day of the murder. The coroner then formally asked, 'Mr Walter Hensby, did you murder Mrs McGrath?' 'No, sir,' replied Hensby. The coroner then asked the jury whether they were satisfied with Hensby's account of his movements on the evening of the murder, and if they were satisfied with his account of the marks on his arm. The murderer, he reminded them, was likely to be a person who was known to Mrs McGrath, and whom she would admit to the flat. The jury retired for nearly an hour, and Hensby must have been seriously worried that they would name him as the suspected murderer, but a verdict of murder by a person or persons unknown was returned.[32] He spoke out in the *News of the World*, denying any knowledge of the murder or its motive.

The police investigation of the murder of Violet McGrath made no further headway, and Hensby remains the only credible suspect today. Still, it must be admitted that the evidence against him is far from strong; he did not have a criminal record, and probably would have been unable to keep such a cool head if he had really murdered her. Would such a desperately poor man, who was constantly borrowing money from pub landladies to finance his gambling, not have found the time to steal some money and valuables from the flat? The last we hear of Hensby is that, as a result of his brief newspaper notoriety, his estranged wife's solicitors caught up with him, and he was summoned to Marylebone Magistrates' Court to pay ten guineas in maintenance arrears.[33]

Murder in Thurloe Square, 1955

Alfred Brunton, a young London labouring man, found employment as a grocer's assistant and as a cellarman. Since his sister had died in an asylum, and he had received inpatient treatment for depression himself, he was not considered for war service in 1939. Instead, he became a nightwatchman, a line of work he would pursue throughout the remainder of his career. He married and had twin sons, before settling down in a Paddington slum tenement. The family were soon at loggerheads with the Nigerian landlord of the house, who behaved

Thurloe Square, from an old postcard. The murder house at No. 21 can be clearly seen in the terrace to the right.

obnoxiously and made noise to prevent poor Alfred from sleeping during the daytime hours.

After finally leaving the Paddington slum, the Bruntons landed on their feet: Mrs Nancy Brunton obtained a position as cook to a wealthy lady, Mrs Rosemary Inchbold, who lived at No. 21 Thurloe Square, Kensington. A large basement flat came with the job and, although it was rather dark and old-fashioned, it was vastly preferable to the slum dwelling the family had just vacated. Mrs Inchbold found the Bruntons very satisfactory live-in servants. Nancy Brunton was an excellent cook, and Alfred helped with the cleaning and other household chores, in spite of his work as a nightwatchman.

But in early 1955, Alfred Brunton's mind was becoming increasingly clouded and confused. Although he and the family were doing much better at Thurloe Square, he blamed himself for not standing up to his obnoxious former landlord in Paddington. On 3 March 1955, there was a commotion at No. 21 Thurloe Square, with the eleven-year-old Peter Brunton running from the house shouting for help, and the emergency services were called. The police arrested Alfred Brunton, and an ambulance removed the corpse of his son John, who had been strangled to death with a tie. The dazed Alfred Brunton admitted to the police that he had tried to kill his son. A psychiatrist found clear signs of melancholia, and it turned out that he had previously received electroconvulsive treatment for this condition. His mother had committed suicide, and his sister had spent much of her life in an asylum. The following month, at the Central Criminal Court, Alfred Brunton was found guilty of murder, but insane, and Mr Justice Byrne ordered him to be detained until His Majesty's pleasure be known.[34]

Murder in Earl's Court Square, 1956

Eric Samuel Dique was born in India in 1931, the youngest of a family of nine. After his parents had both died, he was brought up by an older sister. At school, he was clever and industrious. In 1951, he came to London, and decided to stay there although he could only get an unqualified job as a laundry hand. He lived in a shabby lodging house at No. 49 Earl's Court Square, and tried his best to save money from his paltry salary.

In early 1954, Eric Dique met the fourteen-year-old Annabel Wheatley, who was working as a cinema usherette although she was supposed to be at school. Having a confirmed liking for swarthy 'gentleman friends', she needed little persuasion to move in with him at No. 49 Earl's Court Square. Eric was very fond of his young 'wife', who might well have lied to him about her true age. Still, he disapproved of her consorting with 'loose girls' and going out partying in the evening without him. He also disapproved of the low moral standards of the other lodgers at No. 49 Earl's Court Square, and removed Annabel to more salubrious lodgings at No. 74 Comeragh Road, where they lived happily for a while. Eric did his best to save money so that they could get married, but the thoughtless young Annabel preferred to spend it on her various amusements. In February 1955, she gave birth to a son.

Becoming a mother at the age of fifteen did not curb Annabel's flighty tendencies, however. She became very friendly with Sheikh Hassan, a native of British Guyana who had come to London in 1954 and described himself as a medical student. He lodged at No. 49 Earl's Court Square, and she might well have met him there. In June 1956, she eloped to Edinburgh with her new swain, and they got married at the register office. Annabel was of course seriously worried about what Eric might do when he found out what she had been up to, particularly since the young Indian was a tough character who did not take nonsense from anyone. When Annabel and Sheikh Hassan confronted Eric Dique face to face, however, Eric was completely flabbergasted by her devious behaviour. Far from showing any inclination to beat up Sheikh Hassan, he pleaded with her to return to him. Annabel screamed back that he should care for her happiness, and offered him the little boy to take care of. Still, the gloomy Indian returned to his lodgings without resorting to violence against the guilty pair.

A few days later, the volatile Annabel invited Eric to come visit her at the room she shared with Sheikh Hassan at No. 49 Earl's Court Square. Exactly what this young floozie had planned to discuss with her erstwhile 'husband' is not known, but their brief reunion did not end well. Eric attacked her in a furious rage and strangled her to death with his tie. He then returned to his own lodgings, where he made a full confession to his landlord and willingly went along to the police station. In court charged with murder, Dique pleaded guilty, and his trial took less than a minute and a half. Later, he was reprieved by the Home Secretary on account of his youth, and sentenced to imprisonment for life.[35]

The name of Eric Dique again hit the newspaper headlines in December 1959, when he and two other villains broke out of Wormwood Scrubs Prison. Together with armed robber Ronald Pearson and rapist Brian Harry Davidson, Dique made haste through the London streets, aiming to put as much distance as possible between himself and Wormwood Scrubs. Unfortunately for him, an off-duty prison officer saw that the three men wore prison-issue trousers underneath their raincoats, and recaptured Dique and Davidson with the help of an off-duty police constable. Pearson was also taken into custody after a few days. The newspapers criticised the security at Wormwood Scrubs, where some of the most hardened villains of the land were incarcerated. There was no barbed wire on top of its walls, and for two years there had been building works and scaffolding on the premises, something that had greatly helped Dique and his two cohorts when they escaped from prison.[36] There is reason to believe that Eric Dique was released from prison in the 1960s, and that he died in Brighton in 2001. The murder house at No. 49 Earl's Court Square is today the Olympia Hotel.

Another Murder in Onslow Square, 1959

Günther Fritz Podola was a young German ruffian, who became a keen member of the *Hitlerjugend* in the 1940s. Having survived the war, he emigrated to Canada in 1952, to make a living as a thief and burglar. In 1957, the law caught up with him, and he was sentenced to two years in prison, although he was deported back to Germany the year after. Podola had an ambition to visit London, and the slack immigration officials could not prevent him from fulfilling it. He soon established himself as a professional burglar. In July 1959, he robbed some flats at Roland House, Roland Gardens. One of them belonged to Mrs Verne Schiffman, an American model. Podola helped himself to £2,000 worth of furs and jewellery. Then this German crook had what he believed was an excellent idea: he would contact Mrs Schiffman, tell her that he had found various discreditable letters in her flat, and offer to return these, for a fee.

Many American models in London in the late 1950s may have kept material of an immoral nature in their flats, but virtuous Mrs Schiffman was not one of them. She agreed to receive another phone call from the burglar, and promptly contacted the police. Thus her telephone was monitored on 12 July 1959, when Podola called her from a public box in the South Kensington underground station. Although this German crook was far from a criminal genius, he was not a total blockhead. He felt that something was wrong, and saw the detectives trying to surround him. He ran out into Onslow Square, and raced up the steps of No. 105, a large town house that had been converted into flats. Taking cover behind a pillar in the entrance, he pulled a small revolver that he had purchased for £5 for use as protection against angry householders who objected to him burgling their houses. When Detective Sergeant Raymond Purdy came searching for Podola at No. 105, the cowardly German shot him through the heart.

Günther Podola took refuge in a hotel at No. 95 Queen's Gate nearby (it still stands). However, the police were after him, and they soon tracked him down. A task force of armed officers broke the door of his hotel room down and bravely charged the armed murderer. Podola received a well-deserved black eye and some bruising, possibly from taking a hit in the face when the door was burst open. As a result of this ill-treatment, he claimed to have completely lost his memory. The start of his trial for murder was delayed for nine days while a jury heard evidence of whether Podola was medically fit to stand trial. After three and a half hours of deliberation, they decided he was. A fresh jury was called to hear the trial itself. When asked for his plea, Podola replied, 'I do not remember the crime for which I stand accused … I am unable to answer the charges.' There was no question that Podola was guilty of wilfully murdering an unarmed policeman, but a surprising number of foolish busybodies made it their business to save him from the gallows, some of them out of murky political motives of their own. Podola's alleged amnesia was a problem for the medical witnesses. Neurologist Dr Michael Ashby gave evidence as an expert medical witness at his trial, as did psychiatrist Dr Archibald Leigh, who claimed Podola was feigning his illness.

In the end, the jury took thirty-eight minutes to find Podola guilty of murder, and Mr Justice Davies sentenced him to death. The Home Secretary referred the Podola case to the Court of Criminal Appeal, which upheld the conviction, and the Attorney-General's refusal of leave to appeal to the House of Lords brought the case to a close in a fresh outburst of public controversy. This cowardly German murderer, a worthy member of the *Hitlerjugend* if there ever was one, was hanged at Wandsworth Prison on 5 November 1959.[37]

Murder in Redcliffe Square, 1962

Marilyn Anne Bain was born in Scotland in 1937. She became an army nurse, serving in the Far East, but was discharged in 1959. A bisexual, she lived with her lesbian partner Jean McVitie in various small London apartments, ending up in a tiny ground-floor flat at No. 60 Redcliffe Square. Here, they led what can only be called quite immoral lives. They 'cruised' various gay clubs, Marilyn had short-lived affairs with various dodgy blokes, and Jean prostituted herself to gain money, although she was not attracted to men. They were both hard drinkers, and their quarrels sometimes ended in blows.

On 13 September 1962, Jean had earned some money by entertaining a 'customer', and she suggested that Marilyn should go out and buy booze for a grand drinking party. For £4, she purchased a bottle of Scotch whisky, a quarter bottle of brandy, three quarts of ale, and various 'mixers'; surely generous provisions for two young females; the two got very drunk indeed. After a game of poker had been aborted, the cards were flung on the floor, and the two angry young women quarrelled over who should pick them up. Their downstairs neighbour could hear them screaming at each other at around three in the morning, just like they had done the previous day.

This time, however, the quarrel ended in blows. Making use of the unarmed combat training from her army days, Marilyn knocked Jean down with a well-aimed punch, or so she thought. After she had visited the toilet to be sick, she saw that Jean was lying lifeless on the floor, in a pool of blood. In a panic, she phoned for an ambulance, and Jean was taken to the Princess Beatrice Hospital. On the way there, Jean regained consciousness and said, 'She knifed me ... She does not know anything about it.' Jean's recovery proved short-lived: she died on 17 September from a wound infection. Since the autopsy showed that a stab wound in the chest was the direct cause of death, Marilyn Anne Bain was charged with murder.

The police got a good impression of Marilyn Anne Bain, however. Once she had sobered up, she did what she could to help the police with their inquiries, and appeared to regret her foolish actions. She made no attempt to hide her guilt, and she gave the detectives the murder weapon, a bloodstained knife she had retrieved when tidying up the flat. In spite of their frequent drunken brawls, Marilyn and Jean had been good friends when sober, and Marilyn had nothing to gain from murdering her flatmate. It might well be that after being knocked down, Jean had fallen onto the knife. A psychiatrist found her 'a well built rather plain Scots girl of average intelligence', adding that, since her EEG was normal and since she did not have a history of epilepsy or mental disease, she was fit to stand trial.

On trial for murder, Marilyn Anne Bain was ably defended by Mr Sebag Shaw, who argued that this was not a case of murder, rather a tragic accident, bitterly regretted by the prisoner. Marilyn pleaded guilty to manslaughter, and this plea was accepted and the murder charge not proceeded with. She was sentenced to just three years' imprisonment, and disappeared into obscurity.[38]

3

Chelsea and Fulham

*There are mysteries in splendid mansions and in squalid garrets which
contain all the elements of criminal romance, and yet pass with the police
and the press as matter-of-fact incidents of London's daily life.*

George R. Sims, *Mysteries of Modern London*

The quiet garden squares of Chelsea have seen a fair amount of murder
and mayhem over the years, including a horrific double murder in
Paulton's Square and Wellington Square in 1870. There is a contrast
between the elegant Chelsea murder houses, home to the misdeeds
of the rich and famous, and the rather mean-looking terraced murder
houses of Fulham, where various domestic disputes ended badly and
gangsters shot their enemies dead. Chelsea and Westminster have their
own serial killer: the psychopath Patrick Mackay, who decimated the
wealthy old ladies of these parts with impunity, during a short but ultra-
violent reign of terror in the early 1970s. Still, Fulham contains one of
the most famous murder houses of London, No. 29 Gowan Avenue,
where TV presenter Jill Dando was shot dead by an unknown gunman.
Local weirdo Barry George was convicted for the murder on some fairly
flimsy evidence, but later freed after an appeal. Visit the murder house
and ponder one of the greatest unsolved mysteries of modern London.

An excursion to the murder houses of Chelsea should end at the
Cross Keys public house near the Thames, a pleasant historic pub in
Lawrence Street, where the landlady Mrs Buxton was murdered by a
mystery assailant in 1920. When work on this book was well advanced, I
received the unwelcome news that the Cross Keys was in danger of being
'developed' into flats. A very persistent company of developers have
proposed to turn the pub into what the disgusted locals have called a

'McMansion', complete with its own underground swimming pool. After being turned down, they have launched an appeal. Understandably, the local inhabitants are opposing this project, pointing out that Dylan Thomas, Bob Marley and various members of the Rolling Stones had been regulars at the Cross Keys. If you find the Cross Keys still open, enjoy a small ginger ale – ahem! – and sign the petition to Save our Murder Pub.[1]

The Chelsea Double Murder, 1870

The Revd Elias Huelin was a French Protestant clergyman. A native of Jersey, he became minister of the French Conformist church in Soho, and assistant chaplain at Brompton Cemetery. Retiring early, he built up an impressive portfolio of fashionable Chelsea houses. In 1870, when the eighty-four-year-old clergyman was living at No. 15 Paulton's Square, he also owned Nos 24 and 32 in the same square, as well as No. 24 Wellington Square and various other houses. Letting out all these valuable houses gave him a very considerable income. This capitalist clergyman, who was clearly no close student of the respective sizes of a camel and the eye of a needle, collected his rents in person, walking his little dog through the elegant Chelsea squares and streets to call on his many tenants, the golden guineas jingling in his pockets as he went along.

In May 1870, Mr Huelin wanted to renovate his unlet property at No. 24 Wellington Square. Some workmen were recruited to do the plastering and papering, one of them the thirty-one-year-old Scot Walter Miller. When Mr Huelin paid his workers, their eyes were attracted to the many golden guineas in his well-filled purse. The old clergyman seemed to like to show off his wealth. After work on the house was well under way, Mr Huelin told the workmen that he wanted to go to Lincolnshire for a while, to spend some time at a farm property owned by a friend.

When nothing more was seen of Mr Huelin for several days, it was presumed that he had left for the countryside. Instead, his French nephew appeared in London. A foppish, foreign-looking individual with a pince-nez and waxed moustaches, and an exaggerated accent, he took up residence at No. 15 Paulton's Square. He told people that Mr Huelin's housekeeper Ann Boss had accompanied her master to Lincolnshire, and hired a sluttish-looking woman as her replacement. The young Frenchman took charge of his uncle's affairs, collected his rent, ate his food and drank his wine, making merry with his female companion for several days.

One evening, young Mr Huelin sent for a removal man named Henry Piper and ordered him to take a large trunk from the back kitchen of No. 15 Paulton's Square to a small house in Fulham. When Piper lifted the heavy trunk, he could see blood seeping from it. 'What does blood do here?' he asked confusedly, retreating into the kitchen. 'Go back, you *carman*, cord the box, and do your work!' the Frenchman commanded, but Piper steadfastly refused. 'Go back and cord that box!' the 'nephew' insisted, but this time in a broad Scottish accent rather than a French one. Sensing that something was very wrong, Piper sent his assistant for the police. Suddenly, the mystery 'Frenchman' bolted out of the house, with Piper in hot pursuit.

In a long and furious chase through the quiet Chelsea squares and streets, the agile Piper pursued the 'nephew' for half a mile, with a sturdy, panting police sergeant bringing up the rear. Finally, after the exhausted 'Frenchman' slipped and fell, he was collared by Piper and secured by some police constables. With the aptly named Sergeant Large, Piper returned to No. 15 Paulton's Square. When the box was prised open, it was found to contain the doubled-up body of Ann Boss. The harmless old domestic had been strangled with a rope that still dangled from her neck. There was consternation when the mysterious 'Frenchman' turned out to be identical to the Scottish workman Walter Miller, who had donned an elaborate disguise and faked a French accent. It was remembered that, when working at No. 24 Wellington Square, Miller had ordered a large hole to be dug in the garden, and sure enough it was found to contain the body of Elias Huelin. The old clergyman had been knocked down from behind with a shovel, and then strangled to death. An empty brandy bottle was also found in the pit, indicating that the Scotsman had required some Dutch courage before embarking on his murderous career.

The Chelsea Double Murder of 1870 caused widespread revulsion and alarm among the Londoners. That some conniving menial could deliberately plan the destruction of two blameless, respectable people, and come quite close to getting away with it, was an alarming thought for many a well-to-do London resident. Miller had always been a mean-spirited, jealous man, and very envious of his betters. Although often thinking up various schemes to get rich quick, the Scot had never before set any of them in motion with such lethal effect; in fact, he did not even have a criminal record. His plan appears to have been to murder Mr Huelin and Ann Boss, steal their money and valuables in the guise of the French nephew, and then escape to America. The Scotsman's greed was his undoing: he sold the contents of No. 15 Paulton's Square, and dallied too long to collect the rental money. When the remains of Ann Boss became too 'high' to be kept indoors, he rented a little house in Fulham and planned to send the box there, but the seepage of blood and body fluids from it sealed his fate.

Sentenced to death at the Old Bailey on 14 July 1870, Walter Miller was executed at Newgate on 1 August. He died impenitent, in a manner corresponding to the brutality of his crimes. Tearing free from the keepers when he was to be pinioned, he ran head first into the unyielding stone wall of his cell, perhaps hoping to commit suicide by 'dashing his brains out'. However, that kind of thing only works in French novels – the human skull is thicker and more solid than people think – and, still conscious, the groaning, dazed Miller was pinioned and put on a chair on the scaffold. When the bolt was drawn, both convict and chair fell, but the hangman had got his calculations wrong; the drop was too short and Miller was strangulated rather than executed cleanly. For his heroism in tackling Miller, the removal man Piper was voted a reward of £50. He politely asked if he could also be allowed to see the execution, a privilege that was granted him.[2]

Elias Huelin's property, including the two murder houses, was inherited by his real nephew Edward. Ann Boss had been left a legacy in Mr Huelin's will, but the greedy nephew argued that, since she had been killed before him, her descendants were not in a position to claim a penny. It took a year of legal wrangling to work out a compromise, largely in favour of the relatives of Ann Boss.[3] Walter Miller's young son Stocks Miller was sent to America, where he became postmaster in Moorcroft, Wyoming, before dying of pneumonia after working in an irrigation ditch. The two murder houses turned out to be hard to let: people did not like to live in houses where two respectable Chelsea citizens had recently been done to death in a horrible manner. It took decades for their reputation to be forgotten. When murder house devotee George R. Sims visited them in 1907, however, he found that they were both inhabited by people who knew nothing about their sinister past: 'In the room the murder was committed, the children romp and play.'[4] The celebrated occultist Aleister Crowley, who lived at No. 31 Wellington Square in the 1920s, is said to have taken an interest in the neighbouring property at No. 24, expressing disappointment that it was not haunted.

Above left: The body of Mr Huelin is found, from the *Illustrated Police News*, 21 May 1870.

Above right: The finding of the body of Ann Boss, from the *Illustrated Police News*, 21 May 1870.

Below left: Miller is taken into custody, from the *Illustrated Police News*, 21 May 1870.

Below right: People stand gawping outside the Wellington Square murder house, from the *Illustrated Police News*, 21 May 1870.

Double murder at Chelsea: portraits of the major players in the drama, from the *Illustrated Police News*, 28 May 1870.

Murder at Langton Street, 1872

Paul Julius May and Hermann Nagel, two jolly young German hooligans, came to London in the summer of 1872. They were well supplied with money, and spent it lavishly. They were on their way to America, they said, but showed no urgency in getting there. For a while, the two Germans stayed at a hotel in Finsbury, before settling down in a brothel at No. 21 Langton Street with their two favourite floozies, Ellen Gordon and Augusta Burgess. They attended the Cremorne and other places of amusement until they had spent all their money.

On 21 August 1872, May and Nagel sat at No. 21 Langton Street pondering their misfortunes. They did not even have the money to pay the rent, let alone travel to America. They pawned some of their clothes to purchase a pistol and ammunition. Not long after the Germans had returned home with the pistol, the two girls were alarmed to hear shots fired from the second-floor bedroom. When the door was broken open, May was lying on the floor, bleeding from a wound in the side. Nagel lay on a couch on the other side of the room, quite dead.

Above: The Shocking Tragedy at Chelsea, from the *Illustrated Police News*, 31 August 1872.

Below: More images about the Paul May case, from the *Illustrated Police News*, 7 September 1872.

The wounded Paul May was removed to St George's Hospital, where the police made sure that he was constantly watched, since they suspected that he was only slightly injured and feared that he would abscond. Inquiries with the Berlin police showed that the two young Germans were in fact wanted men. Paul May, a clerk apprenticed to a brewery firm, had stolen 1,000 Thalers, aided and abetted by his friend Hermann Nagel. Even before the Langton Street murder, the Berlin police had found out that the two miscreants were in London, and steps had already been taken to have them extradited.

Paul May was fit to attend the coroner's inquest on Hermann Nagel, held at the Victoria Tavern on 26 August. He said that he and Nagel had decided to commit suicide together, rather than to disgrace their friends with the knowledge of their extravagance and dissipation. Nagel first shot May in the belly, before putting the pistol to his own heart and firing off the second barrel. The police thought this story sounded very fishy indeed, particularly since the pistol had been lying on the floor not far from May. Had May in fact been the person holding the pistol, shooting Nagel with a well-aimed bullet to the heart but 'chickening out' and only wounding himself slightly? Or had he deliberately murdered Nagel, and then wounded himself and made up the story of a 'suicide pact'. The German girl Augusta Burgess testified that, on the day of the murder, May and Nagel had been quarrelling angrily about money. When he was committed for trial at the Old Bailey for the wilful murder of Hermann Nagel, Paul May wept bitterly, saying that he did not have a friend in the world, and that even his father had refused to come and see him.

There was an old legal tradition, dating back to the times of James I, that if two people made a 'suicide pact' and one survived the survivor should be charged with murder. There was a precedent of this as recently as 1838. On trial at the Old Bailey, Paul May was evasive when questioned about what he was doing in London, and how he and his deceased friend had got hold of such an amount of money. Otherwise, he stuck to his story, adding that he believed that his own wound had in fact been very serious, and that he still 'might be lying upon his death-bed'. In his summing-up, Mr Justice Grove was very favourable to the prisoner, accepting that Nagel had met his death by his own independent act, and that a 'suicide pact' was not proven. Accordingly, the jury found Paul May not guilty.[5]

A newspaper reported that Paul May smiled and seemed agreeably surprised by the lenience of British justice. Still, he was promptly extradited back to his native land, where he was charged with embezzling 1,000 Thaler from his employer, and rewarded with an eighteen-month prison term. The newspapers commented that the mystery of how May and Nagel had got their money, and why they had left Germany in such a hurry, had belatedly been solved.[6] It is a pity that this information had not been available to the Old Bailey jury, and an even greater pity that the exact positioning of the two men and the pistol had not been satisfactorily documented. It is quite possible that, although he ended up in a German prison for his original crime, Paul May was a very lucky man.

The Rylston Terrace Murder, 1885

In 1885, the forty-five-year-old Henry Norman, a painter and decorator, was working for a company in Fulham and lodging at No. 10 Rylston

Terrace, Rylston Road. Six days a week, he rose at 5 a.m. to go to work, returning home at 9 p.m. very tired and bedraggled. His wife Ellen worked part time as a washerwoman, as well as looking after the children Henry Jr and Annie, the sole survivors of a brood of seven. During the ten years they had been married, Henry and Ellen had generally been on good terms, although the death of their children at regular intervals had been a great disappointment. Henry's fondness for drink, and inability to save money, also put a strain on the marriage.

In 1885, the dutiful husband Henry Norman became a changed man. He got the fixed idea that Ellen was cheating on him with various men, including the landlord at No. 10 Rylston Terrace, the shopkeeper John Batten. The parsimonious Mr Batten lived, with his entire family, in the first-floor front room over the shop, renting the other three rooms out to lodgers. Henry Norman lived with his wife and children in the second-floor front room. On 15 July 1885, Henry Norman came into his mother's laundry, where Ellen worked, saying, 'Mother, my wife has been unfaithful to me, what am I to do?' 'Forgive her!' the generous Mrs Norman replied. Henry threw his hat down and exclaimed, 'No I cannot! I love my wife, but I will kill that man!' He then made his way into the laundry room to beat up his wife, but fortunately his sister-in-law interceded.

On the evening of 16 July, a very drunk Henry Norman came knocking at John Batten's door, challenging him to come out and have a fight. Batten told him to return when he was sober, but the truculent Henry kept accusing him of adultery with his wife. Batten told his son to go and fetch Ellen Norman. When he told her about her husband's accusations, she vehemently protested her innocence. The two men parted on acrimonious terms, with Mr Batten calling his lodger a damned liar and threatening to take out a summons against him.

Later the same evening, Henry and Ellen Norman visited the Lord Clyde public house. They again began quarrelling, and Ellen wept bitterly, saying that she was fearful of returning home with her husband, since he had a dagger. Nevertheless, the Normans went back to Rylston Terrace. At about five o'clock the following morning, John Batten heard Henry run out of the house. Soon after, Henry Jr screamed, 'Murder!' Batten ran upstairs, opened the door, and saw the dying Ellen Norman lying on the bed. She had been stabbed hard in the chest while asleep. The two children 'were continuing to scream in the most dreadful manner'.

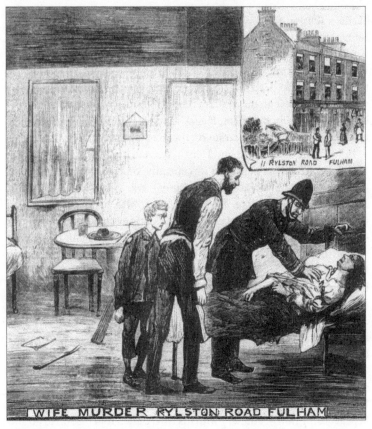

Wife murder in Fulham, from the *Illustrated Police News*, 1 August 1885.

Batten sent for the police, but the culprit was already in custody. Henry Norman had run straight to the Fulham Road police station, doffed his cap to the inspector on duty, and said, 'I have killed my wife!'

The coroner's inquest on Ellen Norman revealed Henry's insane jealousy of his wife, and his unfounded accusations against Mr Batten the landlord. In fact, Ellen Norman had lived an exemplary life, without any extramarital affairs. On trial at the Old Bailey, Henry Norman was convicted of murdering his wife, and sentenced to death by Mr Justice Hawkins. He was executed at Newgate on 5 October. A short, stout man, he was given a drop of 7 feet and died instantaneously.[7]

The situation of the Rylston Terrace murder house was not immediately easy to figure out. In Victorian times, such a 'Terrace' was a row of terraced houses in a certain road, similar in build and structure. Sometimes, the terrace was named after the builder who had financed and constructed it, sometimes after the road itself, and at other times from patriotic motives. The profusion of 'George Terraces', 'Queen's Terraces' and 'King's Terraces' confounded the Victorian postmen, since provincial letter-writers often did not include the name of the road on which the terrace stood. In the 1880s and 1890s, when the London street nomenclature and house numbering had become insufferably confused, there was a determined move to abolish all these 'Terraces', 'Places' and 'Rows', to rename the streets in a more imaginative manner, and to renumber the houses going from the centre to the periphery.

The present-day No. 10 Rylston Road is a two-storey end-of-terrace house, the ground floor of which is home to the 'Poochie Galore' dog-grooming salon. Since we know that the murder house had two storeys above a shop, 'Poochie Galore' is definitely innocent. Instead, it turns out that 'Rylston Terrace' was the name for part of Rylston Road, consisting of ten terraced three-storey houses divided by Mendora Road. No. 10 Rylston Terrace, today known as No. 44 Rylston Road, is still standing. It remains more or less unchanged in structure since the 1885 *Illustrated Police News* drawing of the murder house, although the terrace has been extended to the south, with houses of a different style.

The Waterford Road Murder, 1902

Henry Williams, a thirty-one-year-old Fulham bootmaker, was also a reservist in the 14th Surrey Militia. He was recalled to arms in April 1900, and served in the militia for the duration of the Second Boer War, finally returning home in July 1902. There was some worrying news for the returning soldier, however. His common-law wife Ellen Andrews had been more than friendly with a sailor named Baker while he had been away, and their five-year-old daughter Margaret was in a sadly neglected state, wearing stockings with large holes in them, and lacking many buttons. Nevertheless, Henry moved in with Ellen and Margaret in two rooms on the upper floor of No. 40 Waterford Road, Fulham, and got work at Mr Cohen's boot shop nearby.

However, Henry Williams, who had been a jolly young labourer before he went off to South Africa, had become a changed man. He constantly ruminated about Ellen's unfaithfulness, drank too much, and threatened violence against the sailor Baker. He used to carry a large black razor in his pocket at all times, occasionally threatening to cut Ellen's throat with it. Mrs Elizabeth Annie Helms, landlady of the house at No. 40 Waterford Road, found him a very disturbing presence. So did his employer, the bootmaker George Cohen. Henry confided in him that his faithless Ellen had not just been 'carrying on' with the obnoxious seafaring man Baker while he had been serving his country; she was still seeing him, and other men as well, at regular intervals. Moreover, he suspected that Baker was a 'fancy man' who acted as Ellen's pimp, and that this disreputable pair were also 'grooming' the little girl Margaret to become a prostitute. Surely, such dreadful things could not be happening, the old bootmaker replied. Before leaving the boot shop, for the final time, Henry gave Cohen a piece of paper with the words, 'Take care of my tools. Henry Williams.'

On the afternoon of 10 September 1902, Henry Williams went to visit the wife of a neighbour in Waterford Road. He was weeping and seemed quite distraught. With difficulty, he explained that he had just cut his little daughter's throat to prevent her from becoming a prostitute like her mother. Raising his hands to the sky, he exclaimed, 'Thank God, I shall soon be in my grave with my child! I long for the time to come to go to my grave, she shall be in heaven and I long to go with her!' The neighbour fetched the bootmaker Cohen, and sent for a policeman. Cohen thought Henry needed a glass of brandy to steady his nerve, and bought him one at the Lord Palmerston pub (today Morrisons) in nearby King's Road. In the meantime, Police Constable Lewis Harrison had been let into No. 40 Waterford Road, where he found the little girl's corpse on the blood-soaked bed. He proceeded to the Lord Palmerston, where he took Henry Williams into custody. Just at that moment, Ellen Andrews came into the pub, throwing up her arms and screaming, 'Is Maggie dead?' 'Yes, Maggie is dead; now go to your bloody fancy man!' Henry gruffly retorted.

When questioned by Detective Inspector Walter Dew, later to be famous as the man who caught Crippen, at the Fulham police station, Henry Williams made a full confession. Feeling the effects of the stiff brandy he had taken on board, he exclaimed,

> I did kill my lovely daughter to save her from becoming a prostitute! It is not many men who would have had the heart to do it, but I bleeding

well did it, and now I shall hang for it. I did it to save my old woman from putting her into bed with other men. God blind me, she was my child, and I loved her, and I will walk like a man to the scaffold!

At the inquest on little Margaret Andrews, her mother needed police protection from the hostile crowd. She denied ever having been unfaithful to her common-law husband. When Henry accused her of once having made 'a repulsive admission' to him, she denied it vehemently. Henry did not believe her, nor did the crowd of spectators. A neighbour in Waterford Road testified that, before the murder, Henry had spoken of Ellen to her, saying 'I will not hurt a hair on her head, but break her heart another way!' To another person, he had said that it would make him stark raving mad if his little girl would ever call another man 'daddy'. When committed for trial at the Old Bailey, Henry exclaimed, 'I only want a fair trial so that people can see what a miserable time I have had!'

Giving evidence at the Old Bailey, Ellen Andrews said that Henry's demeanour had changed very much after he had returned from the war. He was unreasonably jealous and once said, 'I cannot trust you again! I have found another way of breaking your heart and brand you so that you will never hold up your head in the world again.' The jury found Henry guilty, but added a recommendation to mercy, because of the 'somewhat honourable motives he had of saving the little girl from a life of prostitution'. However, Mr Justice Jelp calmly sentenced the prisoner to death.[8] Awaiting execution at Pentonville Prison, Henry Williams impressed the warders with his calm and courageous behaviour. The hangman Henry Pierrepoint, who executed him on 11 November 1902, thought him the bravest person he had ever hanged.

Despite this, this strange Henry Williams, who met death with such impressive courage, had been something of a coward in life. If the sailor Baker really was a 'fancy man' living off his wife, and having designs on his little daughter, then why not seek him out and beat him up? If his common-law wife was notoriously unfaithful to him, then why not kick her out, keep the little daughter he was so very fond of, and find another wife? Either of these stratagems would have appealed to the moral code of the time. To kill a child to get revenge on a faithless wife was not unheard of in Victorian and Edwardian times, but it was the crime of a worthless scoundrel. The murder of little Maggie Andrews is today quite forgotten, the murder house at No. 40 Waterford Road its only memorial.

The Tragic Tale of John Currie, 1915

John S. Currie was born in Staffordshire in 1884, the illegitimate son of an Ulster-Scottish navvy working on the railways. In spite of this unpromising start to his life, he became quite an aesthete. His talent for painting soon became obvious, and after school he was employed in painting ceramics in the Staffordshire Potteries. He studied at the Newcastle and Hanley schools of art, where he won a British Institution Scholarship, and went on to become an art teacher in Bristol.

Currie married in 1907 and moved to London, where he tried to establish himself as a full-time artist. He studied at the Slade School of Art and made friends with some other talented young artists, including Mark Gertler, Edward Wadsworth and Rudolph Ihlee. The young aesthetes called themselves the Later Primitives and liked to dress up in black jerseys, scarlet mufflers and black hats like the costermongers. When they had enjoyed a few pints, the gang of aesthetes became extremely combative and liked nothing better than a good fight with some medical students or other street roughs.

John Currie was somewhat overshadowed by his friend Mark Gertler, but his characteristic neoclassical portraits won many admirers, among them the aesthetes Michael Sadleir and Edward Marsh. In 1910, however, the jolly young artist met his nemesis: the beautiful seventeen-year-old model Dorothy 'Dolly' Henry. He became infatuated with her and deserted his wife and child to move in with his beloved Dolly at Primrose Hill. In spite of her undoubted physical attraction, Dolly was a stupid, tactless young woman, who knew nothing of art, and who freely flirted with other men to make John jealous. In this respect, the fiery Irishman seldom disappointed her: they had many fierce quarrels, which sometimes ended in blows. John more than once threatened to murder her when he suspected she had cheated on him, and, as we will find out, these were not empty threats.

Although John Currie feared that his period of genius as a painter had passed, Mark Gertler encouraged him to carry on, and Edward Marsh purchased a collection of his paintings in 1913. The year after, the volatile Dolly moved out on him, but she returned just a few weeks later and they moved to Brittany together. Unfortunately Dolly was not cut out for rural life, and she went back to Chelsea, where she took a flat at No. 50 Paultons Square, not far from No. 15 where Miller had murdered Mr Huelin back in 1870. Hoping for yet another reconciliation, John followed Dolly back to London in 1915, but he became furious when he heard rumours that she had been modelling for pornographic photographs, and that she was spreading untruths about him to wreck his artistic career. In a furious rage, John Currie purchased a handgun and went to see Dolly at No. 50 Paultons Square. He shot her several times at close range, and she died at Chelsea infirmary before she had been seen by a doctor. The demented artist, who had turned his gun on himself, also died a few days later. His final words were, 'It was all so ugly!'[9]

Due to the ongoing First World War, there was comparatively little newspaper publicity about the tragic murder and suicide at No. 50 Paultons Square. Several of Currie's unsold paintings were auctioned off for a few shillings after his death. However, the shrewd Michael Sadleir and Edward Marsh, who had recognised Currie's talent and supported his work, would have the last laugh: his art has appreciated steadily, and is represented in several major collections, including the Tate Gallery. The Potteries Museum and Art Gallery has his famous painting of Dolly Henry, entitled 'The Witch'. The coquettish young woman sits toying with her russet tresses, with an enigmatic half-smile at the artist, who would end her life just a few months later.

The Mysterious Murder of Mrs Buxton, 1920

In 1920, the fifty-three-year-old Mrs Frances Buxton was the landlady of the Cross Keys public house, situated at No. 1 Lawrence Street, Chelsea. She had married one Frank Buxton in Toronto in 1888, and they had at least one daughter alive. Mrs Buxton had separated from her husband in 1908, after he had given her venereal disease. She had kept the Cross Keys, a nice early-Georgian pub not far from the Chelsea Embankment, since April 1915, with her business partner Arthur Cutting. In spite of her age, Frances Buxton was quite fond of 'chasing the chaps'. She still had some claims to good looks, and liked to wear expensive jewellery when she tended the bar. A potman and two barmaids were employed at the Cross Keys, but Mrs Buxton was the only person who slept on the premises. The old pub had two public bars on the ground floor, and three cellars. The first floor had a large clubroom, a storeroom and a kitchen. Mrs Buxton slept in a small second-floor room. Her only companions were a little biscuit-coloured Pomeranian dog and an old cat.

Just after midnight on Sunday 18 January 1920, the policeman on the beat in Lawrence Street found the door to the saloon bar of the

Mrs Buxton's body is discovered, from the *Illustrated Police News*, 22 January 1920.

Cross Keys unlocked. When he opened it, he found that the bar was full of smoke. He quickly ran to call police reinforcements, and the fire brigade. After the fire had been extinguished, the police found Mrs Buxton's body in the back cellar, partially covered with sawdust; she had been brutally beaten to death. The murderer had evidently hoped to burn the pub down to conceal his crime, but without success due to the vigilance of the police constable. Mrs Buxton kept her Pomeranian dog on the premises, but although this animal had been in the habit of annoying the neighbours with its shrill barking it had kept quiet the night its mistress had been done to death. Giving proof of its excitable nature, the little dog had started jumping round, barking loudly, when the police and fire brigade arrived.

The police could discern three alternative murder scenarios. Firstly, it might be that an old enemy, or former lover, of Mrs Buxton had murdered her for revenge, possibly because she had given him VD. Secondly, some casual acquaintance or random pub customer might have murdered her to steal her valuables. Two brooches and three rings were missing. Thirdly, it might have been a burglary gone wrong. The latter theory was considered less likely, since Mrs Buxton was quite security-conscious, and there were no marks of a forced entry to the premises. Why, if a burglar or robber entered the Cross Keys, had the little dog not barked in the night? Most of the drinkers at the pub the Saturday preceding the murder had been regulars, but one of them definitely was not. Perhaps, one witness suggested, he was the man who had been making Mrs Buxton 'the glad eye' a few evenings before the murder? The medical evidence indicated that the murder had been committed with considerable brutality. Mrs Buxton had been battered with both fists and a blunt instrument (a large bottle made of coloured glass), and then strangled to death with a cord.

The police made a huge trawl of Mrs Buxton's friends and acquaintances. Her estranged husband Frank was still alive, and the proprietor of the Sussex Hotel in Bexhill-on-Sea. He had a solid alibi, and so did the person benefiting from Mrs Buxton's will, her old friend Henry John Penn. Mrs Buxton's business partner Arthur Cutting was known as a somewhat dubious character, and had often quarrelled with Mrs Buxton when they were living together at the pub. He claimed not to have been in Chelsea for three years, but the police found two witnesses who independently claimed to have seen him near the Cross Keys three weeks before the murder. Cutting also had an alibi for the evening of the murder, however, and the time sheets from his employer proved that he could not have been in Chelsea the day he had allegedly been spotted by the witnesses. The most noteworthy of the many men in Mrs Buxton's life was the famous Scottish architect Charles Rennie Mackintosh, who enjoyed a brief affair with her when his wife was away in 1917, and had kept in touch with the Cross Keys landlady ever since. At one stage he had possessed a key to the pub, but he claimed that he had returned it. Mackintosh was also eliminated from the police inquiries, since he had a solid alibi.

In 1922, a woman named Polly Wilson pointed the finger at the railwayman Charles Clay, who she claimed had some of the jewellery stolen from Mrs Buxton. When questioned, Clay said that Mr Buxton was his cousin, and that he had attended the inquest. He had been at work at the time of the murder, and the police found nothing to connect him with the crime. In 1927, the author Netley Lucas claimed that a Liverpool thief named Francis O'Connor had told him that a convict named Burte had murdered Mrs Buxton. There was some newspaper publicity about this, but since Lucas was well known as a hoaxer and confidence man, the police did not take him seriously. As late as 1932, a letter from New York accused the American ex-convict Edward Cooney of murdering Mrs Buxton, but although he had been released from prison as recently as 1931, his whereabouts could not be tracked down.[10]

A somewhat more promising suspect is the army deserter Percy Toplis, known as 'the Monocled Mutineer' since he used to dress in an officer's uniform and wear a monocle. He used to boast that he had a wealthy lady friend in London who would send him money if he needed it. Toplis was definitely in London in January 1920. In April the same year, he robbed and murdered the cab driver Sidney George Spicer near Andover. Pursued by the police, Toplis escaped to Scotland. When challenged by two police constables, he shot and wounded them both, but a party of armed police put an end to his career in early June. Still, there is nothing to directly connect Toplis with the murder of Frances Buxton.

The Fastest Milkman in the West, 1939

Winifred Tedder, an eighteen-year-old Ealing girl, worked behind the till at the Express Dairies milk shop at No. 797 Fulham Road. She lived with her parents, who themselves kept a general shop. In 1938, Winifred got engaged to a young milkman named Harry Crees, a native of Hampton Wick. At the milk shop in Fulham Road, though, she met more attractive male companions than the bumpkin Harry. After a quarrel, the couple broke up their engagement for good. Winifred seems to have taken this with equanimity, but Harry was devastated. Far from the cheerful, cheeky milkman with a twinkle in his eye, portrayed with such bravura by Benny Hill, he was a gloomy, introspective lad, and very fond of his faithless Winifred.

In the evening of 27 February 1939, Harry Crees came into the milk shop at No. 797 Fulham Road, asking for Winifred. Mrs Laura Waite, the manageress, sternly told him to leave, since she knew that Winifred wanted nothing to do with him. However, Harry was angry and persistent, and Winifred came out to reason with him. He was carrying a large brown parcel, and after some angry words had been exchanged she said, 'I know what you have got there, and if you think you can frighten me, you are mistaken!' With alarm and trepidation, Mrs Waite saw that Harry was unwrapping a large black shotgun. 'Stop, you fool!' she cried, but Harry fired both barrels at Winifred, who fell to the floor mortally wounded. He then walked out into the yard and shot himself dead with a revolver.

At the coroner's inquest on Winifred Tedder, members of the family of Harry Crees testified that the young milkman had always been of a particularly morose and taciturn temperament. In 1935, after being jilted by another girl, he had shot himself with a powerful shotgun. Although not less than eighty pellets had been extracted from various parts of his anatomy, he had survived, only to be charged with attempting suicide at Frome Court. He was bound over for two years, but unfortunately no steps were taken to keep this rash young milkman under some degree of supervision, or at least to make sure that he did not have access to loaded firearms.[11] The murder shop at No. 797 Fulham Road still stands today, although it sells wine instead of milk.

Wife Murder in Armadale Road, 1945

Although not considered among Wilkie Collins's finest work, his 1863 novel *Armadale* is an enjoyable Victorian murder mystery. In Fulham, there is an Armadale Road, just off North End Road. Back in the 1940s, a middle-aged couple, Arthur Edward Wright and his wife Emily, lived in one of the flats at No. 4 Armadale Road. They had been living there for more than twenty years, and were known as a devoted couple, fond of playing whist at the local Conservative Club. However, Arthur Edward Wright's life went downhill in the 1940s: a shell-shocked, disabled veteran of the First World War, he was well-nigh unable to secure employment, except as a handyman or a night-time fire-watcher, and the family finances suffered badly as a result.

In February Emily Wright was found dead in the kitchen, her head battered with an axe. It attracted tabloid newspaper curiosity that the murderer, termed 'The Man with a Thirst', had asked a neighbour for a glass of water after committing the crime. Arthur Edward Wright had gone missing, and since the description of the suspected killer matched him very well Scotland Yard made it known that he was wanted for interrogation in connection with the murder of his wife. Late in the evening of 1 March, however, a middle-aged man jumped or fell in front of a train at Earl's Court station. Before dying from his injuries at St Mary Abbot's Hospital, Kensington, he told the doctors that he was Arthur Edward Wright, wanted for the murder of his wife.[12]

The Perham Road Murder, 1951

In 1951, No. 15 Perham Road was a lodging house run by the eighty-four-year-old Belgian immigrant Madame Eugenie le Maire. She had resided at No. 15 for not less than forty-eight years, living in two basement rooms, both of them dirty and full of cobwebs. The remainder of the house was in a similar state of decay. Nevertheless, Madame le Maire had several lodgers, one of them the twenty-nine-year-old labourer John O'Connor, a native of Londonderry. He was often grumbling about the filthy state of the house, and the indifferent cooking, but still he remained in the gloomy little room he was letting, probably since he could not afford to live in the better class of lodging house.

On 11 August 1951, Madame le Maire was found murdered in her basement kitchen. Since her lodger John O'Connor was missing from the premises, he became the prime suspect. On 13 August, several newspapers published his description, adding that Scotland Yard wanted him to help in the inquiry. At the time when these articles were published, however, O'Connor was already in custody. He had walked into the local police station, confessed to the murder, and described exactly what had happened that fateful evening.

It turned out that John O'Connor had gone for a prolonged pub crawl on the evening of 11 August, returning home quite late in a very drunken state. Madame le Maire invited him into her kitchen for a cup of tea, and he accepted her offer. All of a sudden, he got the impulse to destroy her. He seized the feeble old woman by the throat and throttled her until she was unconscious, before raping her. O'Connor then returned to his own room, where he tried to gather his thoughts. After a while, he went back down into the kitchen, grabbed a large bread knife, and stabbed his landlady hard in the chest several times before leaving the house for good. After just a few days on the run, he turned himself in to the police, however.

On trial at the Old Bailey for the murder of Eugenie le Maire, things were not looking good for John O'Connor. Since he had made a full confession to the murder, the verdict had to be one of guilty, although his solicitor had prepared an insanity defence. O'Connor wanted nothing of this. He expressly forbade any evidence to be introduced with regard to his sanity, or lack of it. Even when challenged by the judge, he stubbornly refused to have any such evidence presented in court. It took the jury just ten minutes to find him guilty, and he was hanged at Pentonville Prison on 2 October 1951.[13]

The Tragic Tale of the Battens, 1958

John Thomas Batten was a retired civil servant living at No. 28 Chiddingstone Street, Fulham, off New King's Road, with his wife Elizabeth Frances. They had been married for thirty years, and had always been a very happy couple. However, in 1958, the now seventy-eight-year-old Mr Batten was becoming increasingly infirm: his eyesight and hearing were failing, and his mind became increasingly gloomy and depressed. He feared becoming an invalid and a burden on others. As for his wife, she was just sixty-three and in reasonable physical health, but the victim of repeated nervous attacks.

On 25 July 1958, Elizabeth Frances Batten had yet another of her attacks, and her elderly husband became furious as she screamed hysterically. He grabbed a length of pipe and struck her repeatedly on the head until she was dead. The confused old man first tried to conceal his crime, through washing the pipe and putting it in the basement. He then wrote a full confession in a notebook and took barbiturates, intending to destroy himself, but the emergency services found him alive and he had to stand trial at the Old Bailey on 9 September for murdering his wife. He was found to be insane and unfit to plead, and was incarcerated in Broadmoor.

However, this tragic case does not end there: it resurfaced in 1961 at the Chancery Division of the High Court of Justice, before Mr Justice Pennycuick. There had been a dispute between the now seventy-nine-year-old Broadmoor inmate John Thomas Batten and the relations of his murdered wife about the £2,500 in her estate. Since Batten had been insane at the time of the murder, and since his wife had bequeathed her estate to him, the Broadmoor inmate actually won the day, in spite of the convention that a person who feloniously killed another should not inherit him or her.[14]

Murder of the 'Dancing Granny', 1965

Annie Doohan, a middle-aged widow hailing from Glasgow, came to Fulham in 1960 with her daughter Helen. She had four other children alive, and ten grandchildren. Annie Doohan got a job as an attendant at the Fulham baths, and she lodged in a flat nearby together with Helen. A friendly, cheery 'granny', with boundless energy when it came to partying, she soon became quite popular locally. In late 1965, Helen got engaged, and she was planning to move to Newport, South Wales, taking her mother with her.

Annie Doohan was happy for the sake of her daughter, although sad to have to leave her old stomping ground in Fulham. On 5 December 1965, she went to the Old Oak pub, at the corner of North End Road and Star Road (it still stands), and was soon the life and soul of the party, singing and dancing to belie her sixty-two years. Leaving the pub late in the evening to return to the flat where she lodged at No. 86C Lillie Road, Annie Doohan went north on North End Road, but she never arrived at the flat. Helen got worried and contacted the police, and early the following morning Annie Doohan's naked and battered body was found in the basement of a disused church at No. 222A North End Road, at the corner with Chesson Road; she had been brutally murdered on her short walk home.

In London's criminal history, 1965 was the year of 'Jack the Stripper', a serial killer who preyed on prostitutes and deposited his victims naked. 'New Nude Murder – But No Link!' exclaimed the *Daily Mirror*. The *Daily Express* provided some further particulars: Annie Doohan had neither been robbed nor sexually assaulted, and the derelict church where she was found was Bullen's warehouse for second-hand furniture. Detective Superintendent Richard Chitty of Scotland Yard said that this was clearly not a 'Jack the Stripper' crime, but rather a random, possibly sexually motivated slaying in Fulham's seedy night-time underworld. Although some individual at the pub might well have thought that the 'dancing granny' who led the community singing with such gusto might prove to be sexually 'easy', Annie Doohan had been a very respectable woman. Helen Doohan was heartbroken: the day after the murder of her mother, they were supposed to have left Fulham for her own wedding in Newport.

When the *Fulham Chronicle* reported on the inquest on Annie Doohan on 10 December, there was already a suspect in custody: the unemployed thirty-year-old local man Morgan Williams, of no fixed address. On 17 December, the same newspaper could report that Williams had been remanded in custody, and that the body of Annie Doohan had been identified by her son. Morgan Williams, a native of Merthyr Tydfil, had many convictions for theft and burglary, and had been in prison more than once. He drank and smoked excessively, and admitted having consumed nine pints of strong beer and seven double whiskies the night of the murder. He had been seen with Annie Doohan at the Old Oak the evening of the murder, and when taken into custody at the Southwark police station he admitted descending to the basement of the 'murder church' with her, hoping for some casual sex. He had been almost paralytic with drink, and when he recovered his senses he was standing over her naked, blood-spattered body. Although a 'borderline defective' of low intelligence, he was considered fit to plead.

It turned out that, after the murder, Morgan Williams had pawned Annie Doohan's watch. He was seen returning to the Church Army hostel at No. 8 Star Street with his clothes liberally sprinkled with blood. Williams was found guilty of murder at the Old Bailey in March 1966, and sentenced to life imprisonment.[15] The old 'murder church' at No. 222A North End Road still stands, and it is still a furniture shop.

The Walpole Street Hippie Murder Mystery, 1967

Claudie Danielle Delbarre was a young French girl who first came to London as an au pair in 1965, at the age of just sixteen. Attracted by the 'Swinging London' lifestyle, she returned a few months later hoping to become a model, but instead she descended into the dangerous drug culture of the time. To pay for her addiction, Claudie became a club hostess and a prostitute. A card-carrying member of the raffish Chelsea *demi-monde*, she was known for her large blonde wig and extremely short skirts.

On 19 September 1967, Claudie went partying at various London clubs. She 'picked up' a tall American hippie with long blond hair, and in the wee hours she brought this individual back to her fourth-floor bed-sitting room at No. 17 Walpole Street. The following morning, Claudie was found dead on a divan, murdered by repeated heavy blows to the head from a blunt instrument. There was considerable newspaper publicity about the murder of Claudie Delbarre, since she was young and quite attractive. Although she was referred to as a 'model' or 'good-time girl', lurid revelations about her life were released at regular intervals. Some photographs of her, taken by the celebrated Chelsea photographer John Bignall, were used as illustrations. The police were interviewing Claudie's various boyfriends, but this would take time, since there were more than 200 of them.

The police soon found the murder weapon: a heavy glass tumbler. It had the fingerprints of both Claudie and another person. In a vital breakthrough, it was found that the other prints matched those of the American hippie Robert Lipman, who had previously been arrested for possession of cannabis. It turned out that, after the murder, Lipman had speedily absconded back to his native New York, where he had checked into St Luke's mental hospital in a state of emotional distress. Lipman came from a wealthy New York family. He had once been an estate agent, but became an alcoholic and drug addict, using quantities of cannabis, cocaine, amphetamine and LSD. Since there was solid technical evidence against Lipman, he was extradited to London in May 1968 to stand trial at the Old Bailey for the murder of Claudie Delbarre.

Robert Lipman's family had made sure that, before the extradition, the hippie had been kept in a secure mental institution without access to illicit drugs. His hair had been cut and his appearance tidied up. As a result, the tall American gave a good impression in court: he seemed like a decent person, reserved and well spoken. A high-quality legal team had been briefed to defend him, led by the celebrated David Napley, a veteran solicitor who knew all the tricks of his trade. The defence was a startling one: Robert Lipman and Claudie Delbarre had both taken LSD prior to going to bed, the American in such a quantity that he suffered a seriously 'bad trip', imagining himself to be fighting huge snakes somewhere in space! When Lipman recovered, he was horrified to see that 'thrashing about' during his 'trip', he had accidentally killed Claudie. Amazingly, the jury accepted this argument, and Lipman got off with just six years in prison for manslaughter.[16] The life of young Claudie Delbarre was clearly not valued particularly highly.

In his memoirs, Sir David Napley (as he had become) reviewed the many *causes célèbres* of his illustrious career. A long chapter is dedicated to his most newsworthy exploit: successfully defending the notorious politician Jeremy Thorpe from a charge of conspiring to murder his homosexual lover. Nor could Sir David refrain from crowing about his clever defence of Robert Lipman, in another chapter of his memoirs. In rather dubious taste, it is illustrated with a photograph of poor Claudie's half-naked body. Sir David argues that Lipman should really have walked free, since if there had been a law regarding 'dangerous intoxication' the American could surely not have been found guilty of manslaughter.[17]

In spite of all Sir David Napley's arguments, there is reason to believe that Robert Lipman was a very lucky man. Firstly, we only have his own word that he took any LSD at all. Secondly, would not an experienced 'walking pharmacy' like Lipman have the sense to make sure he got hold of high-quality LSD from a pusher who did not deal in 'bad acid'? Thirdly, Lipman himself stated that he arrived at Claudie's flat at 4.15 a.m., and there is evidence that he left it at 7.30 a.m., dashing back to his own flat and booking a flight to escape. This seems like a very short LSD trip to me, and it is equally telling that this alleged 'trip' was followed by shrewd and logical behaviour as the hippie planned his flight from justice. Fourthly, although drug takers high on LSD have been known to leap out of windows thinking they can fly, there are very few examples of them being violent to other people during their 'trips'. Fifthly and most damningly, Lipman had clearly not been 'thrashing about' in a drug-induced frenzy, as was alleged in court, as he had stuffed sheeting into Claudie's mouth to prevent her from screaming as he battered her head with the heavy tumbler. An alternative hypothesis is that Lipman had become impotent from his extensive drug-taking. Perhaps Claudie had made fun of his inability to 'get it up', triggering a furious assault from the tall American?

There are two versions of the later career of the creature Lipman. According to the first one, he was killed in a railway accident in Austria, not long after being released from prison. According to the other version, his wealthy family helped him to change his name and set up a new career for himself, and he lived happily ever after, still being alive today. A curious sidelight on the case is that, in his youth, Lipman had married the wealthy New York socialite Lynn Sakowitz. Before she walked out on him in 1962, they had two sons, both later adopted by Lynn Sakowitz's second husband, the Texas oil billionaire Oscar Wyatt Jr. One of these sons was a member of Eternal Values, a weird American gay Nazi sect, whereas the other is said to have become one of the many lovers of that fun-loving royal, Sarah, Duchess of York.

Walpole Street, full of seedy bedsits back in the 1960s, is today a fashionable Chelsea street. The tall houses have mostly been subdivided into flats. The spectre of Claudie Delbarre, the Chelsea good-time girl with her blonde wig and short skirt, seems to have faded away, as has that of the skulking hippie who brutally ended her young life.

A Fulham Gangster Murder, 1968

In the 1960s, Fulham was home to a healthy population of gangsters. In 1967, a gang war broke out. As the gangsters fought for the control of the Fulham underworld, a man had his leg blasted off with a shotgun, hand grenades were thrown through windows, and the Queen Elizabeth public house in Bagley's Lane was damaged by a bomb.

One of the Fulham villains taking part in this gangster war was the scrap metal dealer Anthony Lawrence. On 10 February 1968, Lawrence and his scrapyard labourer Terence 'Ba-Ba' Elgar went to call on the rival gangster George Marshall in his flat at No. 51 Hazlebury Road. Not long after, a volley of revolver shots rang out, and Lawrence and Elgar came running out of the house. Bleeding profusely, they staggered into the front gardens of the adjoining houses looking for help, but nobody wanted to let them in. The police and ambulance services were quickly on the spot. Lawrence, who had been shot twice in the head, was still alive, but Elgar was dead from a shot to the chest.

The police sealed off Hazlebury Road, and No. 51 was closely examined by the forensic technicians. George Marshall and his friend Ian Horton, who had been with him prior to the murder, were nowhere to be found. 'Wanted by the Yard!' exclaimed the front page of next day's *Daily Mirror*, illustrated with mugshots of the two gunmen. Marshall gave himself up the day after, but Horton went on the run. He was apprehended in a raid on a Bolton flat on 20 February. He had clearly made some other enemy in the meantime, since he greeted the police with the words, 'I'm glad it is you. I thought it might have been the other bastard.'

On trial at the Central Criminal Court for the murder of Terence Elgar, Marshall and Horton pleaded not guilty. Their story was that Lawrence had previously offered them £250 to murder James Sullivan, a rival scrap metal dealer. They had taken the money but not carried out the hit. When Lawrence and Elgar came calling at No. 51 Hazlebury Road, Marshall and Horton were quite apprehensive, since Lawrence had a fearsome reputation for violence. Nor was this Fulham gangster exactly in a friendly mood; he remarked that he had once murdered a man and disposed of the corpse in a swamp, and that there was plenty of room there for others who double-crossed him. He wanted to see Marshall's arsenal of firearms, which he kept in the basement. When Lawrence grabbed a rifle and loaded it, they first thought that he had picked out the weapon they were supposed to use against Sullivan, but they soon realised that he planned to murder them. Horton grabbed Lawrence by the collar, but the scrap metal dealer gave him a hard knock on the head with the rifle barrel. When Lawrence aimed at them with the rifle, Marshall and Horton opened fire with their own revolvers, hitting their enemy twice. The unarmed 'Ba-Ba' Elgar had also been gunned down by this fusillade of bullets.

Marshall and Horton received some unexpected help from some police detectives, who testified that Anthony Lawrence had several convictions for violent crime, and that he could behave like a complete lunatic on occasions. The two gunmen were not taken in a lie, and their story was roughly consistent with the technical evidence, except that it was thought that Elgar might have been shot when he tried to escape up the stairs. In the end, George Marshall was found guilty of murder and sentenced to life imprisonment, but Ian Horton was acquitted. In May 1969, however, Marshall also walked free after a successful appeal.[18] The Appeal Court rightly found that the judge's summing-up had been flawed, since he had not put to the jury the possibility that Elgar might have been shot by a man in a crouching position. Waiting to shake Marshall's hand when he came out of court was his friend Ian Horton, and also the scrap metal dealer James Sullivan. A newspaper article on the unsatisfactory outcome of the Terence Elgar murder investigation pointed out that, although the two gunmen were walking free, Anthony Lawrence was serving a fifteen-year sentence for a string of serious offences. This forthright Fulham gangster's reaction to the lenient treatment of the two men who had gunned down his friend, and done their best to kill him as well, has unfortunately not been recorded.

The Butcher of Petley Road, 1971

In late 1971, the forty-eight-year-old Florence Lee, the estranged wife of the London postal worker Harry Lee, was homeless and in dire straits. When she asked the forty-year-old minicab driver Peter Nutkins for a lift, he offered her a roof over her head in his flat at No. 50 Petley Road, Fulham, and she gratefully accepted. For no obvious reason, the demented Nutkins murdered her after they had had intercourse. He then dismembered her body using a carpenter's saw. He first thought it would be a good idea to throw the remains into Thames, but changed his mind and decided to bury them somewhere in the countryside.

When Peter Nutkins drove to Henley-on-Thames with the car boot full of body parts, he was stopped by a policeman for driving too slowly. When the constable showed an interest in the contents of his car boot, Nutkins cried out, 'All right, don't open it! There's a body in there!' The gruff constable first made an incredulous remark, but Nutkins opened the boot and was of course promptly arrested to face a murder charge. He seemed quite sane, but could not provide an explanation why he had murdered a complete stranger he had taken back to his flat. It turned out that Florence Lee was the younger sister of Mr Raymond Bellisario, a photographer who specialised in taking pictures of the royal family, and he was the person who identified her body. Nutkins was found guilty of murder and sentenced to a lengthy prison sentence; he died at Wormwood Scrubs in January 1975.[19]

Depravity and Murder in Cadogan Square, 1972

Leo Baekeland was a Belgian scientist who invented Bakelite, earning a future as a result, and settling in the United States. His grandson, the immensely rich American playboy Brooks Baekeland, trained as a pilot in the 1930s, but was more interested in pursuing various attractive women, with considerable success. One of his girlfriends was the vivacious, red-haired young fashion model Barbara Daly. Her father had gassed himself when she was ten, to the detriment of the family finances, and her mother wanted to marry her off to the richest man possible. Barbara was in love with the handsome Brooks, but he preferred 'playing the field'. After she had tricked him into believing that she was pregnant, he reluctantly married her, and they settled down in a large house in New York's fashionable Upper East Side.

For a few years, the Baekelands lived reasonably happily together. They spent lavishly, and their parties were legendary, even by New York standards. Barbara became well known as a leading society hostess. In 1946, she gave birth to their only son Tony. It did not take long for the marriage to break down, however. Both the Baekelands were notoriously unfaithful, they quarrelled fiercely and frequently, and Barbara's mental health left much to be desired. When Brooks wanted to divorce her, she took one of several drugs overdoses, and he eventually relented. The son

Cadogan Square, from an old postcard.

Tony was a bad egg even as a youngster: cruel to animals, constantly dishonest, and given to severe temper tantrums. From an early age, he showed strong homosexual tendencies, befriending various undesirable types to the despair of his long-suffering parents.

Eventually, Brooks Baekeland had had enough. He left his wife and son and moved in with a younger woman, whom he later married. Barbara Baekeland, a volatile woman with negligible parenting skills, had to take care of Tony as well as she could. They were both under treatment by psychiatrists, and Tony soon showed worrying signs of 'losing it' altogether. Several doctors were of the opinion that he suffered from schizophrenia. A sinister-looking cove with an interest in Satanism, he kept collecting some very dubious boyfriends. Barbara tried various strategies to make him 'straight'; according to rumour, she herself seduced him, in order to teach him about the pleasures of heterosexual love. These weird activities were taking place in the expensive penthouse flat at No. 81 Cadogan Square, Knightsbridge, where Barbara and Tony lived with their maid and their cat.

In time, Tony Baekeland's behaviour became increasingly erratic. He repeatedly attacked his mother, knocking her out cold with a walking cane, smashing an egg into her face, attempting to blind her with a pencil, and even seizing her by the hair to throw her in front of a car. Many people advised her that Tony belonged inside a mental hospital, but the volatile Barbara Baekeland, whose instincts of self-preservation were quite defective, pooh-poohed their concerns. Dismayed by her foolish actions, Brooks Baekeland cut her allowance to make her see sense, but the stubborn former society hostess did not budge. Brooks also refused to fund Tony's care, since he did not believe in psychiatry. Instead, he described his lunatic son as the personification of evil, predicting that he would be up to further mischief unless he was safely locked up.

One day in November 1972, Barbara Baekeland went out to luncheon with a friend of hers, mentioning that Tony was waiting at home at No. 81 Cadogan Square, and that he would be cooking her dinner. However, when she returned home, the demented Tony stabbed her hard with a kitchen knife, killing her instantly. The lunatic was unable to provide a motive for murdering his mother. The old rumours of an incestuous affair resurfaced, but others thought that the frenzied attack had been provoked by Barbara throwing the collar of a long-dead Pekingese dog, of which Tony had been very fond, out of the window.

The tragic murder of Barbara Baekeland made headline news on both sides of the Atlantic. After all, a member of one of America's richest dynasties had been murdered in the heart of one of London's most affluent neighbourhoods. Defended at the Old Bailey by none less than John Mortimer, later the creator of the famous 'Rumpole' character, Tony was found guilty of manslaughter with diminished responsibility, and sent to Broadmoor for an indefinite period of time.

Here the story of the Cadogan Square murder should have ended, had not a number of foolish society busybodies, on both sides of the Atlantic, taken an interest in the plight of Tony Baekeland. Egged on by Tony's grandmother Nini Daly, who may well have been as crazy as the rest of the family, they used their money to lobby those in power, with unexpected success. Amazingly, they succeeded in getting the Cadogan Square matricide out of Broadmoor in July 1980. Brooks Baekeland strongly opposed this move, since he felt that Tony belonged behind bars for life. The lunatic had written his father a number of abusive letters, threatening to murder his second wife as well, and sent Brooks's little son some very obscene toys, manufactured in the Broadmoor workshops. The Broadmoor psychiatrists had agreed to release Tony only under the condition that he was taken care of in some kind of halfway house, but since this had not been put in writing, the sinister murderer was able to move into the New York flat of his grandmother. Six days later, he stabbed this harmless old woman nine times in a frenzied attack, nearly killing her.

Awaiting trial for the attempted murder of his grandmother at Riker's Island, the ever reckless Tony started an affair with one of the prison guards, and another with a murderer who had raped and decapitated a young boy. Although a pervert himself, he was worried about being brutalised by the prison 'rough trade', and paid them more than $20,000 in protection money. On 20 March 1981, Tony Baekeland was found dead in his bunk, suffocated with a plastic bag.[20] It was never definitely resolved whether it was murder or suicide, but it remains quite ironic that the career of the Cadogan Square matricide was ended by a bag of the very same material that had made his family's fortune.

Patrick Mackay's Murder Houses, 1973–1975

Patrick Mackay, a relatively little-known serial killer active in the 1970s, has a strong claim to be the record holder for the number of London murder houses he left behind. This sinister individual was born in 1952, the son of the accountant Henry Mackay and his wife Marion. Henry Mackay had once been a private in the Eighth Army, serving with commendable gallantry. After being promoted to corporal, he once had his entire patrol wiped out by German gunfire in an ambush and was himself severely wounded. Later, having qualified as an accountant, Henry Mackay went to British Guyana, where he met his wife Marion and took her back to London. Settling down in Dartford, they built up a family of three children.

Henry Mackay's life steadily went downhill in the 1950s, however. He became an alcoholic and beat up his wife and his son Patrick at the slightest provocation. It has to be admitted that young Patrick was a very nasty piece of work, however, and he may well have been deserving of some parental discipline. He was disrespectful to his mother, cruel to animals, bullied small children, and made a habit of constantly thieving and pilfering. Henry Mackay died in 1962, and from that time Patrick's behaviour went from bad to worse. He was soon big and strong enough to beat up his mother and sisters, and poor Marion Mackay, a foolish and volatile woman with negligible parenting skills, was quite unable to control him.

His incessant thieving meant that Patrick soon came into contact with the police. He spent lengthy periods of time in various approved

Old houses in Cheyne Walk, from an early postcard.

An old postcard of Lowndes Square.

schools and psychiatric units for young offenders, but, although one doctor proclaimed him a very dangerous young psychopath who might one day become a murderer, he was each time released on probation into the care of his dysfunctional family. He repeatedly beat his long-suffering mother up, but each time she pleaded for him to be released and sent back home, since he had promised to be good. His sister Ruth also spent considerable time inside various psychiatric hospitals, before being committed to Broadmoor for attempting to burn one of these hospitals down.

In 1973, the hard-drinking, work-shy Patrick Mackay began a career of mugging well-to-do old ladies in central London. At the time, such a cowardly crime was quite uncommon, and the trusting old women even allowed Mackay to carry their shopping home for them, and invited him into their flats. The psychopath Mackay repaid them by knocking them down, stealing their handbags, and ransacking their flats or houses. He used to prowl about outside Harrods, looking for some well-dressed old lady to follow home.

One of the victims Mackay had been 'setting up' was the eighty-four-year-old widow Mrs Isabella Griffiths, who lived at No. 19 Cheyne Walk, an elegant and historic Chelsea house. After the old Chelsea manor house had been demolished following the death of Sir Hans Sloane in 1753, Nos 19–26 Cheyne Walk had been built on the site. A personable young rogue when he made the effort, Patrick Mackay had befriended Mrs Griffiths, done her shopping, and even been invited inside her house. On 14 February 1974, Mackay thought the time had come to rob her. However, when he called at No. 19 Cheyne Walk, something made Mrs Griffiths suspicious of his intentions. She told him that she did not need any shopping done and refused to let him in. Enraged, the powerful young Mackay pushed hard at the door, breaking the chain. He seized hold of Mrs Griffiths and throttled her until she was unconscious, before stabbing her in the stomach with a large kitchen knife to make sure she was dead. Since the old lady lived alone, it took twelve days before the body was discovered. There were no relevant witnesses, and Mackay had left no technical evidence behind.

Throughout 1974 and early 1975, Mackay kept robbing old women at regular intervals. He was cunning enough not to be caught, although he was not the shrewdest of men: once, he threw some very valuable jewellery he had stolen into a dustbin, since he believed it to be fake. On 10 March

1975, he was on the prowl in Lowndes Square, home to many wealthy pensioners. He spotted the eighty-nine-year-old widow Mrs Adele Price taking out her keys to enter No. 13 Lowndes Square, where she lived in a third-floor flat. Mackay approached her from behind, jangling his own keys as if to enter as a resident. The unsuspecting Mrs Price admitted him. Halfway up the stairs, he complained of feeling faint. Kind Mrs Price invited him into her own flat for a glass of water. Mackay followed her into the kitchen, grabbed her by the throat, and strangled her to death. He helped himself to some whisky, and stole money and two transistor radios. Again there were no worthwhile clues to the identity of the murderer.

Father Anthony Crean, a kind but foolish semi-retired Roman Catholic priest, lived in a small cottage just by the convent chapel at Shorne in Kent. Fond of the outcasts of society, he befriended the worthless Patrick Mackay and gave him financial support. He continued to help Mackay even after the miscreant had repaid him by burgling his cottage. However, the naïve old priest would pay even more dearly for his kindness to the murderous young psychopath. Later in March 1975, another thug taunted Mackay for his friendship with the old priest, suggesting that they were homosexuals. In the psychopath's warped mind, the only way to remove this slur was to murder Father Crean. He went down to Shorne, burst into the cottage, and beat up the defenceless old man with an axe, before drowning him in the bath.

Since Mackay was a repeat violent offender, and since he was known to have associated with Father Crean, he soon became the prime suspect for the old priest's murder. A fingerprint from one of his robberies fitted one found at the murder scene in the cottage. When arrested and questioned by the police, Mackay confessed to the murder of Father Crean. In custody, he also freely admitted the murders of Isabella Griffiths and Adele Price. As befitting a proper psychopath, he showed no remorse whatsoever for his terrible crimes. He also blabbered to the other prisoners, boasting that he had committed many more murders, some of which he described in some detail. For example, he boasted of having attacked an old tramp on Hungerford Bridge, throwing him headlong into Thames. The police got interested, since there had been several other unsolved murders in 1973–1975, some of which fitted Mackay's *modus operandi* perfectly.

In July 1973, at the height of Mackay's murder spree, the seventy-three-year-old spinster Mary Hynes was murdered in her ground-floor flat at No. 4 Willes Road, Kentish Town. She had been savagely beaten about the head with a wooden club, and her stockings had been stuffed into her mouth. Mackay was strongly suspected of having committed this murder. During police questioning, he let slip some details that could have been known only to the murderer, for example that the back door to the flat had been nailed shut. At the time of the murder, Mackay had been awaiting trial for assault at the Ashford remand centre, but the discipline and security at the centre was quite defective, and he could easily have absconded for the day.

In January 1974, the wealthy fifty-seven-year-old widow Stephanie Britton was brutally stabbed to death at 'The Mercers', an elegant and historic house at Hadley Green. Her four-year-old grandson Christopher Martin was also murdered. At the time, Mackay was working as a groundsman at the Tudor sports field in Barnet, less than a mile from the house. Mackay is said to have confessed to these murders when boasting to a fellow inmate. He later retracted his confession, however, possibly from fear of being roughly handled by the other prisoners after it had become known that he was a child killer. In his confession to the murder of Isabella Griffiths, Mackay graphically described how he had pinned her to the floorboards with a powerful stab. Mrs Griffiths' stab wound was a shallow one, however, although Stephanie Britton had been pinned to the floor with a knife.

The sixty-two-year-old Frank Goodman was a harmless old bloke who rented a small tobacconist's shop at No. 26 Rock Street, Finsbury Park. One evening in June 1974, he was attacked by a person bursting into the shop as he was about to close it, and was murdered with repeated blows from a lead pipe. The till was emptied and a quantity of cigarettes stolen. All the murderer left behind was a bloody footprint. There is a strong case for Patrick Mackay being the guilty man. His landlord identified the lead piping, and associates of Mackay could remember him returning late in the evening, his pockets bulging with money and cigarettes. When questioned by the police, Mackay readily admitted robbing the shop, but he denied murdering Frank Goodman. He spoke about his bloodstained boots, and described how he had discarded them in Finchley cemetery. The boots were retrieved by the police, with stains of human blood on them.

On trial at the Old Bailey, Mackay admitted the manslaughter of Isabella Griffiths, Adele Price and Father Crean.[21] The prosecution accepted this plea, leaving the murders of Mary Hynes and Frank Goodman on file. There is a moderately solid case for him being responsible also for the murders of Stephanie Britton and Christopher Martin at 'The Mercers', and he may well have been involved in three other unsolved murders during his killing spree. Patrick Mackay was imprisoned for life. He has been reported by some to be among the fifty or so prisoners in the UK who have been issued with a whole-life tariff, meaning that he will never walk free, but will leave prison in a coffin. By 2014, he will have been behind bars for thirty-nine years.

Of Patrick Mackay's murder houses, Isabella Griffiths's attractive house at No. 19 Cheyne Walk is of course still standing, as are No. 13 Lowndes Square, once home to Adele Price, and No. 4 Willes Road where Mary Hynes once lived. 'The Mercers' also still exists, and Frank Goodman's tobacconist's shop at No. 26 Rock Street is today a small café. Father Crean's cottage at Shorne was still standing in 2003, and is likely still to be in existence today, although it does not of course qualify as a London murder house. Hopefully, Patrick Mackay's macabre record of (perhaps) five London murder houses will never be broken.

The Monster Butler, 1977

Archibald Thomson Hall was born in Glasgow in 1924. From an early age, he established himself as a thief and burglar, serving several prison sentences. A clever man, who was sometimes capable of hatching original plans to get rich, he got the idea of posing as a butler to infiltrate the households of wealthy people, win their confidence, and then steal their valuables. A plausible rogue, he looked the perfect 'gentleman's gentleman'. In prison, he studied genealogy and etiquette, and tried his best to lose his Scottish accent. He was also a keen student of antiques, so that he would know what to steal once he got employment at some stately home.

Although Archibald Hall was more than once caught pilfering and sent back to prison, he was always able to get yet another job as a butler. In 1975, he was butler to Lady Hudson, a wealthy Dumfriesshire dowager. Since he liked both his job and his employer, he decided to 'go straight' for a change, and not steal anything. However, there were other 'complications', namely that Hall was bisexual, and that he had made sure his ex-boyfriend David Wright got a job as Lady Hudson's gardener in 1977. Wright was a 'bad hat' who wanted to burgle the house and steal

Lady Hudson's jewellery, and when Hall objected Wright threatened to expose him as a crook. Hall was not having any of that: when they were out hunting, he shot Wright dead and buried him in the grounds of Lady Hudson's estate.

Having 'disposed of' his friend, Archibald Hall went back to his old haunts in London, again securing employment as a butler with the greatest of ease. His new employers were the eighty-two-year-old former Labour MP Walter Scott-Elliott and his wife Dorothy, living in Flat 22 at Richmond Court, a prestigious apartment block situated at No. 200 Sloane Street. Scott-Elliott was a very wealthy man, and the flat full of valuable antiques. Planning to empty the flat in a simulated burglary, the Monster Butler recruited two accomplices: the thief Michael Kitto and the prostitute Mary Coggle. However, their plan went badly wrong when Mrs Scott-Elliott, who Hall thought was in a nursing home, unexpectedly returned and confronted Hall and Kitto at Flat 22. The two ruffians attacked and murdered her without any further ado.

For it to be possible for the gang to continue stealing money and antiques, Mr Scott-Elliott also had to disappear. Hall thought up another cunning plan. With himself and Kitto acting the parts of butler and chauffeur, Mary Coggle dressed up as Mrs Scott-Elliott, wearing her fur coat and a large wig. The dotard Walter Scott-Elliott, whom the villains had dosed with sedatives, did not notice the difference, although the befuddled ex-legislator must have found his 'wife's' plebeian accent very odd indeed. They all went for a drive to Scotland in a hired Ford Cortina, with the corpse of Mrs Scott-Elliott travelling in the boot of the car. Here Hall and Kitto murdered Walter Scott-Elliott and buried him and his wife in the countryside. Next to go was the foolish and volatile Mary Coggle, who had taken too much of a liking to Mrs Scott-Elliott's expensive clothes, and was becoming a liability. Hall and Kitto murdered her and put her body in a barn in Dumfriesshire. Hall then murdered his half-brother Donald, a convicted paedophile he had always detested, but when their car was searched by the police at a hotel Donald's body was found in the boot. The Monster Butler escaped through a lavatory window, but was later captured at a police roadblock.

The police traced the car to the Scott-Elliotts in London, and Flat 22 was found to be robbed of many of its antiques, and spattered with blood. All the bodies were recovered, and Hall and Kitto charged with five counts of murder. In courts in London and Edinburgh, they were both sentenced to life imprisonment, Hall with the recommendation that he should never be released.[22] Indeed, the Monster Butler had to serve a full twenty-five years in prison. When he died of a stroke at Kingston Prison, Portsmouth, in 2002 at the age of seventy-eight, he was one of the oldest prisoners in Britain, and the oldest serving a whole-life tariff. Richmond Court still stands, and there is still a Flat 22. A two-bedroom flat in this prestigious block costs a cool £8,000 per month to rent; whether the resident ghost of the murdered former occupant is included in this price is not stated in the advertisement.

The Murder of Peter Arne, 1983
Peter Arne Albrecht was born in Kuala Lumpur, British Malaya, in 1920, the son of an American father and a Swiss-French mother. In spite of his cosmopolitan background, he considered himself traditionally British. Indeed, he spent his youth as an actor touring various provincial theatres all over the British Isles, under his acting name Peter Arne. A rash homosexual and something of a rogue, he more than once got into scrapes with the law. In 1946, Peter Arne and his boyfriend Jack Corke decided to go to South Africa to make their fortunes. On their way there as passengers on a steamer, they met the novelist Mary Renault, whom they decided to 'fleece' in a swindle involving a company building houses for South African immigrants. After she had been relieved of several thousand pounds, Peter Arne made his escape back to Britain, having spent all the money on high living.

Back on the acting circuit, Peter Arne decided to take his career more seriously. As a result, he became quite a famous character actor, both on film and TV. He had parts in *The Cockleshell Heroes*, *Chitty Chitty Bang Bang*, and three of the *Pink Panther* films. A man of a somewhat sinister aspect, with an excellent voice and the ability to mimic various foreign accents to perfection, he often played the villain. In his TV career, he appeared in *Danger Man*, *The Saint* and *The Avengers*, before turning out a bravura performance as a Nazi officer in the popular *Secret Army* TV series.

By the 1960s, Peter Arne was quite a wealthy man. He could afford to buy a flat at No. 54 Hans Place, one of Chelsea's historic garden squares. It was named after the celebrated physician Sir Hans Sloane, whose collections formed the basis of the British Museum, and whose name also lives on in Sloane Square and other Chelsea landmarks. The

Hans Place, from an old postcard.

handsome Georgian houses in Hans Place were modified in Victorian times, giving rise to an unfortunate architectural trend referred to by Osbert Lancaster as 'Pont Street Dutch'. Nevertheless, in the 1970s and 1980s Hans Place was exceedingly fashionable: Peter Arne hobnobbed with leading politicians, businessmen and media personalities. Still, his own private life remained a very shady business. He was said to have intimate knowledge of a not inconsiderable proportion of London's various 'rent boys', and he also made a habit of 'picking up' unknown young vagabonds in the street and taking them back to No. 54 Hans Place for some casual sex.

On 1 August 1983, the now sixty-one-year-old Peter Arne attended a costume-fitting for an episode of the *Doctor Who* TV series 'Frontios', in which he was to play the character 'Mr Range'. After the fitting, he returned home to No. 54. Not long after, the sound of a violent quarrel was heard from the premises. When a neighbour came to investigate, he was shocked to find Peter Arne's body inside the flat, beaten to death with a stool and with a log from the fireplace. The bloodstained log was later found in the communal hallway of No. 54. The police were well aware of Peter Arne's double life: the distinguished character actor had been consorting with some very queer people. In his diary, the names of some of the highest in the land were found alongside those of rent boys and convicted criminals. Rumours that Peter Arne was a member of a paedophile ring, or that he was a part-time pimp supplying some very wealthy and influential people with rent boys, could never be substantiated at the time.

A scruffy, foreign-looking young man had been seen skulking outside No. 54 earlier in the day, and on 10 August the police released an e-fit image of him. Four days later, a man exactly matching this e-fit was found drowned in the Thames near Wandsworth. He turned out to be the Italian former schoolteacher Giuseppe Perusi, who had met with hard times and was sleeping rough in Hyde Park. Traces of Peter Arne's blood were found on his clothes, and his fingerprints matched those found at No. 54. It was presumed that Arne had picked the homosexual vagabond up for some casual sex, and that the Italian had returned a few days later, perhaps to demand money. An argument had ensued, costing Arne his life.[23] The murder house at No. 54 Hans Place still stands. It may well have been partially rebuilt as a result of damage during the Second World War, but is virtually unchanged since the time Peter Arne lived there. The part of 'Mr Range' in the *Doctor Who* series was eventually played by William Lucas; it is not known whether the costume fitted for Peter Arne matched his measurements.

The Murder of Jill Dando, 1999

Jill Dando was one of the BBC's best-known TV presenters, famous for co-presenting the popular *Crimewatch* show. In 1999, she became engaged to marry the wealthy and successful gynaecologist Alan Farthing. She moved into his Chiswick house, and put her own house at No. 29 Gowan Avenue, Fulham, on the market.

On 26 April 1999, Jill Dando left Farthing's house just after 10 a.m., in her distinctive blue BMW convertible, to do some shopping and to pick up mail and faxes from No. 29 Gowan Avenue. Stopping on the way to buy some stationery, an ink cartridge for her fax machine, and two filleted Dover soles, she arrived at her small terraced house at around 11.30. She managed to find an empty parking space just by her house, something that was normally quite difficult in this crowded street. She set her car alarm and walked up to No. 29. However, as she put the key into the lock, a strong man, who must have hidden behind the hedge in her front garden, seized hold of her arm with enough force to leave a bruise, and forced her to the ground. Holding her down with his right arm, and pressing the muzzle of his gun so hard against her temple that its imprint could be seen afterwards, he murdered her with a single shot.

There was no witness to the murder of Jill Dando, but two people saw the killer escape. Her neighbour Richard Hughes heard her scream but did not hear the shot. When he heard her front gate shut, he looked out and saw a sturdy, muscular man with a full, jowly face and a mop of straight black hair walk off quite calmly. The neighbour across the road, Geoffrey Upfill-Brown, saw a man fitting the same description jog off towards Fulham Palace Road. He slowed to a walk when he perceived he was being observed. Interestingly, the witness thought he might well be wearing a wig. Since the murderer had pressed the gun so very hard against Jill Dando's temple, neither of these two men had actually heard the shot, nor did they discover the murder victim. However, when another neighbour, Helen Doble, walked past Jill Dando's house about ten minutes later, she saw the murdered woman lying slumped at the front door. She called the emergency services, but Jill Dando was already dead.

As the hunt for the murderer began, the police were deluged with tips. A number of mysterious men had been spotted in the region of Gowan Avenue and Fulham Palace Road. One of them, a smartly dressed bloke looking like an Englishman, had been walking down Gowan Avenue at around 9.30 a.m. A Mediterranean-looking man had been seen in Gowan Avenue just before 7 a.m., and later about 10.30 a.m. A number of witnesses had seen an agitated-looking man run across Fulham Palace Road, speak on a mobile phone in Bishop's Park, and wait for a bus at the stop outside No. 389 Fulham Palace Road. Several witnesses had seen a dark blue Range Rover nearby. One of them had seen this vehicle take off at speed from Doneraile Street, the westward continuation of Gowan Avenue, and travel south on Fulham Palace Road. It was later seen on CCTV heading south across Putney Bridge. These sightings suggested that the killer and an accomplice had staked out the murder house, waiting for Jill Dando to arrive. The killer might well have been wearing a disguise, with over-large spectacles and a wig. Had he been picked up by the accomplice in the blue Range Rover that disappeared without trace after crossing Putney Bridge?

The Dando task force made a huge trawl of possible suspects: former boyfriends of Jill Dando, women who might have had designs to marry Alan Farthing, obsessed fans with an unhealthy interest in the attractive

TV presenter, and criminals brought to book through the *Crimewatch* show. Shortly before the murder, NATO had bombed the Serbian TV headquarters in Belgrade, killing seventeen people. The Serbs had threatened revenge. After Jill Dando had appeared in a TV appeal to help Kosovan refugees, the BBC directors had received death threats from angry Serbs, and Jill herself had been sent a letter, presumably by a Serb, criticising her meddling in the conflict. 'You Evil Bastard, Slobbo, You Murdered Our Jill!' exclaimed a breathless tabloid newspaper headline when the Serb conspiracy became known, pointing the finger at President Slobodan Milosevic himself. The police thought Jill Dando an unlikely victim of a Serbian hitman. Still, they were impressed by the swiftness of the execution and the killer's calm escape from the scene. The murder weapon had been a 9-mm Remington-made pistol, and the bullet had been 'crimped' – altered to reduce the amount of gunpowder, and thus the sound of the explosion, when it was fired.

The early murder investigation served to eliminate many people from suspicion. Jill Dando's ex-boyfriends were all 'regular Joes' without any ambitions to murder her, or access to firearms. Alan Farthing's previous life did not contain any skeletons in the closet. When some underworld sources were interviewed, they merely ridiculed the notion that organised criminals would take revenge on the *Crimewatch* presenter. Several men had had an unhealthy interest in Jill Dando, and at least one of them knew where she lived, but again these stalkers proved to be timid and unadventurous men, without access to firearms. The greatest mystery of the murder of Jill Dando was how the killer could have known that she would be at No. 29 Gowan Avenue the day of the murder. She did not have a fixed routine, but visited the house at quite irregular intervals. CCTV footage did not indicate that she was followed from the Chiswick house. If the killer had kept staking out the murder house day after day, waiting for her to arrive, then surely he would have been spotted by the paranoid Fulham householders, who saw burglars everywhere.

After thirteen months, the Dando task force finally made the breakthrough, when unemployed local weirdo Barry George, alias Barry Bulsara, was arrested. He lived in a flat at No. 2B Crookham Road, not far from Gowan Avenue. When searched by the police, this flat was cluttered with old newspapers and junk of every description. 'Mad Barry', as he was called, was a well-known street pest, who used to follow attractive women around in the streets, and photograph them clandestinely. He had a liking for celebrities, and frequently changed his name by deed poll in order to fraudulently claim kinship with people like Paul Gadd (the now notorious 'Gary Glitter'), SAS soldier Thomas Palmer, actor Lee Majors, and Freddie Mercury (whose real name was Bulsara). 'Mad Barry' had previous convictions for attempted rape, indecent assault (twice) and impersonating a police officer. The police were shocked to find out that he had been an admirer of Diana, Princess of Wales, and that he had once been discovered hiding in bushes near Kensington Palace, dressed in combat gear, and carrying a knife and a length of rope.

The evidence against Barry George was that he was a stalker with an interest in celebrities, and that he had once belonged to the Territorials and knew how to handle firearms. In a bizarre photograph, a man alleged to be him is wearing a gas mask and brandishing a pistol. One witness identified him as the man she had seen in Gowan Avenue earlier in the morning on the day Jill Dando was murdered. Employees of a benefits office, and of a taxicab firm nearby, had seen 'Mad Barry' later on the day of the murder. The following day he had returned, trying to convince them to give him an alibi for the murder. A particle found on his coat matched microscopic firearm discharge residue found on Jill Dando. This latter circumstance was given very considerable importance when Barry George was on trial at the Old Bailey. On a majority vote, he was convicted of murder and sentenced to life imprisonment.

However, there are also strong arguments in favour of Barry George's innocence. Although he was a stalker of women, there is nothing to suggest that he had a fixation with Jill Dando. There is no evidence that he owned a firearm or ammunition. The 'crimping' of the murder ammunition would surely have been beyond him. Would a man of such low intellect (the bottom 1 per cent of the population) be able to commit the perfect murder, and would a man of such fragile mental health (he suffered from Asperger's syndrome, anxiety and panic attacks) be able to keep quiet about it and protest his innocence with such impressive candour? As for the woman who picked him out as the man she had seen in Gowan Avenue the day of the murder, she had previously given a description of this individual that did not fit Barry George at all. Neither of the two witnesses who actually saw the killer could identify Barry George. It is of course a damning circumstance that several witnesses claimed that Barry tried to persuade them to concoct an alibi for him, but as author Scott Lomax has argued Barry was a known sex offender and had previously been questioned in the investigation of the murder of Rachel Nickell. Perhaps Barry felt paranoid and was fearful of being 'framed' by the police? The particle on his coat is another damning circumstance, but its importance has been challenged: it might have come from fireworks that Barry had collected, it might have been the result of armed police entering his flat, and it might have been the result of contamination. As a result of these doubts, particularly with regard to the origins of the suspected firearms discharge residue, Barry George was freed after a retrial in 2008. After emerging from prison, 'Mad Barry' gave an exclusive interview to *News of the World*, saying that at the time of the murder of Jill Dando he had been busy stalking another woman. Being a street pest did not make him a murderer, he argued. He must have been annoyed when this notorious (and fortunately now defunct) newspaper referred to him as a 'bug-eyed oddball' and in other terms of disrespect. Helped by his loyal sister, Barry has been able to stay out of trouble since his release. He is still attempting to obtain compensation for the eight years he spent behind bars.

If Barry George did not murder Jill Dando, then who did? Was the murder the result of a skilfully carried out covert operation, in which one agent monitored the Chiswick house, letting the part of the team staking out Gowan Avenue know that Jill Dando was coming? In his memoirs, Barry George's defence council Michael Mansfield claimed that someone in a bar in Bosnia had admitted carrying out the killing in revenge for the NATO bombing of a Belgrade TV station during the Balkans war. He also suggested a place in Eastern Europe where the unusual, crimped bullet that killed Jill Dando could have been made. I regard it as ruled out that a Serb team of hitmen had been sent to Britain to murder Jill Dando. It remains possible, however, that a small team of Serb 'moles', already resident in Britain, had been given an official or unofficial order to strike against the BBC. After the Kosovo appeal, they decided to murder Jill Dando. Then they returned to their own country, some dying in the war and the survivor bragging in a Bosnian bar about his great adventure in Fulham.

Still, the murder of Jill Dando is connected with some even greater mysteries. Could a gang of Serbs really carry out such skilful murder without attracting attention to their foreign nationality? The front gate of No. 29 Gowan Avenue only had fingerprints from people who knew Jill Dando, yet there is nothing to suggest that the killer wore gloves. How could a stranger know that the hedge in her front garden was the perfect place to hide? Why did her neighbour describe her scream as one of 'surprise' rather than one of fear; was it because she saw some person she knew, and did not suspect they had any hostile intent? Had a secret enemy of Jill Dando set up a meeting with her at No. 29 Gowan Avenue, and waited for her there with murder in mind?[24]

Jill Dando's house at No. 29 Gowan Avenue was sold for £400,000 just a few days before the murder; the thoughts of the purchasers when they realised they had just become the owners of one of London's most notorious murder houses have not been recorded. Still, they lived at the premises for a number of years, occasionally troubled by journalists but never by ghosts or revenants. In a later interview, the current inhabitant of No. 29 described the house as having a happy and serene atmosphere, not one of murder and bloodshed. Rather understandably, no person was keen to move into Barry George's dump of a flat at No. 2B Crookham Road, and it stood empty for many years. People's memories are short, however, and I note that it now has a tenant.

Murder at Upper Cheyne Row, 2004

Elliot White was a young black man, a drug addict living in London's criminal underworld. Since he had accumulated considerable debts, the drug dealers had 'put out a contract' on him, and he had to keep moving between various squats and hostels to prevent being called on by some very unpleasant people. In November 2004, the only good news for White was that his friend Damien Hanson had just got out of jail. A very dangerous man, Hanson had once been sentenced to twelve years in prison for attempted murder, but he had got out after serving half his term. The two villains, who shared the predicament of being as poor as church mice, made plans to change this state of affairs. Hanson had an obsession with rich people, and in prison he had been collecting press cuttings about wealthy women and their jewellery. No close student of gemmology, he considered the 'green 'uns' the most precious stones, worth £20,000 or more. Hanson also made notes of the registration numbers of expensive cars he saw in the street, and then found out where their owners lived. Full of hate against London's affluent upper class, the two villains spent much time discussing whom they should rob first. Their choice was the wealthy banker John Monckton and his family.

The forty-nine-year-old John Monckton had enjoyed a distinguished banking career, becoming the Managing Director of Bonds at Legal & General PLC. A Roman Catholic, he devoted much time to charity work. He lived in an elegant end-of-terrace Georgian house at No. 30 Upper Cheyne Row, Belgravia, with his wife Homeyra and younger daughter Isabelle; his elder daughter boarded at her public school. This was one of London's most fashionable and expensive streets: the Marquess of Blandford, Bill Wyman, Felicity Kendal, George Best and Sol Campbell all lived near the Moncktons.

On 30 November 2004, the bell rang at No. 30 Upper Cheyne Row. When Mrs Monckton made use of the intercom, the caller said he had a parcel for John Monckton, and the banker went downstairs to get it. Through the spyhole, Monckton could see a black man dressed as a postman with a parcel in his hand. However, when he opened the door, Damien Hanson, who had been crouching down, burst into the house. Elliot White, who had acted the part of the postman, seized hold of Monckton as Hanson pursued Mrs Monckton upstairs brandishing a long knife. He grabbed her, threatened her with the knife, and stole her money and jewellery. When she tried to run upstairs to reach the panic button, he stabbed her twice in the back. When he heard his wife scream, Monckton desperately tried to break free, giving White a couple of hard knocks in the face, but the pseudo-postman managed to hang on with a powerful bear hug. When the wild-eyed Hanson came dashing downstairs, he stabbed Monckton hard five times, and the banker fell to the ground. The two villains were observed by several people as they fled through the quiet Belgravia streets to reach their getaway car. A neighbour heard White praise Hanson with the words, 'You're the business!'

From the second floor, the Moncktons' nine-year-old daughter Isabelle had been a witness to the attack on her mother. Wisely, she did not scream and run downstairs; if she had done so, her life expectancy might well have been counted in seconds when facing the frenzied, knife-wielding intruder. After the villains had left, she sounded the alarm and called 999. Swift and competent medical attention saved the life of Mrs Monckton, whose stab wounds to the lungs had been near fatal. John Monckton himself had died on the spot, from a stab right through the heart.

In the meantime, the two villains had made a clean getaway. They needed to change their clothes, and went to some wasteland to burn the garments they had worn during the murder and robbery. Foolishly, they set fire to the clothes quite close to some houses, and witnesses observed them running away from the fire. The fire brigade swiftly extinguished the blaze, allowing the police to gather valuable evidence. Blood from both Moncktons were found on the clothes. The girl Isabelle had made a drawing of a motif on the murderer's jacket; it exactly matched one found in the fire.

After ditching their clothes, White and Hanson went to refresh themselves with a hearty meal at a fast-food restaurant. White complained that his arm hurt, and requested a plaster, but when he pulled up his sleeve, blood was pouring from a recent stab wound; the frenzied Hanson had knifed his own partner by mistake. When they read about the murder, the observant restaurant staff alerted the police, and valuable CCTV footage of the two men was secured. Even in 2004, London was full of CCTV cameras, which the police found very useful when it came to detailing the movements of White and Hanson on the day of the murder. Both villains were arrested on 15 December. When questioned by the police, the tough Hanson did not say a word, but White soon 'sang like a bird', admitting being present at the robbery but blaming his partner for everything.

At the Old Bailey, Elliot White was sentenced to eighteen years in prison for manslaughter, wounding with intent, and robbery. Damien Hanson was sentenced to life imprisonment, and the judge recommended that he should serve at least thirty-six years in prison. This was one of the heaviest minimum sentences in British legal history, but very well deserved. Hanson will not emerge from prison until 2041, at the age of sixty-one, so wealthy Londoners will be safe from him for the corresponding period of time.[25]

The murder of John Monckton took place before wealthy bankers had become objects of detestation for many 'ordinary people'. Back in 2004, there was nothing but sympathy for the blameless Monckton and his family, and nothing but indignation for the two callous black thugs who had brutally ended his life. That a wealthy gentleman living in a £3-million house, in one of the most prestigious streets of the metropolis, was not safe inside his own home was a worrying reflection for many rich Londoners. Fearful of the criminal underclass, they spent money on CCTV cameras, alarms, and iron doors and grilles, and kept cricket bats and Rottweilers in readiness. Upper Cheyne Row still remains a very expensive and sought-after London street, and the murder house at No. 30 appears to be well looked after.

4

Bloomsbury, Holborn, St Pancras and Camden Town

There are secret chambers in London houses still, the mystery of which has yet to be revealed; some which may remain undiscovered, to be 'mysteries' in the daily press fifty or sixty years hence. The bricked-up cellar that thrills us in the pages of Edgar Allan Poe is playing its part in the criminal tragedies of the modern Babylon.

George R. Sims, *Mysteries of Modern London*

In Victorian times, the part of Bloomsbury and St Pancras bordered by Gower Street, Euston Road, Grey's Inn Road and the British Museum was referred to as the 'Murder Neighbourhood'. Mysterious murders of women, many of them unsolved, abounded in this strange area of flyblown old lodging houses. No. 12 Great Coram Street, where the prostitute Harriet Buswell was murdered by an unknown assailant on Christmas Eve 1872, was one of the most notorious murder houses of its time. After the murder, the house was reported to be haunted; all the tenants moved out, and the house was put up for sale. Miss Sarah Elizabeth Stride saw a good business opportunity in a house that no one else wanted to occupy; she bought it for a song and transformed it into Miss Stride's Home for Destitute Girls and Fallen Women. According to Elliott O'Donnell, the haunting continued for several decades; the second-floor back room, where the murder had been committed, was always kept locked, due to the eerie, unworldly sounds emanating from it at night.[1] The haunted house at No. 12 Great Coram Street stood for many decades to come, even after the street was renamed Coram Street in 1901. In 1912, a woman named Annie Gross shot her rival Jessie Mackintosh dead in the lodging house at No. 2 Coram Street. Both murder houses are gone today, victims of the construction of mansion

Some of Bloomsbury's houses of mystery: the murder houses at No. 4 Euston Square, No. 12 Great Coram Street and No. 4 Burton Crescent, from Ladbroke Black's serial on 'Famous Mysteries' in *Lloyd's Weekly News*, Oct.–Dec. 1907.

flats. No. 53 Whitfield Street, where Elizabeth Stoffel was murdered in 1891, no longer stands; nor does No. 8 in the same street, where the servant girl Sophie Richard was murdered in 1899; or No. 115 Whitfield Street, site of the unsolved murder of the prostitute Dora Piernicke in December 1903.

Cartwright Gardens is today a quiet Bloomsbury backwater, home to a variety of respectable hotels, but in Victorian times it was called Burton Crescent and was situated just at the epicentre of the Murder Neighbourhood. The street name was changed in 1908 because of the unsolved murders of two women: old Mrs Samuels at No. 4 in 1878 and the prostitute Annie Yates at No. 12 in 1884. According to Elliott O'Donnell, both murder houses were haunted at the time, although the ghosts lacked the persistence of the spectre of Harriet Buswell.[2] These two murder houses were later victims of the expansion of the University of London's halls of residence, which destroyed the entire eastern terrace of Cartwright Gardens. Another notorious murder house in these parts was not far away: No. 4 Euston Square, where the elderly spinster Matilda Hacker was found murdered in the coal cellar in 1879. Although the servant girl Hannah Dobbs stood trial for the murder, she was acquitted, and Miss Hacker's murder remains unavenged. The murder house again acquired a very sinister reputation: it was reported to be haunted, and strange groans and screams were heard in Miss Hacker's old room. The bloodstain on the floorboards in the murder room could not be removed by any amount of scrubbing, and no dog would pass this room of horrors without snarling and whining, and giving indications of intense terror.[3] Still, the haunted house stood for several decades before becoming a victim of the reconstruction of Euston station in the 1960s. Some old houses in the southern part of Euston Square, which was renamed Endsleigh Gardens as a result of the murder, still stand.

Throwing a Woman out of the Window, 1872

On Boxing Day 1870, the forty-two-year-old Hungarian meerschaum pipe case maker Martin Janoska, his common-law wife Louisa, and his friend the twenty-six-year-old German pocketbook maker Charles Piker went out for some fun. They had some drinks, went to the theatre, and then had some more drinks before returning to the Janoskas' lodgings on the first floor of No. 40 Bloomsbury Street at just before eleven in the evening. The other lodgers in the house were woken up by their noisy revelling. All of a sudden, there was an outcry as Louisa Janoska was precipitated from the first-floor window onto the pavement below. Only one witness actually saw her fall, but several heard the heavy thud when she landed on her head. Her jaw was broken and her skull fractured, and, although a police constable took her to the university hospital nearby, she expired soon after.

The police took Martin Janoska and Charles Piker into custody. At the Bow Street Police Court, they were charged with throwing Louisa Janoska out of the window. They denied the charge, saying that they had all been drunk, and that she must have fallen down. Janoska said that he had lived happily with his wife, and that he had no motive to murder her. On New Year's Day 1873, the inquest on the twenty-seven-year-old Louisa Janoska was held at the university hospital. She was of English descent, as verified by her mother Elizabeth Elgar. She also said that Louisa had lived in fear of her husband, who was known for his fierce and angry temper. A police constable testified that after he had arrested Janoska and Piker the latter had exclaimed, 'It's not my fault, it's yours!' Janoska had retorted, 'You say nothing!' and placed his hand over his friend's mouth. However, a woman living across the street, who had seen Louisa fall, testified that she had seen no other person at the window.

In the meantime, the police detectives tried some lateral thinking. As we know, the prostitute Harriet Buswell had been murdered at No. 12 Great Coram Street on Christmas Eve, and the murderer was thought to have been a foreigner. Here we had two very dodgy foreigners, who had quite possibly murdered a woman on Boxing Day! It attracted notice that, when the two men had been charged with murder, Janoska had exclaimed, 'My wife went into the front room. I know nothing about it!' He had then turned to Piker, shouting, 'If you are the murderer, speak! You have only known her 24 hours!' The police seriously suspected that Charles Piker had murdered Harriet Buswell. The room at No. 40 Bloomsbury Street was closely searched, as were Piker's own lodgings and wardrobe, but without anything suspicious coming to light. A fruit seller who had seen Harriet Buswell together with the man presumed to be her murderer ruled out Piker as a suspect, because he was much shorter than Harriet's 'customer'. Still, not all students of the Great Coram Street mystery agree that the person seen with Harriet prior to her murder was really the same man who murdered her.

The jurymen still thought there was considerable suspicion against the two foreigners for murdering Louisa Janoska, however. The foreman requested that the coroner should communicate with the Home Secretary to obtain permission to have the two men brought before the coroner's jury for questioning. The Home Secretary replied that this could not be done, and an open verdict was returned. Janoska and Piker returned to well-deserved obscurity, and Louisa's tragic death remains a mystery to this day, as does the Great Coram Street murder of Harriet Buswell.[4]

The Gray's Inn Road Mystery, 1887

In 1887, the situation in life for the sixty-seven-year-old street hawker Frank Fyfield was not an enviable one. He had been blind for several years, and was lame in one leg. For years, he had been in and out of various asylums and other institutions: the 1881 census gives his address as St Pancras workhouse. In 1887, however, he was out of the workhouse, living in a tiny basement room at No. 139 Gray's Inn Road with his wife Ann. Frank's main pleasure in life was drinking beer and gin. Although as poor as the proverbial church mouse, he spent every penny he could lay his hands on on purchasing strong drink. Ann shared his partiality for the bottle. An angry, quarrelsome woman even when sober, she became a perfect virago when drunk. At times, Frank tried to discipline her with his fists, but he was hampered by his sightless condition, which allowed her to dodge him with impunity. Once she cracked him hard on the head with a gin bottle; another time, she set a dog at him, and he had to spend several weeks in hospital.

On 5 May 1887, Frank and Ann went to the Old King's Arms public house in Gray's Inn Road. They were both drunk and jolly, and although Ann had a black eye they seemed to get along quite well. They both swigged hard from their glasses for some time, before reeling out at twenty minutes past midnight. Ann brought some gin with her in a bottle. When the Fyfields came home, they started quarrelling angrily. The landlord at No. 139, Mr Charles Lee, was used to their rowdy behaviour; in fact, he had many times admonished them in the past, although with little effect. After half an hour or so, the Fyfields finally stopped their racket, and for a few hours peace returned to the long-suffering residents of No. 139. At five in the morning, all hell broke loose in the basement room, however. Ann screamed loudly, and Frank began cursing her. The dog gave a howl and ran upstairs, as if it had been struck by some person. Frank kept on incoherently damning and blasting his wife for not less than two hours. Knowing about the Fyfields' drunken and violent habits, none of the other lodgers interfered.

When Mrs Maria Tilbury, who lodged on the second floor, was going downstairs in the early morning, a dishevelled-looking Frank hailed her and said that all was not well with his wife. Indeed, she was quite dead, lying on her back. When Mrs Tilbury asked why her face was bruised and discoloured, Frank said that she had 'knocked herself about' when drunk. She did not believe him, calling out to another lodger, 'Mr Fox, the blind man has done it this time!' The police were called in, and Frank Fyfield taken into custody.

The autopsy revealed that Ann Fyfield had nine ribs broken on the left side, and eight ribs broken on the right. These injuries were not, as medical experts confidently (and rightly) testified, consistent with her falling down and injuring herself, but rather with some person kicking, or rather kneeling hard on, the wretched woman. At the coroner's inquest, Frank was charged with the wilful murder of his wife. On trial at the Old Bailey, the drunken old man had sobered up, and the alcoholic fumes had cleared from what remained of his brain. As a consequence, he gave a slightly better impression in court. Several people testified that he had been quite fond of his wife, and that her behaviour had at times been quite intolerable. It is questionable whether the damning medical evidence against him was understood by the jury. Perhaps they felt pity for the pathetic old man whose life had been so very miserable. As a result, Frank was found guilty only of manslaughter. Believing that he was going to be executed for murder, the muddled Frank cried out, 'I am not guilty! I am not guilty! Have mercy on a poor old man!' He was sentenced to just eighteen months in prison: the judge clearly did not value the life of drunken old Ann Fyfield very highly.[5] It is not known whether Frank was allowed to return to No. 139 Grey's Inn Road after his release, nor what ultimately happened to the old man, except that a Frank Fyfield died at Lambeth in 1892. The murder house still remains today, and appears to be well cared for.

The Murder House in Priory Street, 1890

Mary Eleanor Wheeler, a sinister young woman if there ever was one, was born in Ightham, Kent, in March 1866. Her family moved to Stepney soon after and she spent her youth in East London. After her father's death in 1882, her mother went to Kentish Town, where Mary Eleanor found work at a sealskin factory. In 1885, she became the common-law wife of the carpenter John Charles Pearcey, adopting his name. She cohabited with Pearcey for three years before she became the mistress of a well-to-do local businessman named Charles Creighton. In September 1888, he installed her in the ground-floor flat at No. 2 Priory (now Ivor) Street, Kentish Town. Contemporary accounts agree that, in spite of her indifferent moral qualities, Mary Eleanor was a quite attractive young woman, with long russet hair, fine blue eyes and regular features.

Mr Creighton, who was probably 'running' other mistresses as well, used to visit Mary Eleanor on Monday evenings, and sometimes during the weekends. Since she no longer worked, this arrangement left her with plenty of spare time. She had a piano in her front room, which she learnt to play. She befriended some of the neighbours, particularly the family of a grocer named Hogg, who lived in Prince of Wales Road nearby. She became fond of Frank, the son of the family, who worked as an assistant in the grocer's shop, and gave him the key to No. 2 Priory Street. Frank knew that Mary Eleanor was a 'kept woman' and made sure he stayed away from her flat on Mondays.

As time went by, Mary Eleanor became increasingly fond of Frank. It is difficult to discern what she saw in him, since he was described as a

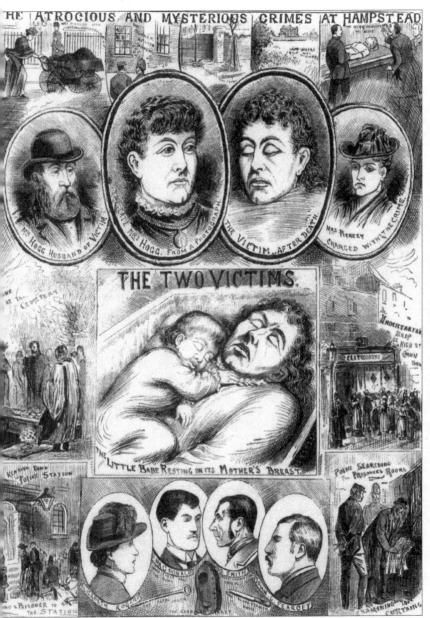

Portraits of all the main players in the Pearcey case, living or dead; from the *Illustrated Police News*, 8 November 1890.

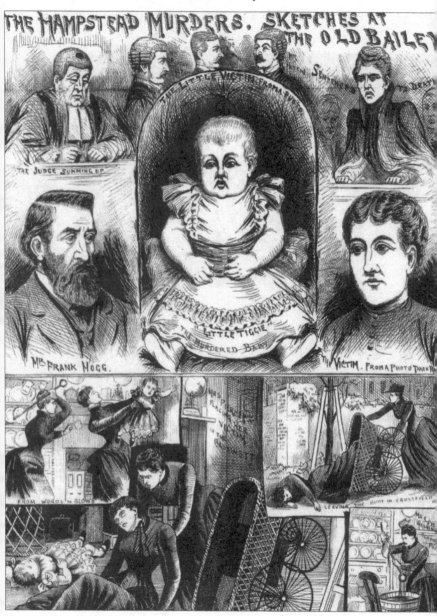

The Hoggs, baby Tiggie, and a reconstruction of the murder, from the *Illustrated Police News*, 13 December 1890.

common-looking little man, with a large unkempt beard, a woebegone appearance, and ill-fitting clothes. Nor was his career in life exactly a success story: after the family lost their grocery, he had to work as a furniture-carrier, relying on the kindness of his elder brother who owned a removal business. Frank's moral qualities were also found wanting: apart from visiting Mary Eleanor at No. 2 Priory Street, he was also 'walking out' with an accommodating young woman named Phoebe Styles. When Phoebe 'got in the family way' in November 1888, Frank felt obliged to marry her. They moved into lodgings at No. 141 Prince of Wales Road, and in April 1889 their little daughter Phoebe Hanslope, called 'Tiggie', was born.

Later in 1889, when Phoebe Hogg fell ill, Frank suggested that Mary Eleanor should nurse her. This unconventional arrangement seems to have had the desired effect, since Mary Eleanor took her duties seriously, and even bought fresh milk and eggs for the patient, who gradually recovered. Although Phoebe was hardly the most perceptive of women, she began to suspect that Frank had been motivated by immoral purposes, rather than concern for her own well-being, when he allowed Mary Eleanor to join their household. She deserted her worthless husband and moved out of No. 141 Prince of Wales Road, rejoining her own family and taking baby Tiggie with her. It was not until her brother had persuaded her that she could not afford a divorce, and that her reputation would suffer if she left Frank, that Phoebe was reunited with her cad of a husband.

In late 1890, Mary Eleanor became increasingly infatuated with Frank. Although he still visited her regularly, she sent him many love letters, begging him to come more frequently. Hogg, however, was under pressure from his family to stay with Phoebe and little Tiggie. He thought of going away, but did not have the willpower to do so. On 23 October 1890, Mary Eleanor paid a boy to take a note to No. 141 Prince of Wales Road inviting Phoebe to come round for tea, and to bring the baby. Phoebe did not come, but when there was a similar message the following day she put baby Tiggie in a large perambulator, left a note for Frank saying, 'Shall not be gone long', and walked to No. 2 Priory Street, arriving around 4 p.m. Not long after, the next-door neighbour heard glass breaking. She called out to Mary Eleanor, but there was no response, and the kitchen blinds were down. The upstairs neighbour at No. 2 heard a baby scream, and later what sounded like several people walking around and moving things about.

The evening of 23 October was cold and quite foggy. Still, several witnesses saw Mary Eleanor wheeling the large perambulator through the streets. Some of them added that, although she was pushing with all her might, she had great difficulty moving the heavily laden vehicle. Nevertheless, the white-faced, breathless woman kept on pushing the perambulator through the endless streets, until she had reached Belsize Park more than 2 miles away. In an area where some houses had recently been erected, by the crossing of Adamson Street and Crossfield Street, she emptied the perambulator of its contents. The overloaded vehicle had broken, so she left it behind in a side street, before walking home. Another witness saw the exhausted Mary Eleanor return to No. 2 Priory Street, reeling as if she was going to fall over at any moment.

Later the same evening, the corpses of a young woman and a baby were found near Adamson Road. Miss Clara Hogg, Frank's sister, saw the description in the newspaper, and suspected that this unidentified woman might be her missing sister-in-law. Although her relatives pooh-poohed her concerns, she wanted to have a look at the bodies. Mary Eleanor went with her to the mortuary. When the two women were taken into the presence of Phoebe Hogg's corpse, Mary Eleanor cried out, 'It is not her! It is not her! Let us go!' and made to pull Clara Hogg away. After a closer inspection, though, Clara identified the body as that of her missing sister-in-law, and proceeded to identify the baby and the perambulator as well. Mary Eleanor's strange behaviour had attracted notice, and after the two women had been taken home in a cab the police kept watch on her house to make sure she did not escape. They found Frank Hogg, who collapsed when he heard his wife was dead, exclaiming that he knew that he himself was partly to fault. He then told them all about his illicit romance with Mary Eleanor.

Later the same day, the police raided No. 2 Priory Street. Mary Eleanor let them in without demur. She sat by the piano in the front room, playing the piano loudly as the detectives inspected her kitchen. They found plenty of bloodstains on the walls, and signs that the floor had been recently cleaned. Mary Eleanor told them that she had been killing mice, but to produce such extensive bloodstaining would have required a veritable massacre of the murine tribe. Her hands were much scratched and bruised from a recent violent struggle. She was duly arrested, and at the coroner's inquest a verdict of wilful murder was returned against her.

On trial at the Old Bailey before Mr Justice Denman, on 24 November 1890, Mrs Pearcey's solicitor Freke Palmer and her barrister Mr Hutton did their best to save their client. The mass of evidence against her was too impressive, however, and an attempt to play the 'insanity card' did not have the desired effect. In his summing-up, Mr Justice Denman was severe on Frank Hogg, saying that no man had ever given himself a viler or more loathsome character. After an absence of an hour, the jury returned a verdict of guilty, and Mr Justice Denman sentenced Mrs Pearcey to death.[6]

There was a fair bit of sympathy for Mrs Pearcey in London society, resulting from squeamishness rather than from doubts about her guilt: surely, they reasoned, it was barbaric to execute an attractive young woman. Freke Palmer made a final attempt to save his client, by demanding that she should be examined by the controversial alienist Forbes Winslow. Instead, three other doctors visited Mrs Pearcey in Newgate, at the orders of the Home Secretary: their verdict was that she was definitely sane. On 22 December, Mrs Pearcey was visited one final time by her mother and her younger sister Charlotte Amy. She sent a letter to Clara Hogg absolving Frank Hogg from complicity in the murder. He had a rock-solid alibi, having been hard at work the entire afternoon, as verified by a number of witnesses. Mary Eleanor was very keen to see her dear Frank one final time, but true to his character the coward refused to meet her. When urged to confess by the prison chaplain, she said, 'The sentence is just, but the evidence was false.' She desired Freke Palmer to place an advertisement in a Madrid newspaper, with the enigmatic words, 'Last wish of M. E. W. Have not betrayed.' When asked what she was alluding to, she said it was a secret marriage she had pledged herself never to reveal.

Mary Eleanor Pearcey was executed on 23 December 1890. Guy Logan and other crime historians have not doubted her guilt, but there has been suspicion that another person had been involved in the murder. In particular, the canny Guy questioned how, alone and unaided, Mrs Pearcey had been able to pack the dead body in the perambulator with the presumably still-living child. However, people *in extremis* sometimes have surprising strength, and the perambulator was the only chance for the desperate woman to dispose of her victims.

Mrs Pearcey awaiting her doom, and a sketch of the murder house, from the *Illustrated Police News*, 20 December 1890.

Execution of the ill-fated Mrs Pearcey, from the *Illustrated Police News*, 27 December 1890.

Two other sketches of the Priory Street murder house, from *Lloyd's Weekly Newspaper*, 26 October 1890, and from *Famous Crimes Past & Present*.

Since the creature Hogg had a rock-sold alibi, amateur criminologists have cast a wide net to find alternative accomplices for Mary Eleanor. It has been speculated that she belonged to a gang of burglars, or alternatively to a secret society of Spanish anarchists (or occultists), and that Phoebe Hogg had been murdered after she had threatened to denounce them. Other conspiracy lovers have implicated the mysterious first husband of Mary Eleanor, whom she married secretly at the age of just sixteen, and who later deserted her and presumably went to Madrid. These speculations have little foundation in fact, however. The motive for the murder was clearly Mary Eleanor's passion for Frank Hogg, and her jealousy of Phoebe. It is notable that she murdered also the innocent little Tiggie, who could not denounce any secret societies; she wanted to destroy not just Phoebe Hogg, but her progeny as well. As Mary Eleanor herself confessed to a wardress, the murder had not been premeditated, but the product of a sudden fury after the two women had quarrelled angrily.

In 1937, Priory Street changed its name to Ivor Street, for reasons unconnected with the murder. Guy Logan called this part of Kentish Town 'as dull, ugly, and lugubrious a portion of London as any I know', but Guy was fortunate to have been spared the horrors of 1960s and 1970s architecture. Indeed, today the relatively isolated area near the Camden Road railway station has a certain old-world attraction, with its cobbled streets and well-kept little terraced houses. When doing some murder house detection in the relevant archives, I noticed that the numbering of the houses on the north side of Ivor Street was more than a little odd. It began with 1, 1A, 2 and 2A, and 3, 4 and so on. Was this an attempt to disguise the identity of the murder house? No, it clearly was not, since three contemporary illustrations clearly show that Mary Eleanor Pearcey's house is the present-day No. 2 Ivor Street: a well-kept house subdivided into flats, still with the characteristic small cast-iron balconies intact. According to a now defunct Internet page, a former resident of the ground-floor flat found it to be haunted by the sound of a child screaming and bloodstains mysteriously appearing on the wall. She called the local vicar to have a ceremony of exorcism performed, and the haunting ceased.

Murder in Jeffery Street, 1891

The forty-nine-year-old William Else was a cab driver living at No. 11 Jeffery Street, Kentish Town, with his wife and two daughters. In February 1891, he fell out of his cab and was run over by another vehicle, breaking his leg. Even after three months in a convalescent home, he still had to walk on crutches and was unable to work. Since Else had some money saved, the family did not face destitution, but their future was not looking particularly bright.

On 2 June 1891, the eldest daughter of the Else family, thirteen-year-old Nellie, was woken up by her father, who said that he wanted to feel her throat. When she saw that he had a large knife in his hand, she leapt out of bed and fled the house. The police later found the body of Mrs Else in the front parlour, and that of seven-year-old Alice in the kitchen. William Else had cut their throats with his knife, before going out into the garden and cutting his own throat herself. Poor Nellie, who had secured such a narrow escape from her murderous father, had her entire family wiped out in one blow. A journalist found it sinister that Jeffery Street, where these sanguinary outrages had taken place, was situated next to Priory (now Ivor) Street, where the murderous Mrs Pearcey had been at large the previous year.[7]

The Camden Town Murder, 1907

Emily Elizabeth Dimmock was born in Standon, Hertfordshire, where her father kept the Red Lion public house. At the age of eleven, she was knocked down by a horse in Hitchin and spent some time in hospital; it was presumed that the head injury resulting from this accident had affected her mind to some degree. Unlike her brothers and sisters, Emily did not go on to become an honest, hard-working member of the lower classes. It is sad but true that she moved to London and became a prostitute, operating in the King's Cross and Euston districts. She was not particularly fastidious when it came to selecting her late-night partners, catching venereal disease more than once, and passing it on to her other partners.

In 1906, 'Phyllis' Dimmock, as she called herself, acquired a permanent boyfriend, the railway cook Bert Shaw, who worked on board the London–Sheffield express. She moved into the two rooms he was renting at No. 29 St Paul's Road (today Agar Grove). He does not seem to have minded that Phyllis kept prostituting herself when he was away working on the trains. She was a regular at the Rising Sun in Euston Road and the Eagle in Great College Street, among other public houses where she could meet her 'gentleman friends'. A busy, low-class prostitute, she was taking quite a few risks, consorting with all kinds of riff-raff. Still, Bert Shaw was keen to maintain a facade of respectability. He got his 'wife' a piano and a sewing machine, and their landlady had no idea that the nice 'Mrs Shaw' was in the habit of smuggling various dodgy blokes into the house for casual sex.

In the evening of 11 September 1907, Phyllis Dimmock went down to her 'local', the Eagle at the corner of Great College Street and Camden Road. She looked down-at-heel and had her hair in curling papers. The following morning, Bert's mother came to visit him and Phyllis at No. 29 St Paul's Road. Phyllis was supposed to have met her at Euston station, but since she was nowhere to be seen Mrs Shaw had to make her own way to No. 29, where she was later joined by Bert, who had just come off duty on the Sheffield express. Although they knocked at the door,

Above: Finding the body of Phyllis Dimmock, from the *Illustrated Police News*, 21 September 1907.

Right: Drawings of the main players in the Camden Town drama, and also a sketch of the murder house, from the *Illustrated Police News*, 21 December 1907.

A drawing of Robert Wood, from B. Hogarth (ed.), *The Trial of Robert Wood* (London, 1936).

Phyllis did not open. Bert borrowed a key from the landlady and entered the flat. Phyllis was lying on the bed quite naked, her throat cut from ear to ear, and the windpipe completely severed.

The police were promptly called, and the crime scene examined. It turned out that Phyllis Dimmock had been murdered after having sex, presumably with one of her 'customers'. Her throat had been cut with great force when she had been asleep. Nothing had been stolen from the flat. In the fireplace was a postcard that some person had tried to burn, although only with partial success. Bert Shaw, the 'obvious suspect', had a rock-solid alibi from his railwayman colleagues, and he could be eliminated from the murder inquiry at a very early stage.

Instead, the police made a trawl of the regulars from the Rising Sun and Eagle pubs, and various other dodgy coves in the Euston and Camden Town districts: pimps, brothel-keepers, violent criminals, and street roughs of every description. Many old customers of Phyllis were tracked down, several of whom had caught venereal disease from her. The brothel-keeper John William Crabtree pointed his finger at a man in a blue suit who had been a long-time customer of Phyllis Dimmock. He had quarrelled with her, possibly because she had infected him with venereal disease, and once he had assaulted her and threatened to kill her. There was also a certain 'Scotch Bob' who had once threatened to do Phyllis harm.

In Edwardian times, sending and collecting picture postcards was highly fashionable. Even the humble prostitute Phyllis Dimmock had several albums of cards. A man named Roberts testified that Phyllis had shown him two cards sent to her by the same person, one of which contained an invitation to meet the sender at the Rising Sun. When the police searched her albums, this particular card was not found. Fortunately, Bert Shaw later found it and handed it in to the police. It had the text: 'Phillis darling. If it pleases you to meet me at 8.15 at the [impression of a rising sun]. Yours to a cinder, Alice.' The sun had clearly been drawn by a person with some degree of artistic talent.

The police suspected that this mysterious 'Alice' was in fact the murderer, who had tried to destroy the other postcard he had sent, but overlooked the 'Rising Sun' one. Inspector Neal smartly decided to release a photograph of the 'Rising Sun' card to the press. A certain Ruby Young, a beautiful 'artist's model' (euphemism for high-class prostitute) living at No. 13 Finsborough Road, Kensington, came forward to denounce her former boyfriend Robert Wood as the writer of the postcard. She clearly recognised his handwriting and style of drawing, she said. Piling sensation upon sensation, she also said that Robert Wood had asked her to provide an alibi for him for the evening of the murder!

It turned out that, outwardly at least, Robert Wood was a respectable middle-class man, employed as a designer of glass tiles and stained-glass windows. After ditching his girlfriend Ruby, he had led a dissolute life, consorting with various low-class prostitutes, one of them Phyllis Dimmock. Plus, Phyllis had clearly been murdered by a person she had known well, since she had gone to sleep and showed no suspicion that she was in danger from her partner.

After Ruby Young had identified Robert Wood to the police, he was taken into custody. Several witnesses identified him as the man they had seen leaving the Rising Sun with Phyllis the evening of the murder. A man named McCowan identified Wood as the person he had seen leaving No. 29 St Paul's Road the night of the murder, but only from the way that he walked. Some witnesses, the helpful Ruby Young prominent among them, agreed that Wood had a strange style of walking, whereas others had found nothing peculiar about his style of locomotion.

Robert Wood had the good fortune of being defended by the brilliant Edward Marshall Hall, who was convinced that he was entirely innocent. Marshall Hall immediately seized upon the weaknesses in the prosecution evidence. Ruby Young was clearly a 'woman scorned', and the quality of their fury and long-mindedness was apparent to every student of plays from the Restoration era. Even if her story of providing an alibi for Wood was true, could it not be that, after the murder, the glass designer had become fearful of becoming involved in the murder investigation, something that would have damaged his reputation? The man McCowan was badly shaken by a hostile cross-examination: he had been untruthful about the state of the street lighting, and was it not absurd to rely on the identification of a man in peril of his life by the way that he walked?

Robert Wood, who was something of a strange character, did not seem to grasp the seriousness of his situation. As Marshall Hall was fighting for his life, Wood amused himself by drawing funny cartoons, including a series of portraits of the people in court. When Marshall Hall asked Wood to testify on his own behalf, however, he gave quite a good impression. Although he may have appeared cruel and selfish when he referred to the murdered woman as 'Dimmock' and denied that a ring he had bought for Ruby Young had any meaning of betrothal, he certainly did not seem like a conniving murderer. The newspapers printed a garbled account of the case, with Wood as the wrongly accused hero, Marshall Hall as his champion, and Ruby Young as the wicked Jezebel perjuring herself in court. Due to this biased reporting, there was great jubilation when the jury delivered a verdict of 'not guilty' after deliberating for just fifteen minutes.[8]

For Ruby Young, the outcome of the trial was a disaster. After Robert Wood had been acquitted, she had to disguise herself as a charwoman to be able to escape the Central Criminal Court, outside which a raucous mob was chanting, 'Ruby, Ruby, won't you come out tonight?' In the pubs, a song beginning

> Ruby Young, Ruby Young,
> Should be hung by the Rising Sun ...

was performed to great acclaim. Ruby left her lodgings at No. 13 Finsborough Road, changed her name and left the country. Fifteen years later, another prostitute, Gertrude Yates alias Olive Young, was murdered in this very house, by the 'toff' Ronald True.

Edward Marjoribanks, one of Sir Edward Marshall Hall's biographers, published an account of the great barrister being approached by a short, contented-looking man sometime after the Camden Town murder trial.[9] When this individual asked him if he remembered him, Marshall Hall thought he recognised Wood, and challenged him. The mystery man just said that his name was not Wood, but that he led a happy life, all thanks to Marshall Hall. In 1949, when the BBC proposed to feature the Camden Town Murder in a series called *Let Justice be Done*, the show was cancelled after relatives of Robert Wood, who was 'believed to be still alive', had objected to it. Mr John Barber, author of the best book on the Camden Town Murder, received private information that Wood never changed his name, but married and led a perfectly normal life, expiring at quite an advanced age.[10]

The debate about Robert Wood's guilt has continued over the years. Several crime historians, Guy Logan and John Rowland among them, have agreed that the evidence against him was insufficient for a verdict of 'guilty'. Although Wood led an immoral life, consorted with Phyllis

THRILLING SCENE IN COURT- THE RUSH TO CONGRATULATE THE ACQUITTED MAN.

Robert Wood is acquitted, from the *Illustrated Police News*, 28 December 1907.

Dimmock with some regularity, and was the last person seen with her alive, it is quite possible that she picked up some other bloke after he had said goodnight to her. Ruby Young's evidence must be viewed with suspicion, and the idea to convict a man for murder because of a funny walk is of course quite preposterous. John Barber has speculated that perhaps Robert Wood had fallen in love with Phyllis Dimmock, and decided to murder her after she had decided to marry Bert Shaw. However, firstly, we do not know if Bert was sincere in wanting to tie the knot with Phyllis; secondly, there is nothing to suggest that the cold, cruel Wood had any warm feeling for the street women he used for casual sex; and thirdly, Wood's respectable family would hardly have approved of him marrying a low-class prostitute.

So if Robert Wood did not murder Phyllis Dimmock, who did? The American popular novelist Patricia Cornwell has suggested that the artist Walter Sickert, or rather Jack the Ripper, had continued his murderous rampage against London's fallen women. However, Cornwell's book has been widely criticised for being inaccurate and speculative, and its theories cannot be taken seriously. There is in fact nothing whatsoever to connect Sickert with the Camden Town Murder, except that this celebrated murder mystery inspired one of his paintings. The killer might have been one of Phyllis Dimmock's many clients, keen for revenge after she had given him venereal disease. This faceless killer, a member of the riff-raff consorting with the prostitutes at the Eagle and the Rising Sun, would then have slithered back into obscurity.

A more adventurous theory links the murder of Phyllis Dimmock, executed with such coolness and precision, with a series of other unsolved murders of prostitutes committed between 1903 and 1909, one of them the luckless Esther Praager in 1908, as recounted below in this book. Although the voluminous police files on the Dimmock case are still kept at the National Archives, the files on Esther Praager and the other presumed victims of this Edwardian 'Jack the Slasher' have not been kept for posterity. According to rumour, they had been kept by a retired Scotland Yard detective, and destroyed after his death.

Since there was more than one St Paul's Road in London, the one in Camden Town was renamed Agar Grove, a more distinctive name, in 1937. When the crime writer John Rowland visited the murder house at No. 29 Agar Grove in 1963, he presumed that this drab old house would soon be pulled down. It was in poor condition, and quite a few of its neighbours had already given way to modern developments.[11] Despite this, the Agar Grove murder house is still there today, in a good state of repair.

Murder in Bernard Street, 1908

Bernard Street, Bloomsbury, was built by James Bruton between 1799 and 1820, and named after Sir Thomas Bernard, Vice President of the nearby Foundlings Hospital. In Victorian times, Bernard Street gradually went downhill, along with the remainder of the district: flyblown old hotels and dubious boarding houses abounded. In 1908, No. 3 Bernard Street, Bloomsbury, at the corner with Herbrand Street and only two houses away from the Russell Square underground station, was one of many shady lodging houses in this part of London. On Friday 16 October, a young woman who called herself 'Miss Smith' moved into a second-floor back room on the premises. The housekeeper Mrs Emily Cook,

Esther Praager is found murdered, from the *Illustrated Police News*, 24 October 1908.

who herself slept in the basement, thought young 'Miss Smith' pretty but rather sluttish-looking, but she asked no questions once she was given a week's rent in advance. There cannot have been any doubt either to 'Miss Smith's' profession, or to the use she was intending to make of the room.

The same evening she had moved into No. 3 Bernard Street, the mysterious 'Miss Smith' went out walking the streets. She returned to the house after midnight with a male companion. At around 2 a.m., one of the other lodgers heard a cry of 'Oy gevalt! Police!' but he thought it was just another drunken quarrel. However, when some of the lodgers at No. 3 Bernard Street had luncheon together on Saturday, it turned out that several of them had heard the outcry in the night. The newest lodger 'Miss Smith', or 'Mrs Marx' as she had introduced herself to some people, was nowhere to be seen, and when the housekeeper knocked at her door, there was no response. Since Mrs Cook did not want to enter the room at her own initiative, she sent a boy to the landlady Mrs Rose, who kept a coffee shop in nearby Marchmont Street. Her son Arthur Chapple, who was in the coffee shop, agreed to come to No. 3 to investigate. He and Mrs Cook made their way to the second floor, where they opened the unlocked door to 'Miss Smith's' room. On the bed was what looked like a bundle of bedclothes, but when Mr Chapple looked closer he could see the contorted face of the murdered woman. A towel had been wrapped round her neck. The mattress and bedclothes were much torn, indicating a fearful struggle.

The police were promptly called in, and so was James O'Donnell, the local doctor. He diagnosed murder by suffocation. Some electrical flex had been wrapped round the murdered woman's neck, and another piece of flex was tied to the bedstead. The wash-hand basin had been used, presumably by the murderer, who had covered his victim's body with a sheet before calmly leaving the room. The police considered it quite extraordinary that he had been able to subdue an able-bodied woman in a lodging house full of people without attracting attention. It was almost as if he had murdered before.

On 18 October, Mrs Selina Cooper, a married young woman living at Colegate Mansions, Whitechapel, came to the mortuary, where she identified the murdered woman as her seventeen-year-old sister Esther Praager. They were Polish Jews, and had come to London from Warsaw. When Selina got married, she provided Esther with employment as a seamstress, taught her English, and allowed her to lodge with the family. However, young Esther had been dissatisfied with her drab existence, and longed for nice clothes and male company. After she had become a prostitute, Selina and her husband wanted nothing further to do with her. Thus she did not know if Esther had any enemies, or felt threatened. The outcry 'Oy gewalt' meant 'Help!' in Hebrew, Esther's native tongue. Esther Praager was buried at the Jewish cemetery, Manor Park, East Ham, on 22 October.

At the coroner's inquest on Esther Praager, several other Bloomsbury prostitutes gave evidence. Although she was just seventeen years old, Esther had been walking the streets for more than a year. She was known as 'die Kleine' ('the Little One' in German) since she was just 5 feet tall. The prostitute Ange Motzmer had been walking with Esther from 9.30 to 10.30 the night of the murder. She later saw Esther leave with a young man in a grey striped suit, remarking, 'We are going home for the night.' Prostitute Margaret Harris had seen Esther on her way back to No. 3 Bernard Street, accompanied by a very short, broad-shouldered man. Shopkeeper George Lupitza had sold Esther some sandwiches at around midnight; he could recall that she had been in a hurry, as if she was fearful that her 'customer', a short man in a dark suit who was waiting outside, would go off with someone else. Professor Augustus Pepper, the Home Office pathologist, explained that Esther had been suffocated, presumably by a strong man holding a towel across her face to prevent

Newspaper sketches of No. 3 Bernard Street, where Esther Praager was murdered in 1908. (Courtesy of Mr Stewart P. Evans)

her from crying out. A verdict of wilful murder against some person unknown was returned.[12]

The police managed to recover three fingerprints, presumed to come from the murderer, from the bedpost and wash-hand basin in Esther Praager's room, but they were not of good quality. In spite of diligent inquiries, the short man she had been seen with the night of the murder could not be traced, nor was there any other worthwhile lead. Like quite a few other Victorian and Edwardian murders of prostitutes, that of Esther Praager has remained unsolved. The culprit is likely to be the short man who accompanied her back to No. 3 Bernard Street, and it is reasonable to assume that he did so with the purpose of murdering her. Esther had a boyfriend named Mark Hert, but he had a solid alibi for the time of the murder. In spite of being described as a waiter, he might well have doubled as Esther's 'fancy man', or she might have had another pimp. Did Esther want to leave this pimp, and was this why she moved into No. 3 Bernard Street? Did the pimp accompany her there, only to kill her when she made her intentions clear?

The police file on the murder of Esther Praager no longer exists, but the murder ledger of the Metropolitan Police contains the interesting information that a certain Julius Cooper, with whom the deceased had cohabited, was strongly suspected of the murder, although the witnesses could not identify him. This is interesting since the report on the inquest makes it clear that Julius Cooper, a chemical dealer of Fieldgate Mansions, Myrtle Street, was the husband of Esther's sister Selina! Indeed, Esther had cohabited with the Coopers for eighteen months, before becoming a full-time prostitute. Had Julius had a fling on the side with his young sister-in-law? The police ledger provides no reason why Julius Cooper was suspected in the first place, however, and after his appearance at the final day of the inquest on Esther Praager, he sank back into obscurity.

The murder of Esther Praager shares many characteristics with the equally unsolved murder of Phyllis Dimmock in 1907. A man named Frank Clarke, one of the witnesses in the Dimmock case, also lodged at No. 3 Bernard Street. Described as a draughtsman, he had several convictions for theft, but there was no direct evidence against him in the Praager murder inquiry. The Bernard Street murder house still stands.

Above left: 1. 99 Stanley (today Alderney) Street, where Frederick Treadaway murdered John Collins in 1876.

Above right: 2. 36 Eaton Place, where two terrorists murdered Sir Henry Wilson in 1922.

Above left: 3. 30 Lowndes Square, where Ernest Albert Walker murdered Raymond Davis in 1922.

Above right: 4. 37 Wardour Street, where Antonio Mancini murdered Harry Distleman in 1941.

5. 24 Charles Street, where Arthur Henry Bishop murdered the butler Frank Edward Rix in 1925.

Above left: 6. 36 Little Newport Street (today 11 Newport Place), where Roger Vernon murdered Red Max Kassel in 1936.

Above right: 7. 44 Duke Street, where Evelyn Hatton was murdered in 1944.

Above left: 8. 42 Rupert Street, where Rita Green was murdered in 1947.

Above right: 9. 46 Broadwick Street, where Rachel Fennick was murdered in 1948.

Above left: 10. 126 Long Acre, where Helen Freedman was murdered in 1948.

Above right: 11. The former antique shop at 23 Cecil Court, where Edwin Bush murdered Elsie May Batten in 1961.

12. 32 Wilton Crescent, where the butler Julian Sesee was murdered by Mustapha Bassaine in 1970.

Above left: 13. Lord Lucan's house at 46 Lower Belgrave Street, where Sandra Rivett was murdered in 1974.

Above right: 14. The basement window at 46 Lower Belgrave Street: is it situated too low for Lord Lucan to see a fight in there?

Above left: 15. The Black Lion at 123 Bayswater Road, where James Hartley murdered George Scott in 1800.

Above right: 16. 13 Clarendon Road, where Norman Cecil Rutherford murdered Miles Seton in 1919.

Above left: 17. 46 Rawlings Street, where Charlie O'Donnell murdered his wife Elizabeth in 1876.

Above right: 18. The lower ground-floor flat at 13a Finborough Road, where Ronald True murdered Gertrude Yates, alias Olive Young, in 1922.

19. The basement of 79 Gloucester Road (the house in the middle; the basement still exists, but has been paved over), where 'Acid Bath' Haigh disposed of three of his victims in 1944.

Above left: 20. The former Pembridge Court Hotel at 34 Pembridge Gardens, where Neville Heath murdered Margery Gardner in 1946.

Above right: 21. 5 Beaufort Gardens, where Jack Mudie was murdered by Thomas Ley and Lawrence John Smith in 1946.

Above left: 22. 15 Paulton's Square, where Walter Miller murdered Ann Boss in 1870.

Above right: 23. 24 Wellington Square, where Walter Miller murdered Elias Huelin in 1870.

Above left: 24. 10 Rylston Terrace, Rylston Road (today 44 Rylston Road), where Henry Norman murdered his wife Ellen in 1885.

Above right: 25. The Cross Keys public house at 1 Lawrence Street, site of the mysterious murder of Mrs Buxton in 1920.

26. The former church at 222A North End Road, where Morgan Williams murdered Annie Doohan in 1965.

Above left: 27. 17 Walpole Street, where Robert Lipman killed Claudie Delbarre in 1967.

Above right: 28. 81 Cadogan Square, where Barbara Baekeland was murdered by her son Tony in 1972.

Above left: 29. 19 Cheyne Walk, where the serial killer Patrick MacKay murdered Isabella Griffiths in 1974.

Above right: 30. 13 Lowndes Square, where the bloodthirsty Patrick MacKay murdered Adele Price in 1974.

Above left: 31. 29 Gowan Avenue, where Jill Dando was murdered in 1999.

Above right: 32. 30 Upper Cheyne Row, where Damien Hanson murdered John Monckton in 2004.

Above left: 33. 2 Priory (today Ivor) Street, where Mary Eleanor Pearcey murdered Phoebe Hogg and baby Tiggie in 1890.

Above centre: 34. 29 St Paul's Road (today Agar Grove), where Phyllis Dimmock was murdered in 1907.

Above right: 35. 3 Bernard Street, where Esther Praager was murdered in 1908.

36. The spooky railway tunnel, through which Mrs Pearcey wheeled the mangled remains of her victims in a perambulator.

Above left: 37. 139 Harley Street, where an unknown woman was found murdered in 1880.

Above right: 38. 40 Market (today St Michael) Street, where Frederick Foster murdered Annia Maria Long in 1893.

Above left: 39. The former Blenheim Hotel at 21 Loudoun Road, where Harry Blackmore was murdered by Thomas Harold Thorne in 1921.

Above right: 40. 9–10 Gosfield Street, where the serial killer Gordon Cummins murdered Margaret Lowe in 1942.

Above left: 41. 187 Sussex Gardens, where Gordon Cummins murdered Doris Jouannet in the ground-floor flat in 1942.

Above right: 42. The former Eastman's Cleaners at 37 St John's Wood High Street, where Emily Armstrong was murdered in 1949.

Above left: 43. 23 Newton Road, where Hannah Newington, alias Flora Davy, stabbed Frederick Graves Moon to death in 1871.

Above right: 44. 32 Westbourne Terrace, where Robina Bolton was murdered in the ground-floor back bedsit in 1956.

Above left: 45. The former Lion Tavern, North Road, where Charles Frederick Bricknell murdered Jane Geary in 1864.

Above right: 46. 19 Canonbury Terrace (today 1 Alwyne Villas), where Frances Maria Wright was murdered in 1888.

47. The former Swan public house at 125 Caledonian Road, where George Ward murdered Lily Allen in 1894, and then committed suicide.

Above left: 48. 11 Danbury Street, where the baby farmer and murderess Annie Walters was at large from 1900 until 1902.

Above right: 49. 63 Tollington Park, where Frederick Seddon murdered Eliza Mary Barrow in 1911.

Above left: 50. The first-floor flat at 14 Bismarck (today Waterlow) Road, where George Joseph 'Brides in the Bath' Smith murdered his latest wife Margaret in 1914.

Above right: 51. The second-floor flat at 25 Noel Road (note the blue plaque), where Kenneth Halliwell murdered Joe Orton in 1967, before committing suicide.

52. 19 Alwyne Road, where the 'author' Douglas Bose was killed by the book reviewer Douglas Burton in 1936.

53. Houses in Whitechapel Road, with the present-day Whitechapel Dental Centre at the site of the former No. 215 where Henry Wainwright murdered Harriet Lane in 1874.

54. The former workshop where Harriet Lane was murdered and dismembered.

Above left: 55. 11 Artillery Passage, where Emma Grossmith was murdered by Alexander Arthur Mackay in 1868.

Above centre: 56. The Blind Beggar at 337 Whitechapel Road, where Ronnie Kray murdered George Cornell in 1966.

Above right: 57. The basement flat at 97 Evering Road, Stoke Newington, where the Krays murdered Jack 'the Hat' McVitie in 1967.

Murder in Warren Street, 1931

Warren Street has lost several of its historic murder houses. Neither Nos 73 and 74, where the Frenchman Emile Barthelemy committed double murder in 1854, nor No. 42, where Charles Francis Cotier murdered Elizabeth Carley in 1862, are in existence today.

In 1931, the twenty-three-year-old Cypriot waiter Alexander Anastassiou lodged at the still-extant No. 65 Warren Street, a narrow Georgian house in a terrace on Fitzroy Street. He shared the top-floor front room with another male lodger, but this was due to penury rather than inclination, because the young Cypriot in fact had a healthy interest in the opposite sex. On the evening of 26 February 1931, Anastassiou smuggled his latest girlfriend, the twenty-two-year-old waitress Evelyn Victoria Holt, up to his room, and the other tenant made himself scarce. In the middle of the night, the landlady of No. 65 heard a woman screaming in Anastassiou's room. She ran upstairs and screamed, 'Open the door!' When Anastassiou opened it, she saw a bloody bundle on the floor. Fearful that she would be murdered herself, the landlady ran downstairs and sent another lodger for the police. It turned out that Evelyn Victoria Holt had been murdered: her throat had been cut with a razor. The injuries to her hands indicated that she had struggled with her assailant. After being cautioned by a detective, Anastassiou made the ill-advised statement, 'I was happy with her. We had been to tea, pictures and supper. But she made me excited – I kill her!'

There was a good deal of sympathy for Alexander Anastassiou among his countrymen in London. He was young and not unattractive, and they thought this wicked English girl had been leading him along. That stalwart spokesman for London's Cypriot community, 'Dr' Angelos Zemenides, later to become a murder victim himself, organised a subscription for his defence. The problem was that Anastassiou's defence council did not have a leg to stand on. Alexander Anastassiou and Evelyn Victoria Holt had been the only people inside the murder room, and the medical evidence spoke strongly against suicide. Then there was the matter of his unwise confession to the detective. Anastassiou did not have a history of psychiatric disease, and the prison doctors thought him fully sane. At the Old Bailey, it was alleged that Evelyn Victoria Holt had attempted suicide with the razor, and that her injuries had been caused when he had tried to stop her. This story was not believed, since her throat had been cut with great force not less than eight times. Anastassiou was found guilty of wilful murder and sentenced to death.[13]

At the Court of Criminal Appeal, the Cypriot's defenders tried another stratagem. Evelyn Victoria Holt had attacked Anastassiou with the razor, and he had acted in self-defence. However, although the Cypriot did have some scratches to his face when first examined by a doctor, these looked like they had been inflicted by fingernails, quite possibly his own. The appeal was turned down and Alexander Anastassiou was hanged at Pentonville Prison on 3 June 1931.

Murder at Gloucester Crescent, 1941

In October 1941, the forty-eight-year-old widow Edith Elizabeth Humphries was living in a two-room ground-floor flat at No. 1 Gloucester Crescent, Regent's Park. She worked as a civilian cook and bookkeeper for the Auxiliary Fire Service. Early in the morning of 17 October, the upstairs neighbour Miss Jill Steele heard Mrs Humphries' little terrier dog barking incessantly. Since the animal was normally quiet and good-natured, she went downstairs to investigate. She found the door to Mrs Humphries' flat wide open. Edith Elizabeth Humphries was lying on the bed, still alive in spite of very serious head injuries. The terrier, who might well have witnessed the murder, was found locked inside a cupboard; it was so frightened that it tried to bolt from the room.

Edith Elizabeth Humphries died at the National Temperance Hospital a few days later. The police found no signs of a forced entry into her flat, so it was presumed that she had brought some male acquaintance home with her to No. 1 Gloucester Crescent, and that this individual had murdered her. Mrs Humphries had been severely beaten about the head after an attempt to strangle her, but she had not been sexually assaulted. Her jaw was broken in several places, and the cause of death was a powerful stab wound to the head, which had penetrated to the brain. There was nothing to suggest that the murderer had attempted to search the flat, since a good deal of valuables, including a gold watch, remained intact.

Mrs Humphries had led a humdrum, uninteresting life, and no motive could be discerned for any person to murder this harmless, middle-aged woman. She was the widow of a taxi driver who had owned the large, semi-detached house at No. 1 Gloucester Crescent. The Scotland Yard detectives thought they had unearthed a vital clue when they found a letter from a fireman's wife in one of Mrs Humphries' drawers. In this letter, she was roundly accused of having an affair with the other woman's husband. Another letter from the same woman retracted the accusation, however. On further investigation, the matter turned out to be a mere misunderstanding. At the coroner's inquest on Edith Elizabeth Humphries, the verdict was murder by some person or persons unknown, and there matters have rested ever since.[14]

It is curious, however, that on 13 October 1941, four days before the murder of Edith Elizabeth Humphries, the body of the nineteen-year-old clerk Mabel Church had been found in a bombed house at No. 225 Hampstead Road. She had been strangled with her own knickers. The evening before, several people had heard loud screams emanating from the bombed-out house in question. It turned out that Mabel Church had been a young woman of dubious moral standards, fond of having a few drinks and meeting young soldiers for casual sex. It was presumed that one of these late-night acquaintances had murdered her, but tracking him down would be very difficult, since in late 1941 London was full of assorted military riff-raff, many of them fond of drinking and chasing girls. Various known criminals and army deserters were rounded up, but the investigation into the murder of Mabel Church made as little headway as that of the brutal killing of Edith Elizabeth Humphries.

It is not unreasonable to suggest that Mabel Church and Edith Elizabeth Humphries were murdered by the same man, a sadistic killer of women, who was probably in uniform at the time and stationed not far from London. Such a man was at large at the time: the 'Blackout Ripper', Gordon Frederick Cummins (more about him in another chapter). At the time, he was serving as an RAF cadet, stationed in Colerne, Wiltshire, but this did not prevent him from prowling around in London when on leave, looking for casual sex. On 10 November 1941, Cummins was posted to Predanneck in Cornwall, and thus removed from his London haunts until early February 1942, when he was transferred to the crew receiving centre in Regent's Park. As is well known, four brutal murders of women followed in quick succession, before this very cunning and dangerous sadistic serial killer of women was arrested and permanently put out of action.[15]

It may be objected that most of Cummins' later victims were prostitutes. Although Mabel Church led an immoral life, there is nothing to suggest that she prostituted herself. As for the middle-aged, respectable Edith

Elizabeth Humphries, she does not fit the profile of a 'Blackout Ripper' victim at all. However, it should be remembered that the woman-hater Cummins sometimes chose his victims at random: his first recognised victim, Evelyn Hamilton, was a respectable schoolteacher. A handsome, personable man, he would have found it easy to persuade young Mabel Church to join him for some 'fun' in the bombed-out house, and to inveigle himself into the lonely Edith Elizabeth Humphries' affections during an evening out. Either Gordon Frederick Cummins murdered Mabel Church and Edith Elizabeth Humphries, or there were *two* sadistic killers of women at large in London in late 1941 and early 1942.

Murder in Bedford Place, 1942

Jean Stafford, a young woman lodging at No. 3 Bedford Place, Bloomsbury, was in the habit of hinting that she led a glamorous life. She had independent means and did not need to work, and even in 1942, in the middle of a devastating war, she had plenty of time for partying. She went out most evenings, sometimes bringing men home with her. The neighbours found her something of a woman of mystery, and called her 'the Blonde in the Leopard-skin Coat'. However, on 16 May 1942, Jean was found strangled in her room. Everything of value had been stolen. The police found that the thirty-three-year-old Jean Stafford was a native of Hull, and there she had married a much older man, whom she had deserted when she went to London to become a hotel waitress. Hard graft was not to her liking, though, and she became a nightclub dancer instead. Her neighbours had always thought her friendly and good-natured, although somewhat reticent about her habits and employment.

At the coroner's inquest on Jean Stafford, in front of Mr W. Bentley Purchase, her body was identified by her husband, the ARP warden James Stafford, an inhabitant of Leeds who had not seen his wife since February 1937. Sir Bernard Spilsbury testified that Jean Stafford had been strangled to death; in addition, her jaw had been broken by a powerful blow, her hair had been pulled hard, and her entire body was much bruised. The housekeeper at No. 3 Bedford Place, Mrs Edith O'Connell, testified that she had more than once let a man known as 'Johnnie' into the house for Jean Stafford. Joseph Lamb, a man who occupied one of the other flats at No. 3, had once dined with Jean Stafford and a man in her flat; she had referred to him as 'Alec'. The coroner's inquest returned a verdict of murder against some person or persons unknown.[16]

The Jean Stafford murder investigation, conducted in the middle of the Second World War, contains statements from more than a hundred people. In particular, the police were keen to track down 'Johnnie', a dapper-looking cove aged 30–40 with a thin face and a long nose, but here they were never successful. No further clue to the identity of the Bedford Place murderer ever emerged, except the strong suspicion that Jean Stafford had been a part-time prostitute, and that one of her less reputable 'clients' had murdered her, and stolen her money and belongings.

Another Gray's Inn Road Murder, 1950

Gray's Inn Road has no shortage of murder houses. We know about No. 139 Gray's Inn Road, where the blind Frank Fyfield put an end to his wife. In 1933, in a small top-floor flat at No. 113, which has since been pulled down, Alexander Lionel Hearne murdered Elsie Winifred de Condappa.

In 1950, the thirty-two-year-old Greek Cypriot wine waiter Socrates Petrides shared the top-floor flat above the restaurant at No. 57 Gray's Inn Road with another waiter named Nicholas Tsanakas. They had a living room and a bedroom each. Petrides was a homosexual who liked to go 'cruising' in Soho's gay bars and cafés. In August 1950, things went

Bedford Place, from an old postcard.

badly awry for the unfortunate Petrides. He picked up the twenty-year-old Blackpool student Fred Hardisty, a naïve provincial youngster who had missed the last train back home. He did not realise the nature of the gay café he had chanced to enter, or the purport of the friendly foreigner's offer of a bed for the night. Petrides locked the door to the bedroom and put a sign saying 'Please do not disturb' on the door, so that Tsanakas would not walk in on them.

However, once the two men were alone in the bedroom at No. 57 Gray's Inn Road, Petrides' true intentions soon became apparent even to the dense Hardisty. The student furiously defended himself against the Cypriot's advances. In a fight lasting fifteen minutes, the brawny student soon got the upper hand, and Petrides feared for his life. He screamed, 'Help, Nick!' to alert his flatmate, but since the door was locked Tsanakas could not come to his aid. To defend himself, Petrides seized an ornamental samurai sword from the wall and stabbed his opponent with it, killing him instantly. At the inquest on Fred Hardisty, Petrides was charged with his murder. On trial at the Old Bailey, he pleaded guilty to manslaughter and was sentenced to five years in prison.[17] There is reason to believe that, after being released, he emigrated to Australia in December 1955.

Murder in Charlotte Street, 1952

The most famous Charlotte Street murder took place at No. 101, where the French butcher Louis Voisin murdered his former mistress Emilienne Gerard in 1917.[18] This particular murder house was demolished after suffering serious structural damage in the Second World War, and nothing remains of it today. However, one of London's many obscure murders took place in a third-floor flat at No. 63 Charlotte Street. Here, in late 1952, lived the West Indian stoker James Philip Smartt, a former professional boxer who lacked one eye. He had married a white woman and had a son with her before she died from natural causes. His second marriage was hardly a success, and Smartt was prosecuted after shooting and wounding his wife when he caught her having an affair.

When James Philip Smartt became unemployed, he allowed another West Indian, the stoker Arthur Claudius Nicols, and his Irish girlfriend, the twenty-three-year-old Eleanor Rose McCombs, to lodge in his flat. On 27 September 1952, Nicols cooked breakfast for the other two, before going to work. When he returned, Nellie McCombs was gone. As cool as a cucumber, Smartt told his compatriot that she had walked out on him, adding, 'Being Irish, maybe she will attend a dance tonight!'

The two West Indians searched various Irish pubs and dance halls, but without finding Nellie. When they returned to No. 63 Charlotte Street, the jovial James Philip Smartt, who had even allowed his friend to borrow a pair of trousers, seemed very reluctant to allow him to remain in the flat. Although he was not the shrewdest of men, Nicols began to suspect that his landlord was up to no good. He went to the police, but when they went to No. 63 to search the premises Smartt harangued them from an upstairs window with such vehemence that the timid constables decided to return to the police station. Instead, they showed some interest in Nicols himself as a suspect in the disappearance of Nellie McCombs, since his trousers were stained with blood. The desperate West Indian tried his best to explain that these very trousers had been lent to him by his 'friend' James Philip Smartt, and that this individual had also offered him a pair of shoes that had looked far from clean!

Suspecting that James Philip Smartt had murdered Nellie McCombs and then deliberately tried to 'frame' her foolish boyfriend for the crime, the police arrested the cunning West Indian and searched the flat at No. 63 Charlotte Street. Under a large pile of dirty laundry, they found the body of Nellie McCombs, who had been beaten down with a heavy shoemaker's last, and then strangled to death. When charged with her murder, Smartt seemed as cool as ever, blaming Nicols for everything. When he was held in the cells at Marlborough Street Police Court, however, the tough West Indian broke down and confessed to the murder. In spite of suffering from gonorrhoea and syphilis, he was otherwise healthy and considered fit to plead. Apart from his confession, there was solid technical evidence against him, including his bloodstained shoes and trousers. On trial at the Central Criminal Court in November 1952, he was found guilty but insane, and incarcerated in Broadmoor.[19]

Curiously, the present-day No. 64 Charlotte Street also has an interesting history. In the 1820s, when it was No. 28, it was London's leading flagellation brothel, kept by Mrs Theresa Berkley. Although there were twenty or so other brothels in the metropolis providing entertainment for those masochistically inclined, Mrs Berkley held the advantage. Not only was her house equipped with a full complement of whips, rods and cats-o'-nine-tails, but she also had the 'Berkley Horse', a curious flagellation machine of her own invention. Today, the murder house at No. 63 has a hairdressing studio on the ground floor, and the former house of infamy at No. 64 not far away was later developed into artists' studios. The name 'Hogarth Studios' can still be seen on the front wall.[20]

5

Bayswater, Paddington
and Marylebone

The secret of many a mysterious disappearance lies buried in the earth,
sometimes in cellars, behind brick walls, beneath the flooring of a kitchen
or an outside, in the garden, or in the farmyard.

George R. Sims, *Mysteries of Modern London*

In this book, I have defined these parts of London as bordered by Kensington and Westminster in the south and west, and extending north as far as Kensal Rise and Willesden, and east as far as St John's Wood and Harley Street. It is quite heterogeneous, with the remaining of Marylebone's elegant Georgian terraces standing side by side with exclusive mansion blocks, new houses, dismal estates and high-rise buildings. Paddington has a different character with its many cheap hotels, a flyblown haven for budget tourists from all over the world. Many of the elegant houses in the western suburbs have been subdivided into flats, and others have become hotels.

Not a few of Paddington and Marylebone's historic murder houses have been lost. The terraced Georgian house at No. 38 George Street, Marylebone, site of the unsolved murder of the milliner Miss Lucy Clarke in 1888, has fallen victim to the developer, as has the Bell public house at No. 15 Little Titchfield Street, where the musician Dan Kildare murdered his wife and sister-in-law in 1920. No. 24 Park Road, where the alcoholic tailor Cecil Maltby murdered his lodger Mrs Alice Middleton in 1922, is buried under a large development of flats and shops.

Not the least curious murder house in this part of London is the grocer's shop at No. 36 Leinster Terrace, just at the crossing with Craven Hill Gardens, where the manager Mr Edward Creed was murdered by an unknown intruder in 1926.[1] The motive was thought to be robbery, but excessive violence had been used against the hapless shopkeeper. The 'Great Ghost-Hunter' Elliott O'Donnell declared the shop to be haunted by Creed's ghost, after staying there overnight and experiencing many unexplained and uncanny phenomena.[2] Steadier and more balanced people than this jittery ghost-hunter also felt the ghost's presence, and as a result the shop became very difficult to let. It is said to have stood until the 1960s, although becoming increasingly derelict. In the end, the murder shop was demolished, along with No. 35, and a small restaurant, hopefully without any resident ghost, was constructed on the spot of these two narrow houses.

In 1916, Lieutenant Douglas Malcolm gunned down a scoundrel who called himself Count de Borsch, at No. 3 Porchester Place, Marylebone.[3] This impostor, who had seduced Malcolm's wife, was actually a Jew named Anton Baumberg, active as a pimp, blackmailer and German spy. There was little sympathy for the murder victim, and, after an emotional trial at the Old Bailey, Malcolm was acquitted to great acclaim. There is a house at No. 3 Porchester Place today, and until a month before the publishers' deadline it was featured in this book. At a very late stage, however, I found out that in the 1930s Porchester Place had been extended to incorporate Lower Porchester Street, and that the houses had been renumbered. The present-day No. 3 Porchester Place was originally part of Lower Porchester Street, and thus had nothing to do with the Malcolm case of 1916; instead, a large and forbidding-looking modern complex has now been erected at the site where the enraged lieutenant dispatched the creature Baumberg to a hotter clime back in 1916. This cautionary tale shows that a murder house detective can never be too careful.

Marylebone and Paddington have a variety of other strange murder mysteries to pore over, however, from the Harley Street Mystery of 1880 to the Ripper of Maida Vale in 1972. Visit the old converted stables where the Cato Street Conspiracy was hatched, follow in the footsteps of Gordon Cummins, the Blackout Ripper, as he prowled the streets in 1942, and ponder the unsolved murders of prostitute Dora Alicia Lloyd and shopkeeper Emily Armstrong.

A Tale of Two Murder Houses, 1820
In the years after the Napoleonic wars, there was a fair amount of political unrest in Britain, fuelled by various radical agitators, Thomas Spence

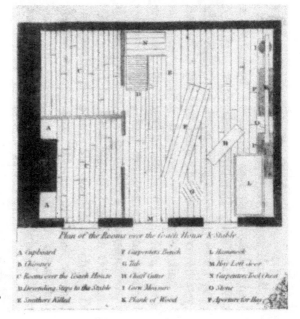

Plan of the Rooms over the Coach House & Stable

A *Cupboard*	F *Carpenters Bench*	L *Hammock*
B *Chimney*	G *Tub*	M *Hay Loft door*
C *Rooms over the Coach House*	H *Chaff Cutter*	N *Carpenters Tool Chest*
D *Descending Steps to the Stable*	I *Corn Measure*	O *Stove*
E *Smithers Killed*	K *Plank of Wood*	P *Aperture for Hay*

Top and bottom: The cow shed in Cato Street, from Major Arthur Griffiths' *Chronicles of Newgate* (London, 1883).

235

Cato Street. A the stable occupied by the Conspirators to assassinate the King's Ministers 23 Feb. 1820. D the windows of the small room into which the Thistlewood retreated at the Horse Patrow in pursuit this he quick reached a bldg of Lundin to Gt. Ceterspore 23 Feb. 1820. Sketched by H.B. Harris Ob. 16 Feb. 1860.

Above: Old houses in Cato Street, from a print.

Left: An old print of the conspirators' house in Cato Street.

Below: An old print of the fight in the Cato Street stables.

Above: Shocking tragedy near Hounslow, from the *Illustrated Police News*, 16 October 1869.

Below: Green shoots Mr Kyezor, from the *Penny Illustrated Paper*, 23 October 1869.

prominent among them. A group of his followers, led by a certain Arthur Thistlewood, called themselves the Spencean Philanthropists. They were serious extremists, who had the aim of overthrowing the government. After the death of George III on 29 January 1820, Thistlewood and his followers hatched an ambitious plot to exploit the governmental crisis triggered by the king's death. They would burst into the house of Lord Harrowby, the Lord President of the Council, at the time of an upcoming cabinet meeting, and kill the entire cabinet with pistols and grenades.

The conspirators had their headquarters in a disused stable in Cato Street, Paddington. Since the muddle-headed Thistlewood thought he needed more manpower for such an ambitious coup d'état, he wanted to swear some new recruits into the conspiracy. By doing so, he unwittingly recruited a police spy named George Edwards, who kept the Home Office well informed of what the Cato Street extremists were up to. Another dubious new recruit was a penniless cow-keeper named Thomas Hidon. James Wilson, one of Thistlewood's lieutenants, had walked up to Hidon in the street and asked him out of the blue if he would 'be one of a party to come forward to destroy His Majesty's ministers?' The cow-keeper was amazed at such a remarkable proposition. He pretended to be up for it, and the naïve conspirators provided him with the full details of the plot. Hidon lost no time in contacting Lord Harrowby and informing him what was happening.

On 23 February 1820, the Bow Street magistrate Richard Birnie led a detachment of twelve Bow Street Runners to the Cato Street stable. A troop of soldiers from the Coldstream Guards were supposed to have assisted them, but they took a wrong turning and ended up at the opposite end of the street by mistake. In the evening, the Runners charged the stable. Thistlewood ran one of them through with a sword, killing him instantly, but the other conspirators had loaded their firearms using low-quality gunpowder, causing them to misfire. Thistlewood and three of his henchmen managed to escape through the back window, but the other conspirators were either collared by the Runners or rounded up by the soldiers, who had belatedly been brought into the action.

Thistlewood and his remaining followers were arrested a few days later. Both Edwards the spy and Hidon the cow-keeper gave evidence against them, and all eleven men charged were found guilty of high treason. Thistlewood and four of his closest associates were publicly hanged at Newgate, in front of a large crowd. A masked man, presumed to have been a bodysnatcher or anatomist's assistant, proceeded to cut Thistlewood's head off, exclaiming, 'This is the head of Arthur Thistlewood – a traitor!' The same operation was repeated on the other four corpses, amid groans and protestations from the spectators, who were horrified by the mutilation of the bodies. For betraying the Cato Street conspirators, both Edwards and Hidon became *marked men*: they were presumed to have changed their names and fled the country.[4]

As forty-nine years went by, the Cato Street conspiracy and the detested traitors, Edwards and Hidon, were gradually forgotten about. However, this all changed in 1869, in the village of Whitton, today absorbed by Greater London, but then quite a rural location. The prime mover in Whitton in those days was Louis Kyezor, a German Jew who had become a successful businessman. He had lived in Whitton since 1839, and done much to improve the housing and public services in this sleepy backwater of a village. He had supervised the construction of several terraces of workmen's cottages, which he rented out at favourable rates. In spite of his foreign origins, Kyezor was very popular locally for his charitable public-spiritedness; there were even those who called him 'The King of Whitton' for his great influence in local affairs. In 1869, the now seventy-four-year-old Kyezor's greatest enemy was an old man known as Thomas Green. This cantankerous old fellow rented the cottage at No. 13 Kyezor Place, one of the terraces built by Kyezor, on very reasonable terms. However, the eighty-three-year-old 'Green' showed Kyezor no gratitude. He found it unnatural to live as the tenant of a damned foreigner, and a filthy Jew at that, and he thought it quite wrong that Kyezor should have so much influence locally. When drunk, this foul-mouthed old man made a habit of damning and blasting Kyezor at the local pub, in the most blood-curdling terms.

'Thomas Green' was very secretive about his own past. To some he said that he had been a captain in the Bengal Navy, to others that he had been employed as a 'stamper' in the Stamp Office at Somerset House. A meanly dressed, common-looking little man, he looked very much unlike a respectable ship's captain, and he possessed neither manners nor education. His main pleasure in life was drinking quantities of beer and gin. He did have some private means, however, through a government pension. Some local people thought 'Green' quite insane. He was often making ferocious threats against Kyezor and other people who had annoyed him. These threats were not idle, since 'Green' had accumulated a collection of old flintlock horse pistols, which he kept ready for use. He was often unkind to his wife, and employed another, younger woman as his housekeeper; there were rumours that the elderly 'Captain Green' was up to no good with the daily help when his wife was away.

One day in early October 1869, 'Green' sat drinking in the local pub. As grumpy as ever, he damned and blasted Louis Kyezor. He ought to be shot, the fierce old man exclaimed, for being responsible for the execution of a Whitton man. When Kyezor heard of this wanton slander against himself, he threatened 'Green' with legal action and eviction. On 8 October, 'Green' accosted Kyezor in the street, making use of his usual insulting language, and attempted to strike his landlord with a stick. Kyezor, who was much the stronger of the two, seized his cantankerous tenant by the scruff of his neck, frogmarched him back to No. 13, and thrust him into the front garden. The following day, Kyezor wrote another letter to his tenant, demanding an apology and threatening legal action. Realising that he was in serious danger of losing his cottage, 'Green' sat brooding in his front room, where he kept his collection of firearms.

In the morning of 11 October, Louis Kyezor wanted to walk to the Whitton and Hounslow railway station. He had not got far when 'Green' accosted him. After a short and angry argument, the old man produced a large flintlock pistol and shot his landlord in the belly. 'Green' then returned to No. 13 Kyezor Place, where he retreated into the outhouse and shot himself through the heart with another of his old pistols. Kyezor lingered on through the rest of the day, in great pain, before expiring near midnight.

At the inquest on Louis Kyezor, there was no doubt that he had been wilfully murdered by the person known as 'Thomas Green', who had then committed suicide.[5] However, when giving evidence, a wine merchant named Agar produced a sensation:

> His name was not Green. He was the principal cause of the exposure of the Cato Street conspiracy in 1820, at which time he was a milkman there. For this service he was granted an appointment at Somerset House and for his own protection was advised to adopt an assumed name, which he did, that of Green.

A correspondent for the *Surrey Comet* newspaper of 16 October 1869 assumed that 'Green' had been the police spy George Edwards, and the same version has been adhered to in Cobbett's *Memorials of Twickenham* and in a number of papers by present-day local historians.[6]

But there are strong arguments against the theory that the murderous 'Green' was the police spy George Edwards. Firstly, there is evidence that in 1820 Edwards went to Guernsey, with plans to emigrate either to South Africa or America. Secondly, Edwards had been an educated man, whereas 'Green' was boorish, ignorant and well-nigh illiterate. Thirdly, 'Green' sometimes used the name 'Thomas Hayden Green', indicating that he might well have been identical to the cow-keeper Thomas Hidon, whose testimony had been instrumental in the conviction of the Cato Street conspirators. At the inquest on Louis Kyezor, 'Green's' wife confirmed that her husband had been superannuated from the Stamping Department at Somerset House. Now, an article on the 'Stamp Office, Somerset House' in a radical newspaper contains the following important information:

> We are fully aware that many of Castlereagh's SPIES are still employed in this rookery, among whom may be particularised some of the traitors who betrayed the high-minded and unfortunate Arthur Thistlewood, whose impetuosity of character led to his ultimate fate. Among this Stamp Office gang, we are positively assured is the vagrant who kept the stable or cow-house in Cato Street, where the 'conspiracy' was concocted, having assumed the name of GREEN, the fellow being employed as a stamper, enjoying a snug salary of £90 per annum![7]

Scenes from the Bayswater Tragedy, from the *Illustrated Police News*, 10 June 1871.

This would appear to confirm that the Whitton murderer 'Green' was identical to the cow-keeper Thomas Hidon, who was given a new identity and employed at the Stamp Office for many years; as previously mentioned, the two newsworthy exploits of his long life came forty-nine years apart.

After the execution of the conspirators, Cato Street had its name changed, but more progressive elements have made sure that it got its old name back. At the western end, remarkably the old stable still stands. It is today a quaint little mews house, and one of the very few London murder houses to bear a blue plaque, this one celebrating the Cato Street Conspiracy. Along the old Whitton High Street, now named Hounslow Road, several of the houses erected by Louis Kyezor still stand, among them the two larger houses (formerly No. 11 and No. 12 Kyezor Place) clearly seen on one of the contemporary illustrations of the murder. However, the murderer's cottage at No. 13 was one of the houses wantonly pulled down in 1960 to make room for the car park of the Prince Albert public house. No local historian or murder house detective was present to throw himself in front of the bulldozers to save this curious relic of London's criminal past.

The Bayswater Mystery, 1871

Mr Frederick Graves Moon was a wealthy brewer of independent means, the son of Alderman Sir Francis Graham Moon, a former Lord Mayor of London. In 1871, the forty-one-year-old Fred Moon was part-owner of the Moon, Cock & Co. Brewery in Leicester. The recipient of an income of £3,000 a year, he had no liking for hard graft, preferring an idle existence in London and living for his various amusements.

On Derby Day, 24 May 1871, Fred Moon decided to visit his long-time mistress, Mrs Flora Davy, who lived in a semi-detached Victorian villa at No. 23 Newton Road, Bayswater. This outwardly respectable house was in reality a concealed brothel, catering for the upper classes of society. It was owned by a retired army officer named Captain Bowes-Elliott. The tall and stout thirty-eight-year-old Flora Davy shared the house with two young floozies named Laura Pook and Catherine Dulin. Flora was a nervous, unpredictable woman with a furious temper and a serious alcohol problem. She drank like the proverbial fish, and had recently been advised, by none less than Dr William Gull, to go for a prolonged 'drying-out' period at a German resort. She lived apart from her husband Captain Davy, a queer-looking cove with an enormous curly black beard, presumed to be a former army officer.

When Fred Moon and Flora Davy met to dine on 24 May, the melancholy Fred was in a gloomy frame of mind. He was fearful that his brewery business would suffer from some novel legislation that had been proposed, and he had lost when backing a horse at the Derby; most of all, he worried that his fickle Flora would find other gentleman friends at the German resort. Still, Flora made sure he received a good dinner, with plenty of champagne, wine and liqueurs. As a result, Fred perked up considerably. Laura Pook and Catherine Dulin joined Fred and Flora for some after-dinner fun: as Catherine played the piano, Laura romped on the floor, catching a decanter Fred threw in her lap. However, after Flora had sent the young ladies away, she and Fred started quarrelling angrily. All of a sudden, there was the sound of a heavy fall, and Flora gave a scream. When the domestics entered the room, Fred was lying dead on the floor, with a large carving knife protruding from his chest.

The police were called, and Flora Davy taken into custody. When she was examined by a police surgeon, she told him she had been drinking; the unchivalrous practitioner just replied, 'Well, you do not need to tell me that!' When Flora appeared at the Marylebone Police Court the next morning, there had been a mishap from the prosecution, and only the police witnesses and a friendly young doctor were available. The charge was one of manslaughter, and the doctor willingly agreed with Flora's defence council Mr George Lewis that Fred Moon might well have inflicted the wound himself. Mr Lewis asked the magistrate Mr Mansfield for bail, and Captain Davy came forward with £200. The next day, though, when Flora was again brought before Mr Mansfield, the outraged magistrate complained that he had been most grossly imposed upon. Captain Davy was not married to Flora, and she had a husband alive in Australia! The mysterious captain, who had wisely made himself scarce, was fortunate not to be criminally prosecuted himself for this caper.[8]

At the coroner's inquest on Fred Moon, it was made clear that 'Flora Davy' was a kept woman, and that No. 23 Newton Road was a high-class brothel. Apart from Fred, 'Flora' also received visits from Captain Davy, from the army surgeon William Pickford, and probably from other fun-loving gentlemen as well. Another spicy revelation was that 'Flora' had been born Hannah Fowler, and married the solicitor William John

Newington in 1856. The marriage had been unhappy, and Newington had left her in 1859 and gone to Australia. Before settling down at No. 23 Newton Road, Hannah Newington had been a professional con woman, operating under the names Flora Newington, Flora Canning, Madame de Morne and Frances S. Canning. She had stayed at expensive hotels without paying the bill, and obtained goods through misrepresentation. When she had been declared bankrupt in 1867, she had owed in excess of £2,300, and six distressed creditors had been clamouring for their money.[9]

It also turned out that 'Flora's' relationship with Fred Moon had been quite tempestuous. Captain Bowes-Elliott testified that Fred had spoken of settling some money on his mistress, and getting rid of her. Once, when he had insulted her, she had threatened to murder him. Mr Pickford, the army surgeon who had shared 'Flora's' favours, had often heard her quarrel with Fred. Once, when she had said, 'I am your wife, Fred!', he had angrily retorted, 'No, you are not, and you never will be as long as I live!' Another time, when she had objected to Fred ordering champagne in her house, he had pointed out that he had *paid for* the house.

The inquest returned a verdict of wilful murder against Hannah Newington, alias Flora Davy, and she stood trial at the Old Bailey before Baron Channell, on 10 July 1871. The grand jury had ignored the bill of murder, however, due to the lack of motive and premeditation, finding a true bill only in respect of manslaughter. Captain Bowes-Elliott and Mr Pickford repeated their damning testimony, but the latter was soon in difficulties after some very spicy letters had been read out in court. These indicated that, in addition to enjoying 'Flora's' favours, he was also keen to spend some time with young Catherine Dulin, to kiss 'his dear little Kitty' like he had done before. There was much newspaper outrage at this discreditable episode, and the constant immorality of the frequenters of No. 23 Newton Road was marvelled at.

As the trial went on, the medical experts for the defence argued that Fred had been stabbed in a scuffle, or even that he might have fallen down and accidentally stabbed himself, but the experts for the prosecution persuasively stated that he had been stabbed hard in the chest, and that 'Flora' had been the only other person in the room at that time. 'Flora' herself stuck to her story that, when they had been sitting together after dinner, Fred had deliberately insulted her. When she asked him not to repeat the insulting words, he threatened to fling a bottle at her head. She then leapt up with the knife in her hand, Fred seized hold of her, and they both fell down. In a two-hour oration to the jury, 'Flora's' barrister Serjeant Parry pointed out that his client had no motive to murder Fred Moon. In spite of their quarrels, they had been quite fond of each other, and Fred had supported her financially for many years. No doubt Captain Bowes-Elliott was trying to be a truthful witness, but he did not think the same could be said of the disgraced Mr Pickford. As for the medical evidence, it was inconclusive, and the jury should not consider it proven that Fred Moon had been deliberately stabbed. In spite of Serjeant Parry's efforts, the jury returned a verdict of guilty. Baron Channell said that he fully agreed with the verdict, commenting that the prisoner should count herself very lucky that she had not been tried for murder! He sentenced Hannah Newington to eight years of penal servitude.[10]

Hannah Newington was taken to Woking Prison, where she took to her bed in the infirmary, suffering from 'exhaustion'. In September 1874, after she had spent more than three years in the infirmary, her solicitors memorialised the Home Secretary, urging that Fred Moon's death had really been the result of an accident, and also pointing out that their client was in very poor health, and that she had suffered a dangerous relapse when she had recently been informed that her only daughter had just died. This petition enjoyed unexpected success, and Hannah Newington was released on ticket of leave on 15 September 1874.[11] It is not known if she was carried out of the prison on a stretcher, or if this wicked woman took a leap out of bed with a merry laugh when informed of the good news from the bonhomous Home Secretary. She may well be the Hannah Newington who died in early 1913 aged seventy-eight. It is not known how she supported herself in the intervening forty years, but it is unlikely to have involved hard graft and honest toil.

As for the murder victim Fred Moon, a disapproving *Times* leader writer commented that, due to his idle, immoral life, his affections were wasted and enfeebled, his temper spoilt, his manners deteriorated, and even his power of decision rendered worthless. It turns out that this unprepossessing specimen of humanity has been effectively removed from the historical record. To avoid unwanted notoriety, Moon, Cock & Co. brewers changed their name to Cock & Langmore. Nor is Fred Moon listed in Burke's *Peerage and Baronetage* among the progeny of Sir

Above: Spendlove the butler finding the body, the front of the murder house, and the jury visiting the cellar, among other images of the Harley Street Mystery, from the *Illustrated Police News*, 19 June 1880.

Below: The cellar entrance, and other images relating to the Harley Street Mystery, from the *Illustrated Police News*, 26 June 1880.

Francis Graham Moon, 1st Baronet. The house at No. 23 Newton Road, described by the aforementioned *Times* leader writer as 'a quicksand of social confusion and moral corruption', still stands today; an expensive and desirable Bayswater residence, it has all the trappings of inner London respectability.

The Harley Street Mystery, 1880

In 1880, the large terraced Georgian town house at No. 139 Harley Street was owned by sixty-eight-year-old Mr Jacob Quixano Henriques, a wealthy Jewish banker and merchant, who had lived there for more than twenty years. At times, when Mr Henriques was travelling abroad, the large house was inhabited only by a caretaker and his wife. Once he was back in London, Mr Henriques had to employ a butler and a full staff of servants. This system did not work particularly well, since the servants hired at such short notice were often of an inferior quality.

In early June 1880, Mr Henriques had been back in residence at No. 139 for around eighteen months. His wife Elizabeth and three adult daughters also lived on the premises. His butler John Spendlove was doing a good job running the household and supervising the other six servants. One day, Spendlove told his master that he had become aware of a very noxious smell emanating from the cellars. At first, the drains were blamed and a plumber was called in, but all the closets and drains were found to be in good working order. In order to find the source of the smell, the butler and the plumber decided to clear the largest cellar room, which extended underneath the pavement. In a corner was a large cistern on four wooden legs; underneath it was a wooden barrel and a quantity of other lumber. When the two men dragged the barrel out, it seemed unexpectedly heavy. The butler peered inside and exclaimed, 'There's somebody in here!'

A party of police constables, led by Chief Inspector Lucas, came to No. 139 to investigate the unexpected finding of a dead body in the cellar of Mr Henriques. When they unceremoniously turned the barrel upside down, a badly decomposed, partially mummified human body hit the floor. It was removed to the infirmary at Marylebone workhouse for a proper medical examination by the pathologist Professor Pepper and two police surgeons. The medical specialists found that the Harley Street cadaver was that of a woman, very short (just 4 feet 7 inches tall), aged between forty and fifty years, and with dark brown hair. Her front teeth

The Harley Street murder house, from
Lloyd's Weekly News, 13 October 1907.

A postcard showing Harley Street in the 1920s.

looked very peculiar: short and with blunt ends, as if they had been cut or filed. The cause of death was that she had been stabbed in the chest. It was estimated that she had been in the barrel for between eighteen and thirty-six months.

At the coroner's inquest on the unknown Harley Street murder victim, the police were roundly criticised for their clumsiness: valuable clues must have been destroyed when the body had been expelled from the barrel. The police had searched London and the Home Counties for former servants in Mr Henriques' household from the last five years; these domestics had all been tracked down, and were in a healthy and living condition. They all denied any knowledge of the body in the barrel, or any acquaintance with a very short woman with dark brown hair and strange-looking teeth. The former butler Henry Smith, who had been sacked for drunkenness by Mr Henriques back in 1878, was now a soldier in the 3rd Surrey Regiment. He testified that, during his tenure in the household, the gate leading to the area steps had regularly been left unlocked on purpose to allow the servants to come and go after hours, as it pleased them, or to smuggle various visitors into the house. The police had been curious as to why some bricks from the cellar floor had been removed, but Henry Smith freely explained that he had been in the habit of burying stale bread down there, so that Mr Henriques would not complain of his wastefulness!

Neither Mr Henriques himself nor Spendlove the butler had anything important or interesting to say at the coroner's inquest, except that the latter admitted that his eagerness to track down the source of the noxious smell had been prompted by the fact that his own bedroom was situated below stairs. Goodley, the plumber who had helped to find the body, provided some light relief when he said that he had not sensed any bad smell in the cellar, since 'plumbers do not notice them so much as other people'. The verdict of the coroner's inquest on the unknown woman was that she had been wilfully murdered by some person unknown. The police did not ever find a suspect, and the Harley Street Mystery remains unsolved today. It was by no means the only unsolved London murder at the time: indeed, the *Illustrated Police News* published a gloomy list of various unavenged outrages in the metropolis. It may be suspected that the dishonest butler Henry Smith, or one of the other servants employed at the time, had smuggled a prostitute into the house through the unlocked gate to the area steps, and later murdered her and hid the body in the barrel. It is true that the victim was an extremely short woman aged between forty and fifty, with very peculiar-looking teeth, but the Victorians were far from fastidious with regard to the prostitutes they went to bed with.[12]

Mr Jacob Quixano Henriques was not afraid of ghosts, nor was he worried about the reputation that often adhered to murder houses in those days. He stayed at No. 139 Harley Street for many years to come, living there until his death in late 1898 at the age of eighty-seven.[13] At some stage, a bay window was added to the ground and lower ground floors. In more recent years, No. 139 Harley Street has been turned into medical and dental consulting rooms, as have so many other houses along this famous avenue of private medical enterprise. Apart from the prominent bay window, the murder house looks very much like it did in 1880; note the railings, steps to the front door, elegant fanlight, and first-floor balcony.

A Murderous Paddington Butler, 1882

Robert Saunders was a respectable and hard-working man who had for many years been butler to a gentleman in Portman Square. Over the years, he built up what would today have been called a property portfolio, buying the leases of various cheap houses and subletting them to tenants. He was able to retire from service some time in the 1870s, when he was just in his fifties, to settle down in a comfortable terraced house at No. 16 Shouldham Street, Paddington, with his wife Mary Jane. The capitalist butler busied himself with his houses and other investments, but not with the same success as before. He became gloomy and introspective, worrying about the expiry of the leases of his houses, and fearing poverty in old age.

One of Saunders' tenants was a cabman named Humphries. One day he fell out of his cab and was run over by another vehicle, sustaining numerous broken ribs and ending up a patient at Marylebone infirmary. Saunders allowed Humphries' wife Louisa to remain in the Humphries apartment as long as she agreed to act as charwoman at No. 16 Shouldham Street. On New Year's Eve 1881, Mrs Humphries was busy cleaning the house. When her work was finished, she went up to the first-floor parlour, where the Saunderses were having tea. They seemed in good spirits, and Mrs Saunders said that, having had hare for dinner, they ought to have pork tomorrow. She wanted her husband to give Mrs

Humphries money to buy some pork, and he gave her three shillings. Saunders then locked the door to the room, drew a small revolver, and shot the charwoman in the head. He then aimed at his wife, but realising the danger she flew at him and tried to seize the revolver. The old butler fired at her twice, but missed both times. Finally, she managed to strike the weapon out of his hand. She quickly unlocked the door, and ran downstairs and out into the street, screaming, 'Murder! Murder!' As she did so, she heard another revolver shot from upstairs.

Police Constable George Stokes soon joined the crowd outside No. 16 Shouldham Street, attracted by the outcry from Mrs Saunders. After she had explained that her husband had shot the charwoman, Stokes bravely entered the house, calling for Saunders to surrender his revolver. When he reached the first-floor parlour, he saw the body of Mrs Humphries stretched out on the floor. Next to her was the body of Robert Saunders himself. He had shot himself in the head, and was quite dead.

At the coroner's inquest, no explanation could be found as to why this respectable old butler had murdered the charwoman, tried to murder his wife, and then committed suicide. Mrs Saunders, who had had such a narrow escape, testified that she had been married to him for thirty years, and that he was quite well off. In recent times, he had become worried about property, and depressed in his mind, but he had mentioned nothing about suicide; nor had he planned other sanguinary outrages.[14] The murder house at No. 16 Shouldham Street is still standing.

Terrible Tragedy at Paddington, 1893

Frederick Foster was a master painter, a steady and industrious thirty-three-year-old man who resided at No. 40 Market (now St Michael) Street, Paddington, with his wife. Prior to 10 December 1893, he had done nothing newsworthy in his life. However, that particular morning, he came running out into the street, shouting that he had just murdered his wife. There were few passers-by on this quiet Sunday morning, and those people who were taking a stroll in Market Street probably thought Foster either mad or delirious. Since nobody took any interest in him, in spite of his wild outcry, Foster desperately ran through the half-empty Paddington streets until he reached St Mary's Hospital nearby. Pushing aside James Huggins, the porter standing at the entrance door, he screamed, 'For God's sake, let me have a doctor, since I have smashed a woman's brains out with a flat-iron!' He was not certain she was dead,

Terrible tragedy
at Paddington,
from the
*Illustrated
Police News*, 16
December 1893.

however, and demanded that a competent doctor should accompany
him back to No. 40 Market Street for this matter to be settled. The house
officer Dr Jones politely explained that the conventional way of treating
cases of serious head injuries was to have the patient transported to
the hospital, but the frenzied Fred Foster was having none of that. A
short, muscular man, he seized hold of the young doctor and prepared
to frogmarch him back to No. 40, but a police constable had heard the
commotion and took Foster into custody.

Clearly thinking that Fred Foster was not right in the head, the
constable offered to accompany him back to No. 40 Market Street to
see if there was any dead woman on the premises. All the way there,
Foster complained that a doctor was needed, not the police; it was the
constable's fault that his poor wife would die. When they arrived, they
found a young woman lying on the back-parlour floor in a pool of blood.

Her head was frightfully battered, the skull smashed in, and the brain protruding. Amazingly, she was still alive. Fred Foster told the constable that she was a 'wife' of the common-law variety: her name was Annie Maria Long and she was twenty-six years old. Clutching his head, he exclaimed, 'It was all her fault. I asked her to come home two or three times, but she would not. When she came into the room I hit her with the iron. It was done through jealousy.' Picking up the broken handle of an iron, which was covered with blood, he added, 'This is part of the flat-iron I hit her with!'

Although it was clear that Annie Maria Long would not live for much longer, she was taken to St Mary's Hospital. As she was lifted into a cab, Fred Foster stood nearby, in dark thoughts, one of which is likely to have been 'I am too young to be hanged for murder.' As a police sergeant collared him to take him off to the station, the muscular Fred wrestled free and ran off into Praed Street. The sergeant pursued him, frantically blowing his whistle for assistance, but Fred outran him and disappeared round a corner. It was speculated that he might have hidden in a cellar or outhouse, or jumped on to a train at nearby Paddington station. The police issued the following description of him: 'Frederick Foster, wanted on a charge of wilful murder, aged 33 years, height 5ft. 3 in., complexion pale, eyes light, dark close eyebrows, mole on left side of the face with three hairs growing therefrom, short side whiskers.'

The inquest on Annie Maria Long was held on 11 December, at the Paddington Coroner's Court. The porter Huggins and the unnamed police constable both gave evidence. Dr Hall, house officer at St Mary's Hospital, testified that, although the murdered woman had twice recovered consciousness, she had been unable to speak. Her death had been caused by five heavy blows to the head, which had broken the skull. The verdict of the coroner's jury was wilful murder against Frederick Foster.[15] In spite of the hue and cry, however, the fugitive was never found. Although there were rumours that he might have committed suicide, no body was ever found. It is likely that Fred left London, where he was reasonably well known as a respectable tradesman. He might have joined the Army under an assumed name, he might have gone to sea before the mast, or he might have become a tramp. The murder house at No. 40 St Michael Street still stands, and its exterior remains unchanged from the time of the Paddington Tragedy of 1893.

The Marylebone Lane Coffee-House Murder, 1896

In the early morning of 19 August 1896, Police Constable James Richardson was patrolling his Marylebone beat. He saw that a crowd of people had gathered outside Aitken's Coffee House at No. 71 Marylebone Lane, and went to investigate. It turned out that someone had heard a cry of 'Murder!' from inside the coffee house. When the resourceful constable entered the premises through a side door, he saw the coffee-house keeper James Aitken sitting on a chair, trying to stem the flow of blood from a deep wound in the neck. His wife Emma stood nearby, weeping miserably, and the constable understood that they had had an angry quarrel, and that she had stabbed him, or possibly thrown a knife at him. A careless young doctor came and dressed the wound, saying that all would be fine! However, instead of recovering, Aitken got worse, and Constable Richardson went to fetch the doctor. When the bungling medical man eventually returned, Aitken had already bled to death. Half an hour before the coffee-house keeper died, he clearly said, 'I annoyed my wife – It is not her fault – I did it myself with a knife!'

The autopsy showed that James Aitken had died from a knife wound to the neck. The wound was consistent with a knife having been thrown at him. At the coroner's inquest on James Aitken, few people had anything good to say about the coffee-house keeper. He had always been a drunken, violent cad, who had more than once beaten his wife or threatened to murder her. Police records showed that Emma Aitken had twice charged her husband for assault, but had later withdrawn the charges. James had been fifty-three years old when his life was cut short by the well-aimed knife throw, nineteen years older than his wife. Her parents had run the coffee house for many years before James took it over. There was much sympathy for Emma Aitken, who had always been considered a sober, respectable and hard-working woman, the very contrast to her idle and sottish husband. The coroner's jury returned the verdict that the deceased had died from the effect of a knife thrown by Emma Aitken, but she had been under great provocation and had not intended to kill him. The coroner said that this amounted to a verdict of manslaughter, and committed her for trial.

On trial at the Old Bailey on 23 October, the fact that Emma Aitken had killed her husband by throwing a knife at him was not disputed, but her barrister argued that she had acted under extreme provocation, since her husband had made use of some very insulting language. Moreover,

The discovery of the body of Archibald Wakley, from the *Illustrated Police News*, 2 June 1906.

A postcard showing Westbourne Grove in the 1910s.

Sensational murder in the West End, from the *Illustrated Police News*, 2 June 1906.

she had been throwing the knife across the length of the room over a partition, without being able to see her husband standing behind it. Mr Justice Wright's summing-up was largely in favour of the accused. The jury failed to agree on a verdict, so a new one was sworn and a retrial was planned for the following week. However, having pondered Mr Justice Wright's comments to the jury, the prosecution decided to withdraw their case, and Emma Aitken was immediately discharged.[16] There is nothing to indicate that she ever remarried, or again made use of her lethal knife-throwing skills. She did not return to the little coffee house at No. 71 Marylebone Lane, since it is recorded that these premises became Mortimer Joseph's Coffee Rooms. Still, the murder house is still standing and was a *crêperie* a few years ago.

The Bayswater Studio Mystery, 1906

Archibald Wakley was a very promising young painter in *fin-de-siècle* London. He worked in both oils and watercolours, and belonged to the late Pre-Raphaelite school, aesthetically akin to Burne-Jones and Spencer-Stanhope. His 1903 painting *A Royal Princess* was inspired by the poem by Christina Rossetti. In 1906, his *A Sleeping Beauty* was exhibited at the Royal Academy. Wakley's artistic output was high in quality but low in quantity, and as a result he could not support himself from the occasional sale of his paintings. He was the second son of the wealthy wine merchant Nathaniel George Wakley, who owned a number of London pubs. In 1906, when he was thirty-three years old, Archibald still lived in the family flat at Oakwood Court, Addison Road, but he also rented a studio at No. 76A Westbourne Grove. He had a couch at his studio and used to spend the night there if he had been working late, or if he had been out partying with his artist friends. No. 76 Westbourne Grove was a large house, situated at the corner of Westbourne Grove and Monmouth Road. The entrance to the studio at No. 76A was (and still is) from Monmouth Road. The larger part of the ground floor of the building was occupied by the Bayswater branch of the London & County Bank.

In the morning of 24 May 1906, the charwoman Mrs Mercer came to clean up Archibald Wakley's studio. To her horror, she found the artist lying slumped by the studio door, his head severely battered, suggesting he was no longer alive. Neither the bank porter, asleep in a small flat adjacent to Wakley's studio, nor the artist Mr Chevalier, asleep in the flat below the studio, had heard any outcry or struggle the night of the murder. At the coroner's inquest on Archibald Wakley, his father testified that Archibald had always been a timid and prudent young man. A former pupil at St Paul's school, he had studied art in France and also qualified as an accountant, helping his father to do the accounts for his pubs. Several of his fellow artists also testified to Archibald's quiet habits and dedication to his aesthetic ideals. They added that, although his paintings often depicted beautiful young women, he was not one for chasing the lasses, preferring a quiet and studious life.

At first, it was suspected that Wakley had surprised burglars who had broken into his studio, but nothing had been stolen and there were no signs of a forced entry. The newspapers thought of another sensational 'solution'. The St James's Place branch of the London & County Bank had recently been broken into by robbers, and some imaginative reporters queried whether the same gang had now targeted the Bayswater branch of the same bank, through the intermediary of Wakley's studio? The police replied that no attempt had been made to break through any door, wall or floor in the studio. Furthermore, the autopsy showed that the murderer had attacked Wakley with great fury, battering his head and upper body with a hammer. Still, Wakley's family and friends firmly denied that the young artist had any enemy, or that he had been involved in an affair with some woman.

The inquest also contained some remarkable evidence that was not immediately published in the newspapers. Professor Augustus Joseph Pepper, the leading forensic pathologist, had noticed some very singular-looking wounds on Wakley's body: on his thighs were a series of small puncture wounds that had not contributed to his death. What instrument would cause such wounds? *Spurs*, the clever pathologist replied. The murderer had worn spurred boots, and the wounds had clearly been caused when he kicked the recumbent Wakley.[17] Now, the only people wearing spurs late in the evening in Bayswater were troopers from the Royal Horse Guards barracks nearby. Had Wakley invited a soldier to his studio? This hypothesis received support from the testimony of the salesman George Miles, who had seen a civilian answering Wakley's description enter No. 76A Westbourne Grove, followed by a uniformed soldier.

Archibald Wakley had written down some names and addresses of various friends and acquaintances on loose pieces of paper, one of them a certain Trooper J. T. Walker of the Royal Horse Guards. Hoping for a vital breakthrough, the police tracked down this soldier, who told them that four months earlier he had met Wakley in Hyde Park. The artist had invited him back to his studio to have a drink. The two had got on perfectly well until Wakley had made Walker a very distasteful suggestion. The virtuous trooper was not having any of that, and he left the studio at once. Nevertheless, Wakley had written to the young soldier, offering to paint his portrait; fearful of what the artist might be up to, Walker had not kept the appointment. Since Trooper Walker had a solid alibi for the night of the murder, the police concluded that the amorous artist had 'picked up' another soldier, and invited him back to the studio to have a drink. When Wakley's real intentions had become obvious, the disgusted soldier had beaten him to death in a frenzy, and kicked him with his spurred boots. The problem was finding this soldier. The witness Miles had never got a close look at him. A parade was held at the Royal Horse Guards, and the troopers were urged to step forward if they had had any dealings with Wakley, but none of them did so.

At the coroner's inquest on Archibald Wakley, the majority verdict was not 'wilful murder' but just 'murder' by some person unknown. They believed that the soldier must have acted under great provocation, and that he had not entered the studio with the intention to murder Wakley.[18] 'Singular Verdict in Studio Murder!' exclaimed the *Daily Mirror*, adding that the police had been culpably negligent and that Sherlock Holmes would have solved the Bayswater Studio Mystery with the greatest of ease.[19] Exactly how the Baker Street sleuth would have accomplished this feat was unfortunately not detailed by the populist newspaper: would he have pulled the troopers' trousers down in search of 'evidence'?

The old bank at No. 76 Westbourne Grove is today part of a large Chinese restaurant. The studio at No. 76A still exists, but it appears to have been converted into offices. Archibald Wakley's *A Royal Princess* is for sale by an Internet art dealer for £8,000.

A Former Police Constable on Trial for Murder, 1912

Harry Day was born in 1873, and after leaving school he became a police constable. In 1896, he married Mary Jane Bennett, the sister of a police colleague. Although they had no children, their marriage was reasonably happy. Harry remained quite a dapper-looking cove, and very strong, but Mary Jane rapidly lost her looks, due to a sedentary life and excessive eating and drinking.

In 1907, Harry Day retired from the police and took over a lodging house at No. 99 Star Street, Paddington. However, having much spare time and relatively little work to do did not suit him. Nor did keeping a lodging house agree with his wife Mary Jane; a very sturdy, corpulent woman, she took to drink in a major way and was rarely seen sober. Although Harry threatened her, and sometimes disciplined her with his fists, her drunken ways continued. The lodgers more than once saw her with bruises to the face, which Harry explained was the result of her falling downstairs.

On 11 May 1912, Harry Day went out to have a few pints with his brother-in-law, the police constable Thomas Bennett. He spoke about his unhappy life with his wife at the lodging house, and said that he very much resented her incessant drunkenness. He threatened to 'do her in' or to 'break her neck' if she did not mend her ways. Harry Day and Thomas Bennett returned to No. 99 Star Street, where they found Mary Jane lying on the bed in a drunken stupor.

On 13 May, a woman named Martha O'Brien, who occupied two second-floor rooms at No. 99 Star Street, saw Mary Jane Day already in a very drunken state at eleven in the morning. Some person, presumably Harry, dragged her into the basement, and she could hear repeated heavy blows, as if some person was being thrashed. When another lodger, the police constable Edward Avery, came into the kitchen an hour later, Harry told him that his wife had gone to sleep in the coal cellar, and that he was about to give her a jug of water. At midnight the same day, Harry made an outcry that his wife was dead. He had dragged her out of the coal cellar and put her fully dressed on a bed in the ground-floor back room, but when he went to see how she was doing before he went to bed himself he found her dead, or so at least he alleged.

Dr Arthur Hobsford Head was fetched, and he declared Mary Jane Day, a very stout and heavy woman, dead from multiple trauma. There were fifty bruises and eleven abrasions on her large, bloated body. A post-mortem examination showed that the cause of death was direct violence to the abdomen, as if she had been run over, kicked very hard, or jumped on. One of her fingers was flattened and its ring deformed, as if it had been heavily trodden or jumped on. As a consequence of the doctor's suspicions, Harry Day was taken into police custody. At the coroner's inquest, he was charged with the wilful murder of his wife.

On trial at the Old Bailey, Harry Day was fortunate to be defended by the eloquent barrister Henry Curtis-Bennett, then at the beginning of his distinguished career. Thomas Bennett gave evidence about Harry's threats against his wife, and the valet George MacNaill testified that, on 11 May, he had heard Harry say, 'The old woman has been on the drink all the week; God blimy, Mac, I'll do the bitch in!' Martha O'Brien provided some very damaging evidence about Harry's ill-treatment of his wife on 13 May, although on cross-examination Curtis-Bennett forced her to admit that she had once quarrelled with Harry after he had accused her of having her little boy fetch drink for his wife. Importantly, Constable Avory testified that on 13 May he had seen Mary Jane fall downstairs; he had tried to catch her, but without success. This might well have accounted for several of her bruises. In contrast, the medical evidence against Harry Day was very damning, particularly when Dr Head spoke of the deceased being likely to have been kicked or jumped on.

Harry Day had given a long statement to Detective Sergeant John Ferrier, who read it aloud in court. His wife had often fallen down when drunk, Harry claimed. In October, she had fallen into the fire and burnt her hand and arm badly. Four months ago, this accident-prone woman had fallen against a fender and broken it into two, driving a curling pin into her eye. He had tried to hide the whisky, but when a lodger had brought some methylated spirits his wife had drunk them. He admitted leaving her sleeping after she had fallen down the stairs into the coal cellar. Some brooms kept in the hallway had been broken, indicating that she had fallen with some force. He admitted thrashing her with a cane, as Mrs O'Brien had heard, to prevent her from going downstairs and looking for the whisky he had hidden. Harry denied making use of the threat spoken to by the witness MacNaill. A medical expert for the defence, Dr Robert Trevor Salisbury, expressed the opinion that the cause of death had been that Mary Jane Day had fallen down the stairs into the basement, and struck her abdomen against the brooms there with some considerable force.

By what must have been a very narrow margin, the jury reached a verdict of not guilty, and Harry Day walked free. He was lucky to have been well defended by a top barrister, who had enrolled a 'tame' expert of his own to 'neutralize' the damning medical evidence.[20] Harry's later fate is unknown, but the murder house at No. 99 Star Street still stands.

Murder at the Blenheim Tavern, from the *Illustrated Police News*, 17 March 1921.

Loudoun Road, from an old postcard.

Triple Outrage in a London Hotel, 1921

In 1921, the Blenheim Hotel at No. 21 Loudoun Road, St John's Wood, was kept by Mr Harry Blackmore and his wife Lucy. In early March that year, a strange young man visited the hotel pub, having a pint of beer and trying to persuade Mr Blackmore to take over another pub, but the elderly publican replied that he was quite content at the Blenheim. On the morning of 10 March, as Mr Blackmore was checking the previous day's takings, the same stranger burst into the pub through the unlocked saloon-bar door. Without a word, he struck the publican a series of crushing blows on the head with a large door bolt.

Mr Blackmore cried out for help, and his wife came to his assistance, along with Mrs Elsie Grimes, the wife of a chauffeur who lived in a flat above the pub. The two women were aghast to find the publican lying motionless on the pub floor, with his assailant standing over him, shaking the bloody door bolt in a threatening manner. The frenzied intruder went for the two women as well, striking out at them with his heavy weapon. With both Mrs Blackmore and Mrs Grimes out for the count, the attacker suddenly and unaccountably ran upstairs and locked himself into one of the second-floor rooms.

Mrs Blackmore managed to reel out of the pub, blood pouring from her lacerated head, to call to her neighbours for assistance. Understanding that a dangerous lunatic was at large, the police superintendent dispatched an inspector and a strong party of police constables to the Blenheim Hotel. The stranger refused to let them in to the room in which he had taken refuge, threatening to take a jump from the second-floor window if they dared to enter. When the police broke down the door, the lunatic jumped 40 feet, landing with a heavy thud on the unyielding flagstones and breaking several bones.

All four people involved in this violent daylight assault were taken to hospital. Mrs Grimes had only suffered a few cuts and bruises, but Mrs Blackmore needed an operation to her broken skull. The intruder, a twenty-seven-year-old man named Thomas Harold Thorn, also needed a lengthy hospital stay for his fractured limbs to be repaired. Poor Harry Blackmore's life could not be saved in spite of an emergency operation; he expired from his serious head injuries on the evening of 12 March. No motive for the lunatic Thorn to attack the harmless publican and his wife could be ascertained. Thorn had been decently educated at King's College London, and had worked at an architect's office for a while, but several members of his family, including his brother, were quite insane. The money in the till was untouched, and nothing else had been stolen; Thorn had nothing coherent to say when asked to explain himself. On trial for murder and attempted murder, Thorn was found guilty but insane, and incarcerated in Broadmoor.[21]

Here the story of this remarkable murderous assault at the Blenheim Hotel should have ended, but Thomas Harold Thorn was adjudged to be making very good progress at Broadmoor, behaving quite sanely and taking part in the social activities of the inmates. In March 1935, he was conditionally discharged and placed in the care of his two sisters at Wallasey. He started business as a tobacconist, but failed. Undaunted, he left his sisters, opened another business in Liverpool, and married his assistant, a girl of eighteen. In 1937, Thomas Harold Thorn was discharged absolutely by the Broadmoor authorities. But in 1938, he had a relapse of his murderous ways, attacking a shopkeeper in Wallasey with a hammer and beating her until she was well-nigh dead. Psychiatrists found him fully sane and he was sentenced to fifteen years' penal servitude for attempted murder.[22] His later activities are unknown, but at least he did not make the newspaper headlines again with further sanguinary outrages.

Sketches from the murder of Lady White, from the *Illustrated Police News*, 23 March 1922.

A photograph of Henry Jacoby, from G. Pollock, *Mr Justice McCardie* (London, 1934).

The Blenheim Hotel, which had been established prior to 1881, remained active as a pub at least until 1944, but it is today the Café Med. The building looks practically unchanged since Thorn went berserk in there back in 1921.

The Pantry Boy and the Toff, 1922

Sir Edward White had been a distinguished politician, and chairman of the London County Council. After he had died, his sixty-five-year-old widow Alice settled at Room 14 at the Spencer Hotel, situated at the corner of Portman Street and Bryanston Street. This hotel had been designed as a private house in Georgian times, and still retains some architectural features of note, like the ornate ceilings of the dining and conference rooms.

Henry Julius Jacoby, a clumsy and stunted lad, was at the bottom of the pecking order at the Spencer Hotel. An eighteen-year-old pantry boy, he was at everybody's beck and call, something that he greatly resented. He had plans to better himself, not through getting an education or a better job, but through robbing one of the permanent residents of the hotel, and 'getting rich quick'.

Lady White was in indifferent health, but she still enjoyed a quiet game of cards with the other residents of the hotel. On 13 March 1922, she returned to her room quite late. After she had gone to sleep, Jacoby sneaked out of his bed in the basement, and made his way through the kitchen up to the first floor, clutching a large hammer that he had taken from a workman's tool bag. Wrongly surmising that a titled lady like Lady White would have hoarded many valuables in her hotel room, the foolish lad entered Room 14 and had a rummage around. There were no witnesses to what happened next, so a believer in human nature would presume that Lady White up and 'disturbed' the thief Jacoby; a less charitable view would be that Jacoby deliberately hammered the defenceless old lady to death.

The following morning, Lady White was found unconscious in bed, having been hammered about the head and face in a brutal manner. A bruise on her left arm suggested that she might have raised it to defend herself, but it is equally possible that she was attacked while asleep. Lady White lingered in hospital until 15 March, when she died without having regained consciousness. The case was now one of murder.

Harmless old Lady White had no known enemies, and nothing had been stolen from her room. There was nothing to suggest that any person had broken into the Spencer Hotel, so the hotel servants came under scrutiny from the police. The foolish Henry Jacoby attracted notice by claiming that he had heard voices whispering the night of the murder and alerted the night porter; they had searched the hotel together, but not seen anything suspicious. Ransacking Jacoby's cupboards, the police found two bloodstained handkerchiefs and a torch; the pantry boy explained the former as the result of having his nose tweaked hard by a fellow servant, but he could not account for the torch. After making various confused statements, Jacoby finally said that, while looking for the suspected intruders, he had heard noises from Lady White's room. Bursting into the room, and lashing out with the hammer he had taken from the workman's toolkit, he had struck down Lady White by mistake, believing her to be a burglar. This story was given little credence, apart from the bit about the hammer. When the workman who had been at the Spencer Hotel was tracked down, he was aghast to find that, for the past few days, he had been hammering in nails with the weapon used to murder Lady White. Although Jacoby had taken care to clean it, it was still stained with her blood.

Although neither mentally retarded nor obviously insane, Henry Jacoby was not particularly bright; his careless blabbing to the police had cost him dearly. A newspaper photograph of him shows a short, foolish-looking lad grinning inanely. On trial for murder at the Central Criminal Court, the evidence against him was solid. Mr Justice McCardie delivered a hostile summing-up, reminding the jury that if Jacoby went into Lady White's room for the purpose of stealing, and struck her down with intent to cause grievous bodily harm, then he was guilty of murder, since his victim had died from his blows. The jury returned a verdict of guilty, adding a strong recommendation to mercy on account of the prisoner's youth. Since Jacoby was a nasty piece of work, and his crime a dastardly one, no reprieve was forthcoming from the Home Secretary.[23]

The Jacoby case hit the newspaper headlines big time when some rabble-rousing editors compared young Jacoby's plight with the lenience shown to the 'toff' Ronald True, the son of a peeress who had murdered a prostitute. When True got a comfortable life in Broadmoor, young Jacoby, the poor servant lad who had murdered a titled lady, would have to swing. 'Baint it all a bleeding shame!' the socialist agitators exclaimed, pointing out that Jacoby's mind had been corrupted by the violent movies he had used to watch, and that the police might well have used the 'third degree' to make him confess.[24] True and Jacoby actually met when they were held at Brixton Prison; the revolting 'hearty' indicated young Jacoby and exclaimed, 'Here's another for our Murderer's Club! We only accept those who kill outright!' However, the authorities did not budge, and Henry Jacoby was executed at Pentonville Prison on 7 June 1922. It is hard to feel much pity for him, in spite of his youth, since he was a scoundrel who, for his own gain, brutally murdered a helpless old lady who had never done him any harm. The Spencer Hotel was for many years the Mostyn, but today it is the Double Tree Hotel.

Murder in Lanark Villas, 1932

Dora Alicia Lloyd was a veteran London prostitute with seventeen convictions for street offences from 1919 until 1928. In happier days, she had been married to the Cardiff music hall artist Walter Lloyd, alias O'Brien, but he had died in 1927, leaving Dora as poor as the proverbial church mouse. A short, very stout woman, she could not afford to be picky about her clients. She had a few steady customers, elderly libertines who were still able to 'get it up' for some perverted 'fun', but not enough to escape the dangers of being a street prostitute. In 1932, when Dora was forty-four years old, she was still walking the Soho streets.

Dora Alicia Lloyd lived in a bed-sitting room at No. 27 Lanark Villas, Maida Vale. She had moved there in early 1932, and her neighbours noted that, when she had been on the drink, she sometimes forgot the number of the house, and had to make use of a 'trial and error' strategy of knocking at all the doors to track it down. One Saturday in 1932, Dora had some port with a friend back at Lanark Villas, before they set out for Soho. Dora had a few drinks at a pub with another veteran prostitute before she went into Air Street to try to find a customer for the night. A prostitute named Florence Crocker, who was also touting for business nearby, was approached by a tall man aged about thirty-five, wearing a blue melton coat and a black trilby. He wore horn-rimmed glasses, and was dark-haired and clean-shaven. He spoke with a cultivated accent, at least by Florence's standards, but since he was unemployed, and only had fifteen shillings handy, she told him to get lost. Dolores Blandford, another prostitute standing nearby, saw this impecunious fellow try to 'pick up' Florence, and also that he later approached Dora Alicia Lloyd and accompanied her into a cab.

Back at Lanark Villas, one of the other lodgers at No. 27, the unemployed motor driver Alexander Fraser, heard a car stop in the road outside the house. He could hear a man's voice in the stairs, and a few minutes later a gurgling sound followed by several thumping noises. The next day, Fraser reported this incident to the landlady, and they knocked on the door to Dora's room. There was no response, so they opened the door, which was unlocked. Dora's dead body was lying on the bed, bruised and battered around the face. Sir Bernard Spilsbury examined the body, concluding that she had been beaten up and then murdered by manual strangulation. She had defended herself as well as she could, and her fists were bruised and bloodied. A pair of brown men's gloves were found in the room, presumably left there by the murderer, and also a ten-shilling note which he had not bothered to retrieve. It was considered curious that the killer did not creep out of the house, but slammed the door and stormed away like a man in a furious temper, his footsteps echoing along the street.

The police concluded that the murderer was almost certainly the same man who had tried to pick up Florence Crocker in Air Street before leaving in a cab with Dora Alicia Lloyd. The impression at the time had been that he was a poor unemployed man who wanted some casual sex with a cheap prostitute. Once inside Dora's bed-sitting

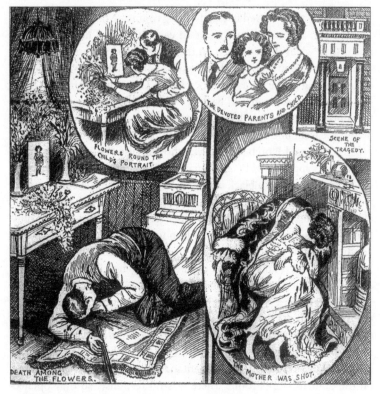

'Colonel and Wife Found Shot!' from the *Illustrated Police News*, 26 January 1933.

room in Lanark Villas, however, he had attacked her ferociously before leaving the premises. It was not obvious whether he had been enraged by some incident, or whether he had intended to murder her all along. Florence Crocker and Dolores Blandford had provided reasonably good descriptions of the suspect, but nobody knew his name. The police advertised in the newspapers to find the cab driver, but without success. They also made a trawl of Dora's regular clients, but they were all too elderly to fit the description of the relatively young suspect.

At the coroner's inquest on Dora Alicia Lloyd, Mr Ingleby Oddie concluded that the man who had murdered her was likely to be the same person who had got into the taxi cab with her at the corner of Air Street and Regent Street. Since the cab driver could not be traced, the killer's identity remained unknown, and the verdict was murder against some person unknown. No worthwhile clues were forthcoming, and the Lanark Villas murder has remained unsolved.[25]

As for the whereabouts of the murder house, it is notable that Lanark Villas was renamed Lanark Road around 1938. According to the Post Office directories, the houses were not renumbered, and No. 27 Lanark Road still stands today, the sole reminder of one of London's many forgotten mysteries.

Murder and Scandal in Clanricarde Gardens, 1933

On 9 February 1933, the cover of the notorious scandal sheet *Illustrated Police News* featured a very tragic story. The retired officer Lt-Colonel Reginald Holloway and his wife had been found dead in their top-floor flat at No. 3 Clanricarde Gardens, Bayswater. He had shot her dead, and then committed suicide. The *Illustrated Police News* speculated that Holloway and his wife had despaired of life after their little daughter Minnie, to whom they had been devoted, had died two years earlier. Her portrait, decorated with flowers, had been on show in the flat. Had Colonel Holloway and his devoted wife decided to end their lives to rejoin their little darling in a better place?

However, at the inquest on Reginald Holloway and his victim, quite a different story emerged. Firstly, Mrs Violet Holloway was very much alive; she attended the inquest as a witness! It had been her sister-in-law Gladys Margaret Bond who had been shot dead by Holloway at No. 3. Mrs Holloway had married her husband in 1913, but he had left her three years later when baby Minnie was just eighteen months old. He had paid her an allowance for a while, before absconding, and she had not heard from him for fourteen years.

A woman named Elizabeth Hill testified that she had once been employed by Reginald Holloway as nurse to Minnie. He had then been in the motor trade after leaving the military, and he lived openly with Gladys Bond, whom he introduced as his wife. Holloway had become a bankrupt in 1933, and his financial worries had continued into recent times. The murder room in Clanricarde Gardens was full of bottles of gin, whisky and vermouth. The coroner's jury returned a verdict of murder against Reginald Holloway, who it is believed then committed suicide while of unsound mind.[26] It is not known whether Mrs Violet Holloway wrote a letter to the *Illustrated Police News* to point out that

The victim of the murderous Harry Tuffney, from the *Illustrated Police News*, 12 July 1934.

she was still alive, but in that case this irrepressible newspaper declined to print it.

Murder in Gosfield Street, 1934

On the morning of 5 April 1934, a man in a sailor's uniform went up to a police constable in Gosfield Street, stating that the previous evening he had murdered a woman. He identified himself as Eric Russell, a twenty-nine-year-old first-class stoker of HMS *Excellent*, Portsmouth, and took the constable to a flat at No. 35 Gosfield Street. Inside was the body of the thirty-five-year-old Frenchwoman Juliette Louise Merrill. She had been a 'kept woman', visited by seaman Russell and by other fun-loving blokes. Russell said that he had known her for half a year, and paid £100 for her services. The evening of the murder, he had run out of money, and Juliette had been screaming at him to get out. In a furious temper, he had grabbed a knife and stabbed her to death.

The findings at the crime scene backed up Russell's story, since his clothes were splashed with blood. When told that he would be taken to the Tottenham Court Road police station, the dazed mariner said, 'Is she really dead, then?' At the police station, he again admitted his guilt. When Russell was tried for murder at the Central Criminal Court on 6 June, his defence team suggested that he had committed the murder when temporarily insane, but this was not believed, and he was found guilty and sentenced to death. After an appeal had failed, the execution was scheduled for 11 July. In the meantime, a petition signed by many Portsmouth sailors was presented to the Home Secretary. They pointed out that Russell had an unblemished record, and that he had always been considered a decent, hard-working man. This petition had the desired effect, and Russell was reprieved.[27]

A Murderous Paddington Motor Mechanic, 1934

Harry Tuffney, a thirty-six-year-old Paddington motor mechanic, lodged in a flat at No. 75 Star Street with his girlfriend, the waitress Edith Longshaw, who was eight years younger. These two were often at loggerheads, particularly when drunk. Harry wanted to marry Edith, but she went out with other blokes and showed no intention of settling down. When he found a letter in Edith's room suggesting that she was planning to run off with another man, Harry became very depressed.

In the evening of 29 June 1934, Harry and Edith drank whisky together. In a sentimental and maudlin state of mind, they spoke of gassing themselves to be together in a better place, but Edith was not ready for such rash acts and went to bed. The gloomy Harry sat drinking alone, brooding over his misfortunes. All of a sudden, he got the impulse to murder Edith. If he could not have her, no other man should! Seizing a large cleaver, he walked into the bedroom and buried it in the sleeping woman's head.

The following morning, a red-eyed and dishevelled Harry came lurching into Marylebone Lane police station, exclaiming, 'I have killed my girl!' He had kept his head over the gas ring since 4 a.m., he said, but, because he had drunk such amounts of whisky, he was immune to the effects of the gas, or so at least he believed. The police went to No. 75 Star Street, where Edith was found dead in the blood-soaked bed.

When Harry Tuffney was committed to stand trial for murder at the Old Bailey, his defence team had no option but to try the insanity defence, since their client had made a full confession of the murder. There was certainly insanity in his family, and Harry had led a far from conventional life. He had become a soldier, serving in the First World War and getting hit on the head by shrapnel. Harry had been twice married before he took up residence at No. 75 Star Street; his first wife had been a very obnoxious woman, he said, and he had once tried to shoot her. Later, when serving as a staff sergeant in Egypt, he had shot and killed three Egyptians during an uprising. Three weeks after this incident, he had gone to the rescue of some military policemen, and shot an Egyptian boy dead. Leaving the army, he became the chauffeur and bodyguard to an Egyptian prince, but without getting any opportunities to decimate that country's population any further.[28]

Harry Tuffney's sanguinary military career brought him brief newspaper notoriety. 'He Admitted Killing Four Men And – MURDERED LOVER WITH CHOPPER!' exclaimed the *Daily Express*.[29] Although a Harley Street specialist consulted by the defence thought Harry far from sane, the Brixton Prison doctor gave evidence that there was nothing to indicate that he was insane. It took the jury just twenty minutes to find him guilty, and he was executed at Pentonville Prison on 20 September 1934.

Saved by King George VI, 1941

Irene Brann was a German Jewess living in Dresden. Rightly fearful of the Nazis and their anti-Semitism, she moved to London in 1937. In an arranged marriage, she wed a British Jew named Aron Coffee, and used her passport to fetch her mother, Margarete Brann. Irene Coffee worked as a bank clerk, and she and her mother lived in the ground-floor rear bedroom at No. 33 Castellain Road, Maida Vale. Not knowing that they were Jewish refugees, the neighbours were suspicious of their German-sounding names, and even accused them of being spies.

Fearful of Hitler's war machine, and unable to appreciate the bulldog-like tenacity of the inhabitants of their adopted country, Irene Coffee and her mother became very depressed in 1940 and 1941. One German victory followed another, and the two foolish and timorous women believed that Britain would be invaded and overrun very soon. To make sure they would not be caught by the SS and sent to a concentration camp when the Nazis took over Britain, Margarete Brann and Irene Coffee decided to commit suicide on 11 October 1941. They both swallowed large amounts of veronal and Phanadorm sleeping tablets, and Irene slashed herself with a razor blade. They left a pathetic letter, saying, 'There is not the slightest hope for us, not now and not in the future. We are in despair because of our enemies, the Nazis, who are making slaves of people in one country after another.'

Seven days later, the police entered the room, finding Margarete Brann dead and Irene Coffee unconscious. Irene was taken to Paddington Hospital, where she recovered completely. Since the law stated that when two people make a 'suicide pact' and one survives the survivor is guilty of murder, Irene Coffee had to stand trial for matricide at the Old Bailey. Although Mr Justice Humphreys stated that he felt the greatest possible sympathy for the wretched woman, she was duly found guilty and sentenced to death; the jury did, however, add a strong recommendation to mercy. The Home Secretary Herbert Morrison commuted the sentence to life imprisonment. From the condemned cell, Irene Coffee had written to King George VI, who also showed sympathy for the poor woman. She was released from prison after just three months.[30]

Irene Coffee lived in the Lake District for a while, before emigrating to Australia and remarrying a man named Schleiss. She committed suicide there in 1968. In 2011, her strange fate was described in German author Heidrun Hannusch's book *Todesstrafe für die Selbstmörderin* ('Death Penalty for the Woman Who Attempted Suicide').[31] The German newspapers criticised British justice for being cruel and old-fashioned, but although a few ignorant London journalists followed suit, in search of some sensational 'copy', it is tempting to retort that at the very same time, *German* justice contained some very unsavoury elements, like allowing wholesale genocide.[32] More than one murderer has faked a 'suicide pact', like our old German 'friend' Paul May back in 1872, and although there is nothing to suggest that Irene Coffee had any motive to murder her mother, some aspects of the case remain obscure. At a time when many Jewish refugees demonstrated admirable courage in actively fighting the Nazi menace, she certainly showed blameworthy cowardice by attempting to destroy herself. The murder house at No. 33 Castellain Road still stands.

The Murder Houses of the Blackout Ripper, 1942

In early 1942, a serial killer was at large in London, taking advantage of the night-time blackout to murder a number of women. On 9 February 1942, the forty-year-old pharmacist Evelyn Hamilton was found murdered in an air-raid shelter at Montagu Place, Marylebone. She had been strangled, and her handbag had been stolen. The following day, the thirty-five-year-old prostitute Evelyn Oatley was found murdered in her flat at No. 153 Wardour Street (the house no longer stands). She had been strangled, her throat had been cut, and she had been sexually mutilated with a can opener. On 11 February, the forty-three-year-old prostitute Margaret Lowe was found murdered in Flat 4, Nos 9–10 Gosfield Street, Marylebone. She had been strangled and her body severely mutilated. Sir Bernard Spilsbury, who examined the body, thought the murderer must be a sexual maniac.

The Blackout Ripper was not done yet. On 12 February, the thirty-two-year-old part-time prostitute Doris Jouannet was strangled and mutilated in her ground-floor flat at No. 187 Sussex Gardens, Paddington. Two days later, a woman named Greta Hayward was attacked near Piccadilly Circus by a young man wearing an RAF uniform. Fortunately for her, a delivery boy came along, interrupting the attack. Greta Hayward and the Blackout Ripper ran off, in different directions, the latter leaving his gas mask container behind. Greta Hayward gave a good description of her assailant, but the problem for the police were that London was full of young men wearing RAF uniforms. A more promising lead was that the gas mask case had the serial number 525987 on the side. The RAF quartermasters kept their records in good order, and the container was found to belong to Leading Aircraftman Gordon Frederick Cummins, who was training to become a pilot. As the police were busy tracking Cummins down, the Ripper struck again. The prostitute Catherine Mulcahy was attacked in her Paddington flat at No. 29 Southwick Street (the house is still standing), but she fought back fiercely, screaming 'Murder!' and the assailant ran off, leaving her an extra £5 as a tip.

Gordon Cummins had been born in York in 1914, and became a leather tanner. In 1935, he moved to London and joined the RAF, and the year after he married a theatre producer's secretary. Cummins was a boastful womaniser who lived beyond his means, but he had never been suspected of committing any serious or violent crime. Good-looking and personable, he affected an upper-class accent and hinted at aristocratic family connections, becoming known as 'the Count' among his fellow aircraftmen. Life in the RAF suited him, particularly after the Second World War had broken out. He made frequent expeditions to central London, looking for casual sex with various floozies.

When questioned by the police in February 1942, the handsome young Gordon Cummins seemed very much unlike the Blackout Ripper. He stoutly denied any involvement in the murders, and claimed that his gas mask container had been stolen. But when his various effects were searched, items belonging to the murdered women were found. Moreover, his fingerprints matched those found in two of the murder flats, and those on the can opener used to mutilate Evelyn Oatley. Found guilty of murder at the Old Bailey, Gordon Cummins was hanged at Wandsworth Prison on 25 June 1942, suitably during an air raid.[33]

For a both prolific and sadistic serial killer, Gordon Cummins is surprisingly little known. There has been speculation that he had claimed his first two victims during air raids in October 1941, namely the respectable middle-aged woman Edith Elizabeth Humphries, murdered at her house at No. 1 Gloucester Crescent (the house stands), and the young floozie Mabel Church, strangled at No. 225 Hampstead Road (the house has been destroyed). It would seem odd for him to have taken a two-month 'break' in his murderous career, but the reason may well be that he was transferred to an air base in Cornwall in early November 1941. Of the murder houses left behind by the Blackout Ripper, those of Margaret Lowe and Doris Jouannet still stand.

The Bryanston Court Murder, 1942

Bryanston Court is a prestigious block of luxury apartments, situated between George Street and Upper Berkeley Street, Marylebone. In 1942, the large and attractive Flat 112 was occupied by Mrs Marion Lees-Smith, an American lady who had married and divorced a rich Englishman, and her twenty-year-old son Derek, a former Cambridge undergraduate. The wealthy Mrs Lees-Smith had spent much time and money opening a club for servicemen, situated not far from Bryanston Court. The work with the club kept her busy and occupied, and her friends thought her happier and more contented than in her rich but idle pre-war days. But on New Year's Eve 1942, Mrs Lees-Smith was found stabbed to death in her bedroom. Next to her body was a table knife, and two empty cash boxes.

There was a good deal of newspaper speculation about the murder of Marion Lees-Smith, due to her obvious wealth and social position. It was said that Flat 112 was the most expensive London flat ever visited by the police in connection with a murder mystery. It had once belonged to the Duchess of Windsor. But the Bryanston Court murder would not remain a mystery for long. It was clearly an 'inside job', since there were no signs of a break-in, and since there was a porter in the block around the clock. Mrs Lees-Smith was not in the habit of inviting strangers into her flat. The main suspect was her son Derek, who was known as an odd cove; there were those who considered him far from sane. Born in Shanghai in 1922, he had been dropped onto the floor by a careless nurse; this injury had left him quite deaf, but did not prevent him from attending a good school, and later spending two years at Trinity College, Cambridge. When apprehended by the police, Derek Lees-Smith made the remarkable statement 'I suppose it means the rope. Don't think I did this because of what's in the will!'

At the Marylebone Police Court, Derek Lees-Smith made a detailed confession. He had been extravagant with money, and felt annoyed with his mother for holding the purse strings. After she had returned home from the servicemen's club, with the cash boxes, he had gone into her bedroom to say goodnight, but she had been in a cantankerous mood, accusing him of being drunk. He had then gone into the kitchen, where he saw a knife in the cutlery drawer. The sight of this instrument transformed him into 'a temporary homicidal maniac', or so at least he claimed. In a furious rage, he burst into his mother's bedroom and stabbed her to death. Afterwards, he acted quite rationally, stealing the money from the cash boxes, wiping the fingerprints from the murder weapon, having a bath and changing his clothes.

This story did not sound overly convincing, and when Lees-Smith stood trial at the Old Bailey charged with matricide, his defence team were racking their brains to think of some stratagem that would save him from the hangman's noose. It was known that he had drunk four pints of bitter beer prior to the murder, and in an experiment, two brain specialists had him drink an equivalent amount of beer, which they found lowered his blood sugar levels. Importantly, this led to abnormalities in his electroencephalogram. This experiment may well have played a crucial part, with regard to the ultimate outcome of the trial, but equally importantly, Lees-Smith was a feeble young man, quite deaf, and certainly looking very much unlike a calculating murderer. He seemed to feel genuine remorse for his actions. In spite of a hostile summing-up from Mr Justice Asquith, who rightly pointed out Lees-Smith's rational behaviour after the murder, the Bryanston Court matricide was found guilty but insane, and he was sentenced to be incarcerated in a lunatic asylum during his Majesty's pleasure.[34]

Derek Lees-Smith was released in the early 1960s, and became a clerical officer at the General Register Office. In 1969, he married a woman named Amy Patrick, and led a quiet life for many years. It is not known who inherited Mrs Lees-Smith's fortune back in 1942, but I can tell you who *did not*: having killed his mother, Derek Lees-Smith was not entitled to a penny, irrespective of the contents of her will, of which he had been so very interested when first questioned by the police.

Murder at the Fursecroft, 1948

In 1948, one of the basement flats at No. 75 Fursecroft, a block situated off George Street, Marylebone, was inhabited by the 'lightning cartoonist' Harry Michaelson, who made his living in the music halls. 'One Minute Michaelson' had appeared many times on the stage and on television, and was reasonably well known. A tall, heavily built Scotsman, he toured theatres all over Britain. On Christmas Day, Michaelson was alone in the flat, since his wife, a professional pianist, was giving a concert in Bournemouth. In the night, the porter at the Fursecroft heard screaming, and saw Michaelson standing by his flat door, bleeding profusely from the head. An ambulance was called, and the cartoonist was taken to

St Mary's Hospital, where he died from his head injuries shortly after arrival, without having been able to speak.

The investigation of the murder of Harry Michaelson was led by Detective Superintendent Peter Beveridge, one of Scotland Yard's best men. It was clear to him that a burglar had made his way into the flat, but as he had been looking for valuables, Michaelson woke up and got out of bed. Lying in wait for him, the burglar struck the startled householder a series of mighty blows on the head with a tubular steel chair, from which one single clear fingerprint was recovered. Mrs Michaelson said that her husband would have had around £5 on him at the time; this money had been stolen. The police made a huge trawl of the neighbourhood, and the fingerprint was compared with those of known burglars and other criminals, but without success. A flippant journalist in the *Daily Mirror* suggested that Michaelson's cartoons should be closely examined: perhaps one of them depicted the murderer, who had returned to settle the score for this unflattering caricature?

The detectives got a lucky break on 19 January, when two police constables picked up a young vagabond named Harry Lewis, a truculent Welshman of no fixed address, who declined to give any information about himself. His fingerprint matched that found at the scene of the crime. When Lewis was challenged with murdering Harry Michaelson, he was shocked and dismayed, wondering how on earth the detectives had been able to catch up with him. He later made a full confession: in search of something to steal, he had entered the flat through an unlocked window. When he was stealing money from Michaelson's trouser pocket, he was challenged by the householder, but the agile young burglar knocked the unfortunate artist down with a series of brutal blows. Bloodstains were found on Lewis's trousers. He usually wore gloves when out burgling houses, but this particular evening he had forgotten to bring them, an omission that would cost this careless housebreaker very dearly.

At the Old Bailey, Lewis had no defence whatsoever, and the case against him was rock solid. He was convicted of murder, and hanged at Pentonville Prison on 21 April 1949.[35] Superintendent Beveridge, who had met Harry Michaelson, and knew him as a kindly man, felt certain that if the young vagabond had asked him for some money, he would have got it. But instead, two men died, one of them for having committed murder for the sake of £5 8s 9d.

St John's Wood High Street, from an undated postcard. The murder shop can be seen in the distance, on the left side of the street.

The St John's Wood Laundry Murder Mystery, 1949

The sixty-nine-year-old Mrs Emily Armstrong lived in Mountbell Road, Stanmore, sharing her little house with her son and daughter-in-law. She was a very respectable old lady, a devout Roman Catholic, and did not have an enemy in the world. In 1949, she was still working as the manageress of Eastman's Cleaners at No. 37 St John's Wood High Street, awaiting her old age pension that would be due the following year. Her duties were to mind the shop and collect money from the customers when they picked up their laundry. The washing was done elsewhere, according to somewhat problematic and unreliable routines; garments were often delayed, and sometimes disappeared in transit, leading to frequent quarrels with the impatient customers.

On 14 April 1949, Mrs Armstrong went to work just as usual. She closed the shop for lunch, went to the bank to withdraw money, and bought some clothes in a shop. At 2 p.m. she returned to open the shop. At 2.30, a female customer came into the shop to pick up some laundry, but it was not ready and she left in a huff. Just five minutes later, another customer trying to enter the shop found that the door was locked. Soon, a queue of puzzled customers stood on the pavement outside No. 37. They knocked at the door and rattled the letter box, but without being acknowledged. Worried that something might have happened to Emily Armstrong, two friends of hers forced the door and entered the shop. They found Mrs Armstrong lying dead in a corner of the shop, her head battered with a blunt instrument. She had been struck more than twenty times by the frenzied attacker. The back door to the shop, which led to a small yard and, via a rear gate, to a small lane behind the row of shops, was open. This was clearly the killer's escape route.

The motive for the murder of Emily Armstrong was clearly robbery, since the shop had been carefully searched; all money on the premises, including the contents of the safe and Mrs Armstrong's handbag, had been stolen. No fingerprints had been left behind, most probably since the murderer had been wearing gloves. A heavily bloodstained handkerchief with a floral pattern and the laundry mark H.621 was found nearby, but its owner could not be traced. Several witnesses had seen suspicious-looking men lurking near the shop, but there was no pattern in their observations. Looking through an album of mugshots of known criminals, one of them picked out a certain Dennis Jones, but he turned out to have an alibi for the time of the murder. Borstal escapee Frederick Jones, ex-Broadmoor inmate George Ratcliffe, and conman James Crosby were also suspected at various times, but no case could be built up against any of them. Army deserters, tramps and vagabonds of every description were questioned by the police, but without any breakthrough being made.

One of the more outlandish theories at the time was that child killer John Allen, known as the 'Mad Parson' since he had escaped from Broadmoor in 1947, disguised in clerical attire, had murdered both Emily Armstrong and another local woman named Gladys Hanrahan, who was found strangled in Regent's Park in late 1948. But when Allen was recaptured after two years on the run, nothing was found to tie him to either crime, except that he had definitely been at large in the St John's Woods area at the time. In 1956, criminal Adam Ogilvie briefly was a suspect, but he turned out to have been in prison at the time of the murder of Emily Armstrong. As late as 1961, a convicted robber named Walter Holland was investigated, but he had been an army sergeant serving in Brighton at the time. Present-day armchair detectives have linked the murder of Emily Armstrong to two other unsolved 'shop murders', those of eighty-two-year-old Margery Wren in Ramsgate in 1930, and Gertrude O'Leary in Stokes Croft in 1939, but it is uncommon for a serial killer to operate with such lengthy intervals between his crimes.[36]

It is clear that Emily Armstrong was murdered by an intruder who had come to steal money and valuables, a callous and powerful man who battered the harmless old woman to death before calmly making his escape through the rear gate. Perhaps Emily Armstrong had tried to raise the alarm when she saw him ransacking the safe, or perhaps the murder was 'insurance' because he wanted to eliminate the only witness who could recognise him. The old murder shop at No. 37 St John's Wood High Street is today a branch of the popular Maison Blanc café and patisserie chain.

Murder at the Laura Hotel, 1950

On the night of 26 May 1950, the young London prostitute Agnes Walsh brought a 'customer' with her to the Laura Hotel at No. 162 Sussex Gardens, Paddington. This hotel was, at the time, a notorious 'knocking shop', where most of the guests checked out before breakfast. Arriving just after midnight, Agnes signed the register 'Mr & Mrs Walsh', although her companion signed it 'Mr Davidson' and gave an illegible address in Co. Durham. The following morning, the hotel proprietor brought some tea up to the fifth-floor room where Agnes Walsh had been entertaining her client. To his horror, he found her bruised and battered body on the bed. She had been strangled to death with one of her own stockings.

Pretty young Agnes Walsh had come to London from Ireland to find work. She had worked as a waitress in small clubs and cafés for a while, but soon became a prostitute, operating from two small Paddington hotels. Not unreasonably, the police initially concentrated their efforts on finding Agnes Walsh's client. A cab driver and other people who had seen him described him as short, pale and thin, with sandy hair and a gloomy expression. He might have been using a black MG sports car. The murderer had stolen a ten-shilling note from Agnes Walsh's handbag, and had ripped off her rings and watch, but the police were speculating that the absconded killer might have tried to make it appear that the murder had been committed for gain. Known violent criminals, perverts and habitual customers of Paddington prostitutes were 'leant on' by the police if they answered the killer's description, but without any breakthroughs being achieved. Then there was the clue of the man's signature 'Davidson', hailing from Co. Durham. Although the police were not convinced that such a cunning murderer would really be foolish enough to give away his real name, they made sure that the Durham newspapers wrote about the search for an MG-driving Davidson who might have gone missing at the time of the murder.

In one of the greatest manhunts London had ever seen, the police kept searching for the 'Nylon Stocking Murderer', as the killer was termed by the newspapers. They described him as a very dangerous, abnormal man, and feared that he might strike again, against another prostitute. In an ambitious trawl through the Paddington underworld, various perverts, American army deserters and assorted foreign riff-raff were flushed out of their hideouts, but none of them matched the description of the killer. On 3 June, there was a breakthrough: the body of the twenty-nine-year-old baker Donald Davidson was found near Sunderland. He had shot himself through the head. Nearby was a black MG sports car, containing a suicide note to his parents, and some press cuttings about the murder of Agnes Walsh.

Investigating Donald Davidson's antecedents, the police found that his parents were prosperous bakers and confectioners. Donald worked in the family business. He was a respectable man without a criminal record, and without any known predilection for consorting with young prostitutes in seedy London hotels. Importantly, he had been away from home, probably in London, at the time Agnes Walsh was murdered, and returned home with scratches to his face. Samples of his handwriting were well-nigh identical to the entry in the register of the Laura Hotel. Hoping for a solution to the mysterious Soho and Covent Garden murders of prostitutes in 1947, the police questioned Davidson's sister at length about his travels to London in recent years, but without any worthwhile clues emerging. The police would have arrested Donald Davidson, Detective Chief Inspector Jamieson told the coroner, and charged him with the murder of Agnes Walsh. Still, the outcome was that the coroner's jury returned a verdict of murder by some person or persons unknown, something that annoyed the Scotland Yard detectives, who felt certain that Davidson was their man.[37]

The Murder of Francis Drake, 1952

Mr Francis John Drake was a gloomy old pensioner, living in his house at No. 79 Warwick Avenue, Maida Vale. Although this wealthy miser owned the entire five-storey house, and the one next door as well, he lived in a dark and insalubrious basement flat. A bearded, scruffy-looking old fellow, he collected the rents from his various houses in person, and was well known to carry a lot of money around. After Mrs Drake had died in 1950, her husband remained in the basement flat at No. 79. Once Drake was alone, he became fearful of robbers and intruders, to the extent that he was very reluctant to open his front door. He seldom spoke to any person, and was always very badly dressed, looking like a tramp.

On 27 February 1952, the tenant Klara Klein found the eighty-seven-year-old Francis Drake lying in the back entrance to his flat. He told her that he had been attacked by a man who he had mistaken for the person who collected his other rents. At Paddington Hospital, he was found to have serious head injuries and six broken ribs. He told the police that his attacker had pushed him down, kicked him hard, and knocked him on the head with great force. This cowardly assailant was described as a clean-shaved, round-faced man, 5 feet 10 in height and 35–40 years old, wearing a dark overcoat with a grey trilby hat and a thick scarf. He had run off without stealing anything.

'Attack Recluse Dies!' was the headline of the *Paddington Mercury* of 3 March 1952: indeed, old Francis Drake had expired from his injuries, and the case was now one of murder. There was further newspaper sensation when the shabby old recluse turned out once to have been an artist of some repute. In 1916, he had exhibited 'The Nativity', a design for stained glass, at the Royal Academy, and his flat was full of fine oil paintings, one of them a self-portrait. Francis Drake's nephew Geoffrey described him as a property owner and art dealer, however.

But although a witness had seen a man fitting Francis Drake's description of his killer staking out the premises at No. 79 Warwick Avenue, and although more than 300 people were interviewed by the police, the murder was never solved. Since the murder of an uninteresting old pensioner remained unrecorded by the national newspapers, it is virtually unknown today. As George R. Sims rightly put it, the most horrible mysteries of London are sometimes its forgotten ones. In yet another of London's forgotten murders, an old man was brutally done to death by some callous brute, in what was presumably a burglary gone wrong. The murder remains unsolved today, but hopefully, the Warwick Avenue murderer has by now faced a higher tribunal.[38]

Murder and Robbery in Lisson Grove, 1954

In the United States, many convenience stores and liquor stores have a bloody history: either crazed robbers, high on crack cocaine, have gunned down the owners and robbed the till, or the shopkeepers have returned fire with their sawn-off shotguns with lethal effect. In contrast, London can boast only a few shops that commemorate murder for robbery; one of them is the aforementioned No. 37 St John's Wood High Street, not far away from Lisson Grove. The milk-shop at No. 92 Bartholomew Road, where Mrs Samuels was murdered and robbed in 1887, no longer exists; nor does Mrs Matilda Farmer's shop at No. 478 Commercial Road, where this harmless old lady was wantonly done to death in 1904. The famous murder shop at No. 36 Leinster Terrace, Bayswater, where shopkeeper Ernest Albert Creed was robbed and bludgeoned to death in 1926, no longer remains.

In 1954, the small shop at No. 39 Lisson Grove was kept by the jeweller Mr Marcus Wehrle. On 24 March that year, the Portuguese crook Justine de Almeida burst into the shop, brandishing a loaded revolver. He tied up the shop assistant Edward Mansfield, but then something must have gone wrong, since two witnesses heard revolver shots from inside the shop. They ran to the post office nearby and made sure that the postmistress called 999. A police car promptly arrived, and Constable Geoffrey Bocking made his way into No. 39 Lisson Grove. He found Mr Wehrle and Edward Mansfield with serious gunshot injuries to the head. When he went into the rear yard, he could see a tall, swarthy man lurking at the bottom of the steps. The suspect pulled a revolver from underneath his raincoat, but with commendable bravery, the sturdy policeman leapt at his adversary and seized hold of his arm. The desperate gunman pulled the trigger, but since the constable had a firm hold of him, all he could accomplish was to shoot himself in the chest.

The Lisson Grove desperado later died in hospital, as did Mr Wehrle; the assistant Mansfield lingered for several days before finally succumbing to his injuries. The deadly encounter inside the little jeweller's shop in Lisson Grove had thus resulted in 100 per cent mortality among its participants. It turned out that although Portuguese by birth, de Almeida had spent much of his life in the United States, where he had learnt his gun-toting ways. He had twice been convicted of armed robbery, and spent lengthy sentences inside tough American prisons. He had later returned to Portugal, where he had spoken of going to London to 'collect a fortune' as he expressed it. He had only been in London five days prior to the murder. There was newspaper speculation that de Almeida had been a hitman, employed by some criminal mastermind to assassinate Mr Wehrle, but the police found nothing to substantiate that the harmless Marylebone jeweller had any dangerous enemies abroad. Despite having been established back in 1880, the narrow little jeweller's shop did not contain many gems worth stealing, but de Almeida did not know that, and he was definitely desperate enough to rob a random shop, and to take a shot at the owner if he tried to fight back.[39]

The Westbourne Terrace Mystery, 1956

In 1956, the thirty-five-year-old Mrs Robina Bolton, 'Ruby' to her friends, was a well-known Paddington prostitute. She and her husband Ernest, who doubled as her pimp and chauffeur, lived in a small ground-floor bedsit at No. 32 Westbourne Terrace. This once grand house, situated just at the crossing with Craven Road, a stone's throw from Paddington station, had its entrance from Craven Road, but the sole window of the Boltons' tiny flat was facing Westbourne Terrace.

Robina Bolton had her 'beat' on Hertford Street, and the evenings she prostituted herself, she had Ernest waiting nearby, ready to take her and the 'customer' back to Westbourne Terrace in his car. On 13 January 1956, business was particularly brisk. Ernest took his wife back and forth to the flat for five or six 'quick 'uns' with various blokes. Later in the evening, she had arranged to pick up a 'special' in a cab: a young 'regular' who liked her very much, and had promised her £15, since he was due a payment of £500 from an Oxford JP for a business deal to do with pornographic literature.

Throughout the wee hours of 14 January, Ernest Bolton kept on telephoning Ruby back at the flat, but there was no answer. Presuming that she was too busy with her customers, he had a nap in the car, before ringing her again at 7.30 a.m. Again there was no answer. The puzzled Ernest Bolton went to No. 32 Westbourne Terrace just before 8 a.m., hoping that by now, all his wife's paying customers had made themselves scarce. He had a look through the window, but could see nothing suspicious. But when he opened the flat door with his key, he was horrified to see poor Ruby lying on the bed, murdered by repeated heavy blows to the head.

Ernest Bolton called the police straight away, and the hunt for the murderer began. The autopsy showed that Robina Bolton had been murdered with an instrument like a heavy chopper. The murder weapon had presumably been purposely brought to the flat by the killer, and then removed from the premises after the deed had been done. The neighbours were used to men coming and going to the Bolton flat, and they had not made any worthwhile observations. But when the detectives used their informants among Paddington's many prostitutes, there was soon a vital lead. One of them knew that one of Ruby's 'regulars' had been a young man called 'Len', known as a pedlar of pornographic books. And indeed, it turned out that the twenty-seven-year-old Leonard Vincent Atter had recently been released from Wormwood Scrubs, after spending 12 months there for selling obscene literature! This sounded promising, the police thought, and Atter was speedily arrested. He freely admitted being Ruby's 'regular', and also that he had been with her between 1 a.m. and 2.15 a.m. the night of the murder. He had left her since she was awaiting yet another customer at 3 a.m.

Leonard Vincent Atter was now the main suspect for the murder of Robina Bolton. A well-dressed, personable young man, he looked very different from the stereotypical furtive, rain-coated pedlar of naughty books and postcards of the time. Led by Detective Superintendent Kennedy and Detective Inspector Cornish, the police worked overtime to find out everything about him. As a young man, Atter had served three and a half years in the army, advancing to become an office-clerk corporal. He married an older German woman in 1950, but they had since separated. He came from a religious family, and his two sisters were Salvation Army soldiers. Atter himself was also involved with the Salvationists, and he played the euphonium in one of their bands. But there was clearly a darker side to his character. He had a strong interest in pornography, and started a small business printing pirated or plagiarised porn books, which he sold to sex shops, pimps and prostitutes. There was a healthy interest in pornographic literature at the time, and soon, Atter earned more from his publishing venture than from his humble daytime job as a clerk. He used this money to set up his mistress, the pretty, twenty-two-year-old window dresser Thelma Rudkin, in a comfortable flat at No. 60 St George's Terrace. But unbeknownst to Atter, the Porn Squad was on his tail, and the pornographer received a well-deserved kick in the backside into a cell at Wormwood Scrubs. Both his wife Lisa and his mistress Thelma visited him in prison, but the fickle Thelma later met another bloke and invited him to move into No. 60 St George's Terrace. When Atter was released in early 1956, he was not at all pleased with this state of affairs. Since the flat was his only asset, he moved in there as well, and went back both to his clerical day job and his evening printing business. Soon, he had another stockpile of naughty books to sell. The police did not believe him when he said that he had not paid Ruby a penny; in fact, *she* had paid *him* £2. The reason is likely to be that Atter had traded her a pile of books for a 'freebie'. Ruby may well have been one of his stable of sellers of pornographic books.

The evidence kept mounting against Leonard Vincent Atter. The police could find no evidence that the 3 a.m. client existed, so Atter was the last person seen with the deceased. Both a cab driver and some other witnesses had spotted them on their way to Westbourne Terrace. It also transpired that the day after the murder, Atter had visited a barber to have most of his beard cut off – surely an attempt to disguise himself! When the inhabitants of No. 60 St George's Terrace were questioned by the police, Thelma Rudkin told all about her former boyfriend, and his deplorable habit of going out to visit prostitutes in the evening, carrying a bag full of books. A copy of *True Detective* magazine was found in the flat: it contained a story about two Americans committing a murder with a hatchet just for the fun of it. Had Atter decided to try this plan out in real life? Most importantly, forensic testing demonstrated traces of blood on his hair and clothes, and he was committed for trial at the Old Bailey.

When Leonard Vincent Atter was on trial for murder before Mr Justice Devlin, Mr Christmas Humphries, for the prosecution, made much of the facts that he had been Robina Bolton's last known customer the night she had been murdered, and that he had cut off most of his beard the day after. *The True Detective* evidence misfired badly, since there was no evidence that Atter had read the magazine; when Thelma Rudkin had recommended it to him, he had said that he was not interested. Things went from bad to worse for the prosecution when the forensic expert witness gave evidence. The technique used to detect blood on Atter's hair and clothes was so sensitive that it tested positive for a sprinkling with a fluid containing one drop of blood dissolved in two gallons of water, and it could not differ between human and animal blood. At this point, Mr Justice Devlin had enough: he directed the jury to find Atter not guilty, and the prisoner walked free.[40] The dapper-looking, bearded pornographer gave an interview to a *Daily Mail* journalist, bemoaning his dismal fate: he was poor as a church mouse, had been fired from his job, and had nowhere to live.[41] His wife Lisa divorced him a few months later, for alleged misconduct with 'a woman now dead'. But Atter remarried in 1960, and he was still alive four years later, hopefully supporting himself by more conventional means.

There is no question that Mr Justice Devlin was right: the evidence against Atter was woefully inadequate, and it can be debated whether he should have been committed for trial in the first place. Even the Brief for the Prosecution, today kept at the National Archives, expresses mild surprise why Atter was 'given a run' at the Old Bailey on purely circumstantial evidence. The police file on the case makes it clear that the detectives involved were convinced that Atter was the guilty man. During gruelling interrogations, they did their best to make him confess, but all they could achieve was that when he was confronted with the presumably damning forensic evidence, he said 'If it is Ruby's blood, it looks though I must have done it.' There was something of a 'moral panic' about the pedlars of pornography in the 1950s: the newspapers depicted them as devils incarnate, and a cancer of society corrupting Britain's youth. Did perhaps one or two of the detectives involved in the Robina Bolton case share these views?

So, was Leonard Vincent Atter the guilty man? I would not think so. He had no history of violent crime, there is no believable motive, and Robina Bolton was his friend and business associate. The forensic evidence is useless, and the story of the detective magazine quite preposterous. The detective story 'A Murderer Walked In', which the jurors were directed to read at the Old Bailey, in fact concerns two transatlantic desperadoes attacking a husband and wife from motives of robbery, killing the woman and badly injuring the man. The Westbourne Terrace murder was clearly premeditated, since the killer brought with him the murder weapon, and took it away with him. Yet Atter did not care if he was spotted with Ruby before the murder, surely careless behaviour for a calculating killer. As for other suspects, it appears as if initially, the movements of Ernest Bolton were investigated by the police, but although he lacked an alibi, he was dropped as a suspect when the case against Atter was being built up. Bolton had an old conviction for keeping a brothel, and no history of violent crime. But why were the Boltons so very poor, and why did they live in such a diminutive flat? And what kind of man can calmly sit behind the driving wheel of a car, night after night, chauffeuring his prostitute wife and her customers? Another potential suspect is of course 'Mr 3 a.m.', Ruby's late-night customer. If we presume that he really existed, it leaves the field open that he was an old enemy coming to settle the score with the prostitute who had given him venereal disease, a blackmailer coming to pick up his weekly fee, or a hatchet-wielding maniac whose ideas of some late-night fun were akin to those of Jack the Ripper.

The Leinster Square House of Death, 1957

Ginter Wiora was born in Poland in 1922. After leaving school in 1941, he was conscripted into the German Army, serving as a radio operator until he was captured by the Americans in March 1945. He then served in a Polish labouring brigade for a while, and was stationed in London. After the war, Ginter Wiora decided to remain in the metropolis rather than return to his country of birth, which had been overrun by the Soviet Russians.

Ginter's first cousin George Wiora, who lived in Dorking, helped him to learn the language properly, and to gain employment as a labouring man and storekeeper. His employers thought the young Pole honest and hardworking, although sometimes clumsy and careless. In 1956, the now twenty-four-year-old Ginter Wiora got a girlfriend, the young art student Shirley Marguerite Allen. She came from a respectable family, and had gone to London against the wishes of her parents. They moved into the basement front room at No. 21 Leinster Square, Bayswater. The shabby lodging house at Nos 21–22 Leinster Square was run by Mrs Doreen Dally. She thought Ginter Wiora, who was known as 'Peter' to his friends, a good young lad, honest and upstanding, and very fond of his 'wife' Shirley.

However, in 1957, Ginter Wiora began to change. He became insanely jealous, accusing Shirley of having affairs with other men behind his back. A young French lodger in the house had been flirting with the pretty young Shirley, and suggested that she should become a model. Ginter Wiora suspected that this French interloper was taking distasteful pornographic photographs, with Shirley as his willing 'victim'. On the morning of 4 May 1957, Mrs Dally was awoken by a loud banging noise followed by a woman crying out, 'No, Peter! No! Oh, Peter, please' and then screaming loudly. She resolutely left her own bedroom, the front basement room at No. 22, and went into No. 21 through a corridor. She saw Shirley emerge from the basement flat opposite her own, with blood flowing from a head wound. When Shirley tried to leave the flat, she was held back, and called out, 'Oh, Mrs Dally – help me, please! Peter has gone mad!' Mrs Dally grabbed the girl's arm and managed to pull her into the hallway, before taking her back to her own bedroom at No. 22. As the brave landlady made her way upstairs, however, to alert the emergency services, she saw Ginter Wiora sneaking up on her with mad staring eyes. He stabbed her hard in the chest with a samurai sword. Leaving Mrs Dally bleeding on the floor, the demented Pole then entered her bedroom, clutching the sword. There was the sound of repeated strokes with the sword, and some bloodcurdling outcries from the poor girl inside.

Regretting that she had not locked the door to her bedroom after admitting Shirley, the bleeding Mrs Dally staggered upstairs, where she and another lodger called the police and an ambulance. When DC Drown and PC Tennyson had ascertained from Mrs Dally what had happened, they descended into the basement, where they found the door to Mrs Dally's flat open and Shirley Allen lying dead on the floor. She had been brutally murdered, and the sword, now badly bent, lay on the floor nearby. When the policemen listened outside the locked door to Wiora's own bedsit, they could hear the sound of a radio and a low moaning, and they could also smell gas. The policemen broke down the door and turned off the gas. Wiora lay on a bed, bleeding from a chest wound and from cuts to his wrists. At the local hospital, emergency surgery was administered to both Mrs Dally and Ginter Wiora, with good effect.

Although the Leinster Square murder never hit the national newspapers, it was quite a sensation locally, with the xenophobic Bayswater and Kensington papers pontificating over the sad effects of a 'Girl Art Student' having an 'Illicit Affair with Pole'. The *St Marylebone & Paddington Mercury* could report that after the murder Nos 21–22 Leinster Square had become known as the 'House of Death'; as Mrs Dally was recuperating in hospital after her ordeal, all her lodgers were leaving the house.

Two weeks after the murder, a handcuffed Ginter Wiora was fit to appear at the Marylebone Magistrates' Court, where he pleaded not guilty to murdering Shirley Marguerite Allen. But the forensic and fingerprint evidence against him was rock solid, and so was the testimony of Mrs Dally. Although he had an excellent character, and had been genuinely fond of Shirley before he developed delusions that she was unfaithful to him, he was found guilty of manslaughter under diminished responsibility, and sent to prison for twelve years.[42] The Leinster Square murderer was later transferred to Broadmoor, where he would spend many years. Ginter Wiora became a useful chess player, and contributor to the *Broadmoor Chronicle* on chess and political subjects.[43] He was definitely a Broadmoor patient as late as 1977, and possibly even longer; in fact, there is no evidence that he has died. The 'House of Death' at Nos 21–22 Leinster Square looks exactly like it did in the 1957 crime scene photographs, even down to the iron bars in front of the basement windows.

The Murderous Istvan Szabo, 1960

Today, most people would associate the name Istvan Szabo with the celebrated Hungarian film director by that name but, in the early 1960s, a namesake and fellow countryman of his achieved brief notoriety in London's calendar of capital crime. This Istvan Szabo was a penniless twenty-one-year-old immigrant who lived in a bedsit at No. 45 St Stephen's Gardens, Paddington. He described himself as a student, but seems to have lived off various odd jobs. Szabo did not drink, but he smoked fifty cigarettes a day and led a vicious life. He had convictions for shop-breaking and theft, and his bad timekeeping led to him becoming well-nigh unemployable.

On 29 October 1960, the fifty-three-year-old part-time waiter William Davies, a native of Wales who was known to his customers as 'Happy Bert', was seen to take a young man with him up to his third-floor flat at No. 5 Westbourne Park Road. The following day, he was found dead in there with a deep stab wound in his chest and a knife in his hand. The police were convinced that this was no suicide, however, since the blade of the knife was the wrong way round, and the stab had been made with considerable force. A witness description of the young man seen with the deceased the evening of the murder led to the arrest of Istvan Szabo, who had bragged to his friends that he had killed a 'dirty bugger' or that he had done the 'Bayswater Job'. The motive was presumed to be that 'Happy Bert' had made the young Hungarian an indecent proposal. When remanded in custody by the Marylebone magistrates on 3 November, the Hungarian objected, 'I did not kill him! I only grabbed his wrist and kicked him!' However, on trial at the Central Criminal Court on 15 December, Szabo was found guilty of murder and was sentenced to life imprisonment.[44]

Poles Apart in Westbourne Terrace, 1961

Kazimerz Gielniewski was a distinguished Polish jurist. In 1939, when he was forty-one years old, he fled the Nazi invaders and joined the Polish Provost Corps as a Judge of Appeal. Judge Gielniewski did a good job in the Provost Corps, but in 1946 there was no longer any need for Polish judges in London, nor would the communists welcome his return to his native land, which had been usurped by another dictatorship. To make ends meet, Gielniewski became a hotel waiter, and his wife Alizija also got a menial job. In 1959, the former judge was able to take over the lease of the large house at No. 11 Westbourne Terrace near Paddington station. Gielniewski kept working at the hotel, but his wife settled down managing No. 11 as a lodging house for Polish immigrants.

In 1960, a Pole named Wladyslaw Marian de Sternberg Stojalowski answered a newspaper advertisement about a room to let, and took up residence in a third-floor room at No. 11 Westbourne Terrace. Apart from an English couple living in the lower-ground-floor flat, all the other lodgers were Polish. The fifty-two-year-old Stojalowski was a very odd cove. He claimed, quite possibly with some right, to be of very high birth. He had served in the French Resistance and in the Polish Army, but because he had done little work since the war he was as poor as a church mouse. He was writing a grand epic poem in the manner of Homer, and also a book about politics, he said. He also wrote numerous letters to the queen and the Duke of Edinburgh containing political advice; they were all signed 'Prince Stojalowski'.

The snobbish and eccentric Stojalowski soon stirred up trouble with the other lodgers at No. 11. He did no work and had plenty of time for debate and intrigue. His room was full of framed portraits of the queen and other royal personages, and the impoverished nobleman hoarded a large collection of old newspapers. For obvious reasons, the exiled Stojalowski did not like communists. He was also given to lengthy and vitriolic anti-Semitic rants: the London police was infiltrated by Jews and communists, who tried to steal his possessions and murder him by putting broken glass into his loaves of bread. Stojalowski claimed to be able to tell from a person's features whether he or she had Jewish blood, and he accused a young lodger named Gregorz Jaskiewicz of being in cahoots with his persecutors.

On 12 June 1961, 'Prince Stojalowski' came running into Paddington police station, complaining that the lad Jaskiewicz had assaulted him. He was sporting two black eyes. Since Stojalowski also said that Jaskiewicz had attacked, and possibly killed, Judge Gielniewski, some constables were sent to No. 11 Westbourne Terrace to see what these excitable foreigners had been up to. They found Gielniewski in the toilet on the landing between the third and fourth floors, with severe head injuries inflicted by repeated blows from a heavy bottle. He died in hospital soon after. Stojalowski was adamant that the lad Jaskiewicz had attacked both him and the judge, but since he was behaving as weirdly as ever the police did not believe him, and both Poles were taken into custody. At the police station, Jaskiewicz said that Stojalowski had attacked him with a large bottle, and although the agile lad had given the madman a couple of hard knocks in the face he had pursued him up the stairs and slashed his leg with the broken bottle.

It turned out that Jaskiewicz's testimony was fully corroborated by the forensic evidence; furthermore, he had been sitting on a bus on his way home at the time when Gielniewski was murdered. It was soon clear to the police that, although he was an intelligent, cultured gentleman, Stojalowski was as mad as the proverbial hatter. He had been invalided out of the Polish forces in 1946 suffering from paranoid psychosis, and he was certified insane in 1948. From that year until 1955, he had spent a good deal of time in various mental hospitals, without any apparent benefit from the treatment he had received.

A leading judge being beaten to death by a prince right in the middle of London would normally have been a good news story for the tabloid press. In this case, however, the judge was no longer a judge, and the prince was a very bogus one; anyway they were just foreigners, and the evening newspapers did not care much about their antics. Only a few brief notes in *The Times* tell us how Stojalowski was found guilty but insane, and incarcerated in Broadmoor.[45] He eventually made it out of there, however, since he is recorded to have died in Malvern, Worcestershire, in 1986. Only the police file at the National Archives and the murder house at No. 11 Westbourne Terrace remain as memorials to this strange crime.

The Hatherley Grove Fratricide, 1961

John Joseph Sheehan, a young Irish labouring man, was born in Limerick in 1923. He left school at fourteen to become a messenger boy, and later worked as a hospital orderly and a bus cleaner. He came to England in 1948, and moved to London in 1960 to work at Bristow & Darlington Ltd. His employers later described him as a good worker, but an erratic and quarrelsome kind of person. John Joseph Sheehan moved in with his younger brother Charles, in a bedsit on the second floor of No. 20 Hatherley Grove, Bayswater. They were both angry, short-tempered Irishmen, and liked to drink quantities of beer and whisky. The neighbours noted the sound of frequent quarrels emanating from the flat, and often saw the brothers the worse for drink.

Close to midnight on Friday 7 April 1961, Charles Sheehan came staggering downstairs at No. 20 Hatherley Grove, and started banging on the door of a neighbour. He was unable to speak, and covered with blood. He was taken to nearby St Mary's Hospital in an ambulance, but he expired there due to the loss of blood from a deep stab wound in the neck, which had severed a major artery. A police constable returned to No. 20 Hatherley Grove and arrested John Joseph Sheehan, the only other person in the flat when his brother got stabbed to death. The Irishman admitted stabbing Charles with a table knife, but denied intending to kill him. Urine specimens showed that both brothers had consumed the equivalent of 5 or 6 pints of strong beer.

On trial at the Old Bailey for murdering his brother, John Joseph Sheehan gave a good account of himself and seemed genuinely contrite. A psychiatrist gave him a favourable report, and a number of witnesses testified that the brothers had got on perfectly well when sober, and that the prisoner had nothing whatsoever to gain by killing his brother. The jury found Sheehan guilty of manslaughter only, and he was sentenced to four years' imprisonment.[46]

A Serial Sexual Strangler on the Loose in London, 1962

Norman Edward Rickard was a respectable, thirty-eight-year-old victualling supply officer at the Admiralty. He earned a good salary of £1,100 a year, but lived in a humble basement flat at No. 264A Elgin Avenue, Maida Vale. The neighbours noted that, although Rickard went to work immaculately dressed in a homburg hat, black jacket and striped trousers, as befitting an Admiralty clerk, he often went out partying in the evening wearing jeans and a black leather jacket, bringing home various dodgy young men in similar attire. The landlord was unhappy when he saw that Rickard had redecorated his flat with pink wallpaper and a blood-red carpet. The neighbours whispered discreetly that Mr Rickard might well be one of those 'queers', but since he was friendly and generally well liked, they did not think any worse of him.

On the evening of Friday 9 February 1962, Norman Rickard went out partying as usual. In a West End pub, he 'picked up' a sturdy, broad-shouldered young man and brought him home to Elgin Avenue. Since Rickard did not come to work the following week, his colleagues at the Admiralty reported him missing. When the police and the landlord went into the flat, all seemed well at first, but a noxious smell was emanating from a wardrobe. When the door was opened, Rickard's naked body was hanging upside down in there, suspended from a clothes hook. He had been dead for around a week. A forensic examination showed that Norman Rickard had been tied up, bludgeoned and strangled. He might well have consented to being tied up by his sinister visitor, who then showed his real intentions when his victim was incapacitated. Rickard had been a strong, muscular man, with an interest in bodybuilding, but once he had been trussed up like a turkey he was helpless when the killer got to work.

At the time the police were rummaging round in Norman Rickard's flat, the twenty-three-year-old wardrobe boy Alan John Vigar was getting ready for some late-night partying in his room at No. 29 St George's Drive, Pimlico. A former male model, he worked as an actor's dresser in a television studio. On 19 February, he 'picked up' a young man near Victoria, and they took the bus back to St George's Drive. The following day, the landlady found Vigar's naked body in his room. Just like Rickard, he had been tied up and strangled.

The obvious similarities between the two murders led to speculations that a serial killer was on the loose, and intense press interest. 'Tied Hands Murder Riddle No. 2 – Dresser to TV Stars Strangled!' exclaimed the *Daily Mirror*. Other papers speculated that Britain might be plagued by another Jack the Ripper, this time preying on homosexual men. This hypothesis received support when the police revealed that they were cooperating with the Derbyshire police, who had two unsolved murders of middle-aged homosexuals in 1960 and 1961. In the so-called 'Bubble Car Murder', sixty-year-old William Elliott had been found murdered at Baslow, his tiny car being abandoned nearby. George Gerald Stobbs, aged forty-eight, was found battered to death at the same location in March 1961. It was believed that both men had been lured to the Baslow 'beauty spot' by a man pretending to be a homosexual, who had then deliberately murdered them. Had this brutal Derbyshire gay-basher come to London to continue his sanguinary campaign?

The newspaper publicity led to many tips reaching the police from the general public. Two young girls had been taken to a flat in Maida Vale by a mystery man, they claimed, and they were almost certain it was Norman Rickard's flat! How frightened they would have been if they had known that the corpse of the householder was hanging in the wardrobe! The man had given them some champagne to drink, but they had given him the slip since he seemed quite sinister. Then another, possibly slightly more reliable, young woman testified that she had met a woman wearing only a nightdress under a man's overcoat in Elgin Avenue. She had looked very shocked, and was exclaiming, 'My God!' Surely, she must have been to Rickard's flat, the newspapers speculated.

The police had a number of witnesses seeing Rickard and Vigar together with the killer, and although their descriptions of him were vague and contradictory, an identikit picture was constructed. The police detectives trawled the 'gay bars' of the West End, carrying leaflets with the identikit, captioned, 'If you see this man, notify us immediately. Do NOT take him home ...' The identikit image was thought to match the mugshot, held at Scotland Yard, of an Irish criminal with violent sadistic tendencies; this man had recently been in London, where he had made his presence felt. A homosexual who had promised to testify against him with regard to an unrelated matter was given round-the-clock police protection, since he feared for his life. However, when the Irishman was later arrested in Glasgow, he was able to clear himself from the suspicion of being involved in the Rickard and Vigar murders.

The vague descriptions of the man seen with Rickard and Vigar, and the reluctance of witnesses from the West End homosexual *demi-monde* to come forward, meant that the police investigation made little headway. There was nothing to suggest that the two victims knew each other: after all, Rickard had been a respectable, middle-class man, whereas Vigar had been an effeminate 'nancy boy'. At the inquests on Rickard and Vigar, a police sergeant who had kept watch at another house in St

George's Drive testified that he had seen Vigar return home the night of the murder with a tall, slim, fair-haired man who was extremely well dressed. His impression was that some 'toff' had 'picked up' young Vigar for some late-night fun. The other sightings of the murderer were of an inferior quality, some of them even raising the suspicion that Vigar might have 'ditched' the unpromising lad he had picked up at Victoria, to go home with a wealthier and more attractive man instead. In April 1962, a former West End club owner was arrested in Zürich, on a warrant issued in Tangiers four years earlier for leading young people into debauchery. He was questioned by the Scotland Yard detectives, since he knew Rickard and Vigar, but without anything worthwhile being concluded. In July, a steward on the liner *Rangitot* was arrested and put on an identification parade, but was released the day after. In May 1963, there were newspaper rumours that a prisoner had hinted that two other convicts had murdered Rickard and Vigar together, but this proved yet another red herring.[47]

In December 1964, there was a brief revival of newspaper interest in the murders of Rickard and Vigar, after the fifty-one-year-old homosexual police canteen manager Vincent Keighery had been found murdered in his flat in Carroll House, Craven Terrace, Paddington (the block still stands). He had been seen returning to his flat with a pale-faced, fair-haired young man in his twenties. There was speculation that Rickard and Keighery had known each other, but this was never confirmed. Instead, the murder of Vincent Keighery was solved by some good old-fashioned police work: fingerprint evidence led to the suspicion of three young thugs, and the clothing they had worn the night of the murder was found in a seaman's bag deposited at Victoria station. In March 1965, twenty-six-year-old John Simpson, twenty-three-year-old William Dunning and the twenty-year-old seaman Michael Odam were convicted for the murder of Vincent Keighery. They were sentenced to death, but this was commuted to life imprisonment.[48] There is nothing to suggest that these three thugs had anything to do with the murders of Rickard and Vigar.

At about the same time, there were some very interesting developments in the investigation of the two unsolved Derbyshire murders of homosexuals, mentioned earlier. A young soldier named Michael Copeland confessed to murdering both these men, as well as a German teenager whom he had dispatched while on active duty in

Germany. He later retracted his confession, but the damage was done: he was convicted of murder and sentenced to death, but again the sentence was commuted.[49] A photograph of Copeland shows a rather thuggish-looking youth with thick dark hair, and so he looked quite unlike the elegantly dressed, fair-haired man who had been seen with Alan John Vigar the evening of the murder. Would a brutal Derbyshire 'gay-basher' like Copeland really have fitted into the London gay scene well enough to be able to gain the confidence of the educated and experienced Norman Rickard, and the pretty young Alan Vigar, who is unlikely to have been short of admirers?

The Scotland Yard police files on Norman Rickard and Alan John Vigar are still closed, and are likely to remain so for some considerable period of time to come, due to their spicy contents. If the police sergeant really saw the murderer with Alan John Vigar, then it is strange that his observation was not given higher weight by the police, since the identikit image showed a more brutal, threatening figure. There has been speculation that elements within the police wanted to 'frame' the aforementioned Irish criminal for the murders, and that they made sure the identikit looked very much like him. The three young toughs who murdered Vincent Keighery were just random violent robbers, and had no pathological hatred against homosexuals, so they can probably be exonerated. Michael Copeland is a more promising candidate, since the two Derbyshire murders were linked to the two London crimes at the time, and since he was definitely a cold-blooded killer with a hatred for homosexuals. Would such a rough country bumpkin, who had been a private soldier in the Army from an early age, really have been able to disguise his homophobia and gain the confidence of his two victims? Nor was Copeland a sophisticated strangler, but a believer in extreme violence: he had brutally bashed his two Derbyshire victims to death with a blunt instrument, and stabbed the young German lad not less than twenty-seven times. Perhaps the murderer of Norman Rickard and Alan Vigar was no gay-basher at all, but a perverted sadist, who was homosexual himself and enjoyed watching his bound and helpless victim die from slow strangulation? Did he commit suicide after the Vigar murder, or did he mend his ways to live happily ever after? The murder flat at No. 264A Elgin Avenue still exists, and so does the house at No. 29 St George's Drive where Alan Vigar's young life was ended.

Murder by a Teenager at Randolph Avenue, 1964

Mr Stanley Bragg, a seventy-seven-year-old pensioner, lived in a small ground-floor flat in the large terraced town house at No. 7 Randolph Avenue, Maida Vale. A scruffy, untidy old fellow, he had a long history of psychiatric disease. Although the recipient of a not ungenerous military pension, he lived in squalor, eating tinned cat food and scraps he had found in the street. Since Mr Bragg did not trust banks, he had in excess of £3,500 locked away in a box in his flat, but he did not touch this money if he could help it. A middle-aged woman named Mrs Cotter looked after him from time to time, and helped him clean his flat. Since the grumpy old recluse did not trust hospitals either, she also nursed him when he was ill. Mrs Cotter lived in a third-floor flat at No. 7 Randolph Avenue with her husband and three children.

There were of course rumours among the neighbours that Mr Bragg was a wealthy miser who hoarded money and valuables in his flat. On 15 June 1964, Mrs Cotter's son, the fourteen-year-old schoolboy Timothy Noel Cotter, sneaked into Mr Bragg's flat through an open window, and began to search it for hidden valuables, as the old man slept next door. However, Mr Bragg woke up and the boy panicked, smothering the old man to death with a pillow. At first, it was thought that Mr Bragg had died from natural causes, but a competent pathologist found clear signs of asphyxiation.

Although the tall, thin Tim Cotter was just fourteen years old, he had shown worrying signs of immaturity and delinquency. He had not coped with a grammar-school education, and truancy was the result. After stealing £26 from Mr Bragg in January 1964, he had been leniently treated, and allowed to repay the money from the 10s a week he earned from his newspaper round. When Mrs Cotter discovered that Tim had Mr Bragg's keys, she asked him where he had got them; he sullenly replied, 'I think I've done him in!' The shocked Mrs Cotter said that she had to inform the police of this, and Tim agreed to come with her to the police station. When examined by a psychiatrist, he was found fit to plead, and of above average intelligence.

On trial at the Central Criminal Court on 15 September, Tim Cotter pleaded guilty to manslaughter, and his plea was accepted by the prosecution. Mr Justice Thesiger sentenced him to be detained at the discretion of the Home Secretary, for at least ten years.[50] Poor Mrs Cotter was led weeping from the court. Ironically, it was divulged during the trial that, when the police searched Mr Bragg's flat, they found £24 in cash and £3,500 in securities, which the clumsy killer had not managed to lay his hands on.

It would appear as if Tim Cotter served his sentence and then disappeared into obscurity; there is nothing to suggest that he was ever guilty of another serious crime. The murder house at No. 7 Randolph Avenue has been renovated throughout, and looks much more presentable than in the days of Stanley Bragg and Tim Cotter.

Clanricarde Gardens Again, 1966

Anthony Milne Creamer, a tough young Glaswegian, left school aged fifteen in 1960 to become a barrow boy. Two years later, he got a job at Oxford, but was dismissed for fighting another employee. Two rounds of borstal did him little good, and in late 1965 he was sentenced to nine months in prison for breaking and entering. Emerging from prison in May 1966, he got a job as a kitchen-boy in London, working long hours for a very low salary, which he usually spent on drink. A strong man with a liking for street-fighting, he was quite good at karate.

Andy Allan, a twenty-year-old barman at the Shakespeare pub near Victoria station, was a well-behaved young man who was good at his job, and did not have a criminal record. He was openly homosexual, and spent much time chasing men at various gay clubs and taking them home to his tiny bedsit at No. 35 Clanricarde Gardens, a number of houses down from where Reginald Holloway had murdered his sister-in-law back in 1933.

Andy Allan and 'Tony' Creamer first met in late June 1966, when the latter had a drink or two at the Shakespeare. Although it was clear to Tony that Andy was a 'queer', they went out on a pub crawl together. Andy said he had a pregnant Doberman bitch, and Tony was keen to buy one of the puppies. After drinking all evening, they went to visit the old couple who were taking care of the dog. Tony was dismayed to see that the animal was just a corgi. The laughing barman was lucky not to have received a karate blow on the spot for this silly joke. When Andy invited his new friend back to No. 35 Clanricarde Gardens for some 'fun', Tony said he was not interested.

Nevertheless, Andy and Tony met again at a pub on 7 July. Andy talked about his most recent boyfriend, a chef, and Tony made jokes about the diminutive 'Doberman'. The day after, Tony went to see Andy again at his bedsit. The following day, young Allan was found murdered in a cupboard. Tony was soon caught in the police trawl of Andy's friends and acquaintances, since several people had seen him with the deceased on 7 July. He admitting knowing Andy, but denied being a homosexual. With a left-luggage ticket found in Tony's flat, the police could retrieve a suitcase full of objects stolen from No. 35 Clanricarde Gardens. Tony's fingerprints were found all over the murder flat.

Tony Creamer told the police that he and another young man named Urquhart had gone to Andy's flat for a marathon drinking session. All of a sudden, a drunken fight had broken out, and when attacked by both men he had made use of his karate skills to defend himself, killing Andy and knocking Urquhart out cold. He was still resentful about the dog incident, saying, 'He told me he had a Doberman which was having pups and I was going to buy one off him, but it was only a fucking Corgi he had!'

The man Urquhart denied having anything to do with the murder, and his fingerprints were not found in the murder flat. Since the police were satisfied that he was not involved, Creamer alone stood trial for the murder of Andy Allan, on 25 October 1966. He had admitted killing Andy with seven karate blows in rapid succession. Mr Justice Glyn-Jones said that two psychiatrists had described him as a dangerous man, and a believer in the use of violence. He was sentenced to life imprisonment, and Mr Justice Glyn-Jones added that he would write to the Home Secretary recommending that he should not be released until the prison authorities were convinced that he could walk the streets without constituting a danger to the public.[51] A *Daily Express* journalist expressed relief that the 'First Karate Killer' had been put behind bars for a very long time. Describing karate as a 'brutal and ugly form of physical violence', he predicted that this dangerous oriental school of martial arts would cause further mischief if it was not speedily prohibited.

Murder and Mystery in Great Portland Street, 1969

Back in 1969, the shop at No. 78 Great Portland Street, at the corner with Riding House Street and not far from the BBC building, was Mr Leon Weinstein's jeweller's and pawnbroker's shop. On 20 February that year, the seventy-three-year-old Mr Weinstein was hard at work on the premises, with his two assistants Charles Day and Frank Biering. Mr Biering was himself past retirement age, at sixty-seven, and he had once owned his own small jeweller's shop. All of a sudden, three masked intruders burst into the shop from the rear entrance, brandishing their shotguns and demanding money. When the three elderly custodians of the shop tried to defend themselves, the robbers knocked down Mr Weinstein and Charles Day with the butts of their shotguns. This did not stop Frank Biering from fighting back, and one of the robbers shot the unarmed old man at point-blank range with a powerful shotgun, killing him instantly.

The three robbers ran out of the shop with £2,500 they had stolen, taking off in a bright red Ford Transit van that had been parked nearby for use as a getaway car. This car was driven by a fourth member of the gang. After Mr Weinstein had recovered from the hard knock he had received, he lurched out into Great Portland Street, shouting, 'They have shot him!' Detective Chief Inspector Bruce Wilson, who led the hunt for the shotgun raiders from the Marylebone Lane police station, realised that he was dealing with professional gangsters. He was surprised that one of them had 'lost his head' and gunned down the harmless old shop assistant. Giving an interview to the *Daily Express*, Mr Weinstein said that this was the third time his shop had been robbed. Thirteen years earlier, the brave shopkeeper had chased an armed robber out of the premises, and six years ago he had attacked another armed robber with a cosh, evicting him from the premises although the robber fired two shots. Keeping a central London pawnbroker's shop was clearly a dangerous business in those days.

It was suspected that the same gang had robbed a jeweller's shop in Balham High Street six days earlier, and soon the police managed to track some suspects down. The motor trader Charles Parsons, the dealer George Smith and the unemployed labourer Arthur Sullivan were all arrested and remanded in police custody, charged with murder at the Marylebone Street Police Court, and two other men were arrested and charged with conspiracy to rob. In the end, the three suspected murderers were all committed for trial at the Central Criminal Court, but the other two men were discharged. It was noted that several relatives of the three men were present in court, loudly protesting their innocence.

In the end, the three suspects were found not guilty of murder, and Parsons was also cleared of both the robberies. Smith and Sullivan were found guilty of conspiracy to rob, and sent to prison. The unsolved murder of Frank Biering is yet another of London's many forgotten mysteries, and the old murder shop is today the Rose Rebel upmarket fashion shop.[52]

The Ripper of Maida Vale, 1972

In 1972, the large and ramshackle detached house at No. 61 Randolph Avenue, Maida Vale, was subdivided into a number of small flats and bedsits. Flat 14, situated on the fourth floor, was home to the twenty-two-year-old Amala de Vere Whelan. She had been a student at Warwick University, but had failed her exams and left without a degree to study part-time at the University of London, supporting herself by working as a waitress and barmaid.

In November 1972, Amala de Vere Whelan had lost her barmaid job and was unemployed. On 16 November, a workman who came to redecorate her bedsit found her body lying in the living area of the flat. She had been raped and strangled, and the black dress she had been wearing was crumpled around her waist. The murderer had doused her body with lemon cleaning fluid, and used the same fluid to write the word 'Ripper' on the wall. He had covered her head with a towel, presumably because he found it spooky to have her dead eyes staring at him as he ransacked her flat.

In the early 1970s, the area around Randolph Avenue was a decidedly shady part of London, with many rundown or derelict houses, and it was known as a red-light area as well. In spite of her unpromising living accommodation and her part-time work as a barmaid, however, the police found that Amala de Vere Whelan had a good reputation, and that she had not been a streetwalking prostitute. She seemed to have taken her university studies reasonably seriously. She had no steady boyfriend at the time of the murder, and none of her previous male acquaintances seemed capable of murdering her. Interviewed by a *Daily Express* reporter, one of the detectives expressed his frustration that so very few people had known the recently arrived out-of-towner Amala de Vere Whelan. He suspected that some of her friends might well know more than they were willing to tell the police.[53]

The police suspected that Amala de Vere Whelan's body had been in the flat since Sunday 12 November, since she had been seen on that day in a public house at Sutherland Avenue, wearing the black evening dress later found around her waist. A man with bushy Afro hair had been with her; in spite of his rough appearance, this individual had spoken with a 'quite educated' accent. The police suspected that he was a local, perhaps another impecunious university student.[54]

The bushy-haired young man was never found, and Maida Vale's 'Ripper' murder was never solved. Randolph Avenue is today a very good address indeed, and the large and impressive murder house at No. 61 has been renovated throughout, and subdivided into six luxury flats.

6

Islington

There are no mysteries of modern London worse than its unrecorded ones. There are disappearances that were never chronicled, murders that are never discovered; victims of foul play who go certified to the grave as having succumbed to 'natural causes'.

George R. Sims, *Mysteries of Modern London*

The present-day London borough of Islington was formed in 1965 through the merger of the former metropolitan boroughs of Islington and Finsbury. Islington itself originated as a small manor north of London. In Georgian times, it was quite unspoilt, and home to fashionable spas, tea gardens and amusements. The development of the Regent's Canal and the growth of the railways caused large parts of Islington and its surroundings to be developed into housing during Victorian times. Largely a working-man's district, it also contained some areas of middle-class respectability.

Wartime damage, and considerable developments and slum clearances, have deprived Islington and its surroundings of many a historic murder house. Nothing remains of the old shop at No. 2 Junction Road, Holloway, where the baker James Sweetland murdered the cheesemaker Mr Buckler in 1880, although Sweetland's own shop at No. 7 still stands. No. 90 Paul Street, Finsbury, where James Finemore murdered his wife in 1887, no longer frowns upon the passer-by. As for the Islington Child Outrages of 1895, nothing remains of No. 41 Parkfield Street, off Liverpool Road, where the appositely named Alfred 'Chopper' Gamble murdered little Sidney Dowling, nor of No. 18 Sidney Grove, where the demented Chopper stabbed and mutilated 'Little Willie' Cattell. Chopper Gamble was incarcerated in Broadmoor, and the mystery of a number of wanton mutilations of young children in the Islington area was solved.[1]

Islington in 1840, from an old postcard.

It is not generally known that not far from Parkfield Street, where Chopper Gamble once preyed on little children, Islington has its own spooky 'murder neighbourhood', home to a surprising number of tragedies over the years. Alight at the Angel and go to the house where the baby farmer and murderess Annie Walters lived, at No. 11 Danbury Street. After speculating about how many shameful little bundles this wicked woman had dropped into the nearby Regent's Canal, go to No. 25 Noel Street, where the brilliant young playwright Joe Orton was murdered by his homosexual lover in 1967. Then round the corner is No. 4 Burgh Street, where the businessman James Cameron was murdered in 1970, and a few streets to the north is No. 81 St Peter's Street, where Thomas Neal murdered his wife in 1890. You will end up at No. 22 Islington Green, where Frederick George Murphy murdered the prostitute Rosina Field in 1937. I am sure that the late Mr Charles Fort, and other 'occult philosophers' believing in hauntings and ley lines, would have objected to settling down in this particular part of London.

Murder at the Lion Tavern, 1864

The Metropolitan Cattle Market, just off the Caledonian Road, was built by the City of London Corporation and opened by Prince Albert in June 1855. The market was established to remove the difficulty of managing live cattle at the meat market at Smithfield. The central market area was arranged in a rectangle with stalls and pens for cattle, sheep and pigs, and a tall central clock tower. A large slaughter yard was nearby. At each of the corners of the main area were five market taverns, built in a similar style, providing accommodation and entertainment for those visiting the market: the Lion, the Lamb, the White Horse, the Black Bull and the Butchers Arms.

The Lion Tavern, an imposing four-storey building, dominated the neighbourhood. It was busy day and night, with thirsty drovers, slaughtermen and carters keen to have a pint or two. The landlord Mr Fred Keeble was assisted by his nephew Henry, and by a large staff of barmaids, waiters and housemaids. The three floors above the pub were used as a private restaurant, and as a hotel.

On the evening of 8 June 1864, when a number of customers were swigging hard from their beer glasses at the Lion Tavern, they heard a loud scream from upstairs. As Henry Keeble ran upstairs to investigate, he was met by the twenty-three-year-old waiter Charles Frederick Bricknell, who told him that he had just committed murder. The victim, the twenty-two-year-old chambermaid Jane Geary, was lying dead at the top of the stairs.

When he was arrested by a police constable, Bricknell said that he would tell all about his crime. Although cautioned by the constable, he went on to say, 'She is the only girl I ever loved; and poor girl she has got it, and I hope she will die!' When the doctor came downstairs to announce that Jane Geary was indeed dead, the sinister Bricknell exclaimed, 'I would rather she was dead than anyone else should have her!'

The police discovered that, for many months, Charles Frederick Bricknell and Jane Geary had been sweethearts. He had expressed a wish to marry her, but she had not shared his enthusiasm in this respect, and the relationship had begun to cool down. Indeed, Jane had started 'walking out' with a young man whom she introduced as her cousin, something that had infuriated Charles. Once, when watching the jolly 'cousin' emptying a pint of ale at the Lion Tavern, he had exclaimed, 'That is the man that has taken my peace of mind!' He had spoken confusedly to his fellow servants about getting his own back on 'the cousin', or even destroying himself and leaving all his worldly belongings to his faithless Jane. She had confided in her fellow servants that she was becoming worried about what Charles might be up to.

At the coroner's inquest on Jane Geary, a verdict of wilful murder against Charles Frederick Bricknell was returned. When the young waiter was on trial for murder at the Old Bailey before Mr Justice Erle, things were not looking good for him. The Lion Tavern witnesses delivered their evidence clearly and without contradiction, making it clear that the jilted Charles had got hold of a knife and kept it in readiness to end the young life of his faithless Jane. His barrister Mr Sleigh tried to convince the jury that his client had been so distressed, and his mind so very unbalanced, at the time of the murder that he should be found guilty only of manslaughter. This feeble defence did not have the desired effect: Charles Frederick Bricknell was found guilty, sentenced to death, and executed outside the Old Bailey on 1 August 1864.[2]

The Metropolitan Cattle Market remained active for many years, although the importance of the trade in livestock diminished after the First World War. It became a market for various furniture and bric-a-brac, before finally closing in 1963. The site has been extensively developed with nondescript modern housing, but four out of the five pubs remain: the Lion, the Lamb, the White Horse and the Butchers Arms. Solidly built, the imposing four-storey Lion Tavern, which today is at No. 98 North Road, still dominates its surroundings, although it has been converted into flats. The Lamb, currently for sale, may well be heading for the same fate.

Murder at Brecknock Road, 1886

In 1886, the ground floor of the house at No. 165 Brecknock Road, Kentish Town, contained a large chemist's shop that doubled as the local sub-post office. On 20 June that year, Mr Hardy the chemist was not at the premises, but his daughter Frances acted as postal clerk, and the shop assistant John William Bowes looked after the druggist's counter. A local youth, the nineteen-year-old George Vincent Finch, who had been loitering outside the shop for several hours, suddenly ran into the post office and seized hold of the cash box that Miss Hardy had left on the counter. 'Stop thief!' cried the assistant Bowes, leaping out to intercept Finch, but the demented youth pulled a revolver and shot him at nearly point-blank range. Miss Hardy heard the shot and came running in to the shop, giving a scream when she saw that Bowes was badly wounded. Finch took a potshot at her as she stood just inside the shop door, but

Murder and robbery in Brecknock Road, from the *Illustrated Police News*, 19 June 1886.

missed. He then ran away clutching the cash box, pursued by a lad named Alfred Partell, who had seen him fire at Miss Hardy.

It turned out that Bowes had received a revolver shot in the head, which had killed him instantly. As the shop was filling up with police constables, the brave lad Partell came running up to tell them that Finch had taken refuge at No. 15 Ospringe Road nearby (the house remains). Since this was actually Finch's mother's address, Chief Inspector Millward and his men realised that they were hardly dealing with a master criminal. The police burst in to the house, but initially they could find no trace of Finch. His mother became quite hysterical when she realised that her son was a murderer. In the meantime, the police found a hidden trapdoor inside a closet, leading to a small hiding place where the demented Finch was lurking. 'Give me the revolver, Finch!' Chief Inspector Millward ordered. 'It was entirely an accident!' a muffled voice replied from the hideout, presumably alluding to the murder of Bowes. The police kept negotiating with the hidden gunman, trying to persuade him to surrender his weapon, but Finch said he would only give it to a detective. The exasperated policemen began pulling up floorboards to get to grips with the hidden murderer, but before they were done, Finch meekly handed his revolver over to Detective Sergeant Miller. A sturdy policeman seized hold of his hand, and he was unceremoniously dragged out of his hideout.

George Vincent Finch's mother freely gave interviews to the press, declaring that, in spite of his shabby appearance, her son had received a superior education and aimed to become an artist. Recently, he had been behaving very strangely, getting involved with private theatrical performances. After he had sold tickets to a play to be staged at Kilburn town hall, the audience was disappointed when the actors went on strike because he had no money to pay them with. Mrs Finch had seen better days, she claimed: her late husband had been an officer related to the Earl of Aylesford. Now, she was reduced to living off a small income, and letting rooms to lodgers. George Vincent had been a worry to her with his strange behaviour, which had deteriorated after he had fallen off a bicycle in Highgate Road and landed on his head. Once, he had pushed down a small boy who had annoyed him, and made to beat him with a walking stick. One of his uncles had died in an asylum, and his cousin went insane from too much study, or so at least Mrs Finch alleged.[3]

At the coroner's inquest, George Vincent Finch cut a sorry figure. Described as an unmanly looking youth with a prominent nose, he sat grinning inanely at the witnesses describing the post office shooting tragedy. When asked if he had anything to contribute himself, he stood up and theatrically exclaimed, 'I simply know nothing about it, your Worship. I don't know the gentlemen who have come here. I don't remember being in the chemist's shop. That is all what I wish to say, thank you!' By the time of the trial of George Vincent Finch at the Old Bailey, he had been examined by Mr Gilbert, the surgeon at Holloway Prison, and the physician Dr Bastian, attached to King's College Hospital, and they were both of the opinion that the prisoner was quite insane and unfit to stand trial. Finch was committed to Broadmoor, and the 1891 census lists him as one of the inmates there. He was released in 1922, into the care of the Salvation Army, and there is good reason to believe that he expired in Brentwood, Essex, as late as 1951. The murder house at No. 165 Brecknock Road is still standing, and has barely changed at all since the time of the shooting tragedy back in 1886.

The Canonbury Murder, 1888

In 1888, the year of Jack the Ripper, No. 19 Canonbury Terrace, Islington, was home to the sixty-nine-year-old bank clerk Charles Cole Wright and his seventy-one-year-old wife Frances Maria. He was in reasonable health, but she was very feeble due to heart disease. She was only just capable of indoor locomotion, but unable ever to leave the house. As housemaid, the Wrights had a young woman who called herself Mrs

Hooker, but she went away in early 1887, and they had to employ various hired helps. Exactly a year after she had disappeared, 'Mrs Hooker' returned out of the blue, and got her old job back without any awkward questions being asked.

No. 19 Canonbury Terrace was (and still is) a three-storey, double-fronted, end-of-terrace residence, with a blind wall facing Canonbury Road. This terrace was a row of nineteen houses, situated in Alwyne Villas. Opposite No. 19 Canonbury Terrace lived two Frenchwomen, Barthe Prevotal and Selina Chefdeville. At close to 3 p.m. on 16 May 1888, Mme Prevotal saw two men go up the steps of Mrs Wright's house, and knock on the door. When the door was opened, the men went in, and three screams were heard. One of the men hastily shut the door. This looked quite sinister, Mme Prevotal thought. Being elderly and timid, she called her younger friend Mme Chefdeville, and that lady donned her shawl and bonnet to investigate. She crossed the road and knocked on the door of No. 19, but there was no response. The sturdy Frenchwoman thought of fetching a police constable, when the neighbour at No. 18 called out that two men had just climbed out of the garden of No. 19!

Mme Chefdeville ran out into Canonbury Road, where she saw a tall man carrying a bag, and a shorter man. Most Victorian ladies would have hesitated to tackle two burglars, as she presumed them to be, but Mme Chefdeville was made of sterner stuff. A tall, sturdy woman, she charged the two men, calling out the French equivalent of 'Stop thief!' Presumably quite astounded by this sudden assault, the shorter man turned into Alwyne Road, and his taller companion made off into Astley Road opposite. Mme Chefdeville pursued the taller man. In spite of her corpulence, she was still capable of a sprint, and for a while she was just a few yards behind the fugitive.

There were several workmen and cab drivers in the road and, had Mme Chefdeville screamed out to them that she was pursuing a thief, the fugitive would have been promptly tackled. The problem was that the monoglot Frenchwoman hardly knew a word of English; the reaction of the bystanders as she ran after the man, gabbling volubly in her native tongue, was one of derision. As a result, the workmen merely stood astounded when she came pounding past them, since, although she 'was halloaing and making motions to stop him', as one of them expressed it, they could not understand a word she was saying. A woman living in

Mme Chefdeville challenges the Canonbury Terrace burglars, from the *Penny Illustrated Paper*, 26 May 1888.

Mme Chefdeville chases the person she presumes to be the murderer, and a view of the murder house, from the *Penny Illustrated Paper*, 26 May 1888.

Astley Road saw the tall man come running past her into River Street, pursued by a crowd of mischievous street boys, and by the panting Mme Chefdeville. He dropped his bag to distract the boys, ran across busy Essex Street, and was gone.

Mme Chefdeville found a police constable in Canonbury Road, but he turned out to be yet another poor linguist, merely scratching his head as the excited Frenchwoman gabbled away in her own language. In the end, using sign language, she made him follow her to No. 19 Canonbury Terrace. In the passage, at the foot of the stairs, they found the body of Mrs Wright in a sitting position against the wall. The unfortunate old lady had a large bruise below the left eye, indicating that one of the ruffians had felled her with a blow. The autopsy showed that her heart had been much diseased, so that the shock of being knocked down might well have killed her. Mrs Wright had two pockets in her skirts, one containing some keys and a few silver coins, the other seventeen gold sovereigns and a half sovereign. Neither had been touched by the murderer or murderers.

At the inquest on Frances Maria Wright, her husband testified to her bad health. The house had been burgled five years earlier, when the Wrights had been on a seaside holiday, and he had lost all his valuable plate. He had not replaced it, instead making sure that the house contained nothing of any value, apart from 'an accumulation of old clothes'. Mr Wright was very wary of burglars, and so was his wife. The day before the murder, a man had come up to No. 19 'asking an obviously useless and "fishing" question, as though to gain either admittance or information about the inmates'. The following morning, Mr Wright had warned his wife not to answer any knock without putting the chain on the door, advice that the feeble old lady unfortunately had left unheeded. The inquest returned a verdict of wilful murder against some person or persons unknown. There was a good deal of newspaper publicity about the 'Canonbury Murder'. Not without reason, it was considered particularly reprehensible that a respectable, elderly householder had been done to death by a callous burglar. A *Penny Illustrated Paper* journalist reminded his readers that 'London residents cannot be too strongly reminded that there are wild beasts in human form about, ever seeking prey ...'[4]

Police Inspector Davies and Detective Sergeant Maroney, the officers in charge of the Wright murder inquiry, were convinced that two

Above: The Canonbury Terrace murder house and other images, from the *Illustrated Police News*, 26 May 1888.

Left: The murder house, and other sketches in connection with the Canonbury Murder, from the *Pall Mall Gazette*, 19 May 1888.

burglars had entered No. 19 Canonbury Terrace with intent to steal, and that one of them had knocked the old lady down, killing her. Such a gang of burglars needed an 'inside man' – or perhaps an 'inside woman' – to know which house to target, however. The servant girl 'Mrs Hooker' turned out to be a 'wife' of the common-law variety, and her 'husband' Hooker was currently serving a long sentence for highway robbery. The twenty-one-year-old Mary Dominey, to call her by her proper name, had given birth to two children, both presumed to have been fathered by Hooker the highwayman. After he had been incarcerated, she had suffered great difficulties in supporting herself and the children, in spite of returning to work with Mrs Wright. Although Mary Dominey was repeatedly questioned and bullied by the police, she vehemently denied tipping the burglars off about the unprotected house. At the inquest, she had told a story about being accompanied to No. 19 Canonbury Terrace by another girl named Amy White, but Mr Wright had never seen or heard about this person. Sergeant Maroney suggested that Amy was an invented character to cover up Mary's own misdeeds, but, as tough as ever, Mary gave nothing away.

For several months to come, the Wright murder investigation made very little progress. However, in the evening of 27 August 1888, it had a lucky break when a nineteen-year-old woman named Phoebe Field was arrested for drunkenness. She sported a formidable-looking black eye, the result of a blow from her former boyfriend Alfred Edwards. Phoebe also told the constable that her current boyfriend Henry Glimmon had been involved in the Canonbury Murder. Another burglar, known only as 'Long Jack', had knocked Mrs Wright down, and they had stolen £17 in gold and some coppers.

Once she had sobered up, Phoebe was formally questioned about the murder. She said that, seven weeks earlier, she had been living with a man named Alfred Edwards, as his common-law wife. One day she met Henry Glimmon in a pub, and after an acquaintance of just a few hours she left Alfred and became Henry's 'wife' instead! Alfred was far from happy about this, but he did not dare to challenge Henry, a dangerous character who hinted that he had killed before, and might just as well be hanged for six or seven as for one, as he expressed it. One night, talking in his sleep, Henry admitted having committed the Canonbury Murder, adding, 'Never mind, mother, it will soon be all right.' When Phoebe confronted him with this nocturnal confession, he said that he had burgled No. 19 Canonbury Terrace together with a man known as 'Long Bob', with a man named Charles Parsons acting as lookout and a girl working on the premises doing the 'inside job'. Henry had knocked Mrs Wright down to stop her screaming, but accidentally killed her. 'Long Bob' found the £17 in her pocket, but did not steal the gold coins, exclaiming, 'Now you have killed her I cannot touch it!' as he ran off.

This sounded promising, the police thought. They knew a thief named Henry Glennie, and Phoebe admitted that due to drunkenness and illiteracy she had got his name wrong. Sergeant Maroney went to put more pressure on Mary Dominey; surely, she must have been the gang's female accomplice. However, Mary was adamant that Amy White was the guilty party. She added that she had once quarrelled with the elusive Amy, who had been 'walking out' with Henry Glennie at the time, screaming, 'I will have you locked up for the murder at Mrs Wright's house' at her rival. Later, she had met Henry in the street, and he had freely confessed murdering Mrs Wright, adding that he thought the newspaper illustrations of himself being chased by the portly Mme Chefdeville quite hilarious. This Islington burglar was much less inclined to merriment when he was arrested by the police later the same day, and charged with the Canonbury Murder.[5]

When the twenty-four-year-old Henry Glennie was on trial for murder at the Old Bailey, on 22 October 1888, Mme Chefdeville and others described how they had chased the miscreant. None of Mme Prevotal, Mme Chefdeville or two other witnesses could identify Glennie as the man they had seen. However, the cabbie John Jones picked out Glennie from a crowd of seventeen men as the man he had seen running through the streets, as did the housewife Johanna Rowe. Mr Austin Metcalfe, who defended Henry Glennie, gave Mary Dominey a proper grilling. He accused her of being a prostitute, and exposed that she had once been arrested for theft, but got off through giving evidence against her accomplice. The fact that she had been living in sin with a serious criminal did not help her credibility. Why had the police allowed her a guinea a week until Glennie had stood trial; were they bribing her to make sure she did not refuse to give evidence? Phoebe Smith fared little better: the important discrepancies between her initial evidence and her testimony in court were relentlessly exposed. Had the police perhaps given her some 'help' to adapt her testimony to the known facts of the case? Was it not odd that she could not even tell the correct name of the man whom she cohabited with, and then accused of murder? The police had to admit that 'Long Jack', or 'Long Bob' for that matter, could not be traced. The man Parsons, implicated by Phoebe Smith, had just been sentenced to five years' penal servitude for a watch robbery. Glennie's defence was a moderately solid alibi: his sister, and three other people, testified that he had been at Neasden the afternoon of the murder. The jury found Glennie not guilty, and the murder of Mrs Wright remains unsolved to this day.[6]

The jury probably did the right thing in acquitting Henry Glennie, since the evidence of Phoebe Smith and Mary Dominey seems far from convincing. Had Phoebe decided to 'frame' Henry for the murder after he had gone out with some other floozie? The tale of the burglar who did not steal £17 in gold sounds too good to be true. If, as must be presumed, 'Long Bob' got his name because of his tall stature, then surely *he* would have been the taller of the two miscreants, and thus the person chased by Mme Chefdeville. It also seems highly likely that Mary Dominey was the gang's female accomplice, that she invented the character 'Amy White', and that she made up her evidence against Glennie when the police put her under serious pressure.

Henry Glennie got married in 1890, and the 1901 census lists him as a hot water boiler fitter. At the time of the 1911 census, he was also gainfully employed. He is likely to be the Henry Glennie who died in Hammersmith in 1930, aged sixty-seven. Charles Cole Wright did not mourn his murdered wife for very long: he remarried later in 1888, although he died less than two years later. Due to their habit of frequently 'changing their names', nothing worthwhile can be unearthed about the latter careers of that deceitful pair, Phoebe Smith and Mary Dominey. In 1890, a burglar named Frederick Bedford confessed to the murder of Frances Maria Wright, but since he was known for his lying habits he was not believed at the Birkenhead Police Court, the magistrate declining to take proceedings.[7]

What *can* be revealed, however, is the location of the murder house. Canonbury Terrace is today part of Alwyne Villas, and the nineteen houses in this terrace have been renumbered. There is only one house that has a blind wall facing Canonbury Road and matches the three original drawings of the murder house: the present-day No. 1 Alwyne Villas, the nineteenth house in what was once Canonbury Terrace. It is also possible to follow in Mme Chefdeville's footsteps from the murder house, along Canonbury Road, Astey Road (today Astey Way) and River Street (today River Place), where the presumed murderer crossed Essex Road.

A Murderous Islington Sailor, 1890

For many years, the seaman Thomas Neal sailed the seven seas before the mast, accumulating a considerable amount of money, before stepping ashore sometime in the 1870s and settling down in Islington. Here, he built up a bricklaying business with some degree of success. A short and sturdy man, he dressed in old-fashioned nautical attire. Being quite deaf, he spoke in a stentorian voice, frequently making use of coarse and earthy language. He drank quantities of beer and 'grog', and was more than once in trouble for getting into fights and knocking his opponents senseless.

In 1883, it occurred to the now sixty-year-old Thomas Neal that perhaps he ought to marry. Since this Islington Popeye wanted a young wife, he paid court to the sixteen-year-old Teresa Gray. Her father was impressed with Neal's apparent wealth, and this mismatched couple were duly married. In spite of his age, the former sailor still had lead in his pencil: after their marriage, Teresa gave birth to five healthy children in rapid succession. Still, all was not well with Thomas and his family. The old sailor had a furious temper, and he beat his wife up at the slightest provocation. Once, when his mother-in-law Esther Gray objected to him disciplining Teresa using a stick, the sturdy mariner unceremoniously knocked her down. He then threw his wife from the parlour into the passage, seized hold of the mother-in-law and threw her on top of poor Teresa, and thrashed Mrs Gray with the stick until she begged for mercy. For this outrage, Esther Gray had Thomas prosecuted before the magistrates, and he was sentenced to two months in prison.

This short period of incarceration did nothing to improve Thomas Neal's fierce and angry nature. He preferred drinking to bricklaying, and as a consequence was soon short of money. He blamed his young wife for not taking proper care of their children, not entirely without reason, since she had insisted that four out of the five children were 'farmed out'. This cost money, and money should be spent on 'grog', he reasoned. Thomas was also very worried that Teresa was unfaithful to him. He drew dark inferences from her habit sometimes to stray from the family home, to drink at various public houses, and consort with some dubious 'gentleman friends'. On 23 January 1890, Thomas came lurching into the Pied Bull public house asking for his wife. On being told that she had not been there, he exclaimed, 'God blind and punish me, if I catch the bloody pair I will settle them!' The man he was referring to was a certain Harry Day, whom the old sailor suspected to be more than friendly with his faithless Teresa.

A few days later, the rowdy Neal family were evicted from their lodgings, having to find another room at No. 81 Peter (today St Peter) Street at very short notice. Thomas's boxes were still stored with his long-suffering mother-in-law, with whom he and his wife also took their meals. On the morning of 28 January, Thomas came to Esther Gray's house to have his breakfast. Finding that his wife was not there, he suspected she was up to no good. Grasping a hammer in a furious temper, the old sailor stalked off to No. 81 Peter Street to 'have it out' with his wife. When Thomas burst in to the tiny second-floor front bedroom, she was still asleep. He seized hold of her with a hearty goodwill, and the neighbours heard a cry of 'Murder!' and repeated heavy blows. Bleeding profusely, Teresa tried to run downstairs, but Thomas seized hold of her again, and forcibly kicked her out of the front door. He

Shocking wife murder at Islington, from the *Illustrated Police News*, 8 February 1890.

kicked another lodger, Eliza Waterman, after her, shouting, 'They have robbed me enough!' It turned out that Teresa had been stabbed hard in the throat, chest and shoulder, and she expired at St Bartholomew's Hospital a few hours later. The newspapers printed a description of the absconded murderer:

> Thomas Neal, aged 67, height 5 ft 2 in; stout; complexion fair; hair, whiskers and moustache grey, shaved on chin; dress, long brown overcoat, light pepper-and-salt jacket and vest, light grey trousers, side-spring boots, black hard felt hat; very deaf; has been a sailor.

The furniture dealer Benjamin Dawson, with whom Thomas Neal was on good terms and who took care of one of his sons, was surprised when the ex-sailor came to see him at midday on 28 January, looking very dejected. Thomas said goodbye to his son, explaining that he had killed his wife and that he was about to give himself up to the police. On the way to the police station, however, the old sailor changed his mind, deciding to leave the district where he was well known, and think of some stratagem to lie low. The description of him issued by the police proved his undoing, however; late the same evening, two police constables recognised him in Ball's Pond Road, and took him into custody. A bloodstained knife was found in his pocket.

On trial at the Old Bailey for the wilful murder of his young wife, things were looking very black for Thomas Neal. Witness after witness, his mother-in-law prominent among them, outlined how he had been brutally mistreating his wife for many years. Several eyewitnesses had seen him pursue Teresa down the stairs of No. 81 Peter Street, and then kick her out. His bloodstained knife matched the injuries on her body. When asked if he had anything to say, Thomas exclaimed, in his stentorian voice, 'I have got nothing to say, and I have no witnesses; my witnesses have all turned my enemies!' He was found guilty of murder, sentenced to death, and executed at Newgate on 26 March 1890.[8]

Murder at the Swan, 1894

In 1894, the large and prosperous Swan public house, situated at No. 125 Caledonian Road not far from the Regent's Canal, was managed by Mr Francis Christopher Hill. He lived on the premises with his wife, his stepdaughter Lily Kate Allen, and his daughter Violet May Hill. Several servants also slept in the house, one of them the twenty-year-old barman George Ward. The son of an army captain who had died prematurely, he had seen better days, and resented his humble occupation.

The reason George Ward stayed at the Swan was that he had fallen deeply in love with the seventeen-year-old Lily Allen. A tall, attractive girl, and an accomplished singer and musician, she was at first flattered by Ward's attentions, and even wrote him some letters, but she soon tired of him. For her part, Mrs Hill very much disapproved of George Ward, and she thought her daughter could do much better than marrying a penniless barman without prospects in life. She preferred an Australian midshipman named Gohegan, who had also paid Lily attention, and the girl was soon engaged to marry this individual. To get Lily away from the Swan, and the angry, jealous George Ward, she was apprenticed to a milliner.

George Ward murders Lily Allen at the Swan public house, from the *Illustrated Police News*, 24 March 1894.

On the morning of Saturday 17 March 1894, one of the servants brought up some tea for Lily Allen and young Violet Hill, who shared a bedroom on the upper floor of the Swan. The girls were terrified to see George Ward come crawling into the room on his hands and knees after the servant had left. He was carrying a large hatchet, and held a razor between his teeth. Without saying a word, he leapt to his feet and struck Lily hard on the head with the hatchet, rendering her insensible. He then proceeded to cut her throat with the razor, and young Violet Hill, who tried to protect her sister, herself received a serious wound in the arm. The demented Ward then cut his own throat with great violence.

Hearing poor Violet screaming, Mrs Hill ran upstairs. The horrid sight she was met by was vividly described in a newspaper:

> On the floor beside the bed lay the murderer, a ghastly object, bleeding freely from the throat, and on the bed lay Lily Kate Allen, a girl of 17, weltering in a mass of bloodstained bed clothes, with the blood issuing from a fearful gash in her throat. The younger daughter Violet, ten years of age, was kneeling up in bed, screaming frantically.

Mrs Hill did not faint at this dreadful scene, but resolutely threw the window open and called for assistance. When a police constable arrived at the pub, Mr Hill, clearly a man who did not waste words, said, 'Go and fetch the doctor, that barman of mine has cut my daughter's throat, and also his own.'

There was much uproar in the King's Cross area after this dreadful murder and suicide, and it is stated that 'during the whole of Saturday and yesterday the house in which the double crime was perpetrated was literally besieged'. The bodies of the dead were removed to the mortuary. Violet Hill was put under the chloroform and had her arm stitched up by a doctor. At the time of the inquest, a week later, she was still in hospital. At the inquest, some papers found at Ward's lodgings were examined. He was the son of the late Captain A. Ward of the 3rd Dragoons. Ward had saved some letters he had received from Lily Allen, couched in affectionate terms. Ward's uncle claimed that Lily Allen had once given Ward a card case, and that he had given her an umbrella and an engagement ring. There was a heated quarrel between Mr Hill and the uncle about whether Ward and Lily had ever been out together.[9]

Here this unedifying story ends, except for the good news that Violet May Hill survived Ward's frenzied attack; she married a man named Symons in Plympton in 1903, and seems to have lived to quite a respectable age. As for the murder pub, it remained the Swan for many years, but it is today the Canal 125 bar and restaurant.[10]

The King's Cross Murder, 1896

James Riley was a master builder and consulting engineer, with his office at No. 40 North (today Northdown) Street, King's Cross. He lived in the two floors above the office, with his wife Emma and their three little daughters. Riley also owned No. 42 North Street, which he had let to the young butcher Elijah Galley in 1894. A wealthy capitalist, he owned various other London houses as well.

After Elijah Galley had moved into No. 42, it did not take long for tension to develop between landlord and tenant. Galley called himself 'The Poor Man's Butcher', a title he earnt by undercutting the prices of the other local butchers. Such practices did not make him popular, and he was constantly fearful that the rival butchers would lie in wait to beat him up, or vandalise the butcher's shop. Galley kept a sharp lookout outside the shop, chased impudent boys away, and called the police if he thought some person was spying on him.

With time, the Poor Man's Butcher's Shop did better and better. By mid-1896, Galley was earning more than £55 a month. He was popular among his customers, and everything seemed rosy for him and his family. However, James Riley was becoming increasingly averse to living next door to the Poor Man's Butcher. He did not think it was appropriate to undercut the price of meat, and considered Galley a bounder who stole customers from the other King's Cross butchers. When Riley accused Galley of defaulting on a week's rent, the butcher retorted that he had really paid it. When Galley went round the neighbourhood complaining of Riley's dishonesty, the wealthy builder had finally had enough of his troublesome tenant. On 4 July 1896, he wrote a letter giving Galley notice to leave the premises, and had his clerk deliver it.

To Elijah Galley, who had spent many months building up his flourishing butcher's shop, this was a both cruel and unexpected blow. His customers were mostly local people, and he feared they would not stay loyal if he moved shop. Not unreasonably, he thought Riley a cad for not having the courage to confront him face to face. Without further

Above: Elijah Galley goes on a rampage at No. 40 North Street, from the *Illustrated Police News*, 11 July 1896.

Left: No. 40 and No. 42 North Street, from the *Illustrated Police Budget*, 11 July 1896.

ado, he seized his large butcher's knife, entered Riley's house and walked upstairs. Without knocking, he burst into the front kitchen, where Riley was just unlacing his youngest daughter's shoes. His eldest daughter, nine-year-old Elizabeth Alice, was also in the room. 'What is the meaning of this?' the furious butcher exclaimed, holding up the letter. 'What it is!' Riley curtly replied. When Mrs Riley came into the room and approached Galley, he seized up the butcher's knife and stabbed her hard. Riley grasped a poker and struck Galley a glancing blow on the forehead, but the sturdy butcher did not go down. Instead, he seized hold of his landlord and stabbed him again and again, until he was dead. The two little girls sat petrified, witnessing the murder of their parents.

Having murdered the Rileys, Elijah Galley ran into the back kitchen and down the stairs. His assistant James Holton was surprised to see Galley come lurching into the butcher's shop, bleeding profusely from the forehead. 'Jim, fetch a policeman!' he said. When the assistant asked why the police were needed, Galley just groaned, 'I am done, Jim!' At the same time, young Elizabeth Alice Riley had managed to get the attention of a passer-by, and three police constables came to No. 40 and No. 42 North Street to examine the scene of the murder, take care of the two little girls, and arrest Elijah Galley.

At the coroner's inquest on James and Emma Riley, a verdict of wilful murder was returned against Elijah Galley. On trial at the Old Bailey in early August 1896, the little girl Elizabeth Alice Riley gave pathetic and damning evidence against Galley. Weeping profusely, she described how the butcher had stabbed both her parents to death. The verdict of the jury could be either murder or manslaughter, and the former verdict seemed the more likely one. Galley was an honest, hard-working tradesman, though, and several witnesses testified as to his excellent character and reputation. In court, he seemed extremely dejected, and certainly did not fit the stereotype of a brutal, callous murderer. He was perfectly sane, and not a habitual drunkard. The jurymen clearly found it abhorrent to find him guilty of murder, but the facts of the case were there for all to see. After deliberating for ninety minutes, the jury failed to agree.

Next month, a new jury was sworn and the trial restarted. The evidence from poor little Elizabeth Alice was of the same distressing nature. Defending Elijah Galley, Lord Coleridge contended that the unexpected eviction from the butcher's shop had temporarily unhinged his client's mind. Disputing the little girl's evidence, he suggested that, in fact, Riley had been the one to strike the first blow, with the poker. There had been contradictions in the girl's evidence in the two trials, he claimed (they were in fact very unimportant, but the new jury did not know that). Nor had it been entirely ruled out, the clever Lord Coleridge continued, that Mrs Riley had also had some kind of weapon handy. It was natural for a butcher to carry his knife with him everywhere, and thus there had been no premeditation. Elijah Galley was willing to plead guilty to manslaughter, and rather surprisingly the prosecution accepted this plea. It was noticed that 'the prisoner seemed agreeably surprised at the verdict, and waved his hand to friends in the gallery as he left the dock'.

Mr Justice Kennedy sentenced Elijah Galley to twenty years' penal servitude for each count of manslaughter, the two sentences to be concurrent.[11] At the time of the 1901 census, Galley was in Portland Convict Prison, but in 1911 he was in Maidstone county gaol. He was released not long after and reunited with his family. There is reason to believe that Elijah Galley died in Bromley in early 1944, aged seventy-eight.

The Islington Baby Farmer, 1902

Baby-farming was an unsavoury phenomenon in late Victorian Britain. Catering to pregnant young women who were keen to get rid of their babies, the baby farmers either adopted infants for a lump sum, or undertook to care for them for periodic payments. Most women chose to give their children to baby farmers due to their children's illegitimacy, which at this time carried with it many stigmas. The baby farmer made more money if the child died, especially if the mother had paid a fixed fee, because often this amount of money was too little to pay for the child's care for any substantial period of time.

Some baby farmers adopted numerous children and then either neglected them or murdered them outright. The doyenne of this particular profession was Amelia Dyer, who operated from a small terraced house at No. 45 Kensington Road, Reading (it still stands). Her daughter Polly was her accomplice; she lodged at No. 76 Mayo Road, Willesden (the house no longer stands), and it was from here that Mrs Dyer removed two unwanted babies and disposed of them in the Thames. However, one of the mothers changed her mind and wanted to

The baby farmers Mrs Sachs and Annie Walters are hanged, from the *Illustrated Police Budget*, 7 February 1903.

see her poor little baby one final time! Lacking the innovative thinking to produce *another*, living baby, and show it to the mother before she went to the police, Mrs Dyer and Polly were in dire straits when the two tiny corpses were fished out of the Thames. The harridan Mrs Dyer was executed in 1896; Polly and her husband were very lucky to get off without charge.[12]

Amelia Sachs and Annie Walters were another pair of hardened wretches who made a good profit from the baby-farming trade. Amelia Sachs, who was both clever and enterprising, set up a private nursing home at Claymore House, situated in Hertford Road, East Finchley. Around 1900, she began to advertise that babies 'could be left', and took money for adoptions. The clients, judging from the witness accounts, were mostly servants from local houses, who had become pregnant and had employers who were keen for the matter to be resolved discreetly. Having learnt from Amelia Dyer's dismal end, she made *damned* sure that her 'clients' were determined never to set eyes on their 'shameful bundles' again, before the babies were murdered. Acting the part of a professional foster parent, Annie Walters offered to adopt the babies for a fee of £25 or £30. She then took the poor little creatures to her lodgings at No. 11 Danbury Street, Islington, where they soon ceased to exist.

However, the rather foolish Annie Walters had chosen the wrong house to lodge in, since it was owned by a policeman named Seal. He and his wife soon became suspicious of their sinister lodger's extremely rapid turnover of babies. When the careless Annie gave another lodger at No. 11 some money to buy poison, Constable Seal called in his police colleagues. On 18 November 1902, Annie Walters boarded an omnibus and went to South Kensington. She was followed by a detective named Wright, and when he saw that she was carrying a baby-sized bundle he arrested her and demanded to see its contents. The dead baby inside was just a day or two old. When charged with murdering it, Annie exclaimed, 'I never murdered the dear! I only gave it two little drops in its bottle, the same as I take myself!'

The clumsy excuses of Annie Walters led the police on to Amelia Sachs, who was also arrested. The 'Islington Baby-Farming Case' was headline news. Many people marvelled at the hardened cruelty of these two inhuman women. Annie Walters had deliberately smothered or poisoned the babies, before dumping the corpses in waste ground, or 'leaving them behind' in public houses. An unknown number of babies were murdered this way, quite possibly dozens. The evidence against Amelia Sachs and Annie Walters was rock solid; they were found guilty of murder and executed at Holloway Prison on 3 February 1903. This was the only double execution of women that had taken place in modern times. Still, there were not many people who felt much pity for such hardened wretches; the usual squeamishness with regard to hanging women did not apply to baby farmers.[13]

A descendant of Amelia Sachs has recently managed to track down Claymore House, and found that it had acquired a bad reputation due to the criminal activities that had taken place there. Sometime after the trial of Sachs and Walters, the building had its name chiselled off the stone plaque above the window, and it is now just plain No. 5 Hertford Road.[14] The house where most of the babies were murdered, No. 11 Danbury Street, also still stands. It is a small terraced house, early Victorian in style, and not unpleasantly situated, without any modern buildings nearby. Not far away is the Regent's Canal: how many pathetic little bundles did Annie Walters feed the fishes with, dropping them from the bridge near the house where she lodged?

Murder by 'Poor Wally', 1907

Walter Edward Fensham was a young Islington labouring man. He had been a carter, but after being thrown from a horse he had become apprentice to a bookbinder. Although 'Poor Wally' was just thirty years old in 1907, his general health was far from good: he suffered from scrofulous glands on the neck, had twice been operated on for some internal complaint thought to be appendicitis, and was lame in one leg after being kicked by a horse. These disagreeable ailments caused him to drink heavily, and a foolish doctor prescribed him laudanum, to which he became addicted.

Nor was 'Poor Wally's' family life particularly happy. He was very fond of his father James, but disliked his stepmother Harriett, since she bullied and mistreated the doting old man and treated the children from his first marriage with disrespect. Although he was as poor as a church mouse, Walter could not stand living in the same house as this virago of a stepmother, and he left the family home at No. 15 St James Road, Islington, and moved into some very insalubrious lodgings on King's Cross Road. He often came to visit the family home, to see that all was well with his father and to have a hearty meal; in spite of her mean-spirited nature, his stepmother was an excellent cook.

On 28 December 1907, Walter Fensham came to visit No. 15 St James Road, where his stepmother cooked him a pork chop, which he devoured. Then there was an angry altercation, which deaf old James Fensham, who was sitting in the front room having a discussion with his landlord, did not hear. When James Fensham heard his daughter Florence cry out, he went into the kitchen, where he found his wife lying on the floor, with a knife embedded in her throat. Florence explained that 'Poor Wally' had stabbed her, before making a hasty escape from the premises. A doctor was called, and Harriett's lifeless body was removed to the Great Northern Hospital, where she died the following day.

The hue and cry was up for Walter Fensham, who had taken refuge in the house where his brother lodged, at Granville Place, Marylebone. He was talking confusedly about stabbing his stepmother, but the brother thought he was just drunk as usual. When the maudlin Wally finally reeled off towards his own lodgings, the brother felt uneasy, and he went straight to No. 15 St James Road to find out what had happened. Once he was informed that Harriett Fensham had really been stabbed, he directed the police to Walter's lodgings, where the culprit was arrested.

After recovering from a powerful bout of delirium tremens, Walter was declared fit to stand trial for murder, which he did at the Old Bailey before Mr Justice Phillimore. Things were not looking good for him: there was no doubt that he had wilfully murdered his stepmother with a knife he had brought with him on purpose, since Dr Scott, medical officer of Brixton Prison, was of the opinion that he was fully sane. Before stabbing Harriett, he had exclaimed, 'I don't care if I get hung for poor father!' Walter's defence team did their best to emphasise their client's failing health and unhappy position in life. There was no doubt that the stepmother had been a very angry, mean-spirited woman. Hoping to replicate the success of his near-contemporary Robert Wood, Walter Fensham stepped into the witness box. He gave a realistic account of his miserable life, adding that when he had been working for the London Omnibus Carriage Company he had fallen off a large dray horse and landed on his head. The large lump on the back of his head still remained, as did his terrible headaches, which forced him to take whisky and laudanum every day.

The day before the murder, Walter had been drinking very hard, and this drinking binge had continued the following day. He could vaguely remember eating the pork chop, and hearing his stepmother exclaim, 'You are only a bastard and come here to get what you can out of your father!' but he could not remember stabbing her, he claimed. Several witnesses came forward to testify that Walter had been very drunk the day of the murder, and that he had become addicted to laudanum after undergoing an operation to have tubercular glands removed from his neck. He was sentenced to death, but with a strong recommendation to mercy.[15]

Surprisingly many people did what they could to save 'Poor Wally' from the gallows. There was a petition among family members, and another among the medical profession. Mr Justice Phillimore did not support the recommendation to mercy, but Mr Herbert Gladstone, the Home Secretary, gave Walter a conditional pardon in February 1908. His health improved in prison, and he was released in 1920. He married a woman named Maud Anderson the year after, and enjoyed a normal family life for a while, but in 1931 he was lost sight of after leaving his wife. He was found in Banstead Mental Hospital the year after, was discharged from the asylum in March 1933, and lived on until 1943.[16] The murder house at No. 15 St James (now Mackenzie) Road still stands.

Murder at the Home for Aged Hebrew Christians, 1910

In 1910, the house at No. 43 St John's Villas, Upper Holloway, belonged to the British Society for the Propagation of the Gospel among the Jews. The idea of promoting Christianity among the Hebrews was a popular one in Victorian times, and the British Society had been founded in 1842, to become the Presbyterian and Dissenting churches' counterpart to another Hebrew gospel society run by the Anglicans. The British Society made No. 43 St John's Villas into The Home for Aged Hebrew Christians, filling it to the rafters with impoverished old Jews who had rescinded the faith of their fathers.

One of the inmates of The Home for Aged Hebrew Christians was the fifty-eight-year-old Noah Woolf, a German Jew who had lived in Britain since 1871. He had worked as a bookbinder, but now he claimed to be crippled due to varicose veins. In spite of his venerable name, shared with the great seafaring patriarch, he had been converted to Christianity. By 1907, Noah and his wife had been admitted to the Home, taking early retirement and leading a comfortable life. Since he was rather a work-shy, idle fellow, life at the Home suited him to perfection. The other Aged Hebrew Christians began murmuring against Noah, however, since he was not only relatively young and able-bodied, but he occasionally smuggled alcoholic beverages into the Home and used coarse language unfitting to a respectable Hebrew Christian. Through toadying to Mr Levinson, the superintendent of the Home, and various other clergymen, Noah managed to stay in residence. His wife died in March 1909, but this did not induce Noah to change his habits of life.

In February 1910, the sixty-eight-year-old former hawker Aaron Simon took up residence at the Home. A very quarrelsome man, he soon became Noah's particular enemy. The Aged Hebrew Christians did not do much work, and had plenty of time for theological debate, gossip, and intriguing against each other. Simon ceaselessly murmured and agitated against Noah: was it not a shame that the Home should be polluted with such a vagabond, who drank beer and whisky, and did not believe in the prophecies in the Bible. Simon cunningly persuaded the superintendent of the Home to call a general meeting of the Aged Hebrew Christians. At this meeting, he himself detailed all Noah's faults, and called a vote of no confidence in him. Not a single Hebrew Christian had any confidence in poor Noah, and Simon urged the superintendent to expel him from the Home. Noah objected that Simon had been lying,

St John's Villas, from an old postcard; the murder house can be seen on the left side of the street.

Man murdered in an Islington Jew's Home, from the *Illustrated Police News*, 5 November 1910.

and that there was a conspiracy against him, but he had to leave the Home on 4 July. The Secretary of the British Society agreed to pay him eight shillings and sixpence a week for three months.

Noah Woolf moved into lodgings at No. 68 Myddelton Street, Clerkenwell. He mended the occasional book, and managed to keep poverty from the door for as long as the British Society kept paying their weekly grant. After three months, however, Noah had to seek cheaper lodgings in Canonbury Road, Islington, and sell all his goods to stay alive. Desperately, Noah wrote to various officials at the British Society, saying that he was a poor helpless cripple who had led a true Christian life at the Home for three years, and begging that he should be readmitted to No. 43 St John's Villas, but without the desired result. As winter approached, the gloomy Jew sat ruminating in the cold, draughty room, dreaming of his former security at the Home for Aged Hebrew Christians, and plotting revenge against the scoundrel Aaron Simon, who had wantonly ended his tenure there. He bought a large knife and had it sharpened for use against his old enemy.

At 9.45 in the evening of 27 October, Noah Woolf came calling at the Home for Aged Hebrew Christians. The matron, who had only been employed at the premises for a few weeks, did not recognise him. Noah asked to see Aaron Simon, but the matron told him that Simon was asleep and should not be disturbed. Without arguing, Noah crept off. When he returned the next morning, again asking for Simon, the matron offered to take him to Simon's room, but Noah said, 'All right, don't trouble, I know where his room is.' Bursting into Simon's room, Noah collared the old hawker with a hearty goodwill, brandishing his large knife. He demanded that Simon should withdraw his accusations against him, so that he could be readmitted into the Home, but even with a knife against his throat the stubborn old man refused. Without further ado, Noah stabbed his enemy hard in the neck and chest, and Simon dropped to the floor. Noah then ran out of the Home, down the front doorsteps, and disappeared.

Trudging back to his lodgings, his final hope of returning to the Home crushed, Noah Woolf realised that he had had enough. Instead of trying to escape, the broken-spirited Jew went to the nearest police station, and admitted the murder of Aaron Simon. Although cautioned by the police, he described how he had purchased the knife, made his way into the Home, and murdered his enemy. On trial at the Old Bailey, Noah made no efforts to save himself from the gallows, nor did the barrister employed to defend him make any worthwhile exertions; in fact, the defence did not call a single witness. The jury returned a verdict of 'guilty', although with a recommendation to mercy. Mr Justice Darling donned the black cap and told the weeping Noah Woolf that he had committed a deliberate and cruel murder, and begged him to make his peace with God. The Home Secretary ignored the recommendation to mercy, and Noah Woolf was executed at Pentonville Prison on 21 December 1910.[17]

Since the interest in converting Jews to Christianity was waning in the 1920s and 1930s, the Home for Aged Hebrew Christians had to close. Eventually, the British Society for the Propagation of the Gospel among the Jews merged with several other agencies for gospel work among the Jews; it is today part of the Christian Witnesses to Israel. The murder house at No. 43 St John's Villas, Upper Holloway, is today a private residence. Is it haunted by the ghost by a gloomy old Jew, who had once found it his sole ark of security in a hostile world?

Murder in Tollington Park, 1911

Frederick Seddon was a miserly, penny-pinching Lancastrian who made his living as the superintendent of collectors for a national insurance company. His wife Margaret Ann, whom he had married in Derby in 1893, ran a down-at-heel second-hand clothes shop at No. 276 Seven Sisters Road (it still stands) and the Seddon family, including the five children and Seddon's elderly father, lived in the three floors over the shop. Seddon had been a Freemason, although he resigned from his lodge in 1906.

In 1909, the shrewd Frederick Seddon made some successful property deals, enabling him to take the lease of a fourteen-room house at No. 63 Tollington Park, near Finsbury Park. With his usual astuteness, he rented the lower ground floor to the insurance company for use as his office. The entire Seddon family were crammed into the three first-floor bedrooms to enable him to rent out the second floor.

In 1910, the second-floor rooms were taken by forty-nine-year-old spinster Eliza Mary Barrow, who moved in, along with her young ward Ernest Grant. She had fallen out with her previous landlord, Frank Vonderahe, her cousin, and the rent on these rooms was cheaper. Miss Barrow was a far from attractive person: prematurely aged, quite deaf,

Right: Frederick Seddon, from F. Young (ed.), *Trial of the Seddons* (London, 1925).

Below Sketches of the Seddons, from the *Illustrated Police News*, 16 March 1912.

reluctant to wash, and drinking like the proverbial fish. She owned capital to the tune of £4,000, including the lease of a pub and a barber's shop, and a quantity of India stocks. The Vonderahes had of course hoped that they would one day inherit her fortune, but Miss Barrow had proven too angry and mean-spirited to have in the house.

Frederick Seddon and Eliza Barrow had one big interest in common: the acquisition of money. Miss Barrow confided in her landlord that after Lloyd George's controversial 1909 budget, she had become concerned about her investments, fearing poverty in old age. He offered to take over the lease of the pub and the barber's shop in return for a small annuity and the remission of her rent. Early in 1911, he increased her annuity in exchange for £1,600 in India stocks. Miss Barrow did not have long to enjoy this annuity, however: just a few months later, she fell ill with incessant diarrhoea and vomiting. Doctors could do nothing for her, and she died of heart failure two weeks later. There was no suggestion of foul play, and the doctor willingly signed her death certificate.

Frederick Seddon made sure that Miss Barrow was buried in the cheapest possible manner, in a public grave. He did not notify her family about the funeral. He would probably have lived happily ever after, enjoying Miss Barrow's fortune, had it not been for her previous landlords, the Vonderahes. Their reaction, when they found out that Eliza Barrow had expired, is likely to have been one of jubilation. However, when Miss Barrow's cousin, Frank Vonderahe, came to No. 63 Tollington Park to take possession of her estate, Seddon informed him that nothing was left after he had paid both the substantial funeral expenses and the cost of Ernest Grant's upkeep from his own pocket. Suspicious over the suddenness of Miss Barrow's death and the clandestine funeral arrangements, the Vonderahes began to think that Seddon had poisoned their relative after first having 'fleeced' her out of her money. They went to the police and demanded an exhumation and autopsy. Miss Barrow's body was examined by Sir William Willcox and Bernard Spilsbury in 15 November 1911; it was discovered that there were about two grains of arsenic in her body.

Frederick and Margaret Seddon were put on trial at the Old Bailey for murder, and it emerged that Margaret had bought a large amount of flypaper. Flypaper contains arsenic, so could have been related to the murder of Miss Barrow. The defence argued that Eliza Barrow could have been taking medicine containing arsenic, and claimed that the defendants were not aware of the existence of arsenic in flypaper. Frederick Seddon's downfall came in his insistence upon giving evidence; his attitude was abhorrent to the jury, who found him guilty. His wife, however, was acquitted.

On hearing the sentence, Mr Seddon made one last effort to secure his future – he knew that the judge was a Freemason, and appealed to him to overturn the verdict in the name of this link. The judge, despite being moved by the plea, was unwilling to reverse the sentence, reminding Seddon that the Freemasons taught against crime and suggesting that he make his peace with God.

On Seddon replying that he had already done so, the judge sentenced him to death.[18] Doubt about his guilt has persisted over the years. He was certainly guilty of being a mean, money-loving swindler, but the chain of evidence linking him to the purchase of flypaper, and the extraction of arsenic from them, remains obscure. There has been speculation that Miss Barrow after all died of natural causes, namely acute gastroenteritis aggravated by dehydration that led to secondary heart failure. Mrs Seddon, who certainly got off very easily, has been accused by some of being the driving force behind the murder plot.

There was an appeal, but this failed, and Seddon was hanged on 18 April 1912 at Pentonville Prison. Mrs Seddon rapidly moved out of the murder house, which was of course not easy to sell. It remains practically unchanged today – a large Victorian semi-detached property in a convenient North London location.

Mercy Killing in Widdenham Road, 1913

In 1913, the flat at No. 137 Widdenham Road, Holloway, was home to the electroplater William Charles Wood, his forty-four-year-old wife Edith, and their thirteen-year-old invalid daughter Ethel. Poor Ethel had been ailing since birth, with severe epilepsy. The pioneer neurosurgeon Sir Victor Horsley had attempted an operation in April 1912, but Ethel's fits continued. On 4 January 1913, Edith Wood entered the Holloway police station in a hysterical condition, exclaiming that she had just murdered her daughter. When Ethel had a very bad fit, she had strangled her to death with a cord. At the coroner's inquest, William Charles Wood and a number of other local people testified that Edith had always been the model parent, and very fond of her invalid daughter. She had neglected everything to look after the ailing girl, and it had distressed her very much that the operation did not have the desired effect. Edith Wood, who was incarcerated in Holloway Prison, was not in a fit state to attend the inquest, which returned a verdict of wilful murder against her, with a rider recommending that the state of her mind should be looked into. Indeed, when Edith Wood was on trial for murdering her daughter, she was found guilty but insane, and was ordered to be detained until His Majesty's pleasure be known.[19]

Brides in the Bath, 1914

On 17 December 1914, a recently married couple calling themselves Mr and Mrs Lloyd rented a first-floor room at No. 14 Bismarck Road, Holloway, a small and nondescript terraced house. Before agreeing to take the room, Mr Lloyd made sure that there was a bath on the premises. He was most solicitous of his wife's health, and took her to see a doctor named Bates, telling a story of some quite dangerous-sounding dizzy spells on her behalf. He also made haste to get his wife to draw up a new will, with himself as the sole beneficiary, at the office of a local solicitor. The same day, he persuaded her to withdraw the entire balance of her savings bank account, amounting to nearly £20. Many recently married wives would have found such a combination of events a little sinister, but Mrs Margaret Lloyd was a simple, naïve woman who had great trust in her husband.

On the evening of 18 December, Mrs Lloyd asked for a hot bath. Her husband sat playing 'Nearer, my God, to Thee' on a harmonium, before going out to buy some tomatoes for their evening meal. When he returned, he found his wife dead in the bath, or so he claimed. When Dr Bates was called in, he agreed that she must have suffered another of her dizzy spells, passing out in the bath and drowning. With unseemly haste, Mr Lloyd arranged for his wife to be buried, and for a solicitor to obtain probate. The London newspapers found it tragic that a recently married young woman would perish in her bathtub. These articles were noticed by two families in Herne Bay and Southsea, whose recently married young relatives had also tragically drowned in their baths! In both these instances, the husband had used gullible doctors to establish a diagnosis of 'fits' before the drowning incidents, before rapidly absconding after having cashed in on the bride's life savings. Surely, this was too much of a coincidence!

Above: George Joseph Smith goes to see the solicitor with his wife, from the pamphlet *Sensational Crimes and Trials*.

Right: A portrait of George Joseph Smith. (Courtesy of Mr Stewart P. Evans)

George Joseph Smith inspects the bath, from *Sensational Crimes and Trials*.

The execution of George Joseph Smith, from the *Illustrated Police News*.

When the police looked into the antecedents of 'Mr Lloyd', he turned out to be a thief, swindler and bigamist whose real name was George Joseph Smith. Born in Bethnal Green in 1872, he had been an extremely bad egg since an early age, constantly thieving and pilfering. Aged just nine, he was carted off to Gravesend reformatory, where he remained until he was sixteen. This lengthy incarceration in the gloomy Victorian reformatory did nothing to improve his character, however: he was soon sentenced to six months' hard labour for stealing a bicycle, and later served time for receiving stolen goods. In 1898, in his only legal marriage, he married Caroline Beatrice Thornhill, although he also married another woman bigamously the following year. Caroline worked as a maid for a number of employers, stealing from them for her husband. She was eventually caught and sentenced to twelve months. On her release, she incriminated her husband, and he was imprisoned for two years in January 1901.

Since Smith was virile and good-looking, he could make a career of offering lonely women marriage, and then deserting them after he had relieved them of their savings. By continuously changing his name, he kept one step ahead of the authorities, and was able to keep adding to his list of 'wives'. To be able to keep 'running' his stable of wives, he faked an identity as an antiques dealer, who had to travel a lot to attend sales and auctions. In 1910, George Joseph Smith had bigamously married Beatrice Mundy. He stole her money and drowned her in a specially installed bath at No. 80 High Street, Herne Bay (the house remains, but it is today No. 159, and part of the Herne Bay Culture Trail). In 1913, he married Alice Burnham, in spite of the determined opposition of her family, who had recognised him as the scoundrel he was. He drowned her in the bath at the lodging house at No. 16 Regent Road, Blackpool (it still stands). These two swindles brought Smith considerable sums of money, but he spent lavishly, meaning that he once more had to resort to his newly invented system of matrimonial assassination. In Bath, he married naïve young Margaret Lofty under an assumed name, and took her to No. 14 Bismarck Road, where she became his third 'bride in the bath'.

Detective Inspector Arthur Neil was suspicious about the likelihood of an adult woman drowning in such a small bath. The only sign of violence was a tiny bruise above her left elbow. Inspector Neil soon knew all about Smith's swindles and his very suspicious doings before his most recent wife's demise. Certain that John Lloyd and George Joseph Smith were the same man, Neil told him that he would take him for questioning on suspicion of bigamy. The man finally admitted that he was indeed George Joseph Smith.

Still, it was necessary to find evidence that Smith had really murdered his wives. Sir Bernard Spilsbury spent weeks trying to establish how a woman of Margaret Lofty's size could have drowned. Finally, he came to the realisation that the lower half of her body must have been pulled in order to bring her head under water. If this were done suddenly and forcefully, the water flooding in to the nose and throat would cause loss of consciousness without signs of drowning. To test his hypothesis, Neil hired some divers of the same measurements as the victims – he found that pushing them under the water would result in visible signs of a struggle, but on jerking one of the women's feet she became unconscious. It took over half an hour for her to come to, and thus proved Spilsbury's theory.

In spite of the ongoing First World War, the trial of George Joseph Smith, which began on 22 June 1915, was quite a media event. The businesslike callousness of the triple murderer was much abhorred, and he was likened to an equally cool customer, Palmer the Poisoner. Smith was only tried for one murder, but the other two deaths were used to explain how the defendant killed. Sir Bernard Spilsbury presented the medical evidence with his usual brilliance, and Smith was found guilty of murder and sentenced to death.[20]

George Joseph Smith was executed at Maidstone gaol on 13 August 1915. The murder house still remains, although Bismarck Road is today known as Waterlow Road, partly because of the murder, but mainly because the local inhabitants did not care to live in a street named after a Hun.

The Islington Barmaid Murder Mystery, 1915

On 23 March 1915, the twenty-nine-year-old Mrs Annie Josephine Wootten, the wife of Lieutenant Albert Wootten of the 10th Bedfordshire Regiment, was found dead on the staircase of their house at No. 114 Rotherfield Street, Islington. A careless doctor thought she had fallen downstairs and broken her neck, but a more prudent colleague at the mortuary, who actually bothered to undress the corpse, discovered that she had in fact been shot in the chest with a small-calibre revolver.

The case was now one of murder, and the detectives took care to question the only two witnesses available: Mrs Wootten's two little daughters. They had heard their mother talking to a person whom she referred to as 'Mrs Higson's friend'. Then there had been two muffled bangs, a cry of pain, and the sound of a heavy fall. The girls had seen their mother with blood on her blouse. The detectives went to call on Mrs Cora Higson, who declared herself certain that the only person in London to whom Mrs Wootten would refer as 'Mrs Higson's friend' was Mrs Marie Lanteri, a barmaid at the Gun public house in Lupus Street, Pimlico. Mrs Higson also knew that Marie Lanteri had been 'carrying on' with Lieutenant Wootten!

Sensing that a vital breakthrough was near, the detectives went to the Gun, where the jolly-looking twenty-two-year-old Marie Lanteri was busy pulling pints. They asked some questions about her in the neighbourhood, and found out that she was using the names Marie Lanteri, Alice Mary Wheatley and Alice Wootten on alternate days, and that she had a keen interest in chasing the lads. The detectives went into the pub and confronted Marie Lanteri, who was soon in difficulties when it came to explaining her use of three different names. Nor did she deny being on very friendly terms with that amorous warrior, Lieutenant Albert Wootten; she had in fact told several people that she was going to marry him. She had previously been married to a bloke named Lanteri, she said, but he had died after just four months, and the marriage might not have been a legal one anyway. When she was arrested and charged with the murder of Mrs Wootten, the cheeky young barmaid exclaimed, 'Cor blimey! That is a nice thing to be charged with!'

Alice Mary Wheatley, to call her by her right name, was clearly a floozie of the first order. Was she also a murderess? Much depended on the evidence from the two children, which was repeated clearly and without contradictions at the coroner's inquest, and a verdict of wilful murder against Alice Mary Wheatley was returned. Before the Old Bailey trial, the detectives worked overtime to find further evidence against the Pimlico barmaid. She had been 'carrying on' with Albert Wootten for several months, and both Mr and Mrs Higson knew all about the intrigue. Since Alice Mary had been talking freely about her plans to marry the lieutenant, Mrs Wootten had also found out about her husband's infidelity. She had forbidden him to see this floozie of a barmaid ever again, but he had clandestinely kept meeting his paramour.

In other words, although Lieutenant Wootten qualified as a 'temporary gentleman' due to his wartime commission, he was a permanent cad. His infidelity to his wife had been bad enough, but his treatment of his mistress was quite reprehensible. He had seduced a young barmaid of twenty and then cast her aside, and when the guilty pair had been living together he had written a letter to her parents, starting, 'Dear Dad and Mother', to convince them that their daughter was really married to him. The police and prosecutors knew that the lieutenant could not have murdered his wife himself, since he had a solid alibi. Nor was there anything to suggest that this 'officer and gentleman' had been sincere in his alleged intention to leave his wife for Alice Mary Wheatley; in fact, he himself freely admitted that the only reason he had kept 'taking care of' his mistress was that he was concerned that she might be 'in the family way'. Lieutenant Wootten agreed to appear in court as a prosecution witness, to testify that Alice Mary had had access to a revolver.[21]

The trial of Alice Mary Wheatley before Mr Justice Lush in June 1915 was quite a media event. Although there was a war on, and the sensational trial of 'Brides in the Bath' Smith was ongoing, there was a fair amount of newspaper interest in the Barmaid Murder Mystery of Islington. The tribulations of young Alice Mary Wheatley, her own loose ideas of morality, the perfidy of the bounder Albert Wootten, and the uncertain outcome of the trial all contributed to keeping the journalists interested. The trial did not disappoint anyone. The prosecution case against Alice Mary Wheatley seemed moderately solid, but her defence team had success in glossing over their client's lurid past and depicting her as a wronged woman, the victim of a much older man. The outcome appeared certain when the far from bonhomous Mr Justice Lush lambasted Lieutenant Wootten for his outrageous conduct, which should give him cause for reflection and shame as long as he lived. He directed the jury to regard the lieutenant as a discredited witness, whose evidence was of no value. As a consequence, the jury was out for only twelve minutes before returning to deliver a verdict of not guilty. Alice Mary Wheatley, who had previously been sitting erect with arms folded during the judge's summing-up, left the dock smiling merrily.[22]

Giving interviews to the journalists after the trial, Alice Mary Wheatley declared that being on trial for murder had been a most tiring experience. She needed a lengthy holiday to recover, and to be capable of pulling pints (and perhaps also men) once more. As for her views on the 'Barmaid Murder Mystery', they would have to purchase the coming weekend's copy of *Lloyd's News*, since this newspaper had just bought the exclusive rights to her story. The weekend feature in *Lloyd's News* contained no further lurid revelations, however, nor any hints about who Alice Mary thought was the guilty party.[23] Thus, after the jolly young barmaid had gone off on her holiday, clutching the cheque from *Lloyd's News*, the mystery remained unsolved. Lieutenant Wootten was clearly a cad, but he had a solid alibi for the time of the murder. Nor had he any motive to murder (or employ some person to murder) the mother of his children, since his intentions towards Alice Mary Wheatley had been wholly dishonourable. The police found nothing to suggest that he had been 'running' any other mistresses on the side. A burglary or robbery gone wrong is not an option, since Mrs Wootten had been shot by a person she had known and voluntarily invited into the house. In contrast to her husband, Mrs Wootten had led a blameless life, without any secret enemies or illicit affairs. If it is true that 'Mrs Higson's friend' could apply only to Alice Mary Wheatley, then things are looking black for our heroine. A neurotic young woman of low morality and violent passions, she would have been perfectly capable of shooting her rival. If there had been reliable evidence that she had access to loaded firearms, her position in court would have been a far from enviable one.

It is not known what happened to Alice Mary Wheatley after the verdict: her habit of changing her name has allowed her to dodge the genealogists with impunity. As for that howling cad Albert Wootten, whose moral defects were so skilfully used by the defence to save Alice Mary from the gallows, the last we hear of him is that the *Gazette* of 13 July 1915 announced that he had relinquished his commission. He may well have been the Albert Wootten who ended the First World War as a private soldier in a labouring battalion.

Mystery of the Thirteenth House, 1919
Lucy Nightingale, a young woman hailing from Liverpool, left her husband in 1919 and took a room at a small brothel at No. 13 Prah Road, Finsbury Park, kept by the retired butcher Henry Ball. Being young and quite pretty, with long dark hair, she made a good living as a London prostitute for several months. However, on 28 July 1919, Lucy Nightingale was found bound, gagged and strangled to death in her room at No. 13, and a murder investigation began.

Sketches from the murder of Lucy Nightingale, from the *Illustrated Police News*, 7 August 1919.

The motive for the murder of Lucy Nightingale was likely to have been plunder, the police thought, since the room had been ransacked by the murderer or murderers, and Lucy Nightingale's rings had been stolen. They had failed to detect £8 in treasury notes, and thirty-one shillings in silver, which the murdered woman had hidden in a wooden box. The police 'leant on' Ball the brothel-keeper, and accused him of being an accessory to the murder. The worried brothel-keeper soon 'sang like a bird'. Lucy Nightingale had led a quiet life at No. 13, he said, occasionally taking men home with her. Her husband, who worked as a coal porter in Manchester, had come to see her in late April, but she had not wanted anything to do with him. The day of the murder, Ball had visited his wife in the lunatic asylum where she was an inmate. Returning late in the evening, he had found Lucy Nightingale's body. Lucy had had a few regular customers, one of them a piano-playing seaman known as 'Taffy' Morgan, believed to be a native of Cardiff. Taffy had given Lucy his framed photograph, which was exhibited on a piano in Ball's sitting room.

Since Ball was such an unattractive individual, the police first disbelieved his story about the 'convenient' visit to the asylum, but it turned out that he was telling the truth. Thus it was unlikely that Ball was directly involved in the murder. In search of 'Taffy' Morgan, the police struck lucky. It turned out that the nineteen-year-old sailor Harold Horatio Morgan was already a wanted man, for stealing twenty-one bottles of whisky, 1,500 cigarettes and various other items from the lockers of his ship. His accomplice had been the forty-one-year-old ship's cook Frank George Warren, who sometimes used the name Burke, and had a reputation as a serious criminal. The two thieving mariners had initially taken refuge with a Cardiff floozie named Olive Parton, who had agreed to become Warren's 'wife'. After drinking the whisky and smoking the cigarettes, in an orgy lasting several weeks, they wanted to put some ground between themselves and the *heddlu*, and took lodgings in North London.

Young Taffy Morgan went to play the piano to his favourite prostitute Lucy Nightingale, but their meeting was not a success. Olive Parton was surprised when Morgan returned to their lodgings in an angry temper. He said that a woman had done him out of thirty shillings, and that he would have the money back somehow. By this time, the two Welshmen were once more as poor as church mice, and they spoke of doing another 'job' to alter this state of affairs. Olive was beginning to tire of the sinister Warren, and she contemplated returning to Cardiff to get herself another 'husband'.

The night of the murder of Lucy Nightingale, Warren and Morgan had returned to their lodgings early in the morning. Warren carefully washed his shirt, something Olive had never seen him do before. She noticed that he had a scratch on his chin, which he explained as the result of a fight with a man, although she thought it looked more like it had been inflicted by a woman. She was surprised to see that Warren trimmed his moustache, shaved carefully, and washed his face, again actions she had never before observed her hygienically challenged 'husband' undertake. He gave her three gold rings without explaining where they came from. The next morning, Warren and Morgan took Olive for a walk. When they saw a newspaper placard with the words 'Finsbury Park Murder', Warren and Morgan exchanged glances. 'My God, you have nothing to do with that!' Olive exclaimed. 'Why should you think we had anything to do with it?' replied her 'husband' evasively.

When the police came knocking at the lodgings to take Warren and Morgan into custody, the faithless Olive Parton told them all they wanted to know about the two Welshmen. Showing no adherence to the musical exhortations of her buxom namesake 'Dolly', she did not 'Stand by her Man', but readily agreed to testify against him in court! A neighbour at Prah Road, who had seen a young man outside No. 13 on the evening of the murder, identified this individual as Morgan. The police believed that the two Welsh ruffians had decided to rob Lucy Nightingale, after Morgan had reported that she had a good deal of money saved. Having made sure that Ball was away, Morgan had come to call on Lucy Nightingale the evening of the murder. When young 'Taffy' had been invited to her room, the sinister Warren sneaked into the house and burst into Lucy's bedroom, knocking the woman down and throttling her, as Morgan held her legs and tied her up. The two villains then ransacked the room, and Warren pulled off Lucy Nightingale's rings, to give to his faithless 'wife'.[24]

When Warren and Morgan were on trial at the Central Criminal Court for the wilful murder of Lucy Nightingale, things were not looking good for them. Olive Parton and various other witnesses provided some very damning evidence against them. The handkerchief used to gag the murdered woman matched one in Warren's possession. To save himself, Morgan changed his story. The evening of the murder, he had accompanied Warren to No. 13 Prah Road, he said. He had drunk much gin, and, after playing the piano for a while, he sat down in an armchair as Warren took Lucy Nightingale upstairs. After a while, Warren came downstairs and persuaded Morgan to accompany him to their lodgings. Morgan had begun to suspect Warren of being the murderer after he had given the rings to Olive, but he had been too frightened of his sinister countryman to openly accuse him. In a hostile cross-examination, he denied holding Lucy Nightingale down, tying her up, or helping to ransack the room. In his summing-up, Mr Justice Darling pointed out that, although Warren's barrister had hinted at a murder conspiracy involving Morgan and Ball, his client had not gone into the witness box to explain his movements the night of the murder. The jury took the hint and Warren was found guilty, whereas Morgan was acquitted. Donning his black cap, Mr Justice Darling sentenced Warren to death. Turning to Morgan, he addressed the young Welshman with the remarkable words:

> Let me say a word to you. You have been in a very unpleasant position for a long time owing to the company you keep, and your own immorality. You are now undergoing sentence for theft from your ship, and when you come out, make up your mind to lead a better life![25]

It is not known whether Harold Horatio Morgan followed Mr Justice Darling's advice and became a model citizen. The police thought him a very lucky man, since Warren had an old arm injury that incapacitated him, and the technical evidence was in favour of one person holding Lucy Nightingale down, and another making use of excessive force to strangle her. Frank George Warren, alias Burke, was hanged at Pentonville Prison on 7 October 1919. It is to be hoped, for his own sake, that young 'Taffy' Morgan had told the truth at the Old Bailey, since otherwise he might have been haunted, on alternate nights, by the ghost of the woman he had helped to murder, and that of the former shipmate he had helped to convict for the crime. The murder house at No. 13 Prah Road is still standing, and has changed little since 1919. For a while, the former brothel was the headquarters of the local Conservative Club, but nowadays it is a private house.

The Blackstock Road Murder, 1933

In early 1933, the printer Walter Standley and his wife Elizabeth moved into a large flat over a shop at No. 13 Blackstock Road, Finsbury Park. They had been married for many years, but had no children. Two lodgers also lived in the flat. The forty-four-year-old Elizabeth Standley seemed the typical lower-middle-class London housewife, taking an interest in cooking, looking after the lodgers, and dressing in the latest fashions as well as she could afford.

On 4 March 1933, Mr Standley and the lodgers had their breakfasts cooked by Elizabeth, before going to work. One of the lodgers, a man named Cox, returned for luncheon, which he of course wanted to have cooked by the ever-reliable Elizabeth Standley. He was puzzled that she was nowhere to be found. Rather daringly, he knocked at her bedroom door. When there was no response, he carefully opened the door and went inside. He saw two legs protruding from underneath the bed and again called Elizabeth Standley's name. Since there was again no response, he seized hold of the legs and pulled Elizabeth's dead body out from underneath the bed. She had been murdered by repeated heavy blows to the head, and strangled by a piece of wire flex tied round her neck.

The police found evidence that Elizabeth Standley had been knocked down with an iron trivet, and then purposely strangled with the wire. There was no sign of a break-in, so she had clearly let her murderer into the flat. Mr Standley himself had a solid alibi, as did both the lodgers; furthermore, neither of these men had a motive to kill the meek and inoffensive housewife. Instead, the police soon suspected her nephew, the thirty-one-year-old Jack Samuel Puttnam, who had been on indifferent terms with his aunt. They had more than once quarrelled about money, and Elizabeth had also been unhappy about Jack's private life. Shortly after the murder, the omnibus conductor Louis Zackis had seen a young man fitting Puttnam's description come running out from No. 13 Blackstock Road to board his vehicle.

Jack Samuel Puttnam was arrested by the police and brought to the Highbury Vale police station for questioning. After talking about his life as a soldier in India, he suddenly and unexpectedly admitted to killing his aunt. She had upbraided him for having an affair with his own sister-in-law, and threatened to expose him. In a furious rage, he had struck her down and strangled her with the wire. The police lost

The murder of Mrs Standley, from the *Illustrated Police News*, 9 March 1933.

no time in urging him to sign a written confession to the murder of Elizabeth Standley.

On trial at the Central Criminal Court for the murder of Elizabeth Standley, Puttnam pleaded 'not guilty'. Mr Standley and others testified that Puttnam had been in the habit of borrowing money from his aunt. The murderer had stolen at least £150 from the flat, and he seemed to have had knowledge of where the money was kept. The omnibus conductor Zackis picked Puttnam out as the man he had seen leaving No. 13 Blackstock Road. Then there was the matter of the written confession, and, although Puttnam claimed that he had been coerced by the police to sign it, or alternatively that he had signed it in the hope that his immoral dealings with the sister-in-law would remain unexposed if he did so, the jury believed neither of these versions. Jack

Samuel Puttnam was found guilty, sentenced to death, and executed at Pentonville Prison on 8 June 1933.[26]

Reviewer Murders Author, 1936

The twenty-one-year-old Douglas Bose was a clever young lad, who did very well at school and got a partial tuition scholarship to the University of Oxford in 1932. He did well initially, but got mixed up with a Bohemian set of 'fast' people, and was sent down in 1934. Young Bose was the son of a commercial secretary, who was now dead, and his widow Mrs Marjorie Bose had no control over her scapegrace son, who moved out of the parental home and took lodgings in London. He tried to establish himself as an author and journalist, and is believed to have written some articles, although there is nothing to suggest that they ever got published. Bose continued to consort with a very raffish set of people, and moved into the flat of Sylvia Gough, a well-born good-time girl who had once been a model of Augustus John. They led a riotous life together, and drank to excess.

The thirty-year-old Douglas Burton was one of London's many literary hangers-on. A short, stunted man with an ugly, disfigured face, he kept poverty from the door by reading proofs and writing book reviews. He befriended the religious writer John Beevors, who tried his best to find him work. Beevors wrote to Edith Sitwell, the celebrated poetess, describing Burton as 'a wretched deformed semi-dwarf'. Edith Sitwell, who was a very charitable lady, met Burton and tried to find him work as a publisher's reader.

Douglas Bose and Douglas Burton did not know each other, but Burton knew Sylvia Gough. On 14 February 1936, he saw that she had a black eye, and she told him that her author boyfriend had thrown a large Brazil nut at her. The chivalrous Burton found this a very caddish thing to do. It turned out that all three were going to the same party that evening, at No. 19 Alwyne Road, Islington. When the two men met, Burton, who did not lack courage in spite of his diminutive stature, confronted his opponent, saying that it was a far from gentlemanly thing to throw nuts at ladies. Bose tried his best to laugh the matter off, looking down at his much shorter adversary and teasing him. After dinner, there was still tension between the two men, and, although the cad Bose was no longer teasing his opponent, Burton suddenly attacked him with a sculptor's hammer, which had been left on a cupboard after having been made use of to hang pictures. One single blow behind the ear was enough to send Bose crashing to the floor. There was much alarm among the partygoers, and Burton could make his escape unimpeded.

The shaken book reviewer took refuge in the flat of another lady friend of his. When he tried to explain that he believed that he had killed a man, she did not believe him. The next morning, Burton gave himself up at the Tottenham Court Road police station. When the constable on duty asked him, jokingly, whether he had killed someone, the gloomy-looking literary man replied, 'I hope not. I don't know yet.' It turned out that Douglas Bose, who had an abnormally thin skull, had died on the spot, and Burton was committed to the Central Criminal Court charged with his murder.

While in custody awaiting trial, Douglas Burton behaved extremely weirdly. He claimed to have become infatuated with the celebrated cabaret artiste Betty May. Her indifference to him had driven him over the edge. He wrote a number of letters detailing his affairs with various women, who were all just substitutes for his beloved Betty. In the meantime, his legal counsel were working hard to save him from the gallows. Since many witnesses had seen Bose being knocked down, the 'insanity defence' was the only option, and it turned out that the weirdo Burton had been behaving strangely even in 1931. He was fond of befriending beautiful women, particularly if they resembled Betty May, and some of them felt pity for the stunted little wretch; this was how he had met Sylvia Gough in the first place.

Edith Sitwell was approached by John Beevors, and agreed to appear as a character witness, testifying that Burton was insane. The brother of the accused also approached her, asking for £1,000 to support Burton's defence. Edith Sitwell's friend, the academic John Sparrow, dissuaded her from appearing in court, however, since it was apparent to him that the trial would be a squalid one, and since her testimony would have no direct bearing on the case anyway. Burton's enterprising legal team instead got hold of a Belgian woman who had been one of Burton's 'conquests', and who was willing to tell all about his various peculiarities; she later told an Australian journalist that after a visit to that continent, Douglas Burton and his twin brother Donald had made love to her all the way back to England.

A number of witnesses testified in court about Burton's various peculiarities, and his barrister made a brilliant speech alleging that although Dr Grierson, the prison doctor who had examined Douglas Burton, had merely found him 'eccentric', his client was really quite insane, and more a subject for pity than for punishment. Summing up, Mr Justice Finlay declared that he found this case singularly squalid and unpleasant, due to the vicious lives of both murderer and victim, and many of the other people connected with the case. Burton's letters were disgusting documents, expressing his infatuation with Betty May, whose identity the learned judge did not know, in very emotional language. The jury found Burton guilty but insane, and he was committed to a lunatic asylum.[27]

There was a good deal of newspaper interest in this sensational case, and Sylvia Gough sold her story to the *Daily Mirror*.[28] She explained that a witch had once put a black magic spell on her, resulting in misery not only for herself, but every person she came into contact with. Once the daughter of a millionaire and the wife of an army captain, a leader of the 'Bright Young Things' and the toast of London society, she was now alone and destitute. Her lover Douglas Bose, who also dabbled in black magic, had often been cruel to her, but each time she had wanted to leave him he had threatened to take poison and end his young life. Douglas Burton, a very chivalrous and old-fashioned man, had once branded the initial of his current lady friend on his arm with a red-hot poker. He had been enraged by Bose's cruelty to her, with fatal results for the young author turned black magician. It is not known how many were taken in by this farrago of tabloid newspaper nonsense, but there is reason to believe that there was eventually a happy ending for the unfortunate Douglas Bose, whose clouded mind improved a good deal in the asylum. The amorous book reviewer is said to have emerged from its walls after just a few years, and led a quiet existence thereafter.

Murder in Islington Green, 1937

In the 1930s, Rosina Field was a middle-aged Islington prostitute with several convictions for streetwalking. In 1935, when she was forty-seven years old, she walked out of the Clerkenwell Police Court while waiting to appear on a charge of loitering, but she was rearrested, brought before the magistrate, and sentenced to six weeks' imprisonment with hard labour.

In spite of this period of incarceration, Rosina Field continued her vicious life. It must have been a concern for her that, since her attractions

Islington Green, from an old postcard.

as a prostitute were well-nigh gone, she had to accept all comers, even the most unattractive and perverted ones. On 14 May 1937, her dead body was found in the basement of Mr Harding's furniture warehouse at No. 22 Islington Green. An autopsy by Sir Bernard Spilsbury showed that she had been brutally knocked down and then strangled to death.

The local police, who knew Rosina Field well, were probably not all that surprised that she had come to a sad end. It did not take long before some important witnesses came forward in the hunt for the murderer. On 12 May, Coronation Day, Rosina Field had been seen on Islington Green, walking towards the furniture shop at No. 22 in company with a well-known local crook, the fifty-two-year-old Frederick George Murphy, who actually worked as handyman in the shop. On 13 May, when Murphy had a drink with one of his female colleagues at the shop, he told her that there was a dead body in the cellar, asking her not to tell any person about this, since he himself wanted to approach the boss when back to work the day after. A quantity of debris, including a leather suitcase, was removed from the basement at No. 22 Islington Green to be examined for fingerprints. The creature Murphy, who himself went to the police with an implausible story about finding a dead body in the basement of the shop, was taken into police custody. The coroner's inquest on Rosina Field returned a verdict of wilful murder against him.[29]

When Frederick George Murphy, a short and sturdy bloke who looked very much like the hardened criminal he was, faced a murder trial at the Old Bailey before Lord Hewart, things were looking very black for him. He was the last person seen with the murdered woman, he possessed a key to the shop, and he admitted handling the dead body. 'Tough Mick', as he was called, had five previous prison sentences for assault, pimping and burglary. A stocky, red-faced 'bully' with a coarse voice, he had quite a formidable reputation locally. Not a single person was willing to testify in his favour, not even the woman who had lived with him for five years as his 'wife'. There was no immediate motive for him to murder Rosina Field, but he was an inveterate pimp and a customer of various low-class prostitutes, and a violent quarrel might well have ensued if he had tried to persuade Rosina to give him a 'quick 'un' after he had lured her into the furniture shop.

The chain of evidence against Frederick George Murphy appeared rock solid, and after Lord Hewart had delivered a hostile summing-up the jury found him guilty of murder. Described by the *Daily Express* as 'a London-born Irishman, pug-nosed and squat', 'Tough Mick' boldly spoke up when he was asked if he had anything to say before sentence was passed. The prisoner berated Lord Hewart for his harsh summing-up, which had not contained a single word in his favour. The police were all corrupt, and they had finally succeeded in 'framing' him for murder after several previous attempts. Lord Hewart paid little attention to the outburst from the angry little man, but calmly sentenced him to death. After the final words of the ritual, which would have put terror into the hearts of most people, Tough Mick just sneered 'Mercy on my soul, oh yeah …' He would have had more to say had the warders not taken him away with commendable expedition.

'Condemned Man Accuses the Lord Chief Justice!' exclaimed the headline of the *Daily Express*.[30] The *Daily Mirror* preferred the version 'Crook Twice Tried for Murder now to Die!'[31] Indeed, Frederick George Murphy had once stood trial for the murder of Katherine Peck, a hawker's wife also known as 'Singing Rosie', who had been found dead in a Walworth street back in 1929. Murphy did not deny being with Katherine Peck when she was murdered, and in a pub he had boasted to two men that he had killed her. The exact circumstances of this murder remain obscure, and at the time the bonhomous Mr Justice McCardie had said that he fully concurred with the 'not guilty' verdict, due to lack of evidence. The murder of 'Singing Rosie' formally remains unsolved, but the police detectives involved in the case must have felt vindicated when the sinister Tough Mick was convicted of the murder of Rosina Field in 1937. The Court of Criminal Appeal turned a deaf ear to the exhortations of Frederick George Murphy's legal counsel, and the Islington Green murderer was hanged on 17 August. There has been speculation that Murphy might well have been involved in the unsolved murder of Dora Alicia Lloyd, and perhaps in the aforementioned 'Soho Stranglings' as well, but no conclusive evidence has been brought forward regarding this. The murder house, which was Osborn John House Furnishers back in the 1930s, today appears to be a private house in this busy Islington location; very few people, even among the locals, know its terrible secret.

The Murder Houses of Argyle Street, 1951

For many years, Miss Esther Bowen kept a small hotel at No. 3 Argyle Street, King's Cross. In November 1918, when she was in her eighties and semi-retired from running the hotel, she was found dead in her room, tied and gagged with a large towel that had suffocated her. The motive for the murder was clearly robbery, since Miss Bowen was reputed to have hoarded a good deal of money on the premises. The two men who had discovered the body, named Bray and Clauson, came under scrutiny, since their stories contradicted each other. However, the coroner's inquest on Esther Bowen returned a verdict of murder against some person or persons unknown, and the Argyle Street murder remains one of London's many unsolved mysteries.[32]

In the 1970s, a large modern building replaced the ramshackle old hotels at Nos 1, 3 and 5 Argyle Street. There is no reason to believe that Miss Bowen's murder hotel looked much different from the still-existing three-storey terraced houses at No. 7 and No. 9 Argyle Street. The latter building was the Newlyn House Hotel back in November 1951, when the young labouring man Herbert Bass-Woodcock checked in there with his teenage sister-in-law Annie Thorne. Bass-Woodcock's life had been very unfortunate from the start. In spite of their double-barrelled name, his parents had been very poor and mean-spirited, and Herbert had been one of their fifteen living children in a small Nottinghamshire farmhouse. Both parents had been imprisoned for child neglect in 1941. Herbert was educationally subnormal, and an inveterate thief. He became a bricklayer's labourer, and married a young woman named

Jean Thorne in 1950. He moved in with her parents and siblings, but they were very unkind to him.

Fed up with the endless jibes from the rest of the household, Herbert Bass-Woodcock eloped to London with his seventeen-year-old sister-in-law Annie Thorne, with whom he had fallen in love, leaving his wife and child behind. At the Newlyn House Hotel, the guilty pair were in a gloomy frame of mind and, according to Herbert, Annie said that, if he died, she would want to live no longer. Accordingly, he strangled her to death in her second-floor room at the hotel. Much more squeamish about putting an end to his own existence, he then gave himself up to the police.

When the dismal Herbert Bass-Woodcock was on trial for murder at the Old Bailey, his defence team made the most of his singularly unhappy background: in fact, he had been 'born a monstrosity'! Mistreated by his parents, bullied at school for being backward, tormented by a disagreeable skin disease, disciplined in borstal for his incessant pilfering, and being

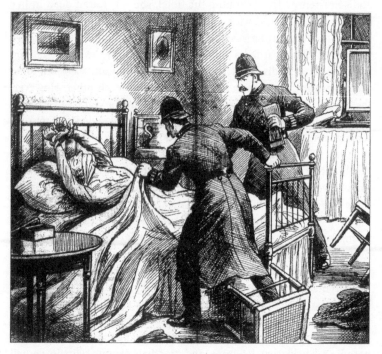

Miss Bowen is found murdered, from the *Illustrated Police News*, 14 November 1918.

the butt of every joke in his wife's parental home, had this wretched young man not suffered enough? Mr Christmas Humphreys, for the prosecution, struck a more sombre note when he reminded the jury that the prisoner had in fact seduced and murdered his sister-in-law, a girl of 17. Herbert Bass-Woodcock was found guilty but insane, and was incarcerated in Broadmoor.[33] There is an encouraging hint that he might have made his way out of the asylum, hopefully to start a new and happier life: a man named Herbert Bass-Woodcock, of the relevant age, married a woman in Basford in late 1963. The murder house at No. 9 Argyle Street, not far from King's Cross station, is today the Florence Hotel.

Brecknock Road Again, 1957

In 1957, the house at No. 13 Brecknock Road, Holloway, was the printing works of Mr W. P. Griffiths & Sons Ltd. A long, narrow building, it was (and still is) much larger than it seems from its narrow frontage on Brecknock Road. Mr Griffiths employed a caretaker named John Folkard, who lived in a flat above the works with his wife, son and elderly mother. On the night of 16 December 1957, Folkard came staggering into this flat, bleeding from the head. His wife and mother, who were not the brightest of women, suspected that he had had an accident while being 'on the drink' and simply put him to bed, but the following morning he was observed to be comatose. He was taken to hospital and the police were called in. They believed that the fifty-five-year-old caretaker had surprised some thieves who had broken into the printing works, and it turned out that a suitcase full of bottles of wine and spirits, the property of the workmen's 'Christmas club', had been stolen. On 22 December, Folkard died without regaining consciousness, and the case was now one of murder.

Ransacking the printing works, the police found evidence of a break-in through a window, and also a plentiful supply of fingerprints that did not match those of the workmen. They suspected that the murder had been committed by some inexperienced young thieves, who did not have enough sense to wear gloves. When the caretaker had disturbed them, they had panicked, knocking him down with a 'jemmy' or similar instrument. In a trawl of local juvenile delinquents with burglarious habits, the detectives found the seventeen-year-old hat blocker Francis Jacobs, a nasty piece of work who had already made his presence felt in the neighbourhood. His fingerprints matched those found at No. 13 Brecknock Road.

After receiving a proper grilling from the Islington detectives, Jacobs blamed a certain 'Skouse Eddy', who had persuaded him to take part in burgling No. 13 Brecknock Road through an unlocked rear window. It was Eddy who had 'coshed' the watchman, and the two burglars had later sold the spirits to a Maltese 'fence'. Seeming genuinely contrite after he had appreciated that Folkard was dead, Jacobs drew a plan of the printing works to explain how the burglary had been committed, and he also drew a picture of Eddy's distinctive tattoo. The search was on for Eddy in Liverpool when the Islington detectives received notice that a young thief had just been arrested in Ross-on-Wye: the twenty-year-old Arthur John Bosworth, whose fingerprints matched the second set at No. 13 Brecknock Road.

On trial for murder at the Central Criminal Court, both burglars admitted breaking into No. 13 Brecknock Road and stealing the suitcase full of bottles. Jacobs denied any participation in the murder, claiming that he had even tried to restrain Bosworth when he had attacked the nightwatchman. Bosworth eventually admitted that he had hit Folkard twice with a mallet, after the caretaker had first struck him with a hard object. There was no solid evidence that Bosworth had been injured, and Folkard had in fact been struck four times; nor was the prosecution satisfied with Jacobs' version of events, suspecting that he was lying and that his involvement in the assault was much greater than he had indicated.

In the end, Bosworth was found guilty of murder and sentenced to death. Jacobs was found not guilty of murder but guilty of burglary, and was eventually sentenced to borstal. With remarkable leniency, considering that Jacobs had taken an active part in a burglary that had resulted in murder, Mr Justice Jones pointed out that his aim was not just to punish the young man, but to take a course that was really the best for him. Albeit of no fixed address, he was said to have good parents, and had received a positive report from his probation officer. As for Bosworth, the more hardened wretch, he was made to sweat for several weeks before the Home Secretary finally recommended a reprieve.[34] The murder house at No. 13 Brecknock Road retained its layout for many years, with a large workshop on the ground floor, and some flats above. With time, the ground floor became a restaurant, and the flats above were converted into offices. It is likely to be well guarded by its ghostly nightwatchman, making his rounds in the dead of night to look for thieves and murderers.

Murder by a Lesbian, 1961

Norma Rose Everson was a strong, tough thirty-three-year-old woman, who had been in the Army in her youth. She worked as a van driver and lived at No. 56 Battledean Road, Highbury, with her girlfriend Gladys. However, Norma and Gladys were often at loggerheads, since, in the long hours when Norma was out driving her van, Gladys was far from faithful to her. It particularly annoyed her that Gladys was having an affair with their neighbour Mrs Winifred Lord, a mother of two. One day in early June 1961, Norma came home to Battledean Road to find Gladys in bed with Winifred Lord. At first, Gladys managed to calm her down, but Winifred was a little too cheeky for Norma's liking, and the tough ex-army lesbian stabbed her to death with a kitchen knife. Norma Rose Everson was found guilty of murder, but since there had been great provocation her sentence was penal servitude for life.

In June 1966, Norma Rose Everson again hit the news when she broke out of Styal Prison, near Wilmslow in Cheshire, taking two other dangerous convicts with her. When the three tough female prisoners took a breather, they were spotted by a man walking his dog. The jailbreakers were recaptured after only six hours of freedom, and Norma Rose Everson once more disappeared back behind the prison walls.[35]

A Gloomy Tale of Beresford Road, 1962

In 1962, the end-of-terrace house at No. 26 Beresford Road was owned by the fifty-year-old Jamaican Cyrene Emmanuel Wright. In the 1950s and 1960s, it was a profitable business for Caribbean capitalists to purchase rundown old London houses and sublet the premises to various impecunious countrymen. Mr Wright had a nephew named Selvin George Williamson, a bad hat who was unemployed and had various mental-health issues. Still, his uncle gave him a roof over his head at No. 26 Beresford Road, and tried to help him secure paid employment.

On 16 April 1962, Selvin was behaving weirdly, and the other lodgers told Mr Wright about his antics. The landlord went up to his nephew's top-floor bedroom to investigate, but the deranged Selvin was waiting for him in there. Using a chair and a marble-topped table, the lunatic attacked his uncle in a furious rage, belabouring his head until he was dead. One of the other lodgers called the police, but when they arrived Selvin leapt out of the window and climbed on to the roof of No. 26. He then took a huge leap on to the roof of Beresford Lodge, a four-storey block of flats detached from the terrace of older houses in the road (it still stands, as does the murder house). The lunatic tried to lower himself over the edge of the building, but fell heavily to the ground and died in hospital soon after.[36]

The Sad Tale of Joe Meek, 1967

Robert George 'Joe' Meek was born in Newent, Gloucestershire, in 1929. He moved to London in 1954, hoping to establish himself as a songwriter and music producer. Although unable to play a musical instrument or write notation, it did not take long for him to find success. His innovative use of electronic sounds and effects made him an iconic figure of the 1960s, and a pioneer of space-age pop. His most famous work was the Tornadoes' 1962 smash hit 'Telstar', the first pop single by a UK artist to reach No. 1 in America, and said to have been Margaret Thatcher's favourite song.

Joe Meek set up his own studio at No. 304 Holloway Road, in the three floors above what was then a leather goods shop. He was one of the first producers to grasp and fully exploit the potential of a modern recording studio. He developed sound effects like echo, and tools such as dubbing. His aim was to produce perfect songs, rather than gain commercial successes.

Joe produced everything on the three floors of his studio, and was never afraid to distort or manipulate the sound if it created the effect he was seeking. His landlords, who lived downstairs, were often unhappy with the amount of noise he made, but when they knocked a broom against the ceiling, Joe instead turned up the volume.

In his studio at No. 304 Holloway Road, Joe Meek wrote and produced a number of successful recordings. He worked with the Kinks, with Lonnie Donegan, and with Tom Jones. His career was hampered by his hasty temper and strong musical likes and dislikes: he passed up the chance to work with the then unknown David Bowie, and he did not think the Beatles were any good. When he heard Rod Stewart sing for the first time, Joe rushed into the studio, put his fingers in his ears and screamed until Stewart had left.

Joe Meek was obsessed with space exploration, and with spiritualism. He set up tape machines in cemeteries to communicate with the dead, hoping to make contact with his idol Buddy Holly. He used drugs to excess, and suffered from recurrent paranoia and depression. A rash homosexual, he had been fined for 'cottaging' by the police, and subsequently blackmailed. In January 1967, the police discovered a suitcase containing the mutilated body of the homosexual Bernard Oliver. For some reason or other, Joe became concerned that he would be implicated in the murder investigation when the Metropolitan Police said they would be interviewing all known homosexual men in the city. By this time, his career was on the rocks: the hits had dried out, and although he had earned considerable royalties, he had spent them all on high living. It did not help that the French composer Jean Ledrut had accused Joe of plagiarism, claiming that the tune of 'Telstar' had been copied from one of his own musical scores.

At this time, Joe Meek sometimes lived with his musician boyfriend Heinz Burt. This individual had brought with him a single-barrelled shotgun that he wanted to use to shoot birds with while on tour, but Joe had taken it away from him and hidden it under his bed. Joe normally got on well with his landlady Violet Shenton, who ran the leather goods shop at No. 304, and lived in a small flat behind it, although they regularly quarrelled about Joe's lack of punctuality in paying the rent, and his noisy parties and jam sessions. On 3 February 1967, Joe's young assistant Patrick Pink saw that his unbalanced boss was burning paper and other material in his studio. He called Violet Shenton, who tried to reason with Joe, but soon they were quarrelling angrily about his various demerits. In a furious rage, Joe went to get the shotgun, and made use of it to shoot his landlady in the back, killing her instantly. He then reloaded and turned the gun on himself.[37] Since the shotgun had been registered to Burt, he was questioned by the police, before being eliminated from their enquiries, since the assistant Pink had heard what had been going on the day of the murder. Just a few weeks after this rash murder and suicide, the plagiarism lawsuit was ruled in Joe's favour.

Joe Meek is today quite a cult figure in London's musical world. Nobody cares much about the landlady whose life he wantonly ended: she is quite forgotten, but the murder house at No. 304 Holloway Road has a blue plaque commemorating Joe's life and work.

The Murder of Joe Orton, 1967

Joe Orton, a young working-class lad from Leicester, took an interest in the theatre and won a scholarship to the Royal Academy of Dramatic Art in 1950. Here, he met the homosexual Kenneth Halliwell, who was six years older and whose early life had been both dramatic and unhappy. His mother had died before his eyes after being stung by a bee, and when his father later gassed himself it was Kenneth who found the body. Having inherited substantial means, Kenneth purchased a flat in West Hampstead, and Joe moved in with him. They became very close and started a relationship.

In spite of being indifferent students at the Royal Academy of Dramatic Art, Kenneth and Joe both had strong literary ambitions. They wrote novels together in the style of Ronald Firbank, but without being able to get them published. In 1959, Kenneth spent much of what remained of his inheritance on a small second-floor flat at No. 25 Noel Street, Islington. Kenneth wrote a pile of novels that nobody wanted to publish, and plays that nobody wanted to perform. He and Joe amused themselves by stealing library books, and defacing them by adding various obscene images. They were eventually discovered and prosecuted for stealing and damaging library books in May 1962, and they were each sentenced to six months in prison.

This harsh sentence seems to have given Joe Orton's dormant literary ambitions a jolt. His play *Entertaining Mr Sloane* became a surprise hit in 1964, and was praised by Terence Rattigan. When his black comedy *Loot* shot to fame in 1966, with rave reviews in the media, Joe was considered the most exciting young playwright in Britain. A witty, amusing character, he was equally at home in a Chelsea literary salon as he was in some sleazy Soho gay club. In spite of his mainstream literary fame, he was sexually very promiscuous, and at a time when homosexuality was still a criminal offence, he took part in veritable orgies in the public lavatories.

Kenneth Halliwell did not approve of Joe Orton's meteoric success. He himself remained incapable of getting anything published, and as a result he became increasingly morose and depressed. Joe had friends in all walks of life, and many of these friends did not make it a secret that they thought his boyfriend Kenneth a very queer fish, in more ways than one. A short, awkward-looking cove with a bald head and an ill-fitting wig, Kenneth thought it amusing to wear an Old Etonian tie to which he was not entitled. He had little to say that was novel or interesting, and many of Joe's friends disliked him. Although Kenneth was not above some serious hanky-panky himself, he was pained by Joe's continuing promiscuity, which the latter openly flaunted. Many of Joe's friends thought it only a matter of time before the wealthy and successful playwright left his dull boyfriend and the little flat at No. 25 Noel Road for good.

On 9 August 1967, a driver came to take Joe Orton to Twickenham Studios for a meeting to discuss a script. Since nobody answered his knock, he had a look through the letter box and saw a man lying on the floor. When the police broke down the door, they found that Kenneth Halliwell had murdered Joe Orton with repeated hammer blows to the head. He had then committed suicide through a massive overdose of Nembutal.[38] The murder house at No. 25 Noel Road today has a blue plaque celebrating Joe Orton. Since it is placed at second-floor level, many people miss it. Fittingly, the murderer Kenneth Halliwell, who brutally cut short Joe's very promising literary career, is not mentioned at all; his fame, or rather notoriety, remains that of Herostratos.

The Photofit Murder, 1970

Mr James Cameron was a well-to-do businessman, head of the Beecham Group's market research department. He lived alone in an expensive Georgian terraced house at No. 4 Burgh Street, Islington. A very respectable, immaculately dressed bachelor, he was popular among his neighbours in this well-to-do part of Islington. His elegant house contained a valuable collection of antiques.

On 14 October 1970, one of the neighbours thought it very odd that she had not seen Mr Cameron for several days. She called the police, and after they had forced the door to No. 4 Burgh Street they found Cameron's dead body in the upstairs front bedroom. He had been tied up, and shot in the head. Furniture in the room had been knocked over, and the bed and carpet were heavily bloodstained.

The police searched the garden for the murder weapon, or other clues, but found nothing. Nor were any suspicious fingerprints found in the house. The neighbours had nothing bad to say about Mr Cameron: he had always been the perfect gentleman, very polite and always saying, 'Hello', although he liked to keep very much to himself. Apart from his antique-collecting hobby, he had also had a fondness for classical music, sometimes playing his records as early as 6.30 in the morning.

The police set up a special murder-squad team, led by Detective Chief Superintendent Bill Wright, at Islington police station. Their main clue was a witness who had seen a man exiting Mr Cameron's house shortly after the murder. He had worn glasses and carried an umbrella. The clever Scotland Yard detectives soon found evidence that the murderer had forced Cameron to sign several cheques, for a total of just £60, before shooting him dead. An individual had made use of one of these cheques to book a flight from London to Edinburgh. Was this the killer making his escape to the Scottish capital? Several passengers on the plane remembered a young man who very much resembled the description of the killer. They helped the police to build up a photofit of him, which was advertised in the newspapers and on the *Police 5* TV programme. Soon, a vital tip came from a Dulwich viewer of *Police 5*, who had sold an umbrella to a man exactly fitting the description shortly after the murder. Another viewer from Nottingham was certain that the twenty-four-year-old unemployed drifter John Ernest Bennett was the wanted man.

After Bennett had been arrested, and after the witnesses had picked him out from an identity parade, Bennett admitted that he had met Cameron in a London 'gay bar', and accompanied him back to No. 4 Burgh Street. Finding Cameron quite creepy, Bennett 'chickened out' and refused to go to bed with him, however. Ten days later, he returned to No. 4 Burgh Street, where James Cameron was pleased to see him, offering him money and a job at Beecham's. He then made homosexual advances to the young man, but Bennett overpowered him, tied him up and threatened him with the gun, which then went off accidentally. This did not sound like a very convincing story, and Bennett would probably have been better off if he had just 'clammed up' and denied everything. In particular, it hardly took Sherlock Holmes to figure out that the motive for his return to Burgh Street had been to rob the 'poofter' who had earlier made advances to him.

At the Old Bailey, John Ernest Bennett was sentenced to life imprisonment for the murder of James Cameron, with the recommendation that he should spend at least seventeen years behind bars. Mr Justice Eveleigh said, 'You have not displayed the slightest concern for the death of this man. It was a cold and deliberate murder for money.' James Cameron, the quiet gentleman who led a double life, was brutally murdered for just £60. His house at No. 4 Burgh Street is still standing, a memorial to the first murder solved through a police 'photofit'.[39]

The Cross Street Murder, 1971

The forty-seven-year-old Mr James Hails was an honest, hard-working master butcher, employed at A. Costas Butcher's in No. 44 Cross Street, Islington. On 17 December 1971, he was hard at work preparing some Christmas fare. However, outside the shop, two teenage hoodlums were making plans to rob the butcher's. When the shop was empty of customers, they suddenly burst in and demanded money. Mr Hails was not having any of that, however. He threw chunks of meat at the intruders, one of whom responded by lunging across the counter and stabbing him hard with a long boning-knife he had picked up from the counter. The two boys ran off with £4, leaving the badly wounded James Hails behind. The robbers were seen by Mr Costas's old mother, and two Greek women could report that they had nearly been run down by two tall, slim coloured youths not far from the butcher's shop. These two individuals were later observed boarding a bus in Essex Road.

Mr Hails died a week later after emergency surgery at St Leonard's Hospital, and a murder investigation began. The police trawled the Islington teenage criminal underworld for quite some time, finding evidence that a gang of six young black men had been terrorising the neighbourhood for several months, robbing shops, burgling houses and snatching handbags. They strongly suspected that the Cross Street murderers were members of this teenage mob.

On New Year's Day 1972, a young black man snatched a handbag near Islington Green, but two civilians pursued and captured him. There was no such thing as honesty among thieves in the Islington criminal underworld at the time, and the sixteen-year-old Clive Flemming soon 'sang like a bird', admitting being present at No. 44 Cross Street when the butcher was murdered, but blaming seventeen-year-old Donald Lewis for the murder. Lewis had 'overdone it' while 'taking care of the geezer' as Flemming helped himself to some money from the till. When arrested, Lewis was equally quick to blame his former partner in crime for the murder.

On trial at the Old Bailey in May 1972, Lewis was found guilty of murder and sentenced to life imprisonment. Mr Justice Thesiger recommended that he should spend at least fifteen years in prison. Flemming was found guilty of manslaughter, and the judge recommended that he should serve at least ten years behind bars.[40] According to the police files on the case at the National Archives, Lewis was alive, and out on probation, in 1998.

The mindless killing of the respectable butcher James Hails by two brutal young hooligans is one of London's forgotten murders. It did not receive much newspaper publicity even at the time, and today nobody knows that the gentleman's outfitters at No. 44 Cross Street was once a butcher's shop, where the butcher had to pay a high price for his have-a-go heroics.

7

Tower Hamlets

*The warehouse in the Whitechapel Road, in which Henry Wainwright killed
and buried his paramour, Harriett Lane, has not been done away with, and
the dwelling in which the ruffian Seaman killed Mr Levi and his housekeeper
– hard by the Commercial Road East – still frowns upon the passer-by.*

Guy Logan, from *Famous Crimes Past & Present*

Few parts of London have changed as much as the Tower Hamlets. Slum
clearances, wartime carnage, and extensive development have all taken
their toll on the region's historic murder houses. Nothing today remains
of No. 9 Grove Road, Stepney, where James Mullins murdered Mrs
Elmsley in 1860, or of the house at No. 17 Grove (now Golding) Street
where the Jew Marks Goodmacher murdered his daughter in 1920. The
murder shop at No. 96 Green Street, Bethnal Green, where Matilda
Moore was slain in 1860, no longer frowns upon the passer-by; nor does
No. 478 Commercial Road, where Matilda Farmer was murdered by the
half-brothers Conrad Donovan and Charles Wade in 1904. No. 10 Peel
Grove, where the reputed miser Miss Margaret Marshall was slain by
a mystery assailant in 1897, was demolished when the Bethnal Green
infirmary was constructed.

Of the highways and byways of Jack the Ripper, very little remains,
although, after receiving your not inconsiderable fee, the Ripper tour
guides would like to tell you otherwise. The murder house at No. 29
Hanbury Street, where Jack left his second victim Annie Chapman dead
in the back yard, stood until 1970, when it was demolished along with
the entire north side of the street to make way for extensions to Truman's
Brewery. Of Miller's Court – the alleyway entered from a passageway
by No. 26 Dorset Street – where Jack committed his most sanguinary

outrage when he murdered and mutilated Mary Jane Kelly at No. 13, not a single brick remains.[1] As one of the last to see it before it was demolished in a slum clearance, the old Ripper author Leonard Matters left the following sinister description behind:

> Miller's Court, when I saw it, was nothing but a stone flagged passage between two houses, the upper stories of which united and so formed an arch over the entrance. Over this arch there was an iron plate bearing the legend, 'Miller's Court.' The passage was three feet wide and about twenty feet long, and at the end of it there was a small paved yard, about fifteen feet square. Abutting on this yard, or 'court', was the small back room in which the woman Kelly was killed – a dirty, damp and dismal hovel, with boarded-up windows and a padlocked door as though the place had not been occupied since the crime was committed.[2]

Dorset (later Duval) Street was rightly called 'the worst street in London', due to the amount of crime and vice taking place in these parts. It is not generally known that the sinister Miller's Court was home to two other murders: Kate Marshall murdered Eliza Roberts at No. 19 in 1898, and the young prostitute Kitty Roman was found with her throat cut at No. 12 in 1909.[3] A man named Harold Hall was later tried and convicted of the Roman murder, but doubts have persisted concerning his guilt. In 1901, Mary Ann Austin was murdered with ten wounds to her abdomen at Annie Chapman's former home, Crossingham's Lodging House, at No. 35 Dorset Street. Nothing whatsoever remains of Dorset Street today, although it is still possible to see where it once was located.[4] The locations where Jack the Ripper left victims behind in the street, namely Buck's Row (now Durward Street), Berner (now Henriques) Street, Mitre Square and perhaps also George Yard (now Gunthorpe Street) have also changed beyond recognition.

The reader of this book would be well advised to avoid the much-touted Ripper rip-off tours through Whitechapel, and instead go for a short excursion round some of the existing historic murder houses of these parts. It makes good sense to start at Alexander Arthur Mackay's murder house at No. 11 Artillery Passage, going east to No. 62 Hanbury Street, 16 Batty Street and 31 Turner Street, before visiting No. 5 Fulbourne Street and what remains of Henry Wainwright's murder house in Vine Court off Whitechapel Road. Going east past Dan Mendoza's former murder pub at No. 299, the tour can be ended at the Kray twins' murder pub, the Blind Beggar at No. 337 Whitechapel Road, where refreshments are available.

Murder in Artillery Passage, 1868

For the student of London architecture visiting the East End, a good place to go is the Artillery Passage conservation area, situated not far from Spitalfields Market. This relatively little-known part of London has an interesting history. The name Spitalfields originally came from the fields outside the Hospital of the Blessed Virgin Mary without Bishopsgate, established in the late twelfth century. During the Dissolution of the Monasteries, the Priory of St Mary Spital was closed, and in 1537 part of the fields was designated as an artillery ground, for members of the Guild of Artillery to practice with their longbows, crossbows and guns. In 1682, the old artillery ground was purchased by four wealthy Londoners, who wanted to develop the area into housing. The street layout remains more or less unchanged from their plans, with Artillery Lane becoming the main thoroughfare from Bishopsgate, and Gun, Steward and Fort Streets running off it to the north. Artillery Passage, a narrow alley even by the standards of the time, connects Artillery Lane with Sandys Row.[5]

In 1868, the small eating house at No. 11 Artillery Passage was kept by Mr George Grossmith and his wife Emma, who had lived there since at least 1862. They had an eighteen-year-old servant named Alexander Arthur Mackay, who helped in the kitchen and waited at table. Their eldest son, the eleven-year-old Walter Grossmith, ran errands and worked as a kitchen-boy when he was not at school. The forty-five-year-old Emma Grossmith was a fierce, angry woman, who had little patience with the clumsy, ignorant Alexander Arthur Mackay, who for some reason or other was nicknamed 'John'. She lost no opportunity to scold him for his sloth and general incompetence. When it was discovered that John had spoilt a dish of potatoes, and then hidden it to conceal his 'crime', he was shouted at by both the Grossmiths. The nasty boy Walter also had some 'fun' at the hapless John's expense.

On the morning of 8 May 1868, Walter asked John to fetch him some water so he could wash his feet, but the truculent servant said he would be damned if he did. John got hold of a rolling pin and made a threatening gesture towards the boy, but Mrs Grossmith came into

Above: Attempted murder in Norton Folgate, a dramatic sketch of Alexander Mackay's assault on Mrs Grossmith, from the *Illustrated Police News*, 16 May 1868.

Below: Alexander Mackay murders Emma Grossmith, from *Famous Crimes Past & Present*, issue 56.

the room and scolded him. After she had left, Walter could hear John mutter, 'If that damned bitch does not mind, she could get into the wrong box, and get something for her trouble!' Walter lingered in the house, thinking it would be very funny to watch yet another quarrel between his mother and John. However, the servant, who was busy cleaning the shop windows, saw Walter lurking inside the restaurant, and called out, 'The boy is not gone to school!' Mrs Grossmith ordered Walter to get going. The mischievous lad went away with great reluctance, since he would have greatly liked to see a proper 'scrap' between his mother and John.

The next drama in Artillery Passage was that several neighbours heard loud screams emanating from No. 11. There was also the sound of repeated heavy blows. One neighbour heard Mrs Grossmith scream, 'Oh, John, you will kill me!' and a hoarse voice replying, 'Hold your row!' The widow Mrs Mary Sandiford, who lived at No. 13 Artillery Passage, went knocking at the door of the restaurant at No. 11. When John opened it, she could see that he had a scratch on his cheek, and that his clothes were stained with blood. Going inside, she was shocked to see Mrs Grossmith lying motionless on the floor, covered in blood. 'Oh, John, you have done this!' she exclaimed. 'No, Ma'am, I have not,' the servant replied, as cool as a cucumber. 'Where is Mr Grossmith?' asked Mrs Sandiford. 'Just round the corner. I will go and get him!' said John and made off. Several people saw the wild-eyed, bloodstained youth running through the streets, but John managed to make his escape.

When the local doctor arrived at No. 11 Artillery Passage, he found that, although Mrs Grossmith's head had been very badly beaten with a large rolling pin, she was still alive. Her face was so swollen and distorted that Mr Grossmith could not recognise her. After a few days in hospital, she recovered enough to tell her husband what had happened the day she was assaulted. She had been making pastries, and the clumsy John had given her a very dirty and greasy cloth to wrap them in. When she had reproached him, he had gone for her with a large rolling pin, beating her until she was well-nigh dead. The hue and cry was now up for Alexander Arthur Mackay, also known as John. A friend of his could report that, a few days after Mrs Grossmith was assaulted, he had met John at Woolwich, near the Marine Barracks. When asked what he was doing in these parts, he had replied, 'Oh, just looking for a job!' with the greatest coolness.

Mrs Grossmith died a few days later, and the case was now one of murder. At the coroner's inquest on Emma Grossmith, her husband testified that Alexander Arthur Mackay was the son of an old friend of his, and that he had previously spent three years at Feltham reformatory for larceny. He had worked long hours at the restaurant, for a low salary. Once, when the mischievous Walter Grossmith had smeared, with some foul-smelling grease, some forks that John had just cleaned, the long-suffering servant had nearly had a fit from impotent rage. Another time, when Walter had told his father that John was in the habit of helping himself to some beer from the tap, John had told the boy that he had twice dreamt that he had murdered him. It was probably lucky for Walter that he had gone to school so promptly the day of the murder, since the frenzied John is unlikely to have spared this thoroughly nasty boy when he went on a rampage with the rolling pin. Another time, Mr Grossmith had seen John strike a chopper into a large piece of meat. When asked what he was doing, the sinister servant had replied, 'I am practising how to serve those that don't do as I like!'

The coroner's jury returned a verdict of wilful murder against Alexander Arthur Mackay. The problem was that no further clues were forthcoming about the Artillery Passage murderer's current whereabouts. In July, however, a clever detective had a brilliant idea. It had happened before that wanted fugitives had been incarcerated in provincial prisons under false names. A recent photograph of Mackay had been found in his bedroom at No. 11 Artillery Passage, and copies were circulated to all provincial police forces and to all prisons. It did not take long for Maidstone gaol to report back that a young man matching the photograph was currently imprisoned for theft under the name George Jackson. He was promptly brought to London, where the Artillery Passage witnesses recognised him as the murderer Alexander Arthur Mackay. On trial at the Old Bailey on 17 August, the evidence against Alexander Arthur Mackay was rock solid, and he was found guilty and sentenced to death. This extraordinary eighteen-year-old murderer was executed at Newgate on 8 September 1868.[6] The old eating house at No. 11 Artillery Passage was still kept by the Grossmith family in 1881, but today it is a Chinese restaurant.

Henry Wainwright's Murder House in Whitechapel Road, 1874

Henry Wainwright was a respectable and successful East End business man, trading as a brush manufacturer, with one factory at No. 84

Whitechapel Road and another at No. 215 across the road, not far from where the Whitechapel tube station is today. He lived at No. 40 Tredegar Square, Bow (the house still stands), with his wife and four children. Well into his thirties, Henry was something of a ladies' man, seducing various actresses and domestic servants with gusto. A rather good-looking, bushy-bearded cove, he had vague thespian ambitions himself, and his sonorous recitations of Thomas Hood's *The Dream of Eugene Aram* attracted some notice in Whitechapel theatrical circles.

One of Henry Wainwright's many mistresses was the nineteen-year-old Harriet Lane. He had met her in 1871, and later set her up in various lodgings, allowing her £5 per week. In the coming years, Harriet gave birth to two children, likely to have been fathered by Henry. In spite of having a wife and family, and keeping a pretty young mistress as well, this bushy-bearded East End Lothario kept 'playing the field'. Harriet became increasingly annoyed by his pursuit of various floozies associated with the stage. Things went from bad to worse when she discovered that Henry kept another permanent mistress, the young ballet dancer Alice Day.

In the meantime, Henry Wainwright's financial position had deteriorated markedly. He had inherited the brush-making business from his father, and was not capable of running it successfully. His immoral and expensive private life, supporting two mistresses, cannot have helped either. The creditors were moving in, and Henry feared bankruptcy. He had to move his family from the elegant house in Tredegar Square to humble lodgings in Chingford. In September 1874, Henry realised that he needed to solve the problem of his superannuated mistress Harriet Lane. Not only was she expensive to keep, but he no longer had any use for her, preferring Alice Day. Furthermore, Harriet kept making angry scenes, particularly when drunk, infuriated by the caddish behaviour of her inconstant lover. On 10 September 1874, Henry invited Harriet to the brush factory at No. 215 Whitechapel Road. He shot her in the head, cut her throat, and buried her body in a shallow grave underneath the floorboards in the rearmost workshop of the long and narrow brush factory.

Not many people missed Harriet Lane, and Henry told them that she had gone off to Continental Europe with a friend of his. Although he had secured the permanent silence of his former mistress, Henry's situation in life remained a far from pleasant one. In November 1874,

A photograph of Henry
Wainwright, from H. B.
Irving (ed.), *The Trial of the
Wainwrights* (Edinburgh,
1920).

Henry Wainwright shoots
Harriet Lane, from *Famous
Crimes Past & Present*,
issue 50.

the factory at No. 84 Whitechapel Road burnt down, but the insurers refused to pay out, since they knew about Henry's straitened financial situation and suspected arson. In June 1875, when Henry finally went bankrupt, a solicitor named Behrend took over the lease of the house at No. 215 Whitechapel Road. Some tenants moved into the house, and in the hot summer months they complained about a very foul smell that seemed to emanate from the rear paint shop. Henry blamed it on some rotting cabbages, but the tenants moved away for good.

When Behrend advertised No. 215 Whitechapel Road for sale, Henry realised that he had to act fast. The new owner of the house would not be as easily fobbed off with regard to the foul smell emanating from the rear workshop. His brother Thomas, who had previously impersonated Harriet's new suitor, with whom she was supposed to have gone to Europe, was again ready to help. Like his brother, Thomas was a careless businessman, and an ironmonger's shop that he had kept in an old pub called the Hen and Chickens at No. 54 Borough High Street had just failed. Just like the cunning Henry had kept a key to No. 215 Whitechapel Road, Thomas had kept the keys to the Hen and Chickens. The old pub had deep cellars, very suitable for hiding unsavoury relics of past crimes.

Henry Wainwright tries to persuade the constable not to open the parcel containing Harriet's mangled remains, from *Famous Crimes Past & Present*, issue 51.

On 10 September 1875, Henry Wainwright let himself into the empty house at No. 215 Whitechapel Road, lifted the floorboards in the rear workshop, and unearthed the remains of poor Harriet. They were surprisingly well preserved, since the careless murderer had buried them in chloride of lime, which acts as a disinfectant and preservative, rather than in quicklime. It was tough work for Henry to dismember the body using a large chopper, and pack the various body parts into two large canvas parcels. The following day, Henry went to a former workman of his named Alfred Stokes, and asked him, 'Will you carry a parcel for me, Stokes?' 'Yes, with the greatest of pleasure!' the polite labourer replied. They entered No. 215 through the rear entrance, accessed through a covered alleyway called Vine Court leading off Whitechapel Road. This took them straight in to the workshop where Henry had unearthed and packaged Harriet's remains. He took the lighter of the two parcels and let Stokes carry the heavy one. They had not got very far, however, when Stokes complained that the parcel was very heavy, and that it stank terribly. Henry did what he should have done in the first place, namely got a cab. When he went off to the cab rank, however, Stokes could not resist having a look inside the parcel. To his horror, he saw a severed human hand and wrist, among other body parts. When Henry arrived with the cab, he loaded both parcels into it, thanked Stokes for his troubles, and went off.

Alfred Stokes was no fool, however, and he realised that some terrible crime must have been committed. He ran after the cab, and at the crossing of Aldgate and Leadenhall Street he tried to convince two policemen to stop it, but they thought him a madman. A few streets away, Stokes saw the cab stop; Henry had spotted Alice Day walking along the street, and he invited her for a ride! As they went riding along, Henry puffed hard at a large cigar to hide the nauseating stench emanating from the two large parcels. As cool as a cucumber, this extraordinary murderer kept up a light conversation with his mistress. The panting Stokes kept pursuing the cab as it crossed the Thames via London Bridge, and finally pulled up in Borough High Street, just outside the Hen and Chickens. Just as Henry unloaded his two parcels, Stokes found a police constable, and managed to get him interested in the cab and its sinister load. In spite of Henry's protestations, the parcels were opened, and various pieces of Harriet Lane's dismembered body tumbled out onto the pavement of Borough High Street.

Nothing was found to incriminate Alice Day, who had enjoyed such a very sinister ride with her bushy-bearded lover and the remains of her predecessor in his affections, and she was released. Thomas Wainwright was sentenced to seven years in prison as an accessory after the fact. He was fortunate to have an alibi for the day when Harriet Lane disappeared, since there was speculation that his help might have come in very handy for Henry, with regard to lifting the heavy floorboards. George R. Sims even speculated that Thomas Wainwright was the true author of the crime, and that Henry was an innocent man who took the blame for his brother.[7]

However, the evidence against Henry Wainwright was rock solid: the revolver bullet in what remained of Harriet's brain, the grave in the rear workshop of No. 215 Whitechapel Road, the spade and chopper found in there, and of course the mangled remains of poor Harriet herself. Found guilty of murder and sentenced to death at the Old Bailey on 22 November 1875, he was taken to the condemned cell at Newgate. During his final night in there, he might well have been pondering some verses in Hood's *The Dream of Eugene Aram*, which he had once been so fond of reciting:

My head was like an ardent coal,
My heart as solid ice;
My wretched, wretched soul, I knew,
Was at the Devil's price;
A dozen times I groan'd: the dead
Had never groan'd but twice.

And now, from forth the frowning sky,
From the Heaven's topmost height,
I heard a voice – the awful voice
Of the blood-avenging sprite:
'Thou guilty man! take up thy dead
And hide it from my sight!'

Still, it must be said that Henry Wainwright died like a man. On 21 December, the day set aside for his execution at Newgate, he calmly smoked one of his large cigars, before walking up to the scaffold. He glared at the people standing nearby, exclaiming, 'Come to see a man

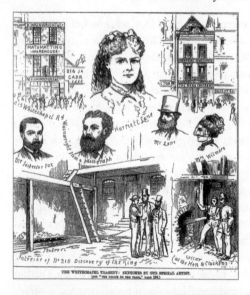

The murder house, the Hen and Chickens, the inside of the workshop and portraits of some of the major players in the Whitechapel Road drama, from the *Penny Illustrated Paper*, 25 September 1874.

Harriet Lane. This image is from a large Victorian scrapbook about criminal matters.

HOUSE WHERE THE BODY WAS CONCEALED.

MR LANE'S HOUSE AT WALTHAM

Above: The murder house, and the house of Harriet Lane's father.

Right: The workman Stokes, who played such an important role in the discovery of the murder.

H. STOKES

die, have you, you curs?' before the executioner Marwood pulled down the hood and launched the Whitechapel Road murderer in to eternity.[8]

Henry Wainwright was buried in the old Newgate burial ground, but when Newgate was being demolished in 1902 his remains were unearthed and taken to a cemetery in Ilford, along with those of Amelia Dyer, Thomas Neill Cream, Mrs Pearcey, and other notorious criminals. The bullets inside Harriet Lane's skull, some skin and hair samples from her body, and the cigar Henry Wainwright had been smoking when he was arrested, were deposited in Scotland Yard's Black Museum, along with the spade and chopper used to dismember the body.[9] These interesting relics of the case are all said to have been lost or stolen over the years; for what was supposed to be a secure museum, accessed by professionals only, the Black Museum certainly guarded its relics of criminal history with blameworthy carelessness. Nor is it certain that the murder house survived. Geoffrey Howse suggested that it was identical to the present-day No. 136 Whitechapel Road, but M. W. Oldridge placed it near the existing modern houses at Nos 128 and 130 Whitechapel Road.[10] It was clearly time to do some good old-fashioned murder house detective work.

Above left: Trial of the Wainwrights, the first page from an old pamphlet.

Above right: A later photograph of the Wainwright murder house, from H. B. Irving (ed.), *The Trial of the Wainwrights* (Edinburgh, 1920).

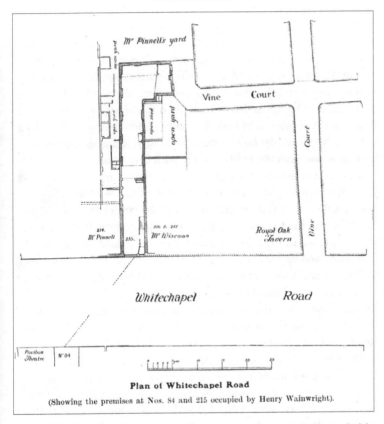

Plan of Whitechapel Road

(Showing the premises at Nos. 84 and 215 occupied by Henry Wainwright).

A plan of the Whitechapel Road murder house, from H. B. Irving (ed.), *The Trial of the Wainwrights* (Edinburgh, 1920).

The contemporary press made much of Henry Wainwright and the Whitechapel Tragedy. The *Illustrated Police News* published Henry's portrait and a drawing depicting the horrified policeman emptying the parcel full of Harriet's body parts into Borough High Street. Not to be outdone, the *Penny Illustrated Paper* published a drawing of the murder house, showing it as a three-storey building at No. 215 Whitechapel Road.[11] To the east is a taller house, to the west a lower workshop marked 'Carr' and numbered 216 (and quite possibly also 217 on the other side of the sign). *The Trial of the Wainwrights* provides valuable additional information, namely a useful plan of the murder house and a photograph of it.[12] This image shows the rather ramshackle murder house, again between a taller house to the east and a lower workshop to the west. The murder house is now home to 'A. Rackow, Wholesale & Export Boot & Shoe Manufacturer' and does not display a number. Carr's workshop now has the sign 'J. Wiseman', and the old numbers 216 and 217 have been replaced by 128 and 126 from when the houses in Whitechapel Road were renumbered in 1898. This might lead the unwary to suggest that, surely, the murder house must now be No. 130, but the experienced murder house detective tends to avoid such conjecture.

Instead, it is time to study the Ordnance Survey maps at the British Library, which display the relevant section of the Whitechapel Road, between the Royal Oak public house and the corner with New Road. The 1874 map has ten houses in this section of the road, from the Royal Oak in the west to the corner house with New Road to the east. An immediate and important conclusion is that the only house with a front to Whitechapel Road and rear access to the end of the eastern branch of Vine Court, as indicated by the plan in *The Trial of the Wainwrights*, is the sixth house from the east. The 1894 map is unchanged from 1874, but the 1913 map has eleven houses in the relevant section of Whitechapel Road, due to one (the seventh from the east) being subdivided into two.

The 1938 Ordnance Survey map has the advantage, compared with the earlier editions, of providing numbers for some of the houses. From west to east, the Royal Oak has Nos 118–120, and it is followed by a very narrow house at No. 122 and a wider one at No. 124. There are two adjacent buildings without numbers provided, followed by No. 132, which is the sixth house from the east and the only one with rear access to the eastern extremity of Vine Court. Then there are five houses, presumably Nos 134–142, with No. 142 the corner house with New Road. Henry Wainwright's murder house is now clearly identical to No. 132 Whitechapel Road, and it is not an unreasonable presumption that the two adjacent buildings to the west are Wiseman's workshop at Nos 126–128, as seen on the photograph in *The Trial of the Wainwrights*.

Having done my homework at the British Library, it was time to don the Sherlock Holmes cap and board the No. 205 bus eastwards to do some proper murder house detective work. Since several of the old houses in the relevant section of Whitechapel Road have been pulled down and replaced with more modern buildings of different proportions, the investigation was not an entirely straightforward one. There are still ten houses to be counted from the former Royal Oak and the corner with New Road, although it is notable that one house has clearly gone missing: the one to the west of the present-day No. 136, where there is a small car park. Audiostar occupies the ground floor of the former Royal Oak, and Khan's Kebab House at No. 122 is clearly situated in the narrow building next to the pub seen on the old Ordnance Survey maps. The house at No. 124, housing the Rahim Business Centre, occupies roughly the same spot as the house with the same number in the 1938 Ordnance Survey map. Then follow three modern houses, Jaan Sports at No. 128, Maryam Oxygen at No. 130 and the Whitechapel Dental Centre at Nos 132–134. Today, there is no No. 126. Then follows the opening to the car park alluded to earlier, and the remaining old houses at Nos 136, 138, 140 and 142.

Thus it can be concluded that the Whitechapel Road front of Henry Wainwright's murder house is no longer standing. Its position is likely to correspond roughly with that of the Whitechapel Dental Centre, a modern building with no similarity to the old murder house, as judged by the original drawing and photograph of it. A look around in Vine Court proves unexpectedly profitable, however. Some of the old houses in there are still standing, and in the south-easterly extremity there is a house with two securely shuttered windows and a padlocked door. Although it ends blindly to the east, and does not correspond with any of the houses in Whitechapel Road, this is clearly Henry Wainwright's old workshop, where he stored the mutilated remains of Harriet Lane. Its position fits perfectly with the rear of the former No. 215, which became No. 132 after the renumbering of the houses. A helpful local, who has heard rumours that a murder once took place in the workshop, informs me that it is today privately owned. Although neither inhabited nor used for storage or business, it is well looked after, presumably by some person who knows its terrible secret.

New Light on the Murder House at No. 16 Batty Street, 1887

On the morning of 28 June 1887, a young woman named Miriam Angel was found dead in bed at her first-floor lodgings at No. 16 Batty Street, off Commercial Road. She had been poisoned with nitric acid, which some person had forced her to swallow. The upstairs lodger, the twenty-two-year-old Jewish stick-maker Israel Lipski, was pulled out from underneath her bed, with acid burns in and around his mouth. Lipski,

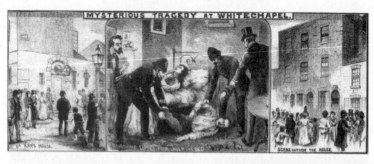

Top: The discovery of the murder of Miriam Angel, flanked by drawings of the murder house at No. 16 Batty Street (right) and the doctor's house (left), from the *Illustrated Police News*, 9 July 1887.

Centre: A villainous-looking Israel Lipski, and other scenes from the Whitechapel Tragedy, from the *Illustrated Police News*, 16 July 1887.

Above: The End of the Whitechapel Tragedy, from the *Illustrated Police News*, 27 August 1887.

born in Poland as Israel Lobulsk, had ambitions to better himself: he hoped for success in his umbrella-stick-manufacturing business, which employed two workmen named Harry Schmuss and Henry Rosenbloom. He was engaged to a Jewish girl named Kate Lance, and was intending to marry her. No motive for Lipski to murder Miriam Angel was apparent, but the police found that he had purchased the nitric acid prior to the murder, and that the door to the room had been locked from the inside.

Israel Lipski did not have a criminal record, and he had nothing to gain from the death of Miriam Angel. During his trial, Lipski claimed that Rosenbloom and Schmuss had committed the murder after being discovered looking for money in Miriam Angel's rooms. Schmuss was in fact a qualified locksmith, able to pick a lock or to give the impression that a door had been locked from the other side. However, the police presumed that Lipski had entered Miriam Angel's rooms with intent to rape her, and this theory was also upheld by the prosecution, and by the far from unbiased judge, Mr Justice Stephen. Israel Lipski was found guilty of murder and sentenced to death. While in custody awaiting execution, he confessed that he had killed Miriam Angel while in the process of robbing her. This confession has been a mainstay for those believing in his guilt, but Lipski's defenders have presumed that he confessed after his reprieve had been turned down, because he did not want to be thought of as having killed Miriam Angel after attempting to rape her.[13]

Israel Lipski was hanged at Newgate on 21 August 1887. The debate about his guilt has continued over the years, and Mr Justice Stephen has been criticised for his needless severity and barely disguised anti-Semitism. Nor has the controversial Home Secretary, Mr Henry Matthews, escaped censure for his refusal to respite Lipski, although he was an opponent of capital punishment. A few days after Lipski had been executed, Isaac Angel, the husband of the murdered woman, led a mob to No. 16 Batty Street. They broke down the door and knocked down Mrs Leah Lipski, the landlady of the house. Angel swore and cursed as he kicked the sturdy landlady, saying that he would not rest until he had had his revenge on her. The disorderly mob broke the windows of No. 16, chanting, 'Lipski! Lipski!' When Isaac Angel was summoned before the Thames Police Court, it turned out that Mrs Leah Lipski was not related to the murderer, and the attack on her had been entirely pointless.

According to Israel Lipski's biographer, Professor Martin Friedland, the murder house at No. 16 Batty Street is no more. It had consisted of two storeys and an attic, he confidently declared, but was pulled down in 1888 for a larger 'blocks of flats' to be constructed. The majority of later students of the Lipski case have accepted this statement as a fact, some of them commenting that, surely, the house had acquired a sinister reputation after the murder, which had prompted its demolition. Some perceptive critics have commented that the facade of the present-day building at No. 16 Batty Street looks very much like the drawing of the murder house in the *Illustrated Police News* of 9 July 1887. Clearly, it was time to do some more murder house detective work, and find out the truth about the house at No. 16 Batty Street.

The northern part of Batty Street was developed in the early 1800s. Horwood's map of 1819 shows houses Nos 1–17 on the eastern side, numbered from north to south, and Nos 18–24 on the western side, numbered from south to north. Berner, Batty and King Streets all led from Commercial Road down to garden land in the south, where they ended blindly. All these streets were later completed from Commercial Road down to Fairclough Street in the south, and the houses in Batty Street were renumbered with even numbers on the western side and odds on the eastern one, from north to south. The 1873 Ordnance Survey map shows the Red Lion public house at No. 24, next to a partially covered alleyway called Hampshire Court, which passes through the narrow house at No. 22. If the aforementioned *Illustrated Police News* illustration is scrutinised, it clearly shows the murder house at No. 16 in the middle, with a police constable in front of it. It is surrounded by two other terraced three-storey houses at No. 14 and No. 18, with the houses at No. 12 and No. 20 being lower and of an older design.

To analyse the fate of the murder house at No. 16 Batty Street, it is essential to compare the Ordnance Survey maps of 1873 and 1894. The most obvious difference is that the houses at Nos 26–42 Batty Street have all been demolished to allow for the construction of a large school at the corner with Fairclough Street. The Red Lion at No. 24 is still there in 1894, as is the Hampshire Court alleyway, but the houses at No. 20 and No. 22 now form one larger house. The shape of the houses at No. 18 and No. 16 has changed: they are wider, and extended towards the rear. The old No. 14 has been much extended towards the north, assimilating the lower house at No. 12 and No. 10 as well. Interestingly, there is no No.

12 Batty Street in the 1901 Survey, just a 'No. 12 Batty Street Buildings', probably indicating an annexe to the rear of No. 14.

Since the doorway of No. 14 Batty Street is inscribed '1888' it is reasonable to suggest that, sometime during the Year of the Ripper, some of the houses on the western side of Batty Street were extensively rebuilt. No. 20 and No. 22 became one house, No. 16 and No. 18 were both widened and enlarged, and No. 14 much enlarged to incorporate the old No. 12 and No. 10. All these houses also acquired another story during these alterations. There is nothing to suggest, from maps or census records, that either of these houses were ever 'blocks of flats' as suggested by Friedland and others: they were humble lodging houses, filled to the rafters with various impecunious East End characters and their large families. The Post Office Directory of 1890 lists a Morris Blanfox, working jeweller, as being active at No. 16, but he is not included in the 1889 or 1891 directories. At the time of the 1901 census, Nos 14, 16 and 18 Batty Street were distinct houses, full of adults, children and boarders. Today, a large part of the western part of Batty Street is occupied by a warehouse, replacing the 'garage' seen on the 1938 Ordnance Survey map, with small shops on the ground floor. It is marked, in white paint, '4–12 Batty Street'. The houses at Nos 14, 16, 18 and 20 still stand, although No. 20 may well have been rebuilt at some stage. Hampshire Court is gone, and so is the old pub at No. 24, pulled down to make room for the large Bernard Baron House block of flats.

A newspaper feature on 'murder houses' contained the breathless words: 'In the heart of Jack the Ripper territory in Whitechapel is 16 Batty Street where, in 1887, a failing umbrella stick salesman named Israel Lipski forced nitric acid down the throat of a fellow boarder as she lay in bed on the second floor.' This ignores, of course, the fact that Lipski's business was far from failing, and that the murder was committed in the front room of the first floor. The journalist interviewed the present-day owner of No. 16, who claimed to have been aware of the history of the house before he bought it. Although one of his friends got a funny feeling about the place, there was nothing to suggest that it was haunted.[14]

In spite of the speculations of this enthusiastic journalist, there is nothing to suggest that the murder house at No. 16 Batty Street survives in its original form. The present-day house is wider, extended to the rear, and since No. 18 was also widened in 1888, it occupies a site slightly to the north of the original No. 16. Since the present-day No. 16 looks not unlike the old murder house, it is quite possible that some of the original brickwork may remain, and that the windows and shutters of the original house were 'recycled' when the house was extended in 1888.[15] So does it still qualify as a 'murder house'? Perhaps not strictly, but it remains a reminder of an obscure and tragic crime committed not far from the alleys where Jack the Ripper once prowled.

'Ripping' Murder in Whitechapel, 1894

In the early 1890s, the house at No. 5 Thomas Street, just off Whitechapel Road, was a small coffee shop kept by the forty-three-year-old George Henry Matthews. Not far away, in Brady Street, lived a fifty-two-year-old woman who called herself Marie Martin or Damyon. She claimed to have been married first to a man named Barker, and then to a blacksmith named William Damyon, who had recently died. Marie Damyon's daughter had been married to the brother of Mrs Sarah Matthews, wife of George Henry the coffee-house keeper, and the two women were very good friends.

In the summer of 1894, George Henry Matthews went hop-picking in Kent, leaving his wife to run the coffee shop. When he returned, he was stark raving mad, screaming and yahooing. After he had beaten his wife black and blue in a furious assault, he was removed to Claybury asylum, where he remained for eight weeks. Eventually, he was released and returned to No. 5 Thomas Street. Although he seemed to have improved a good deal during his time in the asylum, Sarah remained fearful that one day he would cause further mischief.

On Friday 16 November 1894, George Henry Matthews went out drinking. He behaved weirdly, and his incessant 'jawing' caused several other pub customers to leave the premises. Sarah Matthews and Marie Damyon also had a few drinks, but neither was the worse for liquor. They were joined by Marie Damyon's son from her first marriage, the dock labourer William Barker. He was surprised when Mrs Matthews said that the previous night she had been compelled to call someone to stay with her, since she was frightened of what her husband might be up to. When asked the reason for this precaution, she said that she thought he was going wrong in his head.

It was close to midnight when Sarah Mathews and Marie Damyon left the Star and Garter, where they had been drinking beer and gin, and returned to No. 5 Thomas Street. Since Sarah was still fearful of her husband, she asked her friend to remain in the house and sleep in the spare bedroom. George Henry Matthews was nowhere to be seen. Early in the morning of 17 November, Sarah Matthews heard Marie Damyon call out her name. When she opened the door to the stairs, Marie fell into her arms. Blood flowed down the stairs from her cut throat. Sarah hurried to the street door and called for the police, but when they arrived Marie Damyon was dead.

About an hour later, at 4 a.m., Mrs Alice Rogers, wife of a master printer and sister of George Henry Matthews, heard some person shouting outside her house at No. 313 Wick Road, Homerton. After this individual had burst open the workshop door and began to throw things outside, she went down to confront him. It turned out to be George Henry Matthews, soaking wet after having a bath in the River Lea. Foaming at the mouth, he shouted, 'I have ripped Marie up and Sarah!' Mr Rogers went to call in the police, but for some reason they were very reluctant to arrest the lunatic Matthews. After a discussion lasting nearly two hours, they finally took him into custody, to be charged with the murder of his wife's best friend.

While in police custody, George Henry Matthews behaved like a complete madman. He had to be forcibly dressed and undressed, and when brought to the police court he asked for half a pint of water, only to pour it over his head. When arrested, he was carrying £4 10s in gold and a good deal of silver, and another £16 or so was found in the murder house. Matthews agreed to speak to his wife and to give her some money, and for a few seconds he behaved perfectly rationally, before pushing her away and telling her to bring him a cup of tea. It was clear to the police that, in the wee hours, the lunatic Matthews had returned to No. 5 Thomas Street, armed with a razor. It was not obvious whether his original intention had been to murder his wife, particularly since he had told his sister that he had 'ripped' Sarah as well. At any rate, George Henry Matthews was obviously insane and unfit to plead, and he was removed to an asylum by Secretary of State's order.[16] He died in Broadmoor in 1906, aged fifty-five. The murder house at No. 5 Thomas (now Fulbourne) street still stands.

Double Murder in Turner Street, 1896

Mr Jonathan Goodman Levy, a seventy-four-year-old retired umbrella manufacturer, lived at No. 31 Turner Street, Whitechapel, just at the corner of Varden Street. The house faced Varden Street, but had its door in Turner Street. With admirable financial astuteness, this clever old Jew had accumulated quite a fortune, and he could spend his declining years in comfortable idleness, with his housekeeper Annie Gale.

On 4 April 1896, Mr Levy went out on an errand, leaving Annie Gale in charge of the house. However, a professional burglar named William Seaman was lurking nearby. Thinking that the house was empty, he decided to break in to it. Not being quite sure that nobody was at home, he rang the doorbell. When Annie Gale opened the door, he chased her into the house, beat her up with a poker from the grate, and cut her throat with such violence that he nearly took her head off. Seaman then began searching the house, stuffing all the valuables he found into his pockets. When Mr Levy unexpectedly returned, this ultra-violent burglar treated him in the same manner as he had the housekeeper, beating the old man with a poker until he was well-nigh dead, before finishing him off by cutting his throat.

In despatching Mr Levy, William Seaman had used considerable violence, and the next-door neighbour, who heard the commotion, called the police. The veteran burglar heard them coming and tried to leave through the front door, but Mr Levy had locked it and Seaman could not find the key. In desperation, he seized hold of a hammer and cut a large hole through the upper bedroom ceiling and climbed out onto the roof of the house. However, the house was too tall for Seaman to jump down, and the police constables were making their way through the house to apprehend him. When two policemen crawled through the hole in the roof and closed in on him, the desperate murderer jumped 40 feet on to the pavement below.

Landing with a heavy thud, Seaman broke his right shoulder and injured his leg badly. He narrowly avoided flattening a little girl who was just walking past on the pavement, but she got away with a concussion. The groaning murderer was removed to the hospital, and his two victims to the mortuary. There was much speculation about the motive for this frenzied attack. William Seaman was a veteran thief and burglar, who had spent many years in prison, but he had never attempted murder before. A young woman, who asked him why he had murdered Mr Levy and his housekeeper, had heard the murderer mutter that Levy had once done him a great injustice.

Due to Seaman's injuries, the inquest on Mr Levy and Annie Gale was not held until 1 May. Seaman, who had declined the services of a

Above left: Seaman and his victims, from the *Penny Illustrated Paper*, 18 April 1896.

Above right: Seaman murders Mr Levy, from the *Illustrated Police Budget*, 18 April 1896.

Below: Seaman tries to escape over the roof, from *Famous Crimes Past & Present*, issue 88.

solicitor, behaved quite obnoxiously. He accused the police constables of lying, and said that he knew that that Mr Levy had been sleeping with Annie Gale for many years. A detective said that he knew Seaman as a particularly vicious man, who had a long criminal record for repeated burglaries. His landlady was the only person who had anything good to say about him: his disposition was so gentle that if she had caught a mouse in a trap, she said, he would implore her to set it free. On trial at the Old Bailey on 18 May, Seaman offered no defence, and he was found guilty and sentenced to death. He was executed at Newgate on 9 June, in a 'triple event', between the two notorious Muswell Hill murderers Albert Milsom and Henry Fowler. Since Milsom and Fowler had been quarrelling angrily, Seaman was put between them to prevent another fight. Before being launched into eternity along with his two cantankerous fellow murderers, the coarse-looking Seaman commented that this was the first time in his life that he had served as a bloody peacemaker.[17] The murder house at No. 31 Turner Street has been significantly rebuilt, and is today home to Wahab Cleaners. The houses opposite the crossing with Varden Street look just like the old murder house, however.[18]

Murder in Dan Mendoza's Old Pub, 1903

Daniel Mendoza was born in 1764, one of many children in a family of young Jewish refugees from the Spanish Inquisition. A strong, athletic lad, he had little patience with various East End roughs who taunted him with anti-Semitic jibes. After mauling his opponents in a number of bare-knuckle street fights, he became a professional boxer. In his time, boxers usually stood still and swapped punches, but Mendoza developed an entirely new style of boxing, incorporating defensive strategies such as sidestepping, ducking and blocking. At the time, this was quite revolutionary, and Mendoza was able to overcome much heavier opponents as a result of this new style. A series of spectacular wins made him the champion of England, and a household name. Mendoza was so popular that the London press reported news of one of his bouts ahead of the storming of the Bastille. The dashing pugilist single-handedly transformed the English stereotype of a Jew from a weak, defenceless person into someone deserving of respect.

In 1789, Dan Mendoza opened his own boxing academy in London, attended by many young gentlemen with pugilistic ambitions, Lord

Byron among them. Thousands of pounds were riding on the outcome of his matches, some of them wagered by his royal patron, the Prince of Wales. Mendoza published the book *The Art of Boxing* about his modern 'scientific' style, and would have become a wealthy man, had he not been in the habit of spending his guineas as quickly as he earned them. In the late 1790s, when Dan Mendoza's boxing career began to decline, he was constantly in debt, and unable to support his large family. As a consequence, he retired from full-time boxing and took the lease of a small pub, the Lord Nelson at No. 145 Whitechapel Road.[19]

The Father of Boxing, as Dan Mendoza was styled by his admirers, did not remain at the Lord Nelson for very long. The restless pugilist moved on to another pub, and in 1817 a certain Joseph Louch was registered as the keeper of the Lord Nelson. The old pub occasionally hit the news in the century to come: in April 1876, two pugilists were prosecuted for stealing £42 from Mr James Finch, landlord of the Lord Nelson, and in November 1887, the old pub was damaged by fire. In 1890, the Lord Nelson was purchased by a certain George Spinks. On old Ordnance Survey maps, the pub can be seen on the northern side of the

Martha Jane Hardwick is murdered in the Lord Nelson public house, from the *Illustrated Police News*, 3 October 1903.

Whitechapel Road, east of where the Whitechapel tube station is today. There was a covered alleyway just east of the Lord Nelson, leading to a rear alley called Nelson Court, which in its turn led to Winthrop Street.

In 1903, the Lord Nelson was managed by the widow Mrs Hannah Starkey. She employed her unmarried sister Martha Jane Hardwick and her aunt Martha Sophia Brayshaw as barmaids, as well as two potmen named Christopher Pealling and Robert Musgrave. One of the regular customers at the Lord Nelson was the twenty-eight-year-old dock labourer Jeremiah 'Jerry' Slowe. A short, ugly, meanly dressed chap, he very much admired the pretty twenty-year-old Martha Jane Hardwick, but she made it clear that she wanted nothing to do with him. Jerry Slowe did not like being rebuffed, and the short-tempered young dock hand more than once made angry scenes at Mendoza's old pub. Once, he threatened violence if a butcher's hook he had deposited behind the bar was not immediately returned to him; another time, the potman Musgrave heard him mutter, 'I will put her bloody lights out one of these days', referring to Martha Jane, who made no effort to conceal that she did not like serving the scruffy, uncouth Jerry.

In the evening of 23 September 1903, everything seemed normal at the Lord Nelson. Hannah Starkey, Martha Jane Hardwick and Martha Sophia Brayshaw were all busy pulling pints for a crowd of jolly customers, and the two potmen were also hard at work. The taciturn Jerry Slowe was also in attendance, sitting alone at a table and swigging hard from his beer-glass. The Lord Nelson was due to close at half past midnight. By 12.15, the pub was almost empty of customers, and Martha Jane Hardwick was busy tidying up. All of a sudden, Jerry Slowe burst into the pub. Without saying a word, he twice struck out at Martha Jane, and she collapsed on the floor. Mrs Starkey, who had seen the assault, leapt over the counter to pursue the absconding Jerry, calling out to the two potmen Pealling and Musgrave, 'Catch him and kill him!'

The two potmen saw Jerry running out of the pub, and heard Mrs Starkey's agitated outcry. They ran after the fugitive, but the corpulent Musgrave soon ran out of puff. Pealling caught up with Jerry outside Mr Milward's coffee shop, and seized him by the throat, but the sturdy dock labourer sent him staggering with a hard blow to the jaw. Pealling kept pursuing Jerry from a safe distance, since he did not dare to close with his opponent again. His relief was great when he saw a police constable through the fog. Pointing out Jerry, he called out, 'I want that man!'

'What for?' Constable William Bowden calmly replied. 'For assault! He has assaulted the barmaid at the Lord Nelson!' Pealling shouted back. Jerry said that this was all a lot of nonsense: Pealling was clearly drunk, and he was going back to his lodgings. However, Constable Bowden had been able to grasp that something was clearly wrong: he seized hold of Jerry and frogmarched him all the way back to the Lord Nelson. 'Hold me tight, you damned bugger, I have just stabbed a woman!' the drunken Jerry screamed as they went along, the excited Pealling beckoning them on. At the Lord Nelson, another policeman named Hubert Haddock joined the party. A doctor had also arrived on the scene, and declared Martha Jane Hardwick dead from a stab wound to the chest. Even the rowdy, drunken Jerry seemed much awed when he saw her lying in a large pool of blood. 'Is she dead?' he asked the police constables, and seemed much excited when told that she certainly was.

Constable Haddock had found Jerry's bloody knife outside Mr Milward's coffee shop, and he was arrested by a police inspector and charged with the murder of Martha Jane Hardwick. On trial at the Old Bailey on 19 October 1903, the evidence against Jerry Slowe was rock solid.[20] A short, stocky, sinister-looking man with an overlarge moustache, he did not make a particularly good impression in court. Hannah Starkey and Martha Sophia Brayshaw had both seen Jerry stab Martha Jane, and the two potmen had seen him run out of the pub. Although Jerry had a reasonably good reputation, and although he had been drunk at the time of the murder, his crime had been a dastardly and premeditated one. He had stolen the knife from his employer and brought it with him to the Lord Nelson to settle things with Martha Jane once and for all. Found guilty of murder and sentenced to death, he is said by the *Penny Illustrated Paper* never to have entertained any hope of a reprieve, being resigned to his fate and willing to die.[21] He kept annoying the other prisoners by singing music hall songs in the condemned cell, and showed no signs of contrition or remorse. Jerry Slowe was executed at Pentonville Prison on 10 November 1903.

In Edwardian times, social reformers were keen to reduce the number of pubs, rightly pointing out that easy access to cheap beer and gin did not aid the productivity of Britain's labouring men. Indeed, alcohol was a prime source of crime, poverty, and human misery, they claimed. From 1900 until 1908, the number of pubs in Britain fell from 7,800 to 6,700. One of the casualties was the Lord Nelson at No. 145 Whitechapel

Road. In 1907, it belonged to the London City Mission, who held their prayer meetings in Daniel Mendoza's old murder pub, unperturbed by the ghosts of Martha Jane Hardwick and Jerry Slowe.[22] The former pub at what is today No. 299 Whitechapel Road is nowadays a popular shop for Indian fashions. The alleyway to the side has been closed up, and there is no longer any rear access to the premises, due to the development of the railway.

The Two Murder Houses in Hanbury Street, 1912
As murder houses come, No. 29 Hanbury Street is a household name, although it no longer stands. A single-fronted, three-storey dwelling on the north side of this Whitechapel street, it was situated approximately halfway between Commercial Street and Brick Lane. Believed to have been built around 1740 along with adjacent properties by the carpenter Daniel Marsillat, it had two rooms on each floor. In 1888, Jack the Ripper made a visit to No. 29, leaving his second victim Annie Chapman dead in the backyard. This gave the house a sinister reputation, but nobody thought of demolishing it, although it was regularly mentioned in newspaper features on the Ripper murders. Increasingly scruffy and dilapidated, it continued to be occupied until 1969. It was demolished along with the entire north side of the street in early March 1970 to make way for extensions to the Truman Brewery. Prior to its destruction, a number of Ripperologists made sure that it was well documented photographically. One of these photos shows the sinister backyard looking not dissimilar to what it was like in 1888.

The present-day Ripperologist who has come to gaze at the forbidding-looking brewery buildings on the former site of No. 29 is well advised to carry on to No. 62 Hanbury Street, a murder house that has the advantage of still existing and that commemorates a gruesome double murder committed in 1912. By that time, the ground-floor premises at No. 62 was a simple eating house, owned by the Russian Jew Solomon Millstein and his wife Annie. These two had lived in London for twenty years, and had kept the restaurant since their marriage. They had no children themselves, but had adopted a little girl. Although the Millsteins were decent, hard-working people, their restaurant was not the most respectable, even by Whitechapel standards, since the basement of the house was used as a gambling-den, attracting many dodgy characters.

In the early morning of 27 December 1912, smoke was billowing out of the restaurant at No. 62 Hanbury Street. With commendable expedition, the fire brigade arrived at the scene. Entering the first-floor back room, they saw a burning bed, and promptly put the fire out. On the floor, in a pool of blood, was the dead body of Annie Millstein. She had been hit hard over the head with a poker, stabbed, and strangled. A little further towards the eating-house part of the house was the body of Solomon Millstein, who had been knocked down and stabbed to death with his own large carving knife. A doctor called in at 4.30 a.m. believed that they had both been dead for about an hour. Mrs Millstein's jewellery had not been touched, but the murderer had taken the cash box used

The discovery of the murder of the Millsteins, from the *Illustrated Police News*, 6 January 1912.

Left and below: The murder house, and a portrait of Myer Abramovitch, from the *Illustrated Police News*, 6 January 1912.

for the restaurant takings. Having trodden in the pool of blood, he had left several footprints behind. A large, bloodstained scarf, which did not belong to either of the Millsteins, was also found. It was supposed that it had belonged to the murderer, and that one of the Millsteins had torn it off him. The lodger inhabiting the top floor of No. 62, the cabinet maker Marks Verbloot, had heard groaning from downstairs during the night, but he had gone back to sleep. Later, he had smelt smoke, and this had induced him to open the front window, blow a police whistle, and run downstairs.

The police showed the scarf to neighbours, restaurant guests, and gamblers, and some of the latter recognised it as one worn by the young fish porter Myer (or Meyer) Abramovitch. They even offered to help the police find this individual. By that time, though, Abramovitch had already been arrested by Inspector Freeman, and taken to the Leman Street police station. He had several recent cuts to his hands, and he was wearing one of Solomon Millstein's suits over his own bloodstained clothes. He admitted that the scarf was his, and that he had left it behind at No. 62 Hanbury Street. In his pocket was a watch and chain belonging to Mr Millstein. He explained that he had lost all his money gambling at No. 62 on Boxing Day, and that he had decided to 'get even' by robbing the restaurant. The Millsteins had fought back, but he had overpowered and killed them. It turned out that 'Mad Myer', as Abramovitch was called for his unbalanced behaviour, did not have a police record. His first language was Yiddish, but he knew enough English to be able to make himself understood.

At the coroner's inquest on Solomon and Annie Millstein, a linotype operator named Lewis Herscowitz declared that he was Mrs Millstein's brother-in-law. Solomon Millstein had told him that he had lost much custom, and he was even considering selling out. When Herscowitz told him that it was not respectable to operate a gambling-den, Millstein told him not to worry: he was paying the police a very good fee so that they would not close his establishment down! Mrs Millstein had not liked the gambling going on in the basement, since it attracted men of a very low class. A verdict of wilful murder against Myer Abramovitch was returned.

On 30 January 1912, Myer Abramovitch was on trial at the Central Criminal Court. Considering the wealth of evidence against him, and his own damning admissions at the police station, all his defence counsel could try was the 'insanity defence'. However, the prison doctors thought Myer Abramovitch perfectly sane. It took the jury just ten minutes to find him guilty, and Mr Justice Rentoul sentenced him to death.[23] Myer Abramovitch was executed at Pentonville Prison on 8 March 1912.

Murder in Brick Lane, 1960

Frances Tucker was one of the characters of Brick Lane in the 1950s: a hunchback of mixed Scottish and West Indian heritage, she spoke with a strong Caledonian accent, and expressed herself in an earthy and explicit manner. She supported herself mainly through petty crime, and was once imprisoned for peddling drugs. She was well known as a supplier of West Indian 'reefers' and 'hemp'. In spite of her infirmity, Frances Tucker was fond of 'chasing the lads', and in early 1960 the neighbours in Brick Lane noticed that her latest swain was a young West Indian man.

In the evening of 11 January 1960, the house at No. 106 Brick Lane, just at the corner with Princelet Street, where Frances Tucker was living in a first-floor flat, was observed to be on fire. There was serious danger for the inhabitant of the second-floor flat, who shepherded his three children on to a flat roof, from which they were saved by the fire brigade using a long ladder. In all, twenty people were rescued from the burning house, but after the fire had been extinguished Frances Tucker was found dead in her flat.

The police discovered that her death had not been accidental: she had been brutally beaten down, before the murderer had poured paraffin on the floor and tried to burn the house down to conceal his crime. The main suspect was the West Indian boyfriend, an uncouth individual who had previously made various threats against Frances Tucker, among them that he would one day roast her on a Christmas tree with a can of oil. He was identified as the thirty-two-year-old unemployed Jamaican decorator Cleveland Reid, who had previous convictions for theft, assault and unlawful wounding. He had just been released from prison, and a neighbour said that their previous quarrel had been caused by Frances selling some of his effects while he had been 'inside'.

The fugitive Cleveland Reid was tracked down to his married sister's house at No. 7 Mory Road, Cricklewood, where he was found asleep in bed, and promptly arrested. His clothes smelt strongly of paraffin. Reid at first denied any involvement in the murder, but later claimed that he had in fact been blackmailed by Frances Tucker, who had got her hands on a compromising photograph of him, and threatened to send it to his respectable sister. After an angry quarrel, he had strangled her with her scarf and set the house on fire. On trial for murder at the Old Bailey on 17 March 1960, Cleveland Reid was found guilty and sentenced to imprisonment for life.[24]

Murder Houses of the Kray Twins, 1966 and 1967

Those terrible twins, Ronnie and Reggie Kray, are too well known to merit any further description. Tough, resourceful, ruthless gangsters, they ruled their East End 'manor' with an iron hand. They had a fondness for society and 'high life', and associated themselves with elements of the American Mafia wanting to make an impact in London.[25]

The Krays were not armchair gangsters: in spite of having a good supply of trigger-happy hitmen, the short-tempered, volatile twins sometimes personally dealt with enemies who had annoyed them. In 1965, the Krays wanted to muscle in on the Soho pornography organisation run by the gangster George Cornell. In spite of the twins' fearsome reputation, Cornell snubbed them, and even referred to Ronnie as a 'fat poofter'. This was not a smart move on Cornell's part, nor was it prudent of him, on 9 March 1966, to go drinking at the Blind Beggar public house, situated at No. 337 Whitechapel Road, right in the middle of the Krays' 'manor'. When Ronnie heard of this intrusion, he and a friend rushed down to the Blind Beggar. Cornell only had time to say, 'Well, look who's here!' before he was shot between the eyes. The pub was far from empty at the time, but in some strange manner none of the barmaids or drinkers had seen exactly what had happened, or observed what the gunman looked like. Testifying against the Krays could be a very dangerous thing.

In late 1967, a gangster named Jack 'the Hat' McVitie, a minor member of the Kray 'firm', was given an advance of £1,500 to fulfil a 'contract' put out by the twins to kill one of their enemies. However, Jack failed to carry out the 'job' and the Krays decided that, to maintain the discipline in their gang, he should be taught a hard lesson. They invited Jack to a drinking-party in the basement flat at No. 1 Evering Road, Stoke Newington. Hoping that the Krays had forgiven him for his lapse, Jack eagerly accepted the invitation. As he entered the flat, Reggie pointed a handgun at his head and pulled the trigger twice, but the gun jammed. Ronnie then seized hold of Jack, as Reggie stabbed him repeatedly with a carving knife. The flat was cleaned up, and Jack's body disposed of; it has been speculated that it is likely to help prop up a flyover.

The Krays' wholesale criminal activities meant that a special Scotland Yard task force, led by Leonard 'Nipper' Read, was assigned to bring them down. The twins were arrested in May 1968, along with fifteen members of their 'firm'. Many East Enders were pleased that the Krays' reign of terror was finally over: no longer fearing retribution, they freely gave evidence against the twins. In the end, both Krays were sentenced to life imprisonment in March 1969, with a non-parole period of thirty years, for the murders of George Cornell and Jack McVitie. Ronnie was later certified insane, and he died of a heart attack in Broadmoor in 1995.

Reggie was harshly treated, remaining a Category A prisoner for a long period of time, to make sure he was unable to escape and to prevent him from leading the remainder of his 'firm' from within the prison walls. He was finally released, on compassionate grounds, in August 2000, and died of bladder cancer later the same year.

The Blind Beggar murder pub at No. 337 Whitechapel Road is still open for business, although it today caters to tourists and sightseers rather than to gangsters. The murder house at No. 1 Evering Road has also survived.[26]

Above left: 58. 21 Cadogan Place, where William John Marchant murdered Elizabeth Paynton in 1837.

Above right: 59. 55 Greek Street, where William Crees murdered his wife Eliza in 1883.

Above left: 60. 29 Great Windmill Street, where Amelia Pottle was killed in 1887.

Above right: 61. The ornamented door in Maiden Lane, where Richard Archer Prince murdered William Terriss in 1897.

62. The former club at 24 Frith Street, where Charles Emile Berthier murdered Charles Baladda in 1926.

Above left: 63. 66 Old Compton Street, where Leah Hinds was murdered in 1936.

Above middle: 64. 47 Lexington Street, where Marie Jeanet Cotton was murdered in 1936.

Above right: 65. 58 Denbigh Street, where Count Ludomir Cienski gunned down Jan Buchowski in 1943.

Above left: 66. 45 Chester Square, where Elizabeth MacLindon was murdered by Arthur Robert Boyce in 1945.

Above middle: 67. 17 St George's Drive, where Audrey Irene Stewart was murdered in 1945.

Above right: 68. The former club at 3 Carlisle Street, where Amabile Ricca was murdered by Joseph Farrugia in 1948.

Above left: 69. 61 Cadogan Place, where Derek Roberts murdered Valerie Murray in 1956, and then committed suicide.

Above middle: 70. The former club at 48 Dean Street, where Alfred Melvin murdered Big Tony Mella in 1963, and then committed suicide.

Above right: 71. 7 Moreton Place, where Albert Charles Cox was murdered in 1970.

72. The former amusement arcade at 36 Old Compton Street, where Alfredo Zomparelli was murdered in 1974.

Above left: 73. 9 Pembroke Place, where John James Mooney was killed in 1868.

Above middle: 74. 53 Talbot Road, where Frank Mayston killed his wife Gertrude in 1895.

Above right: 75. 59 Onslow Square, where Violet McGrath was murdered in 1954.

76. 105 Onslow Square, where Günther Podola murdered Detective Sergeant Purdy in 1959.

Above left: 77. 20 Pembridge Square, where Alfred Webb was murdered by the burglar Frederick Stewart in 1928.

Above right: 78. The first-floor flat at 17 Finborough Road, where Cyril Epton murdered Winifred Mulholland in 1948 and dumped her body into the area from the still-existing balcony.

79. 6 Pembridge Villas, where James Achew murdered his wife Sybil in 1929.

Above left: 80. 40 Waterford Street, where Henry Williams murdered his common-law wife Ellen in 1902.

Above middle: 81. 50 Paulton's Square, where John Currie murdered Dorothy Henry in 1915, before committing suicide.

Above right: 82. 15 Perham Road, where John O'Connor murdered Eugenie le Maire in 1951.

Opposite: 83. 19 Glazbury Road, where Roderick McKenzie murdered his daughter Dorothy in 1921, and then committed suicide.

Above left: 84. 51 Hazlebury Road, where Terence Elgar was gunned down in 1968.

Above middle: 85. 50 Petley Road, where Peter Nutkins murdered Florence Lee in 1971.

Above right: 86. 54 Hans Place, where Giuseppe Perusi murdered Peter Arne in 1983.

Above left: 87. 3 Bedford Place, where Jean Stafford was murdered in 1942.

Above middle: 88. 57 Gray's Inn Road, where Socrates Petrides killed Fred Hardisty in 1950.

Above right: 89. 63 Charlotte Street, where James Philip Smartt murdered Nellie McCombs in 1952.

Above left: 90. The basement flat at 139 Gray's Inn Road, where Frank Fyfield killed his wife Ann in 1887.

Above right: 91. 65 Warren Street, where Alexander Anastassiou murdered Evelyn Victoria Holt in 1931.

92. 1 Gloucester Crescent, where Edith Elizabeth Humphries was murdered in 1941.

93. The former stables where the Cato Street Conspiracy was hatched, and where Arthur Thistlewood murdered Runner Richard Smithers in 1820.

Above left: 94. The old shop at 71 Marylebone Lane, where Emma Aitken stabbed her husband, James, to death in 1896.

Above right: 95. The former studio at 76A Westbourne Grove, where the artist Archibald Wakley was found murdered in 1906.

Above left: 96. 99 Star Street, where Mary Jane Day was murdered in 1912.

Above middle: 97. 27 Lanark Villas (today Road), where Dora Alicia Lloyd was murdered in 1932.

Above right: 98. 3 Clanricarde Gardens, where Reginald Holloway murdered his sister-in-law Gladys Bond in the top flat in 1933, and then committed suicide.

Above left: 99. 75 Star Street, where Harry Tuffney murdered Edith Longshaw in a second-floor bedsit in 1934.

Above middle: 100. 33 Castellain Road, where Irene Coffee killed her mother Margarete Brann in 1941.

Above right: 101. The former Laura Hotel at 162 Sussex Gardens, where Agnes Walsh was murdered in 1950.

Above left: 102. 79 Warwick Avenue, where Francis Drake was murdered in 1952.

Above middle: 103. 39 Lisson Grove, where Justine de Almeida murdered Marcus Wehrle and Edward Mansfield in 1954.

Above right: 104. The former lodging house at 21–2 Leinster Square, where Ginter Wiora murdered Shirley Allen in 1957.

Above left: 105. 11 Westbourne Terrace, where Wladyslaw de Sternberg Stojalowski murdered Kazimerz Gielniewski in 1961.

Above middle: 106. 29 St George's Drive, Pimlico, where Alan John Vigar was murdered in 1962, presumably by the same man who had killed Norman Rickard.

Above right: 107. 35 Clanricarde Gardens, where Anthony Milne Creamer murdered Andy Allan in 1966.

108. The lower ground-floor flat at 264A Elgin Avenue, where Norman Rickard was murdered in 1962.

Above left: 109. The former pawnshop at 78 Great Portland Street, where Frank Biering was murdered in 1969.

Above right: 110. 61 Randolph Avenue, where Amala de Vere Whelan was murdered in one of the bedsits in 1972.

Above left: 111. The former post office at 165 Brecknock Road, where John William Bowes was murdered by George Vincent Finch in 1886.

Above middle: 112. 81 Peter (today St Peter) Street, where Thomas Neal murdered his wife Teresa in 1890.

Above right: 113. 40 North (today Northdown) Street, where James and Emma Riley were killed by Elijah Galley in 1896.

Above left: 114. The former Jew's home at 43 St John's Villas, where Noah Woolf murdered Aaron Simon in 1910.

Above middle: 115. 114 Rotherfield Street, where Annie Josephine Wootten was murdered in 1915.

Above right: 116. 13 Prah Road, where Lucy Nightingale was murdered by Frank George Warren in 1919.

Above left: 117. The former furniture warehouse at 22 Islington Green, where Frederick George Murphy murdered Rosina Field in 1937.

Above middle: 118. The former Newlyn House Hotel at 9 Argyle Street, where Herbert Bass-Woodcock murdered his sister-in-law Annie Thorne in 1951.

Above right: 119. The former printing works at 13 Brecknock Road, where the night watchman John Folkard was murdered by Arthur John Bosworth in 1957.

Above left: 120. The upper flat at 304 Holloway Road, where Joe Meek murdered his landlady Violet Shenton in 1967, and then committed suicide.

Above middle: 121. 4 Burgh Street, where John Ernest Bennett murdered James Cameron in 1970.

Above right: 122. The former butcher's shop at 44 Cross Street, where James Hails was murdered by Donald Lewis in 1971.

Above left: 123. The present-day house at 16 Batty Street, where Miriam Angel was murdered by Israel Lipski in 1887.

Above right: 124. The house at 31 Varden Street, at the crossing with Turner Street, where Jonathan Goodman Levy and Annie Gale were murdered by William Seaman in 1896. It has been reconstructed and has had another storey added.

Above left: 125. The former pub at 145 (today 299) Whitechapel Road, where Jerry Slowe murdered Martha Jane Hardwick in 1903.

Above right: 126. 62 Hanbury Street, where the Millsteins were murdered by Myer Abramovitch in 1912.

8

Some Final Words

There are streets and squares and terraces in London which have been renamed in order that they may no longer be associated in the public mind with the dark deeds of which they have been the scene. Sometimes, where the renaming has been a difficult one, the houses have been renumbered. But many remain as they were, and Londoners pass them daily and hourly, little dreaming of the drama that once made them notorious.

George R. Sims, *Mysteries of Modern London*

About seven years ago, when walking to the local hospital from my house in Stow Hill, Newport, I noted a considerable police presence outside one of the Victorian terraced houses nearby. Inquiries revealed that there had been a murder. Three young drug addicts had lived in the ground-floor flat and, for reasons unknown, two of them, a man and a woman, had killed the other male occupant of the flat. They had then dumped the body in forest land between Newport and Cardiff, but the police detectives were not fooled by this simple stratagem: the two miscreants were soon in custody, and their flat carefully searched for forensic evidence.

After news of the murder had spread, all the other tenants swiftly moved out of the murder house, and the landlord later put it up for sale. When I went to see it, even the brash young estate agents seemed a bit embarrassed by the situation: it was clearly not every day that they sold a murder house. An experienced estate agent predicted that the property would sell at auction, to a London investor who did not know its history, and this is exactly what happened. The flats soon had tenants once more, and today the Stow Hill murder house looks just like the other houses in the small terrace: drab and rather neglected. Its sinister history has

Dr Palmer's house in Rugeley, from an old postcard.

already become forgotten, although I have more than once seen signs with 'Ground-floor flat to Let' outside.

In his *An Infamous Address*, Roger Wilkes studied the fates of some notorious British murder houses, one of which has been dealt with in this book, namely Seddon's house in Tollington Park.[1] Madeleine Smith's house at No. 7 Blythswood Square, Glasgow, still stands, as does No. 2 Dalton Square, Lancaster, where Dr Buck Ruxton murdered and dismembered his wife and maid in 1935. Ruxton's house stood empty for decades after these grisly murders, since no person would live there, but in the 1970s it was restored by the town council and made into offices. The Villa Madeira, at No. 5 Manor Road, Bournemouth, where Francis Rattenbury was murdered by his wife Alma and her lover George Stoner, still stands today. Providence House in the Suffolk village of Peasenhall, site of the unsolved murder of Rose Harsent in 1901, still frowns upon the passer-by. The elegant villa 'Mayfield', in Cusop just outside Hay-on-Wye, was once home to the local solicitor Major Herbert Rowse Armstrong, hanged for poisoning his wife in 1922. There has been some doubt concerning his guilt, some claiming that Mrs Armstrong succumbed to food poisoning, and others pointing the finger at the rival solicitor Oswald Martin. Mayfield was for many years owned by the solicitor Martin Beales, who restored the old house to its former glory. Mr Beales also occupied Armstrong's office in Hay-on-Wye, and wrote a book on the case.[2] Blackpool's notorious 'murder bungalow' at No. 339 Devonshire Road, where Louisa Merrifield murdered old Mrs Ricketts in 1953, also still stands, conspicuous among the taller houses in this street. Cornwall's two famous murder houses, Trenhorne House near Lewannick, site of the unsolved murder of Alice Thomas in 1931, and 'Blue Waters' in Carrickowl near Porthpean, where Miles Giffard murdered his parents in 1953, also still exist.[3] In 1956, the next owner of 'Blue Waters' successfully applied for a reduction in the ratable assessment of his house, since it was 'plagued by people who come to see where the murders were committed'.[4]

Dr William Palmer's house in Market Street, Rugeley, still stands. This notorious house, from which the mass poisoner set out on his murderous campaign, stood empty for many years, visited only by souvenir hunters. The Talbot Arms, where Palmer murdered the gambler Mr Cook, changed its name to the Shrewsbury Arms, and the Rugeley town council petitioned the Prime Minister to be allowed to change the town's name, since they felt that its reputation would suffer from being too closely associated with Palmer and his crimes. The Prime Minister mischievously replied that they could only change it if they named it after himself – and he was Lord Palmerston! After being shunned for decades, Palmer's house was successively rehabilitated; by the turn of the century, it was the local post office, then an ironmonger's shop, and today it houses two small shops. It is situated directly opposite the old murder pub, now renamed The Shrew, at No. 2 Market Street.[5] The notorious Liverpool murder house at No. 29 Wolverton Street in Anfield, home to the unsolved murder of Julia Wallace in 1931, remains virtually unchanged.[6] Battlecrease House, the Liverpool home of Florence Maybrick, still frowns upon the passer-by.[7] Thus there is evidence that, just like their metropolitan counterparts, many of the historic murder houses of the rest of Great Britain are thriving.

***

As we have seen, the Victorians sometimes changed street names to disguise the identity of a street where a famous murder had been committed. We know how Leveson Street in Liverpool became Upper Grenville Street after the Henrichson bloodbath in 1849. In the metropolis, there are six verified instances of murders changing a street's name. Miniver Place, Bermondsey, became part of Weston Street soon after the Mannings murdered Mr O'Connor at No. 3 in 1849, since the houses would not let.[8] Stanley Street, Pimlico, had its name changed to Alderney Street a year or two after Frederick Treadaway had murdered Mr Collins at No. 99. Then, as we know, the southern part of Euston Square became Endsleigh Gardens in 1880; Ladysmith Road, Kensal Rise, became Wrentham Avenue in 1905; Burton Crescent became Cartwright Gardens in 1908; and finally Rillington Place had its name changed to Ruston Close in 1954.[9] The strategy of renumbering the houses to disguise the identity of a murder house was very infrequently resorted to.[10] Firstly, the murder house would be known by the locals anyway;

The Mannings' murder house at No. 3 Miniver Place, Bermondsey, from the *Illustrated London News*.

The Red Barn and Maria Marten's cottage, from a postcard stamped and posted in 1915.

The Watkins murder house in Llangibby, and other images from this gruesome mass murder, from the *Illustrated Police News*, 3 August 1878.

An old postcard showing the murder house at Denham, where the tramp John Owen murdered the entire Marshall family in a bloodbath. The cottage is said to have stood until the 1950s.

An old postcard showing John Lee's Cellar; all that remained of the famous murder house in Babbacombe, where the servant John Lee murdered his mistress Miss Keyse. When he was to be hanged, the scaffold twice failed to operate, and 'The Man they could not Hang' was reprieved.

Above: The elegant murder house at Muswell Hill, where old Mr Henry Smith was brutally slain by the burglars Milson and Fowler in 1896. The house no longer stands.

Below: The Crumbles murder bungalow, from an old postcard.

secondly, such a renumbering would cost money, and confound the postman; thirdly, nobody wanted the infamous number to be applied to his own house.

How often does it happen that notorious murder houses are demolished? The Red Barn at Polstead, where William Corder murdered Maria Marten in 1828, achieved considerable notoriety, since this was one of the first 'media murders'.[11] Many people who had read about the romantic story of the pretty mole catcher's daughter and her dalliance with the scoundrel Corder came to see Polstead, and the obscure Suffolk village became a tourist venue of some repute. The Red Barn and the Martens' cottage (it still stands today) excited particular interest. The barn was stripped for souvenirs, and even the planks removed from the walls, broken up and sold as toothpicks. The Red Barn was planned to be demolished after the trial, but it was left standing and eventually burnt down in 1842. Even Maria Marten's gravestone, in St Mary's churchyard, Polstead, was eventually chipped away to nothing by souvenir hunters. The same fate befell the murder house in Gill's Hill Lane, where the gambler John Thurtell and his two cronies murdered William Weare in 1824. When Sir Walter Scott visited it a few years after the murder, the principal part of the house was destroyed, and only the kitchen remained standing. George R. Sims later boasted that he had the door knocker from Thurtell's house in his collection of criminal memorabilia. One of the most notorious murder houses of South Wales, the Watkins' cottage in Llangibby near Usk, met with a similar fate. In this humble cottage, the Spanish burglar Joseph Garcia murdered the farm worker William Watkins and his wife and three children, in 1878. The cottage was severely damaged by the souvenir hunters, and later destroyed because nobody would live there. Another well-known murder house in those parts, Tank Cottage in Bassaleg, the scene of the double murder of Charles and Mary Thomas in 1909, was demolished by orders of Lord Tredegar the year after.

In 1924, the career criminal Patrick Mahon murdered and dismembered his mistress Emily Kaye, in a Crumbles bungalow. He was duly hanged for this crime, and the murder bungalow was bought by a showman and exhibited for a one shilling charge. The house was thronged with curious visitors, some of whom took bricks or other objects with them as souvenirs. Since no person would live in this ramshackle bungalow, it was razed to the ground after a few years. The little terraced house at No. 16 Wardle Brook Avenue, where Ian Brady and Myra Hindley murdered Lesley Anne Downey and Edward Evans in 1965 and 1966, stood for more than a decade after the crimes. It was a damp, insalubrious property, however, and people living there had terrible nightmares about murder and mayhem. The haunted house at No. 16 was demolished by Manchester City Council sometime in the 1980s, since it was becoming a target for vandals, and nobody would live there. Today there is just an empty plot between the adjoining houses in the terrace. In 1986, there was mass carnage at Burgate House, Fordingbridge, in the New Forest. Three thieves entered the house and murdered its five occupants, dousing them with petrol and setting the house on fire. This was one of Britain's most horrific mass murders ever. Burgate House, which had been converted from an old barn and was valued at £150,000 prior to the massacre, was put on the market a few years later but, since nobody would buy it, it was ultimately demolished.[12]

The house of horrors at No. 25 Cromwell Street, Gloucester, where Fred and Rosemary West tortured, raped and murdered a number of women in the 1970s, and buried them in the garden, was demolished in 1996, just two years after the Wests had been apprehended. Care was taken to crush all the bricks and destroy all timbers, to deter morbid souvenir hunters. The place where this once notorious murder house once stood is today a small garden. In contrast, the house at No. 25 Midland Road, Gloucester, where the horrible Wests lived for a while in 1973, and where they murdered Fred's daughter by his first marriage and buried her underneath the floorboards in the kitchen, has been allowed to stand. When it came on the market in 2000, there was speculation that it would be bought by the council and destroyed, but it was purchased by a property investor for £57,750, well ahead of its estimate.[13] Its evil reputation has continued, however: in 2011, there were newspaper stories that this shabby-looking little house of horrors was being used as a brothel.[14]

The school gym at Dunblane, where the demented Thomas Hamilton had opened fire on the children, was demolished after the massacre in 1996. The school caretaker's cottage at No. 5 College Close in Soham, once home to the bestial child murderer Ian Huntley and his much-reviled girlfriend Maxine Carr, was quietly pulled down in 2004.[15] In 2006, Fife Council gave orders to demolish the murder house at No. 47 Tay Street, Tayport, where the sex offender Colyn Evans had strangled

Some curious images of Dr Crippen's house.

The postcard showing Sandy McNab standing in front of Dr Crippen's house, which this Caledonian joker has renamed 'McNab House'.

No. 10 Rillington Place at the end of the terrace, with a policeman standing outside. The tall chimney in the background stood for several years after Rillington Place was pulled down.

young Karen Devar, before dumping her body in a rubbish bin and setting it on fire.[16] In 2008, a fire-damaged house in King Street, Higher Broughton, where two young women had been murdered in 2005, was demolished with the case still unsolved.[17] The house in Lammy Crescent, Omagh, Co. Tyrone, where Arthur McElhill murdered his family in 2007, was demolished in 2011.[18] There are also a number of depressingly similar-sounding news stories of notorious American and Australian murder houses being demolished after attracting curiosity seekers, and becoming impossible to sell or let.

These demolished murder houses have several things in common. Murders of extraordinary brutality and savagery have been performed within their walls, and the houses have become closely associated with the crimes in local folklore. Moreover, with the obvious exception of Burgate House, the houses have been nondescript, ramshackle dwellings, and not particularly valuable.[19] In contrast, there is nothing to suggest that any of London's murder houses has been deliberately demolished as a result of its bad reputation. The house at what is today No. 9 Park Road, Richmond, where the servant Kate Webster murdered and dismembered her mistress Mrs Julia Thomas in 1879, before boiling the body parts in the kitchen copper, is recorded to have stood empty for many years, since nobody would live in such a house of horrors. However, in 1897, a lady and her servant moved in, without being disturbed by the ghosts of the brutal Kate pursuing her timid old mistress, brandishing a chopper. When Elliott O'Donnell, the great ghost-hunter, made a polite inquiry about the spectral inhabitants of No. 9, he was surprised and dismayed to find that the place was not haunted.[20] Guy Logan, who took a particular interest in this murder house, even wrote,

> The majority of houses which have been the scenes of murder seem ever after to be under a cloud, and to shudder, as it were, from the public gaze, but this cannot be said of the neat and pretty little villa at Richmond, which was the locale of Kate Webster's horrid crime. I have passed it many times in the course of years, and anything less like the popular conception of a 'murder house' it would be hard to imagine.[21]

The house still stands today, a valuable and well-looked-after semi-detached house in a peaceful Richmond street. Not many people know its horrible secret.

It has wrongly been claimed that Dr Crippen's house at No. 39 Hilldrop Crescent was demolished as a result of its bad reputation. Once the police were done with the house after Crippen had been hanged, it was in fact bought by the Scottish comedian Sandy McNab, who secured it for a very good price. In a newspaper interview, the canny Scot crowed over his good fortune in securing a £1,000 house for just £500. He himself was frightened of nothing that was dead, as he expressed it, but it had proved difficult for him to procure a domestic.[22] McNab issued a picture postcard of himself standing in front of the murder house, and later tried to open it as a museum with Crippen memorabilia, but since this was considered in very bad taste he instead made it a lodging house for music hall performers. The gloomy murder house at No. 39 Hilldrop Crescent stood for thirty years after Crippen had ended his days; it eventually perished from structural damage resulting from bombing during the Second World War. Nor was John Christie's house at No. 10 Rillington Place (soon to become Ruston Close) destroyed as a direct result of the horrors enacted within its walls. In fact, it stood for more than seventeen years after Christie had been executed, before being demolished, along with the rest of the street, as a result of slum clearance in December 1970. Modern houses were built on the cleared site, and not a single brick remains of Christie's murder house today.[23]

In 'God's Own Country' they do nothing by halves, and that also goes for some of the transatlantic murder houses. Top of the list is probably the former Moore residence in Villisca, Iowa, where the entire household, eight people strong, was wiped out by a brutal axe murderer in 1912. The Villisca mass murder remains unsolved to this day, and the house of course retained a very sinister reputation. In 1994, a private investor purchased the dilapidated murder house and restored it to its former glory; it has been featured on several 'spooky' TV shows, and is open for tours and sleepovers for a fee.[24] The celebrated murder house at No. 9337 Columbia Boulevard, Silver Spring, Maryland, also has an adventurous history. In 2002, a little girl and her father were gunned down in this house by a thief who stole $3. When the middle school principal Brian Betts bought No. 9337 the year after, he knew nothing of its sinister history. Once he found out that a double murder had been committed on the premises, the superstitious American did all he could to get out of the deal, but without success. He asked two ministers to bless the house to get rid of any remaining evil spirits, but this strategy clearly did not have the desired effect. In April 2010, Betts was himself murdered inside the murder house by a gang of teenage robbers, one of whom he had befriended on a gay sex chatline. His distraught relatives asked that the house of horrors at No. 9337 be bulldozed, but the bank put it up for sale for $535,000. When its grisly history hit the news, the price was reduced to $515,000.[25]

As the sad tale of Brian Betts indicates, Maryland law contains nothing to force estate agents to disclose various skeletons in the cupboard about a house's murderous past. A recent court case would indicate that the situation is not dissimilar in the UK. A couple who had purchased a house in Stillwell Drive, Wakefield, in 2000, were horrified to find out, through a TV documentary, that a grisly murder had been committed on the premises back in 1985. The dental biologist Dr Samson Perera had murdered his thirteen-year-old adopted daughter, and dismembered her remains into more than 1,000 pieces, which he had hidden in the house. The couple sold the house, at a loss of £8,000, and then proceeded to sue the vendors for failing to adequately inform them about the property's gruesome history. Although the case was taken to the Court of Appeal, the rule of *caveat emptor* was upheld.[26]

***

A murder house goes through three phases: notoriety, rehabilitation and oblivion. A minority of murder houses, mainly cheap and unattractive buildings that had witnessed the grossest and most horrible murders and achieved considerable media publicity, never emerge from the notoriety phase, and as a consequence they are demolished. All the valuable London murder houses have entered the rehabilitation phase, however. Nevertheless, for some notorious Victorian murder houses, it would take a long time for them to become reintegrated into the neighbourhood. As we have seen, the house where Kate Webster murdered Mrs Thomas was shunned for eighteen years, and the two Huelin murder houses became equally notorious. When George R. Sims visited them more than three decades later, he was surprised to find that their sinister past had finally been forgotten.[27]

In contrast, the rehabilitation of most modern murder houses is a comparably swift affair. There are several examples of London and provincial murder houses fetching very good prices and even being quite sought after.[28] One of the most striking examples is the house at No. 20 Dewhurst Road, Brook Green, where the West London mystery man William John Saunderson-Smith was murdered in October 2011. An attractive house in a sought-after part of London, it would normally have been snapped up very rapidly, but would the fact that the former owner had been tortured and brutally murdered on the premises impede the sale? When Tates Estate Agents put the murder house on the market, the *West London Today* had the headline '"Fantastic" Brook Green murder home for sale at £1.8M!' This newspaper did not think that even a grisly murder would put off potential buyers in this very convenient part of London, however, and they were proved right: the murder house was swiftly under offer.[29]

There appear to be several reasons for this change in attitude.[30] Firstly, the increased mobility in modern society has resulted in a decrease in local knowledge and sense of belonging: few modern people, apart from determined amateur historians with a taste for the macabre, bother to record the local murder houses. The gradual decline of the Christian religion, and even stronger decline in various superstitious beliefs, like hauntings and curses, has also played an important part: to a financially astute modern atheist, a murder house is just another house. Unlike the situation in Victorian times, when the *Illustrated Police News* and other newspapers freely published the full address of the most recent murder house and sometimes a drawing of it as well, the numbers of murder houses are rarely divulged in the newspapers today. This means that the identity of a present-day murder house is known to a very limited number of people, and definitely not to out-of-town buyers or London property investors looking to expand their portfolios. Still, this book shows that when you walk the streets of the great metropolis, evidence of its criminal past is everywhere to be seen: part of London's forgotten history is that of its murder houses.

Bibliography of Some Key Works

Aston, M., *Foul Deeds and Suspicious Deaths in Hampstead, Holborn and St Pancras* (Barnsley 2005).

Barker, F. & D. Silvester-Carr, *Crime & Scandal: The Black Plaque Guide to London* (London 1991).

Butler, I., *Murderers' London* (London 1973).

Cargill, D. & J. Holland, *Scenes of Murder* (London 1964).

Downie, R. A., *Murder in London* (London 1973).

Eddleston, J. J., *Foul Deeds in Kensington and Chelsea* (Barnsley 2010).

Eddleston, J. J., *Foul Deeds in Islington* (Barnsley 2010).

Fido, M., *Murder Guide to London* (London 1986).

Howse, G., *North London Murders* (Stroud 2005).

Howse, G., *Foul Deeds and Suspicious Deaths in London's East End* (Barnsley 2005).

Howse, G., *Foul Deeds and Suspicious Deaths in London's West End* (Barnsley 2006).

Howse, G., *A–Z of London Murders* (Barnsley 2007).

Howse, G., *Murder and Mayhem in North London* (Barnsley 2010).

Lane, B., *The Murder Club Guide to London* (London 1988).

Oates, J., *Unsolved Murders in Victorian and Edwardian London* (Barnsley 2007).

Oates, J., *Unsolved London Murders of the 1920s and 1930s* (Barnsley 2009).

Oates, J., *Unsolved London Murders of the 1940s and 1950s* (Barnsley 2009).

Oldridge, M. W., *Murder and Crime: Whitechapel and District* (Stroud 2011).

Shaw, E. S., *A Companion to Murder* (London 1960).

Shaw, E. S., *A Second Companion to Murder* (London 1961).

Storey, N. R., East End Murders (Stroud 2005).

Notes

Major Newspapers Consulted

Introduction

1. On Guy Logan, see J. Bondeson, Introduction to G. Logan, *The True History of Jack the Ripper* (Stroud 2013).

2. There are five worthwhile books on London's criminal topography: Cargill & Holland, *Scenes of Murder*, is a scarce and controversial book which was withdrawn by the publishers due to alleged inaccuracies, but it contains valuable material not available elsewhere. Downie, *Murder in London*, and Butler, *Murderers' London*, are both highly recommended. Fido, *Murder*

Guide to London, is probably the most thorough and systematic early book on London murder houses. Barker & Silvester-Carr, *Crime & Scandal*, deals with all kinds of infamous London addresses, and is a very amusing read. In addition, D. Long, *Murders of London* (London 2012), is a sketchy account sprinkled with errors, but the illustrations are nice.

3. *Famous Crimes Past & Present* 7(82) [1904], p. 56 and G. Logan, *Masters of Crime* (London 1928), pp. 110–26. The murder house no longer stands.
4. The Blandy House dental practice at what is today No. 29 Hart Street, Henley-on-Thames, has an interesting history, since it is situated in the very house where Mary Blandy murdered her father in 1751. See W. Roughead (Ed.), *Trial of Mary Blandy* (Notable British Trials, London 1914), and I. Butler, *Murderers' England* (London 1973), pp. 124–6.
5. Butler, *Murderers' London*, pp. 47–9, Barker & Silvester-Carr, *Crime & Scandal*, pp. 219–20.
6. T. Burke (Ed.), *The Ecstasies of Thomas de Quincey* (London 1928), p. 309.

1 Westminster

1. J. C. Ellis, *Blackmailers & Co.* (London 1928), pp. 236–43, G. Logan, *Guilty or Not Guilty* (London 1931), pp. 249–57.
2. Oates, *Unsolved London Murders of the 1920s and 1930s*, pp. 161–83.
3. G. R. Sims, *Mysteries of Modern London* (London 1906), p. 66. On the Dixblanc case, see J. Smith-Hughes, *Unfair Comment* (London 1951), pp. 248–86.
4. On Marchant, see C. Pelham, *Chronicles of Crime* (London 1887), Vol. 2, pp. 478–9, *Complete Newgate Calendar* (London 1926), Vol. 5, pp. 295–6, and Eddleston, *Foul Deeds in Kensington and Chelsea*, pp. 17–19. Contemporary newspaper coverage included *The Times* 21 May 6c, 22 June 6f and 9 July 7a, 1839; *MP* 21 May 1839, *Era* 26 May 1839, and *MC* 20 and 21 May, and 2 and 8 July 1839.
5. C. Hindley, *The Life and Times of James Catnach* (London 1878), pp. xi–xvi.
6. *The Times* 18 Dec 1876 10f, 20 Dec 1876 10a, 9 Feb 1877 5e; *LWN* 17 and 24 Dec 1876; *MP* 30 Dec 1876 and 26 Feb 1877; *PIP* 30 Dec 1876; *IPN* 30 Dec 1876; *DN* 16, 18 and 19 Dec 1876, 16 Jan and 8 and 9 Feb 1877.
7. *British Medical Journal* i [1877], pp. 215, 226–8, 243–4, *Lancet* i [1877], pp. 293–5.
8. J. P. Eigen, *Unconscious Crime* (Baltimore 2003), pp. 146–50.
9. On the Crees case, see NA CRIM 1/19/9; *The Times* 3 Dec 1883 4a and 5 Dec 1883 10g; *MP* 3, 5, 11 and 13 Dec 1883; *Sta* 3 Dec 1883; *LWN* 9 Dec 1883.

10. *RN* 2 Dec 1883.

11. The trial of Franz Schultz is on the OldBaileyOnline website; see also *The Times* 4 June 12b; *PMG* 3 June 1887 and *LWN* 12 June 1887.

12. See J. Goodman, *Acts of Murder* (London 1986), pp. 1–69 and G. Rowell, *William Terriss and Richard Prince* (The Society for Theatre Research, London 1987); Howse, *Foul Deeds and Suspicious Deaths in London's West End*, pp. 120–47 and *A–Z of London Murders*, pp. 126–9; *IPN* 25 Dec 1897 and 22 Jan 1898.

13. *Timeout London* 25 Oct 2005.

14. On the Bridgewater House murder, see *IPN* 30 March 1901; *Star* 11 May 1901 and *Gippsland Gazette* 4 June 1901.

15. On the Maddox Street murder, see *The Times* 23 Dec 8d, 24 Dec 7b, 28 Dec 3f, 1921; *IPN* 29 Dec 1921, *DE* 23 Dec 1921.

16. On the Walker case, see NA MEPO 3/1574; Shaw, *A Second Companion to Murder*, pp. 246–7; Downie, *Murder in London*, pp. 75–6; *The Times* 24 April 1922 12f, 27 April 1922 11a and 3 May 1922 7e; *DM* 27 April and 3 May 1922.

17. According to the 'British Murders' website.

18. On the life and career of Sir Henry Wilson, see K. Jeffery, *Field Marshal Sir Henry Wilson, a Political Soldier* (Oxford 2006).

19. On his murder, see I. Oddie, *Inquest* (London 1941), pp. 151–3 and Howse, *A–Z of London Murders*, pp. 42–3; *The Times* 23 June 1922 6a, 10a and 14a, 24 June 1922 10a; *IPN* 29 June 1922.

20. On the Madame Fahmy case, the main source is A. Rose, *Scandal at the Savoy* (London 1991). See also E. Marjoribanks, *The Life of Sir Edward Marshall Hall* (London 1930), pp. 434–50; E. Grice, *Great Cases of Sir Henry Curtis Bennett* (London 1937), pp. 55–64; A. E. Bowker, *Behind the Bar* (London 1948), pp. 111–8; M. Hastings, *The Other Mr Churchill* (London 1963), pp. 85–8; N. Warner-Hooke & G. Thomas, *Marshall Hall* (London 1966), pp. 224–30; Barker & Silvester-Carr, *Crime & Scandal*, pp. 16–18; Howse, *Foul Deeds and Suspicious Deaths in London's West End*, pp. 168–75; and *A–Z of London Murders*, pp. 49–53

21. *The Times* 3 Oct 1980 3a, 9 April 1981 4d.

22. On Lord Lloyd, see J. Charmley, *Lord Lloyd* (London 1987) and M. Bloch, *James Lees-Milne* (London 2009), pp. 56–77.

23. On the Rix/Bishop case, see NA MEPO 3/1615; *The Times* 8 June 1925 16c; *DM* 8, 9, 11 and 18 June 1925; *IPN* 11 and 18 June 1925.

24. On the Baladda/Berthier case, see NA MEPO 3/1622 and CRIM 1/357; *The Times* 8 April 9a, 9 April 9d, 15 April 6c, 29 April 22c, 6 July 13c, 7 July 13d, 1926; *DM* 7 and 9 April, and 6 July 1926.

25. *The Times* 29 June 1932 9f.

26. NA MEPO 3/1676; *The Times* 1 Nov 16b, 3 Nov 4g, 5 Nov 7c, 11 Nov 9c, 14 Dec 14b and 22 Dec 9g, 1932; *DM* 1 and 3 Nov 1932; *DE* 1, 3 and 5 Nov 1932.

27. *DE* 5 Dec 1934.

28. The police files on 'French Fifi' and Jeanette Cotton are in NA MEPO 3/1702 and 3/1706. On the 'Soho Stranglings', see Oates, *Unsolved London Murders of the 1920s and 1930s*, pp. 161–83; also *The Times* 27 Nov 1935 8d and 20 April 1936 11f; *DE* 6 Nov 1935; *DM* 6 Nov and 4 Dec 1935, 17 and 18 April 1936.

29. On the case of Leah Hinds, see NA MEPO 3/1707; *DM* 11 May and 16 July 1936.

30. *DM* 23 Aug 1937; *Chicago Tribune* 1 May 1938.

31. On the life and death of Red Max, see A. Tietjen, *Soho* (London 1956), pp. 93–104; *The Times* 27 Jan 7a, 28 Jan 7c, 31 Jan 11e, 4 Feb 12c, 15 Feb 12e, 8 June 11f and 8 Aug 7e, 1936, 29 April 15b and 30 April 15b, 1937.

32. *The Times* 9 June 1937 15f.

33. On McCallum, see NA MEPO 3/2174; *The Times* 1 March 1941 2d; *DM* 21 Dec 1940; *DE* 3 Jan 1941.

34. On the Mancini case, see Shaw, *Second Companion to Murder*, pp. 137–8, E. Glinert, *The West End Chronicles* (London 2007), pp. 195–6; *The Times* 7 May 2a, 6 Sept 9b, 4 Oct 7g, 1941; *DM* 2 May 1941; *DE* 2 May 1941.

35. On the case of Count Cienski, see NA MEPO 3/2253; Sir P. Hastings, *Autobiography* (London 1948), pp. 175–84; W. Bixley, *The Guilty and the Innocent* (London 1957), pp. 40–4; Shaw, *Companion to Murder*, pp. 45–6; M. Hastings, *The Other Mr Churchill* (London 1963), pp. 270–3; *The Times* 25 May 1943 2d and 2 June 1943 2g; *DM* 1 June 1943.

36. *DE* 2 June 1943.

37. The police files on the Evelyn Hatton case are still closed; see the TrueCrimeLibrary database; *DE* 19 and 20 Dec 1944; *DM* 18 and 19 Dec 1944, 7 Feb and 2 March 1945.

38. On the little-known case of Audrey Irene Stewart, see *The Times* 26 Feb 1945 2c; *DM* 6 Jan, 25 Jan and 2 March 1945; *Westminster and Pimlico News* 12 Jan, 9 Feb and 13 April 1945.

39. *DE* 15 Oct 1946.

40. On the McLindon case, see Shaw, *A Companion to Murder*, pp. 175–6; P. Hoskins, *The Sound of Murder* (London 1973), pp. 139–44; Downie, *Murder in London*, pp. 72–4; *Journal of Criminal Law* 11 [1947], pp. 152–6; *The Times* 17 Sept 1946 2d, 18 Sept 1946 2d and 19 Sept 1946 2b; *DM* 19 and 20 Sept 1946.

41. On the Rita Green, Dora Freedman and Rachel Fennick cases, see NA MEPO 3/3027; Shaw, *Second Companion to Murder*, pp. 61–2, Oates, *Unsolved London Murders of the 1940s & 1950s*, pp. 63–72; *The Times* 27 Sept 1947 3b; *DM* 8 Sept 1947, and the TrueCrimeLibrary and JTRForums websites.

42. NA MEPO 3/3014; *DM* 27 March 1947 and 18 June 1948.

43. On the Murray case, see *The Times* 3 March 1956 10g and 24 March 1956 4g; *DE* 26 March; *DM* 16, 17 and 24 March 1956.

44. On the Cecil Court case, see Downie, *Murder in London*, pp. 15–6; Fido, *Murder Guide to London*, p. 47; Lane, *Murder Club Guide to London*, pp. 198–9; A. Moss & K. Skinner, *The Scotland Yard Files* (London 2006), pp. 163–70; Howse, *A–Z of London Murders*, pp. 18–19; *The Times* 4 March 6f, 10 March 8f, 11 May 9d, 12 May 7c, 13 May 6d, 15 June 7f, 1961; *DM* 4 March and 6 April 1961

45. On the Melvin/Mella case, see *The Times* 29 Jan 1963 8c and 15 Feb 1963 4c; *DE* 30 Jan 1963; *DM* 30 Jan and 19 Feb 1963.

46. *DM* 1 Aug 1964; *DMa* 15 June, 16 June, 1 Aug 1964.

47. *DMa* 24 May 1973.

48. On Lord Bernstein, see his obituary in *Ind* 6 Feb 1993.

49. On the Sesee case, see NA MEPO 26/68; *The Times* 2 Oct 1971 2a, 9 Feb 1973 5a and 10 Feb 1973 26d; *DM* 22 and 23 Dec 1970, 10 Oct 1971, 9 Feb 1972 and 13 Feb 1973; *DE* 2 Oct 1971.

50. On the obscure Cox case, see *The Times* 2 July 1970 4c and *Westminster & Pimlico News* 6 and 12 March and 24 April 1972.

51. On the RAC case, see Downie, *Murder in London*, p. 12; *The Times* 19 Dec 1972 2c and 20 Dec 1972 4f; *DM* 3, 4, 6, and 7 July, 19, 20 and 21 Dec 1972.

52. NA MEPO 20/9; *The Times* 6 Sept 1974 3b, 11 Nov 1980 3a, 20 Nov 1980 3a and 28 April 1983 3g, C. Summers in *BBC News* 11 Dec 1999, and N. P. Welsh in *The Guardian* 19 March 2000.

53. Much has been written about the Lucan case: see N. Lucas, *The Lucan Mystery* (London 1975); P. Marnham, *Trail of Havoc* (London 1987); S. Moore, *Lucan Not Guilty* (London 1988); J. Ruddick, *Lord Lucan* (London 1994); D. Gerring, *Lucan Lives* (London 1995); R. Ransom, *Looking for Lucan* (London 1995) and J. Pearson, *The Gamblers* (London 2007). See also C. Smith (*Criminologist* 15 [1991], pp. 156–67), *DM* 26 June, 8 Sept and 6 Nov 1975, 27 April 1976, 22 and 23 Oct 1979, 6 Nov 1999, 14 Feb 2000, *DT* 11 June 2000.

54. D. Maclaughlin, *Dead Lucky* (London 2003). On the real story of Jungle Barry, see *DM* 8, 9 and 13 Sept 2003.

55. *The Times* 3 March 2012, pp. 6–7; *DM* 25 Feb, 8 March, 21 May and 11 Dec 2012, *DMa* 6 March and 3 June 2012.

56. *DM* 4 Feb 2013.

2 Kensington

1. There is an account of the Hartley trial on the OldBaileyOnline website. For newspaper coverage, see *London Chronicle* 30 Jan 1800; *True Briton* 22 Feb 1800 and *Lloyd's Evening Post* 21–24 Feb 1800.

2. The trial of James Mooney is on OldBaileyOnline; Eddleston, *Foul Deeds in Kensington and Chelsea*, pp. 26–8; *The Times* 28 May 1867 13e and 13 June 1867 11c; *Sta* 28 May and 6 June 1867.

3. On the O'Donnell case, see Eddleston, *Foul Deeds in Kensington and Chelsea*, pp. 39–41; *PMG* 20 Oct 1876; *MP* 10 Nov 1876; *DN* 24 Nov 1876; *LWN* 3 Dec 1876.

4. The trial of Frank Mayston is on OldBaileyOnline; see also NA CRIM 1/43/2; *The Times* 27 Aug 1895 8c and 10 Sept 1895 10c; *MP* 23 Oct, 6 Nov and 22 Nov 1895; *RN* 29 Oct 1895; *LWN* 25 Aug, 1 and 15 Sept 1895; *North-Eastern Gazette* 27 Aug 1895.

5. *British Medical Journal* ii [1911], p. 1064 and ii [1917], p. 398; *South African Medical Record* i [1919], p. 30; private information.

6. On the Rutherford trial, see NA MEPO 3/259 and CRIM 1/177/5; P. Savage, *Savage of the Yard* (London 1934), pp. 134–44; D. G. Browne & E. V. Tullett, *Bernard Spilsbury* (London 1951), pp. 109–12; R. Jackson, *The Chief* (London 1959), pp. 88–94; Shaw, *Companion to Murder*, pp. 231–2; Butler, *Murderers' London*, pp. 87–8; *DM* 15, 16, 18, 23, 25 and 30 Jan, 13, 20 and 27 Feb 1919; *IPN* 23 Jan 1919.

7. NA J 77/1692/2649.

8. NA HO 144/22266. See also *DM* 22 July 1922 and 1 and 2 Feb 1929; *NYT* 4 Nov 1922; *SMH* 23 Aug 1929.

9. On the Mackenzie case, see *The Times* 22 Aug 1921 5e, 23 Aug 1921 5b and 24 Aug 1921 8f; *DM* 24 Aug 1921; *IPN* 25 Aug 1921.

10. *NYT* 18 Feb 1905.

11. *NYT* 30 Sept, 19 Oct and 23 Dec 1913; *DM* 29 Sept and 1 Oct 1913; *Adelaide Advertiser* 11 Nov 1913 and *Otautau Standard* 25 Nov 1913.

12. D. Carswell (Ed.), *Trial of Ronald True* (Notable British Trials, London 1925); E. Grice, *Great Cases of Sir Henry Curtis Bennett* (London 1937), pp. 78–88; J. P. Eddy, *Scarlet and Ermine* (London 1960), pp. 113–7; J. Rowland, *Unfit*

to Plead (London 1965), pp. 21–80; Eddleston, *Foul Deeds in Kensington and Chelsea*, pp. 97–102; M. Hamblin Smith (*British Journal of Psychiatry* 68 [1922], pp. 271–8); *DM* 3 and 16 March, 3 May and 12 June 1922; *IPN* 16 March 1922; *NYT* 10 and 11 June 1922; *NZ Truth* 22 Dec 1922.

13. On the batman, see *DM* 11 Sept 1934.

14. *DM* 11 Jan 1951, see also *The Times* 9 Jan 1951 2b and *DE* 9 Jan 1951.

15. J. E. Horwell, *Horwell of the Yard* (London 1947), pp. 29–36; M. Hastings, *The Other Mr Churchill* (London 1963), pp. 149–51; P. Hoskins, *The Sound of Murder* (London 1973), pp. 114–8; Shaw, *Companion to Murder*, pp. 261–2; *The Times* 24 Feb 1928 16e; *DM* 10, 24 and 25 Feb, 30 March, 19 and 22 April 1928; *IPN* 16 Feb and 14 June 1928.

16. On the Achew case, see NA MEPO 3/1652, CRIM 1/486 and PCOM 9/281; *British Journal of Psychiatry* 76 [1930], pp. 322–3; *The Times* 13 Jan 9f, 4 Feb 5d and 11 Feb 11g 1930; *DM* 25 and 27 Nov 1929, 11 Feb 1930; *DE* 18 Jan 1930.

17. K. M. Salfen, *Myth in the Early Collaborations of Benjamin Britten and William Plomer* (Thesis, Univ. of North Texas, Aug 2005), p. 16.

18. *DM* 28 July 1925; *DE* 28 April 1936; *Singapore Free Press* 5 May 1936.

19. On the Trevor case, see NA MEPO 3/2194; Shaw, *Second Companion to Murder*, pp. 234–5; Fido, *Murder Guide to London*, p. 114; Eddleston, *Foul Deeds in Kensington and Chelsea*, pp. 115–8; *The Times* 21 Oct 1941 2d and 24 Feb 1942 6a.

20. Lord Dunboyne (Ed.), *The Trial of John George Haigh* (Notable British Trials, London 1953); A. La Bern, *Haigh, the Acid Bath Murderer* (London 1974); N. Morland, *Hangman's Clutch* (London 1954), pp. 180–207; M. Lefebure, *Murder with a Difference* (London 1958), pp. 3–163; D. G. Browne, *Sir Travers Humphreys* (London 1960), pp. 351–70; Shaw, *Companion to Murder*, pp. 104–8, E. Lustgarten, *The Business of Murder* (London 1968), pp. 13–41; Fido, *Murder Guide to London*, pp. 78–80; Barker & Silvester-Carr, *Crime & Scandal*, pp. 205–6; Howse, *A–Z of London Murders*, pp. 64–6; Eddleston, *Foul Deeds in Kensington and Chelsea*, pp. 131–46.

21. M. Critchley (Ed.), *Trial of Neville Heath* (Notable British Trials, London 1955); F. Selwyn, *Rotten to the Core* (London 1988); S. O'Connor, *Handsome Brute* (London 2013); N. Morland, *Hangman's Clutch* (London 1954), pp. 17–43; E. Lustgarten, *The Business of Murder* (London 1968), pp. 45–74; Downie, *Murder in London*, pp. 98–102; Howse, *A–Z of London Murders*, pp. 73–4.

22. On these actions, see *The Times* 23 June 1934 4a and 25 July 1935 4d.

23. *The Times* 16 Feb 1940 3e.

24. C. E. Bechhofer Roberts, *The Trial of Ley and Smith* (Notable British Trials, London 1947); E. Lustgarten, *The Chalk Pit Murder* (London 1974); J. Rowland, *Unfit to Plead* (London 1965), pp. 103–43; Shaw, *A Companion to Murder*, pp. 160–3; Butler, *Murderers' London*, pp. 144–7; Barker & Silvester-Carr, *Crime & Scandal*, pp. 192–3; Eddleston, *Foul Deeds in Kensington and Chelsea* pp. 125–30; B. York (*National Library of Australia News*, July 2001, pp. 14–7).

25. His obituary was in *The Times* 26 July 1947.

26. *DE* 7 May 1948.

27. On the Epton case, see NA MEPO 3/3007; Eddleston, *Foul Deeds in Kensington and Chelsea*, pp. 119–24; *The Times* 8 May 1948 3b, *DM* 8 May and 18 June 1948, *DE* 8 May 1948.

28. On Christine Granville and her distinguished career, see M. Masson, *Christine* (London 2005) and C. Mulley, *The Spy who Loved* (London 2012).

29. On her murder, see also Eddleston, *Foul Deeds in Kensington and Chelsea*, pp. 149–54; *The Times* 17 June 3e, 21 June 9a, 11 Sept 4b and 12 Sept 3d, 1952, *DM* 12 Sept 1952.

30. On the Aban Court case, see Eddleston, *Foul Deeds in Kensington and Chelsea*, pp. 155–60; *The Times* 10 March 5d, 11 March 6d, 2 April 3b, 11 May 5c, 12 May 3g and 13 May 2c, 1954; *DM* 11 March and 13 May 1954.

31. Interview with Margaret McGrath by Jill Shapiro on www.arthurlloyd.co.uk.

32. The murder of Violet McGrath was featured by R. Furneaux, *Famous Criminal Cases II* (London 1955), pp. 177–87; *The Times* 11 May 8g, 17 May 3e, 12 Aug 3e, 13 Aug 3a, 1954; *DE* 11 and 18 May, 12 and 13 Aug 1954

33. *The Times* 14 Aug 1954 2c.

34. NA DPP 2/2413; also *The Times* 5 March 1955 4f and 26 April 1955 8g.

35. On the Dique case, see NA CRIM 1/2738; *The Times* 7 April 7b, 3 July 10f, 13 Sept 6f and 27 Sept 6b, 1956; *DM* 13 and 29 Sept 1956; *West London Observer* 13 and 20 July, 14 and 28 Sept 1956.

36. On the jailbreak, see *The Times* 7 Dec 1959 10g and 9 Dec 1959 12f; *DM* 7 and 9 Dec 1959.

37. On the Podola case, see J. P. Eddy, *Scarlet and Ermine* (London 1960), pp. 193–218; Fido, *Murder Guide to London*, pp. 80–1; Eddleston, *Foul Deeds in Kensington and Chelsea*, pp. 161–5; *The Times* 18 Sept 6a, 19 Sept 7a, 24 Sept 8c, 25 Sept 6e and 12e, 15 Oct 4b and 21 Oct 4a, 1959.

38. On the Bain case, see NA CRIM 1/4013; Eddleston, *Foul Deeds in Kensington and Chelsea*, pp. 166–70; *The Times* 26 Sept 1962 15g.

3 Chelsea and Fulham

1. On the sad fate of the murder pub, see *DT* 6 Aug 2012; *Evening Standard* 25 Sept 2012.

2. On the Huelin case, see *Famous Crimes Past & Present* 9(114) [1905], pp. 386–92; G. Logan, *Masters of Crime* (London 1928), pp. 209–15 and *Dramas of the Dock* (London 1930), pp. 41–68; Barker & Silvester-Carr, *Crime & Scandal*, pp. 212–3; Eddleston, *Foul Deeds in Kensington and Chelsea*, pp. 29–34. The trial of Walter Miller is available on the OldBaileyOnline website; see also *The Times* 13 May 9f, 14 May 10a, 16 May 12e, 17 May 12a, 19 May 11a, 21 May 11c, 8 June 11b, 9 June 11b, 10 June 11c, 14 July 11a and 15 July 11a, 1870; *SMH* 16 July 1870; *Ashburton Guardian* 15 Jan 1907.

3. *The Times* 24 July 1871 11a.

4. G. R. Sims, *Mysteries of Modern London* (London 1906), pp. 66–8.

5. On the Paul May case, see NA MEPO 3/106; *The Times* 24 Aug 6d, 27 Aug 9a, 28 Aug 12b, 30 Aug 9a and 22 Nov 8c, 1872; *DN* 24, 26 and 28 Aug, 5 Nov 1872; *LWN* 25 Aug and 1 Sept 1872; *RN* 1 Sept and 24 Nov 1872; *IPN* 7 Sept and 9 Nov 1872.

6. *MP* 10 Feb 1873; *Glasgow Herald* 10 Feb 1873.

7. The trial of Henry Norman is available on the OldBaileyOnline website; see also *The Times* 20 July 1885 6c and 18 Sept 1885 12b; *MP* 6 Oct 1885; *PMG* 17 July 1885; *RN* 19 July 1885; *LWN* 19 July 1885; *IPN* 25 July, 1 and 8 Aug 1885; *Manchester The Times* 19 Sept 1885 and *Bristol Mercury* 6 Oct 1885.

8. The trial of Henry Williams is available on the OldBaileyOnline website. See also NA CRIM 1/75/11, the TrueCrimeLibrary and BritishExecutions websites, and *The Times* 17 Sept 1902 11c and 24 Oct 1902 10e.

9. On the John Currie case, see D. B. Haycock, *A Crisis of Brilliance* (London 2009); J. Simkin on the Spartacus Schoolnet website; *The Times* 9 Oct 1914 9c, *This is Staffordshire* 22 Aug 2009.

10. On the unsolved murder of Frances Buxton, see NA MEPO 3/268B; G. Logan, *Guilty or Not Guilty* (London 1929), pp. 140–5; Oates, *Unsolved London Murders of 1920s and 1930s*, pp. 25–36; *The Times* 19 Jan 9c, 20 Jan 7f and 21 Jan 4a, 1920; *DM* 19, 20, 21, 24 and 29 Jan, 5 April and 4 Sept 1920; *IPN* 22 Jan 1920.

11. On the Tedder case, see *The Times* 28 Feb 1939 11b, 3 March 1939 16g; *DE* 28 Feb 1939; *DM* 28 Feb and 1 March 1939.

12. On Wright of Armadale Road, see *The Times* 3 March 1945 2c; *DM* 2 March 1945 and *Fulham Chronicle* 2 and 9 March 1945.

13. On the O'Connor case, see NA MEPO 2/9123; Eddleston, *Foul Deeds in Kensington and Chelsea*, pp. 147–8; *The Times* 13 Aug 2b, 14 Aug 4d, 21 Aug 3b and 3 Oct 2e, 1951; *DE* 13 Aug 1951; *DM* 14 Aug and 25 Oct 1951; *Reading Eagle* 3 Oct 1951.

14. Cargill & Holland, *Scenes of Murder*, p. 20; *The Times* 2 Aug 4e and 9 Aug 3f 1958, 7 June 1961 8e.

15. NA CRIM 1/4479; *DM* 6 Dec 1965, *DE* 6 Dec 1965; *Fulham Chronicle* 10 and 17 Dec 1965.

16. On the murder of Claudie Delbarre, see NA DPP 2/4443; Eddleston, *Foul Deeds in Kensington and Chelsea*, pp. 171–7; P. R. Glazebrook (*Cambridge Law Journal* 28 [1970], pp. 21–3; A. Frewin in *CrimeTime* 1 Oct 2011; *The Times* 9 March 4e, 26 March 5e, 8 Oct 2d, 9 Oct 2d, 10 Oct 2e, 11 Oct 2e, 1968 and 30 July 1969 6e; *DM* 25 Sept 1967, 2 May, 8 Oct, 9 Oct and 11 Oct 1968.

17. Sir D. Napley, *Not Without Prejudice* (London 1982), pp. 238–55.

18. On the Elgar case, see *The Times* 17 Feb 3d, 21 Feb 2d, 23 Feb 4f and 25 May 3f, 1968; *DM* 14, 16 and 21 Feb, 17, 25, 28 and 30 May 1968; *Fulham Chronicle* 1 Jan 1968 and *Ealing Gazette* 31 Oct 2008.

19. On the Nutkins case, see *The Times* 8 Dec 1971 3b and 13 April 1972 2d; *DM* 13 April 1972.

20. On the Baekeland case, see N. Robins & S. M. L. Aronson, *Savage Grace* (London 2008); *The Times* 18 Nov 1972 4d, 21 Nov 1972 2g, 7 June 1973 4g; *DMa* 27 June, 30 June and 12 July 2008.

21. The only full-length book on the Patrick Mackay case is T. Clark & J. Penycate, *Psychopath* (London 1976); see also Fido, *Murder Guide to London*, pp. 82–3; T. Tullett, *Clues to Murder* (London 1986), pp. 148–61; and B. Lane & W. Gregg, *Encyclopedia of Serial Killers* (London 1992), pp. 191–2. There was a long feature on Mackay in *DM* 22 Nov 1975; see also *The Times* 24 April 1975 3e, 22 Nov 1975 3a and 22f.

22. N. Lucas & P. Davies, *The Monster Butler* (London 1990); P. Pender, *The Butler Did It* (Edinburgh 2012); Fido, *Murder Guide to London*, pp. 83–5.

23. On Peter Arne, see Howse, *A–Z of London Murders*, pp. 117–8; *The Times* 3 Aug 10f and 11 Aug 2d, 1983 and *DM* 8, 10, 11 and 12 Aug and 20 Oct 1983.

24. There are many books on the Dando case, of differing quality. B. Cathcart, *Jill Dando* (London 2001) and D. J. Smith, *All About Jill* (London 2002) are competent records of the popular presenter's life and death. J. McVicar, *Dead on Time* (London 2002) is an anti-Barry George book of questionable reliability. In contrast, S. Lomax, *The Case of Barry George* (Hertford 2004) and *Justice for Jill* (London 2007) are admirable accounts of this complex

case, from a pro-Barry George standpoint. J. Phillips, *Who Murdered Jill Dando and Why?* (Bloomington IN 2009) is an unreadable transatlantic rehash of the case.

25. The Monckton case was featured by *DM* 1 Dec 2004 and 22 Nov and 2 Dec 2005; also *This is Local London* 20 Dec 2005.

4 Bloomsbury, Holborn, St Pancras and Camden Town

1. E. O'Donnell, *Ghosts of London* (London 1933), p. 47.

2. E. O'Donnell, *Ghosts of London* (London 1933), pp. 45–6.

3. E. O'Donnell, *Rooms of Mystery* (London 1931), pp. 84–5.

4. On the Janoska case, see NA MEPO 3/108; *The Times* 2 Jan 1873 10b and 6 Jan 1873 5e; *MP* 28 Dec 1872; *LWN* 29 Dec 1872 and 5 Jan 1873; *DN* 2 Jan 1873, *RN* 5 Jan 1873.

5. On the Fyfield case, see his trial on OldBaileyOnline; *IPN* 5 May and 11 June 1887; *RN* 15 May 1887.

6. On the Pearcey case, see G. Logan, *Rope, Knife and Chair* (London 1930), pp. 170–88; J. Laurence, *Extraordinary Crimes* (London 1931), pp. 207–20; R. & M. Whittington-Egan, *The Bedside Book of Murder* (London 1988), pp. 39–54; Lane, *Murder Club Guide to London*, pp. 36–8; Aston, *Foul Deeds and Suspicious Deaths in Hampstead, Holborn and St Pancras*, pp. 98–106. The trial of Mrs Pearcey is on OldBaileyOnline, and the case is extensively discussed on Casebook; see also *Famous Crimes Past & Present* 1(8) [1903], pp. 180–5; *LWN* 26 Oct 1890; *IPN* 8, 22 and 29 Nov, 13, 20 and 27 Dec 1890; *Star* 13 Dec 1890; *Evening Post* 2 Feb 1891.

7. On the obscure Else case, see *The Times* 3 June 1891 12e; *MP* 3 June 1891; *Sta* 3 and 4 June 1891 and *Yorkshire Herald* 6 June 1891.

8. There are three books on the Camden Town case, namely B. Hogarth (Ed.), *Trial of Robert Wood* (Notable British Trials, London 1936); Sir D. Napley, *The Camden Town Murder* (London 1987) and J. Barber, *The Camden Town Murder* (Oxford 2008); the latter is the best and most accessible. See also E. Marjoribanks, *The Life of Sir Edward Marshall Hall* (London 1930), pp. 223–63; G. Logan, *Great Murder Mysteries* (London 1931), pp. 78–98; J. P. Eddy, *Scarlet and Ermine* (London 1960), pp. 41–7; Shaw, *Second Companion to Murder*, pp. 256–61; J. Rowland, *Murder Mistaken* (London 1963), pp. 19–122; N. Warner-Hooke & G. Thomas, *Marshall Hall* (London 1966), pp. 115–35; Aston, *Foul Deeds and Suspicious Deaths in Hampstead, Holborn and St Pancras*, pp. 114–21; Oates, *Unsolved Murders in Victorian and Edwardian London*, pp. 144–52

9. E. Marjoribanks, *The Life of Sir Edward Marshall Hall* (London 1930), p. 261.

10. *DM* 4 Feb 1949; J. Barber, *The Camden Town Murder* (Oxford 2008), pp. 202–3.

11. J. Rowland, *Murder Mistaken* (London 1963), pp. 9–10.

12. On the Praager case, see H. L. Adam, *Murder by Persons Unknown* (London 1931), pp. 117–29; Oates, *Unsolved Murders in Victorian and Edwardian London*, pp. 158–62; *The Times* 22 Oct 2f 1908 and 27 Oct 13d 1908; *IPN* 24 Oct 1908; *Auckland Star* 12 Jan 1910.

13. On the Anastassiou case, see NA MEPO 3/1664; *The Times* 16 March 1931 14b and 19 May 1931 5c; *DM* 28 Feb, 28 April, 19 May and 4 June 1931.

14. NA MEPO 3/2195; Aston, *Foul Deeds and Suspicious Deaths in Hampstead, Holborn and St Pancras*, pp. 143–5; *DM* 18 Oct 1941; *DE* 18 and 20 Oct 1941.

15. G. McKnight, *The Murder Squad* (London 1967), pp. 87–103, S. Read, *In the Dark* (London 2006).

16. On the little-known Jean Stafford case, see *The Times* 23 May 1942 2c; *DM* 23 and 25 May 1942; *Holborn & Finsbury Guardian* 29 May and 26 June 1942. The relevant police file is closed until 2014.

17. On the Petrides case, see NA CRIM 1/2097; Fido, *Murder Guide to London*, p. 42; Aston, *Foul Deeds and Suspicious Deaths in Hampstead, Holborn and St Pancras*, pp. 157–9; *The Times* 10 Aug 3b and 11 Aug 2d, 1950; *DM* 11 Aug and 27 Oct 1950.

18. On Voisin, see Butler, *Murderers' London*, pp. 62–4; Fido, *Murder Guide to London*, pp. 69–70 and Aston, *Foul Deeds and Suspicious Deaths in Hampstead, Holborn and St Pancras*, pp. 130–6.

19. On the obscure Smartt case, see NA CRIM 1/2268; *The Times* 20 Nov 1952 3c.

20. On this remarkable brothel, see Barker & Silvester-Carr, *Crime & Scandal*, p. 132.

5 Bayswater, Paddington and Marylebone

1. H. L. Adam, *Murder Most Mysterious* (London 1932), pp. 128–38; Oates, *Unsolved London Murders of the 1920s and 1930s*, pp. 83–9.

2. E. O'Donnell, *Rooms of Mystery* (London 1931), pp. 270–82.

3. D. Malcolm, *Family Secrets* (London 2004).

4. On the Cato Street Conspiracy, see G. T. Wilkinson, *An Authentic History of the Cato Street Conspiracy* (reissue Aron Press, New York 1972); J. Stanhope, *The Cato Street Conspiracy* (London 1962) and M. J. Trow, *The Cato Street Conspiracy* (Barnsley 2010); Howse, *Foul Deeds and Suspicious Deaths in*

London's West End, pp. 114–9; *West Coast Times* 10 Jan 1870; *Manchester Times* 21 April 1883; *LWN* 24 Dec 1899.

5. *The Times* 12 Oct 10b, 13 Oct 7c, 14 Oct 7e and 16 Oct 10b, 1869; *PIP* 23 Oct 1869; *DN* 14 Oct 1869, *PMG* 15 Oct 1869.

6. T. R. H. Cashmore, *The Mystery of Thomas Hayden Green* (Borough of Twickenham Local History Society Paper 23, 1972); H. Pollins & V. Rosewarne, *Louis Kyezor, 'The King of Whitton'* (Borough of Twickenham Local History Society Paper 82, 2002); K. Quinn Lockyer, *Louis Kyezor in Doncaster* (Jewish Communities & Record 2005).

7. *Poor Man's Guardian* 2 Nov 1832.

8. *The Times* 26 May 12d, 30 May 5e, 2 June 8a and 17 June 10f, 1871; *RN* 4 June 1871; *MP* 30 May 1871.

9. On her early history, see *MP* 6 March 1867 and 14 Jan 1868.

10. J. Smith-Hughes, *Unfair Comment* (London 1951), pp. 212–47; *The Times* 11 July 11e, 12 July 11e, 14 July 11a, 15 July 11a and 17 July 12a, 1871.

11. On her release, see *Sheffield & Rotherham Independent* 21 Sept 1874.

12. On the Harley Street mystery, see Oates, *Unsolved Murders in Victorian and Edwardian London*, pp. 83–7; T. Hughes in *Marylebone Journal*, Feb/March 2010, pp. 57–60; *The Times* 7 June 1880 13g; *MP* 8 and 15 June 1880; *RN* 6 and 13 June 1880; *LWN* 6, 13 and 20 June 1880; *IPN* 12 and 26 June 1880; *Sta* 5 Oct 1880.

13. The obituary of Mr Henriques is in the *Daily Gleaner* 21 Nov 1898.

14. On the Saunders case, see *The Times* 2 Jan 1882 6a and 5 Jan 1882 7g; *MP* 2 Jan 1882; *Sta* 2 and 5 Jan 1882; *DN* 3 and 5 Jan 1882; *LWN* 8 Jan 1882.

15. On the Foster case, see his trial at OldBaileyOnline; also *IPN* 16 Dec 1893; *LWN* 10 Dec 1893; *Leeds Mercury* 12 Dec 1893.

16. On the Aitken case, see *The Times* 19 Sept 1896 11c; *Sta* 20 and 22 Aug, 26 Oct 1896; *MP* 22, 28 and 29 Aug 1896; *RN* 30 Aug and 1 Nov 1896; *IPN* 12 Sept 1896.

17. *The Times* 29 May 1906 15f.

18. On the unsolved murder of Archibald Wakley, see *The Times* 6 June 1906 3e; *IPN* 2 June 1906 and *DM* 25, 26, 28, 29, 30 and 31 May, 22 June 1906. The only modern writer to mention the Wakley case is M. Cook, *London and the Culture of Homosexuality 1885–1914* (Cambridge 1993), pp. 32, 47 and 63–5.

19. *DM* 6 June 1906.

20. On Harry Day, see his trial on OldBaileyOnline and *The Times* 13 June 1912 2g.

21. On the Blackmore case, see *The Times* 11 March 1921 7e, 14 March 1921 9e and 9 May 1921 4e; *DM* 11 March and 24 June 1921; *IPN* 17 March 1921.

22. *The Times* 24 June 1938 13d; *DM* 24 June 1938.

23. On the Jacoby case, see G. W. Cornish, *Cornish of the Yard* (London 1935), pp. 109–18; Shaw, *A Second Companion to Murder*, pp. 108–10; Lane, *Murder Club Guide to London*, pp. 172–3; Howse, *A–Z of London Murders*, pp. 82–4; *The Times* 22 March 9e, 6 April 9c and 23 May 5e, 1922; *IPN* 23 March 1922.

24. The True vs. Jacoby debate was discussed in *The Times* 8 June 1922 5f and 10 June 1922 8e. See also G. Pollock, *Mr Justice McCardie* (London 1934), pp. 217–38; J. Rowland, *Unfit to Plead* (London 1965), pp. 81–102 and J. Goodman, *Murder in Low Places* (London 1988), pp. 155–217.

25. On the unsolved murder of Dora Alicia Lloyd, see NA MEPO 3/1672; G. W. Cornish, *Cornish of the Yard* (London 1935), pp. 295–301; Shaw, *Second Companion to Murder*, p. 123; Oates, *Unsolved London Murders of 1920s and 1930s*, pp. 135–43; *The Times* 22 Feb 14e, 24 Feb 14d, 25 Feb 16b, 26 Feb 9c, 1932; *DM* 23 and 24 Feb, 7 April 1932.

26. *The Times* 8 Feb 1933 6g; *DM* 8 Feb 1933.

27. On the case of Eric Russell, see *The Times* 7 April 7f, 28 May 11e, 7 June 11b and 5 July 4d, 1934; *DM* 26 June 1934.

28. On Harry Tuffney, see M. Hamblin Smith in *British Journal of Psychiatry* 80 [1934], pp. 716–7; *The Times* 16 July 7c, 14 Aug 8e, 21 Sept 9b and 10 Oct 11g, 1934; *DE* 9 July 1934.

29. *DE* 21 Sept 1934.

30. There was very little newspaper publicity about this obscure case, but the debate about Irene Coffee's fate can be followed in NA MEPO 3/2196, CRIM 1/1360 and 1/585/131, and HO 144/21641.

31. H. Hannusch, *Todesstrafe für die Selbstmörderin* (Berlin 2011). See also *Die Zeit* 10 March 2011 and *Der Spiegel* 11 April 2011.

32. *DMa* 9 March 2011; *Ind* 13 March 2011.

33. The only full-length book on the Blackout Ripper is S. Read, *In the Dark* (London 2006). See also G. McKnight, *The Murder Squad* (London 1967), pp. 87–103; Shaw, *Companion to Murder*, pp. 55–7; Fido, *Murder Guide to London*, pp. 53–4; Howse, *A–Z of London Murders*, pp. 39–40.

34. On the Lees-Smith case, see NA MEPO 3/2244; Shaw, *Second Companion to Murder*, pp. 118–20; Butler, *Murderers' London*, p. 73; Fido, *Murder Guide to London*, p. 68; F. K. McCowan, *Journal of Mental Science* 90 [1943], pp. 501–10; *The Times* 18 March 1943 2c; *DM* 1, 2 and 16 Jan, 17 and 18 March 1943.

35. On the Furzecroft murder, see P. Beveridge, *Inside the C.I.D.* (London 1957), pp. 179–85 and Fido, *Murder Guide to London*, pp. 67–8; *The Times* 29 Dec 1948 2d, 20 Jan 1949 2d and 10 March 1949 2e; *DM* 29 Dec 1948; *DE* 28 Dec 1948.

36. On the Armstrong case, see NA MEPO 3/3131; Oates, *Unsolved London Murders of the 1940s & 1950s*, pp. 80–6; *The Times* 16 April 4e; *DM* 16 April 1949. Both Emily Armstrong and Gladys Hanrahan are in the TrueCrimeLibrary database.

37. The main sources on the murder of Agnes Walsh are NA MEPO 2/8771; P. Beveridge, *Inside the C.I.D.* (London 1957), pp. 171–8 and Oates, *Unsolved London Murders of the 1940s & 1950s*, pp. 110–5; see also *The Times* 3 June 4g, 5 June 2e, 14 June 3e, 1950; *DE* 30 May, 2 and 14 June 1950; *DM* 14 June 1950; *Irish Times* 31 May 1950; *Manchester Guardian* 14 June 1950 and *SMH* 5 June 1950.

38. *The Times* 5 April 1952 3c; *Paddington Mercury* 29 Feb, 7 and 14 March, 11 April 1952.

39. On the de Almeida case, see *The Times* 25 March 8d, 26 March 3e, 27 March 3f, 3 April 4e and 29 April 2g, 1954; *DE* 25, 26 and 27 March, and 6 April 1954; *DM* 27 March 1954.

40. On the Atter case, see NA CRIM 1/2701, *The Times* 18 Jan 5b, 23 Feb 4d, 20 March 6b, 21 March 7c, 22 March 16d, 1956.

41. *DMa* 22 March 1956.

42. On the Wiora case, see NA CRIM 1/2831; *DM* 6 and 30 May, 25 and 26 July 1957; *St Marylebone & Paddington Record* 9 and 23 May, 6, 13 and 20 June, 1 Aug 1957.

43. According to streathambrixtonchess.blogspot.com.

44. NA CRIM 1/3569; *The Times* 4 Nov 7g, 25 Nov 17e and 16 Dec 17c, 1960.

45. On the Stojalowski case, see NA CRIM 1/3749; *The Times* 14 June 8b, 15 June 7e, 21 July 5e and 14 Sept 8c, 1961.

46. NA CRIM 1/3638; *The Times* 2 June 1961 8c.

47. B. Galloway, *Prejudice and Pride* (London 1983), pp. 65–7; *The Times* 21 Feb 1962 6g and 22 Feb 1962 6e; *DM* 21, 22, 23, 24, 26 and 27 Feb, 8 March, 11 April, 18 May and 24 July 1962; *Evening Standard* 22 Feb 1962; *News of the World* 25 Feb 1962.

48. On the 'Keighery connection', see *DM* 4 Dec 1964 and 23 March 1965.

49. On Copeland, see *DM* 3 April 1965 and the MurderUK homepage.

50. On the Cotter case, see NA MEPO 20/10 and CRIM 1/4292; *The Times* 25 July 1964 9b and 16 Sept 1964 16d; *DM* 25 July and 16 Sept 1964; *DE* 16 Sept 1964.

51. NA CRIM 1/4581; *The Times* 15 July 14e, 16 July 10e, 16 Aug 5f, 26 Aug 10d, 26 Oct 10d, 1966; *DE* 26 Oct 1966.

52. *DM* 10 and 13 Sept 1969; *DE* 21 Feb 1969; *Westminster and Marylebone Chronicle* 28 Feb, 30 May and 12 Sept 1969; *St Marylebone & Paddington Record* 28 Feb, 14, 21 and 28 March, 30 May and 20 June 1969.

53. *DE* 18 Nov 1972.

54. On the little-known Whelan case, see TrueCrimeLibrary, also *DM* 18 Nov 1972; *Paddington Mercury* 24 Nov and 1 Dec 1972.

6 Islington

1. On 'Chopper' Gamble, see *Famous Crimes Past & Present* 10(117) [1905], pp. 466–8; Eddleston, *Foul Deeds in Islington*, pp. 93–8; and J. Bondeson, *Ripperologist* 131 [2013], pp. 33–7.
2. On the Bricknell case, see Eddleston, *Foul Deeds in Islington*, pp. 55–7; *The Times* 11 June 11f, 12 July 13c and 14 July 10e, 1864; *LWN* 12 June 1864; *Nottinghamshire Guardian* 15 July and 5 Aug 1864.
3. On the Finch case, see *The Times* 11 June 10e, 12 June 6d, 16 June 10d, 1 July 13b, 1886; *IPN* 19 June 1886; *MP* 11 June 1886; *Sta* 19 June and 5 Aug 1886.
4. *PIP* 26 May 1888.
5. *The Times* 18 May 1888 11g, 22 Sept 1888 4f; *IPN* 26 May 1888; *PMG* 13 Oct 1888; *Mataura Ensign* 31 July 1888.
6. The trial of Glennie is available on the OldBaileyOnline website; see also *The Times* 30 Oct 1888 7f; *PIP* 3 Nov 1888.
7. On this confession, see *The Times* 17 June 1890 5e; *Cheshire Observer* 21 June 1890; *Yorkshire Herald* 10 and 20 June 1890.
8. The trial of Neal is available on the OldBaileyOnline website; see also Eddleston, *Foul Deeds in Islington*, pp. 83–6; *The Times* 29 Jan 11f, 30 Jan 4d, 6 Feb 14a, 8 Feb 10c, 10 March 10e and 12 March 10c, 1890; *DN* 1 Jan and 6 Feb 1890; *MP* 29 Jan 1890; *LWN* 9 Feb 1890; *IPN* 8 and 15 Feb 1890; *RN* 16 March 1890; *Birmingham Daily Post* 29 Jan 1890.
9. *Sta* 19 March 1894; *DN* 20 March 1894; *IPN* 24 March 1894; *Royal Cornwall Gazette* 29 March 1894; *The Times* 19 March 6e and 22 March 12a, 1894.
10. The later history of the Swan is told on the 'Beer in the Evening' and 'Pub & Bar Review' homepages.
11. Today quite forgotten, the Galley case was a sensation in its time, see his trial at OldBaileyOnline; also *IPN* 11 and 25 July, 1 Aug and 19 Sept 1896; *RN* 5 and 12 July, 13 Sept 1896; *MP* 6 July and 11 Sept 1896; *DN* 7 July and 10 Oct 1896; *Sta* 9 July and 11 Sept 1896; *LWN* 12 July 1896.
12. On Mrs Dyer and her career, see A. Rattle & A. Vale, *Amelia Dyer, Angel Maker* (London 2007).
13. K. Sugden (Ed.), *Criminal Islington* (Islington Archives and Historical Society, London 1989), pp. 38–41; R. Clark, *Women and the Noose* (Stroud 2007), pp. 208–9; Howse, *A–Z of London Murders*, pp. 81–2.

14. P. Asher in *DMa* 5 June 2011. See also the article by C. Davies in *Camden New Journal*, 12 Nov 2009.

15. On the Walter Fensham case, see Eddleston, *Foul Deeds in Islington*, pp. 140–5; *The Times* 15 Jan 1908 17a and 7 Feb 1908 19b.

16. On Walter Fensham's later career, see NA HO 144/15375 and PCOM 9/734.

17. On Noah Woolf, see NA CRIM 1/118/3 and the OldBaileyOnline website; *The Times* 2 Nov 1910 8d, *DM* 19 Nov 1910, *IPN* 5 Nov 1910.

18. On the Seddon case, see F. Young (Ed.), *Trial of the Seddons* (Notable British Trials, London 1925); E. Marjoribanks, *The Life of Sir Edward Marshall Hall* (London 1930), pp. 289–313; A. E. Bowker, *Behind the Bar* (London 1948), pp. 44–50; D. G. Browne & E. V. Tullett, Bernard Spilsbury (London 1951), pp. 55–69; D. G. Browne, *Sir Travers Humphreys* (London 1960), pp. 79–103; J. P. Eddy, *Scarlet and Ermine* (London 1960), pp. 81–90; Howse, *North London Murders*, pp. 72–84; *IPN* 7 Aug 1919.

19. *The Times* 8 Feb 1913 4c; *DE* 6 Jan 1913; *DM* 8 Jan 1913.

20. On George Joseph Smith, see E. R. Watson (Ed.), *Trial of George Joseph Smith* (Notable British Trials, London 1949); E. Marjoribanks, *The Life of Sir Edward Marshall Hall* (London 1930), pp. 323–56; D. G. Browne & E. V. Tullett, *Bernard Spilsbury* (London 1951), pp. 70–92; D. G. Browne, *Sir Travers Humphreys* (London 1960), pp. 126–48; J. P. Eddy, *Scarlet and Ermine* (London 1960), pp. 91–6; Howse, *North London Murders*, pp. 85–104.

21. On the 'Barmaid Murder Mystery', see *The Times* 27 March 5e, 2 April 3d, 6 April 5d, 9 April 4b, 13 April 3a, 14 April 4e and 21 April 4g; *DE* 27 March and 2 April 1915; *DM* 27 March 1915.

22. NA CRIM 1/156–7; *DM* 24 and 29 June 1915.

23. *Lloyd's Weekly News* 4 July 1915.

24. NA MEPO 3/266; *The Times* 29 July 9a, 8 Aug 4f, 30 Aug 7f, and 19 Sept 7a, 1919; *DM* 30 July, 2, 8, 16, 23 and 30 Aug 1919.

25. On the trial of Warren and Morgan, see *The Times* 18 Sept 4a 1919; *DM* 18 and 19 Sept 1919.

26. NA MEPO 3/1680; *The Times* 6 March 9b, 7 March 16e, 21 March 4g, 2 May 15a, 4 May 6g, 23 May 5c, 1933; *DE* 6 March and 4 May 1933; *DM* 4 and 23 May 1933; *IPN* 9 March and 16 June 1933.

27. *DM* 30 April and 1 May 1936; *The Times* 17 Feb 6g, 20 Feb 4c, 24 Feb 3g, 2 March 3g, 29 April 11c, 1 May 13a; *Fitzrovia News* 127, Winter 2012, 11.

28. *DM* 1 May 1936.

29. On the Islington Green case, see NA MEPO 3/874 and 3/1647; Butler, *Murderers' London*, pp. 122–3 and Eddleston, *Foul Deeds in Islington*, pp.

158–62; *The Times* Oct 29 1935 16d, 15 May 14d, 2 June 4g, 1 July 13e, 2 July 13c, 3 July 11e, 30 July 4f and 18 Aug 7d, 1937.

30. *DM* 3 July 1937. For Lord Hewart's reaction to the murderer's angry outburst, see R. Jackson, *The Chief* (London 1959), pp. 312–4.

31. *DE* 3 July 1937; see also *The Times* 11 June 1929 16d and 12 June 1929 13d.

32. On the unsolved murder of Miss Bowen, see *IPN* 14 Nov 1918.

33. On the Bass-Woodcock case, see NA CRIM 1/2193 and *DE* 11 Dec 1951.

34. On the Folkard case, see NA DPP 2/2770; *The Times* 12 Feb 4f, 19 Feb 4c, 12 March 13e, 1 May 7a, 2 May 6g and 17 May 3a, 1958; *DE* 24 Dec 1957 and 1 May 1958; *DM* 23 Dec 1957, 2 May 1958.

35. L. Seal, *Women, Murder and Femininity* (Basingstoke 2010), pp. 106–16; *The Times* 20 June 1961 8c, 6 June 1966 1e; *DE* 19 June 1961 and 6 June 1966.

36. Cargill & Holland, *Scenes of Murder*, p. 95; *The Times* 17 April 1962 6d.

37. http://en.wikipedia.org/wiki/Joe_Meek. On Joe Meek, see J. Repsch, *The Legendary Joe Meek* (London 1989); M. Moran & J. Hicks, *Telstar: The Joe Meek Story* (London 2007); *Observer Music Monthly* Nov 12 2006 and *Ind* 18 April 2009.

38. On the murder of Joe Orton, see J. Lehr, *Prick up Your Ear* (London 1978) and C. W. E. Bigsby, *Joe Orton* (London 1982); Lane, *Murder Club Guide to London*, pp. 16–18; Howse, *North London Murders*, pp. 124–32; and *A–Z of London Murders*, pp. 66–8; *The Sunday Times Magazine* 22 Nov 1970 and *DMa* 4 April 2009.

39. On the Cameron case, see NA MEPO 26/44; also *The Times* 2 April 1971 4e; *DM* 15 Oct and 5 Dec 1970, and 2 April 1971; *DE* 16 Oct 1970.

40. On the little-known case of James Hails, see NA MEPO 26/165; also *DM* 18 Dec 1971 and 17 May 1972; *DE* 16 Oct 1970; *Islington Gazette* 17, 23 and 31 Dec 1971.

7 Tower Hamlets

1. On topographical aspects of Jack the Ripper, see R. Clack & P. Hutchinson, *The London of Jack the Ripper Then and Now* (Derby 2007).

2. L. Matters, *The Mystery of Jack the Ripper* (London 1960), pp. 91–2.

3. On the sinister history of Miller's Court, see Oldridge, *Murder and Crime: Whitechapel and District*, pp. 62–84.

4. On Dorset Street, see F. Rule, *The Worst Street in London* (London 2008).

5. See the London Borough of Tower Hamlets' pamphlet 'The Artillery Passage Conservation Area' (London 2007).

6. The trial of Alexander Arthur Mackay is available at the OldBaileyOnline website. Newspaper sources include *The Times* 21 Aug 1868 8e; *IPN* 15 May, 6 June, 1 and 29 Aug and 12 Sept 1868; *MP* 9 May, 28 July and 21 Aug 1868; *DN* 9 and 20 May, 21 Aug 1868; *LWN* 31 May and 2 Aug 1868.

7. G. R. Sims, *My Life* (London 1917), pp. 142–3.

8. On the Wainwright case, see H. B. Irving (Ed.), *Trial of the Wainwrights* (Notable British Trials, London 1920); R. D. Altick, *Victorian Studies in Scarlet* (New York 1970), pp. 210–9, Lane, *Murder Club Guide to London*, pp. 136–9, Howse, *Foul Deeds and Suspicious Deaths in London's East End*, pp. 56–82.

9. *IPN* 26 July 1890.

10. Storey, *East End Murders*, pp. 16–30; Oldridge, *Murder and Crime: Whitechapel and District*, pp. 8–19.

11. *PIP* 25 Sept 1874.

12. H. B. Irving (Ed.), *Trial of the Wainwrights* (Notable British Trials, London 1920).

13. The only full-length book on the Lipski case is M. Friedland, *The Trials of Israel Lipski* (New York 1984). See also G. Logan, *Rope, Knife and Chair* (London 1930), pp. 154–69; Storey, *East End Murders*, pp. 31–46; Oldridge, *Murder and Crime: Whitechapel and District*, pp. 20–31. The trial of Israel Lipski is on OldBaileyOnline, and the case has been discussed on the Casebook homepage. See also *Famous Crimes Past & Present* 2(14) [1903], pp. 12–14; *The Times* 2 July 12f, 4 July 4f, 11 July 13a, 30 July 7f, 1887; *MP* 25 and 26 Aug 1887; *IPN* 6 and 27 Aug 1887; G. Bromley in *Ripperologist* 81, July 2007; M. Brooke in *Docklands & East London Advertiser* 22 May 2011; and B. Beadle in *Londonist* 29 Aug 2011.

14. *The Guardian* 13 Dec 2003.

15. J. Bondeson, *Ripperologist* 128 [2012], pp. 80–3.

16. See the Casebook homepage; also *MP* 20 Nov, 8 and 15 Dec 1894; *Sta* 1 and 15 Dec 1894; *IPN* 1 Dec 1894; *Glasgow Herald* 19 Dec 1894; *The Times* 20 Nov 1894 12b.

17. On the Seaman case, see G. Logan, *Masters of Crime* (London 1928), pp. 215–9 and *Wilful Murder* (London 1935), pp. 153–65; Fido, *Murder Guide to London*, pp. 30–1; Howse, *A–Z of London Murders*, pp. 136–8; his trial is on OldBaileyOnline; see also see *Famous Crimes Past & Present* 6(78) [1904], pp. 243–5; *The Times* 2 May 1896 7b and 19 May 1896 5b; *LWN* 3 May 1896; *IPN* 11 April and 9 May 1896; *PIP* 18 April 1896.

18. Howse, *Foul Deeds and Suspicious Deaths in London's East End*, pp. 111–2.

19. On Dan Mendoza and his career, see the articles by L. Edwards, *Transactions of the Jewish Historical Society of England* 15 [1939–45], pp. 73–92 and P. Joy, *Jewish Quarterly* 200, Winter 2005/2006.

20. The trial of Jerry Slowe is on the OldBaileyOnline website; see also Howse, *Foul Deeds and Suspicious Deaths in London's East End*, pp. 168–72 and *A–Z of London Murders*, pp. 145–6; *The Times* 25 Sept 1903 10f; *Auckland Star* 21 Nov 1903; *West Gippsland Gazette* 24 Nov 1903.

21. *PIP* 14 Nov 1903.

22. On the later history of the Lord Nelson, see the DeadPubs homepage. There are photographs of the old pub in the archives of the Museum of London.

23. The trial of Myer Abramovitch is on the OldBaileyOnline database. See also Oldridge, *Murder and Crime: Whitechapel and District*, pp. 85–96; *The Times* 28 Dec 8c, 29 Dec 2e, 30 Dec 2f, 1911, 4 Jan 2e and 12 Jan 2f, 1912; *DM* 29 Dec 1911 and 5 Jan 1912; *DE* 4 Jan 1912; *DMa* 28 Dec 1911.

24. NA DPP 3/3052; *The Times* 12 Jan 12g, 13 Jan 8c, 14 Jan 17b, 18 March 3f, 1960; *DMa* 12 Jan 1960.

25. Among the many books on the Krays are T. Lambrianou, *Inside the Firm* (London 2009) and B. Teale. *Bringing Down the Krays* (London 2012).

26. On murder house aspects of the Krays, see Downie, *Murder in London*, pp. 48–51; Fido, *Murder Guide to London*, pp. 32–5; and Storey, *East End Murders*, pp. 147–52.

8 Some Final Words

1. R. Wilkes, *An Infamous Address* (London 1989).

2. M. Beales, *Dead Not Buried* (London 1995); *The Guardian* 22 July 2010; *DT* 1 Aug 2010.

3. *DT* 10 Oct 2001.

4. *The Times* 15 Dec 1956 6g.

5. G. Fletcher, *The Life & Career of Dr William Palmer of Rugeley* (London 1925), p. 25.

6. *DT* 12 May 2001.

7. *DT* 17 June 2000.

8. *Famous Crimes Past & Present* 1(10) [1903], p. 176. The murder house at No. 3 Miniver Place, later No. 103 Weston Street, stood until 1959; see M. Alpert, *London 1849* (London 2004), p. 93 and plates 20–1.

9. L. Snow, *Queen's Park, Kensal, Brondesbury and Harlesden* (Chichester 2006), 65. As we have seen, a number of 'murder streets' were renamed for

unrelated reasons: street-name reform in late Victorian times, and various street renaming schemes in 1937 and 1939.

10. The houses in Grosvenor Park, Walworth, were renumbered in January 1893, following a murder in the previous year; Fountain Road, Tooting, had its houses renumbered in 1899, following a gruesome mass murder in 1895; the houses in William Mews, Knightsbridge, were renumbered in 1934, following Mrs Barney shooting her lover at the No. 21 in 1932. Elliott O'Donnell wrongly claimed that the murder houses at No. 4 Euston Square, Burton Crescent, No. 12 Great Coram Street and No. 126 Portway, West Ham, were all renumbered in his unreliable books *Rooms of Mystery* (London 1931) and *Ghosts of London* (London 1933).

11. J. Sanders, *The Invention of Murder* (London 2011), pp. 45–62.

12. *The Star* 3 Sept 1986; *Bournemouth Daily Echo* 17 May 2008 and 27 July 2010.

13. *Ind* 19 Dec 1995, 24 May 2000.

14. *DMa* 23 Sept 2011.

15. *DT* 6 Feb 2004.

16. *The Times* 8 March 2006.

17. *Manchester Evening News* 21 Aug 2008.

18. *BBC News* 16 March 2011.

19. The fate of Peter Tobin's shabby little boarded-up house of horrors at No. 50 Irvine Drive, Margate, is yet to be decided, but it may well go the same way as these others. Mick Philpott's fire-damaged council house at No. 18 Victory Road, Derby, must also be in serious danger from the bulldozer. Dr Shipman's old surgery at No. 25 Market Street, Hyde, has become a shop for electrical appliances.

20. E. O'Donnell, *The Trial of Kate Webster* (Edinburgh 1925), p. 82.

21. G. Logan, *Monsters of Crime* (Dublin 1938), pp. 86–7.

22. *Thomson's Weekly News* 19 Nov 1910.

23. www.10-rillington-place.co.uk.

24. www.villiscaiowa.com.

25. *DMa* 27 May 2011.

26. *DT* 28 Feb 2004.

27. G. R. Sims, *Mysteries of Modern London* (London 1906), pp. 66–8.

28. *DM* 3 Feb 1983; D. Lowe in *The Sun* 20 Aug 2010; *Evesham Journal* 17 March 2011.

29. On the Saunderson-Smith case, see *DMa* 4 Nov 2011, 17 July and 10 Aug 2012.

30. Recent articles on murder houses include those by L. Kennedy in *The Times* 8 March 1994; M. Sweet in *Ind* 16 Oct 1999; C. Taylor in *The Guardian* 13 Dec 2003 and D. Lowe in *The Sun* 20 Aug 2010.

Index

Also available from Amberley Publishing

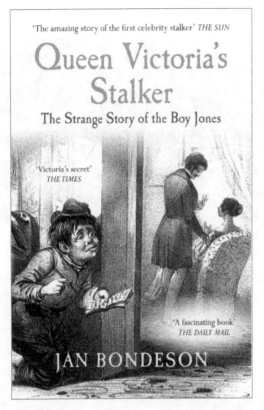

The remarkable tale of Queen Victoria's teenage stalker

£12.99 Paperback
47 illustrations
224 pages
978-1-4456-0697-2

Available from all good bookshops or to order direct
Please call **01453-847-800**
www.amberleybooks.com

Also available from Amberley Publishing

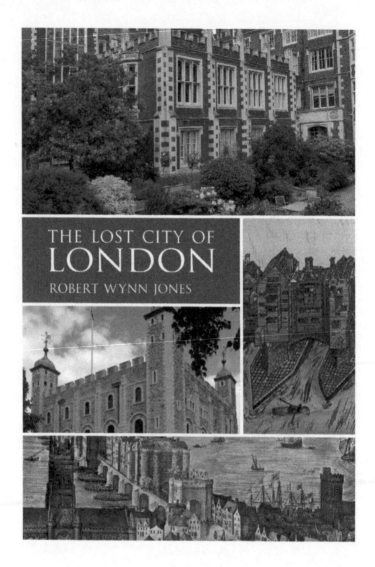

THE LOST CITY OF
LONDON
ROBERT WYNN JONES

Also available from Amberley Publishing

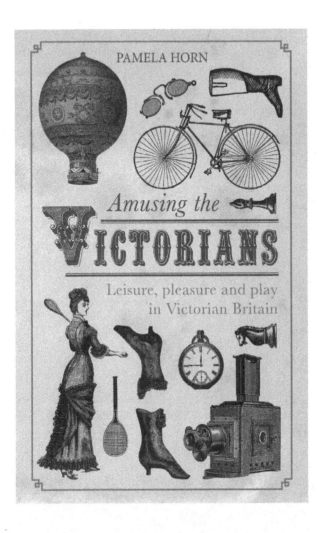

Available from all good bookshops or to order direct
Please call **01453–847–800**
www.amberleybooks.com